FROM 'FAIR SEX' TO FEMINISM

Sport and the Socialization of Women
in the Industrial and Post-Industrial Eras

FROM
'FAIR SEX'
TO
FEMINISM
Sport and the Socialization of Women in the Industrial and Post-Industrial Eras

Edited by
J. A. Mangan and Roberta J. Park

FRANK CASS

First published 1987 in Great Britain by
FRANK CASS AND COMPANY LIMITED
Gainsborough House, 11 Gainsborough Road,
London E11 1RS, England

and in the United States of America by
FRANK CASS AND COMPANY LIMITED
c/o Biblio Distribution Center,
81 Adams Drive, P.O. Box 327, Totowa, NJ 07511

British Library Cataloguing in Publication Data

From 'fair sex' to feminism: sport and the
    socialization of women in the industrial and
    post industrial eras.
    1. Women athletes – History   2. Sports
    – Social aspects
    I. Mangan, J.A.   II. Park, Roberta, J.
    306'.483'088042   GV706.5

Library of Congress Cataloging-in-Publication Data

From 'fair sex' to feminism.
    Bibliography: p.
    Includes index.
    1. Sports for women – Social aspects – History.
    2. Physical education for women – Social aspects –
    History. I. Mangan, J.A. II. Park, Roberta J.
    GV709.F66   1986   796'.01'94   86-17529

ISBN 0-7146-3288-0
ISBN 0-7146-4049-2 (Pbk.)

Typeset by Ann Buchan (Typesetters), Surrey
Printed and bound in Great Britain by
A. Wheaton & Co. Ltd, Exeter

5-28-93

CONTENTS

NOTES ON CONTRIBUTORS

J. A. Mangan is Head of Education, Jordanhill College of Education, Glasgow. He is the author of *Athleticism in the Victorian and Edwardian Public School: The Emergence and Decline of an Educational Ideology* (1981) and *The Games Ethic and Imperialism: Aspects of the Diffusion of an Ideal* (1986). He is also co-editor of *Manliness and Morality: Images of the Male in the Old and New Worlds 1800–1950* (1986) and *Sport in Africa: Essays in Social History* (1986), and he is the founding editor of *The British Journal of Sports History* (now *The International Journal of the History of Sport*).

Roberta J. Park is Professor in and Chairman of the Department of Physical Education at the University of California, Berkeley. Her published articles have appeared in *The Journal of Sport History, The British Journal of Sports History, The Research Quarterly for Exercise and Sport* and other academic journals. Her work has focused upon nineteenth-century sport in Britain and the United States, and health and physical education from the seventeenth to nineteenth centuries. She is co-editor with Janet C. Harris of *Play, Games, and Sports in Cultural Contexts*, an anthology of anthropological readings.

Carroll Smith-Rosenberg is Professor of History and Director of the Alice Paul Research Center, University of Pennsylvania. She has published extensively on the topic of women in recent history.

Charles Rosenberg is Professor in the Department of the History and Sociology of Science, University of Pennsylvania, and the current editor of *Isis*, the History of Science Society journal. His publications include *The Cholera Years. The United States in 1832, 1849 and 1866* (1962); *The Trial of the Assassin Guiteau. Psychiatry* *and Law in the Gilded Age* (1968), and *No Other Gods. On Science and Social Thought in America* (1976).

Paul Atkinson is Reader in Sociology, University College, Cardiff, and is currently Head of the Department of Sociology. His main publications include *The Clinical Experience: The Construction and Reconstruction of Medical Reality* (1981), *Ethnography: Principles in Practice* (with Martyn Hammersley) (1983) and *Language, Structure and Reproduction: An Introduction to the Sociology of Basil Bernstein* (1985).

Kathleen E. McCrone is Professor of History at the University of Windsor, Windsor, Ontario, Canada. Her publications on various aspects of the history of Victorian women have appeared in *Historical Papers, Atlantis,* the *Journal of British Studies*, and *The British Journal of Sports History.*

Jennifer Hargreaves is Senior Lecturer in Sports Studies at Roehampton Institute, London, where she lectures in the history and sociology of sport. She is the editor of *Sport, Culture, Ideology* (1982), and has published widely in a number of books and professional journals. Her present research interest is in women and sport, and she is currently writing a book on that topic.

Sheila Fletcher is a Senior Lecturer in History at the Hertfordshire College of Higher Education, with a special interest in women's history. She has published various articles on the history of women's education and two books in the same area: *Feminists and Bureaucrats: A Study in the Development of Girls' Education in the Nineteenth Century* (1980) and *Women First: The Female Tradition in English Physical Education 1880–1980* (1984).

Scott Crawford is Associate Professor in Health, Sport and Leisure Studies at George Mason University, Virginia. He has published in *Arete, Journal of Popular Culture, International Review of Sport Sociology, The British Journal of Sports History* and other academic journals.

Ray Crawford is Head of the Department of Physical Education, Phillip Institute of Technology, Melbourne. His research interests are in the history of physical education and sport in the schools of Victoria and New South Wales. He has published a number of articles on his interest area and on women and sport in Australia.

Helen Lenskyj is a writer living in Toronto, Canada and the author of *Out of Bounds: Women, Sport and Sexuality* (1986).

Nancy Struna is in the Department of Physical Education at the University of Maryland. Her recent published articles have appeared in *Quest, Canadian Journal of History of Sport*, and the *Journal of Sport History*.

Patricia Vertinsky is an Associate Professor of Education and Physical Education with the University of British Columbia, Vancouver. She has published on topics concerning physical education, curriculum theory and the foundations of curriculum policy; communication and decision-making related to health and exercise behaviour; and socio-historical studies of women and exercise in the nineteenth century.

Donald J. Mrozek is Professor of History at Kansas State University. He is the author of *Sport and American Mentality 1880–1910* (1983) and has edited special issues of the *Journal of the West* on 'Sports and Recreation in the West' (1983). He has also researched and published extensively in American military history and strategic policy.

ACKNOWLEDGEMENTS

The idea for this volume arose out of a set of papers published in *The British Journal of Sports History* in May 1985, and we should like to make the usual acknowledgement with thanks to the Editors for their permission to reproduce the papers in full or in part in Chapters 2, 5 and 6 respectively. In some instances the original papers have been greatly amplified or substantially re-written and we are grateful for the subsequent efforts of contributors to meet our recommendations. We should also like to express our thanks to the Editor of the *Journal of American History* for permission to include Carroll Smith-Rosenberg's and Charles Rosenberg's seminal paper which first appeared in the Journal in September 1973, and to the Editor of *The Journal of British Studies* for permission to use Kathleen McCrone's paper which was first published in the Journal in Spring of 1984, and which is included with additional material in this set of essays. The usual acknowledgements are also due with thanks to *Punch*; to the Hocken Library, University of Otago, Dunedin, New Zealand, for permission to reproduce the photographs of early recreations in the South Island; and to the Library of Congress for the photographs of US sportswomen. Last, but far from least, we owe considerable thanks to Doris Mangan for compiling the index, for unflagging support and for yielding up those lost hours of leisure so graciously.

J.A.M.
R.J.P.

ILLUSTRATIONS

12 Mildred 'Babe' Didrikson Zaharias, champion golfer, was frequently described as a 'tomboy' and broke the mould of the idealized woman amateur (Library of Congress)

13 Gertrude Ederle, long distance swimmer, seen above taking food during her unsuccessful Channel swim of 1925 – she tried again and broke the record in 1928 – had been one of the demurely dressed US Olympic team of 1924 (Library of Congress)

INTRODUCTION

Scarcely more than a decade ago, professional historians paid scant attention to 'sport' as a topic worthy of inquiry. In consequence, as Richard Holt noted in his *Sport and Modern French Society* published as recently as 1981, 'The histories of sport which have been written are not the works of historians but of popular journalists or important officials in the world of sport itself'. In general, their books 'took the form of commentaries on record-breaking performances interspersed with anecdotes evoking the great days of a particular club or a famous sportsman'. Yet any serious social history of sport, Holt continued, has to analyse 'the relationship between changing material and cultural circumstances on the one hand, and the transformation of physical recreation on the other' – in short, how sport evolves in step with society. To add insult to injury, the few substantive studies by historians that we have are mostly concerned with men and their sports. If historical studies of men's sport and recreation were scarce before 1970, those dealing with women and their sports and recreations were virtually non-existent. Little existed apart from a few popular biographies of female athletes, relatively obscure dissertations about influential physical educationists, and highly specialized studies of specific physical education colleges or departments. There was nothing which could be considered a comprehensive study which examined women and sport within broad social, cultural, political, economic or intellectual contexts.

In the 1970s a growing number of academics belatedly turned their attention to the study of sport, recreation and leisure as salient social phenomena. One indication of the extent of this new interest was the appearance of articles dealing with these topics in major historical journals such as *Past and Present*, *Victorian Studies*, *Journal of Social History* and *The American Historical Review*, in specialized journals such as *History of Education*, *Scottish Educational Review*, and *Journal of Educational Administration and History* and in an eclectic variety of journals including *Irish Historical Studies*, *Albion*, *Journal of British Studies*, *Church Quarterly*, and *Workshop History*. And sport eventually spawned its own journals: *Canadian Journal for the History of Sport and Physical Education* (1969), *Journal of Sport History* (1974), *Stadion* (1974), *The British Journal of Sports History* (1984), *Sporting Traditions* (1984) and *Dansk Idpaetstis-torisk Fidsskrift* (1985). Distinguished historians such as Geoffrey Best in his *Mid-Victorian Britain 1857–1875* (1971) and Eric Hobsbawm and Terence Ranger in *The Invention of Tradition* (1983) paid passing but serious attention to sport as part of a broader consideration of the amusements and entertainments of nineteenth-century society. A long neglected and significant aspect of social history was slowly receiving serious attention. By the 1970s Clio's army had gathered to herself shock troops of historians of sport. Yet with notable exceptions, this 'New Army' directed only brief attention to the subject of women, sport and society. Even more oddly, although most sports history conferences for several years now have devoted at least one session to 'woman and sport', very few papers on the subject have been published in symposia or academic journals.

Much of what interest there is in the subject of women, sport, and leisure has emanated from the 'women's movement' of the 1960s and 1970s, and the emergence of publications like *Signs: Journal of Women in Culture and Society*. It has also been stimulated in part by developments in social history, especially those which have directed attention to groups which formerly had been neglected, particularly the urban poor, ethnic minorities and the female sex. Events such as the 1973 Berkshire Conference of Women Historians, and the subsequent publication of a number of papers from that conference as *Clio's Consciousness Raised: New Perspectives on the History of Women*, were instrumental in fostering the new considerable and growing literature which deals with the history of women in all its aspects. With two exceptions, the papers of this small, seminal volume concentrated upon nineteenth-century Britain and America. As Regina Morantz, one of the contributors, pointed out, the Victorian period holds a particular fascination for the historian as it is usually seen as the period during which many of our contemporary notions of women's proper role – and women's 'natural' functions – were firmly embedded in the belief structures of the modern and dominant 'Western World'. However, while a considerable amount of the work of feminist and social historians has been concerned with such topics as female complaints, sexual control, childbirth, and health (topics which can be highly relevant for sport historians), little attention has been directed specifically to sport, recreation and leisure as a source of pleasure, an instrument of control or a symbol of emancipation.

In general, the historiography of these topics has also focused upon the Victorian period, for a good reason. It was in the nineteenth century that social, industrial and technological changes, and an accompanying ideological ferment, gave rise to modern sport. As a consequence, an increasingly substantial and sophisticated picture of male sports has emerged from which mid-range generalizations can be advanced. The picture regarding women, however, is still very hazy. It is becoming apparent that many were far more involved in a wider range of 'athletic' activities than had hitherto been assumed. It is also widely agreed that nineteenth- and twentieth-century sport served as a major vehicle for defining and reinforcing gender differences, at least among the middle and upper classes; but specifically how this operated in various contexts is still unclear. Interestingly, those historical studies which have examined concepts of the female body, beliefs about the 'special physiology' of women, and similar topics, have raised numerous questions which are of major significance to historical investigations of the relationship between women, sport and physical education. While there are some important differences between 'sport' as a social institution and 'physical education', either as formal programmes or, more generally, as part of various exercise and health regimens, they have much in common, and too often have been viewed as conceptually discrete. There is much for the historian of the curriculum at all levels of education to explore here.

And there are other areas of almost unexplored territory. Just as historians of sport, in general, have tended to explore themes which have been facilitated by the ready availability of sources, those who have studied women and sport have relied heavily upon newspapers, health manuals, etiquette guides, and popular journals like the *Fortnightly Review*, *Atlantic Monthly*, and *Godey's Lady's Book*. Considerable use has been made of the publications of education organizations, government agencies and national commissions; and some attention has been directed to the archival collections of selected school, colleges and voluntary sports groups. Consequently the emphasis has been upon middle- and upper-class women. Little or no attention has been given to the pastimes of working-class women, to 'professionals' such as female pedestrians or balloonists, or for that matter to the leisure pursuits of women from Britain and elsewhere who emigrated to countries like Australia, Canada, New Zealand or the United States. And if little has been done as yet to present a comprehensive picture which cuts across class lines, even less has been attempted to provide a cross-cultural historical portrait of women and their sport.

The present collection is intended as a contribution towards filling the many lacunae which currently exist. It is concerned with English-speaking countries, but raises issues of wider relevance. Understandably it reflects current academic preoccupations and interests and is heavily oriented towards the Victorian and Edwardian eras, but it includes work which reaches back into the seventeenth century and extends well into the twentieth century. Concentration on the Victorian period – with the addition of some geographical and chronological breadth – may facilitate the generation of new and much needed mid-range hypotheses.

The twelve papers which comprise this volume are related by a number of important themes, none so central as the persistence of a dominant assumption about the 'inferiority' of the female sex and the unwillingness on the part of some women to be completely constrained by dominant social norms. Sport has had a large part to play in maintaining and sustaining a patriachal social order in Western society. To overlook this is to fail to recognise the potent influence of sport not only in terms of class but also of gender. However, it is as well to recognise that both reality and society are complex. Male domination is far from the whole truth. Individual and group assertiveness even in the alleged heyday of patriarchy – the Victorian era – stimulated diversity in the midst of apparent uniformity.

- Part One serves as an overview of major attitudes to women in both the Old and New Worlds and reveals the close association between European and American ideals and ideas of femininity. It opens with an examination by Carroll Smith-Rosenberg and Charles Rosenberg of ways in which biological and medical thought in the nineteenth century drew upon and reinforced notions of the inherent weaknesses of women. Destined by 'Grand Design' to be limited by their anatomy and physiology, Victorian women were socially – and biologically – relegated to a separate and confined sphere where domesticity and motherhood were the only 'true' vocations. Paradoxically, women were too weak to endure the rigours of even mild exercise, yet programmes of physical education were specifically designed to restore their limited energy. Roberta Park discusses the nature of some of these programmes, as well as various forms of sport considered suitable for American women in the nineteenth century. American middle-class values drew substantially on British traditions in the early and middle Victorian periods, facilitated by the cultural patterns which had been laid down during the Colonial Period, and perpetuated by a shared common language. Although in a country of such vast size there were important regional differences, salient American concepts of 'gender', as well as forms of sport, were derived largely from English sources. By the last decades of the nineteenth century, however, American male sport had been moulded by distinctively 'Yankee' values, competitiveness and an often over-weening preoccupation with winning becoming paramount. Physical education and sport for women on the other hand, especially in educational institutions constrained as a consequence of nineteenth-century notions of proper female behaviour, adhered much longer to Victorian ideals. Paul Atkinson argues that in both Britain and America concerns about the inherent weaknesses of young women resulted in medically determined and defined college programmes of physical education. Nineteenth-century arguments concerning female physical and mental functioning were based upon a model which treated Nature and Culture as opposed categories: women were relegated to an inferior position because they were weak 'by nature', not by social environment, and their capacities were limited compared with those of men. Well controlled programmes of exercise, it was finally believed, might help to alleviate some of their problems. Although they sought to improve women's health and strength through physical education, by adopting the dominant Nature/ Culture model and giving prominence to medical inspection, educational reformers ended up developing an ideology which gave others control of the female body and perpetuated traditional assumptions about female frailties.

In Part II, which concentrates on Victorian and Edwardian Britain, Kathleen McCrone examines the emergence of sport in the late Victorian girls' public school. While intellectual training was the primary goal of the headmistresses of these élite institutions, they believed also that competition in games could provide girls with physical, and much more importantly, moral benefits. They clearly perceived, however, that the aims of games-playing for girls had to be kept distinct from those for boys. Because 'rough' sports like hockey and cricket were often faulted by contemporaries as being physiologically harmful and likely to 'unsex' young women, these types of games, and often all sport for women, had to be hedged by numerous compromises with the powerful existing ideology which continued to relegate women to an inferior position. Jennifer Hargreaves, for her part, narrows the focus from school to home, and examines female sport from the mid-nineteenth century to the early twentieth century through the lens of the 'cult of the family'. In the Victorian and Edwardian eras '. . . the female body was redefined to symbolize a more active, yet nevertheless subordinate role, when compared with men'. Because games-playing was still overwhel-mingly deemed a symbol of masculinity, women games-players were forced to be 'ladylike' in every way possible both on and off the playing-fields if they were not to become objects of ridicule and derision. Not merely headmistresses, but principals of women's physical education colleges, therefore, were careful to construct programmes which differed from those of men. As Sheila Fletcher shows, they promoted a physical education curriculum based upon Swedish gymnastics. The most active and able apologist for this tradition in Britain, Madame Bergman-Osterberg, defined the goals of physical education for women as health, beauty and increased moral consciousness – all important in the perfection of both the individual and the race. The legacy of this tradition, even after the introduction of the work of Rudolph Laban and the ascendency of a non-functional view of Movement, was what Fletcher calls a distinct 'female tradition' in British physical education which resulted in a perpetuation of 'separate spheres' in single-sex teacher-training institutions.

In Part III attention is directed to women and sport in selected Commonwealth countries. Although local circumstances might differ markedly in the various domains of the Empire, a striking persistence underlay dichotomous attitudes toward women and their sports among English-speaking Colonials, as Scott Crawford's examination of the recreational practices of New Zealand women shows. On remote sheep stations and in agricultural settlements where women worked alongside men, their recreations could include such vigorous activities as tobogganing, long horseback rides over rough terrain, even mountain climbing. In more formal recreational activities in both rural and urban settings, however, the tendency was to replicate the customs and values of the mother country. Only after games-playing became an accepted part of elite girls' schooling in England was approval given to New Zealand women to engage in cricket, tennis, swimming, athletics, curling and hockey. Ray Crawford takes up, in an Australian context, the theme of the emergence of schoolgirl sport at the Melbourne Church of England Girls' Grammar School (and more broadly in the State of Victoria) at the turn of the century. His chapter is an interesting case-study of imperial diffusion and adaptation. The Morris sisters, who were instrumental in instituting a more pervasive and dominant role for organized sport for girls, were attracted to developments which were occurring at elite 'public' girls' schools such as Roedean and Godolphin, in England. (Gwynneth Morris studied at Madame Bergman-Osterberg's Physical Training College.) Although sport did perform an important role in the dissemination of British cultural values between 1901 and 1914 it was also shaped by such distinctively

Australian values as '. . . mateship, fierce patriotism, [and] extreme competiveness'. Crawford is concerned with the influence of education; Helen Lenzkyj is interested in the impact of the media. Lenzkyj surveys the views of the Canadian print media towards women in sports from 1890 to 1930. With few exceptions, the newspaper and periodical press stressed a conservative image of women which perpetuated an ideology which assigned females to separate spheres and an inferior status. When the performances of women athletes were discussed in the male-dominated press, and even in women's magazines, considerable attention was devoted to their attire and to things which stressed their femininity. After the 1920s, when such assumedly 'feminine' sports as swimming began to receive somewhat more cordial attention in the press, a concern for grace, beauty, and 'feminine loveliness' still needed to be proclaimed.

The three chapters which comprise Part IV deal with aspects of health, physical education, leisure pursuits and sports for American women from the late seventeenth to the twentieth centuries. All three lend credence to a major theme which is common to all the essays: it has been social convention, not biological potential, which has constrained women's participation in sports, active leisure pursuits, and even healthy exercise. Nancy Struna, one of the few academics currently working on pre-industrial sport, investigates the 'sporting pastimes' of Colonial women, placing these within the context of American society and culture from the late seventeenth century to the decades preceding the war between the States (1861–1865). From about 1680, some middle- and upper-rank American women began to participate socially with men in leisure activities like boating and riding. Competitive events such as horse-racing, however, were strictly male affairs, although women participated freely as spectators. By the middle third of the eighteenth century women had begun to occupy a somewhat more active and public role in American sporting pastimes. In the 1760s, a 'new and distinct phase in the social history of Colonial and early national sporting culture' began to appear. While the types of activities in which women engaged, expanded (and, perhaps, became more competitive), their sport was increasingly 'privatized' and conducted within all-women groups. The emergence of a post-Revolutionary (after 1788) republican notion of motherhood melded with and contributed to the 'cult of domesticity' which arose around 1820. Struna's work also makes evident two other important points which must be dealt with by historians of sport: they must expand their concept of 'sport' if they are to recognize and come to grips with such phenomena in the pre-industrial eras; and they must be more attentive to possible regional differences.

The remaining two essays both speak to the matter of the complexity of the subject matter of sport – particularly women and sport. Patricia Vertinsky discusses ways in which bodily form, style and fashion have served as means of social control. During the nineteenth century 'regular' physicians (as opposed to homeopaths, for example) came to exert a greater role in interpreting new scientific findings regarding health, exercise, physiology and related topics. Perceiving themselves increasingly as guardians of the moral as well as physical well-being of women, many American doctors used their professional authority to control and regulate the bodies of women. After the 1870s, medical doctors and moralists joined forces in an attempt to restore the American 'race' by developing healthier mothers. Their efforts resulted, in the main, in reinforcing traditional ideas regarding appropriate female form and function. In the concluding chapter Donald Mrozek examines reasons for the unequal development of athletic opportunities for women in America in the nineteenth and twentieth centuries, giving particular attention to masculine fears of loss of identity and purpose. The fact that women were considered to be weaker than men did not mean to contemporaries that women could not harm men. Paradoxically, women's role as moral guardian elevated her status, while at the same time what was perceived to be her moral fragility posed grave dangers. The quest for control fostered a separation of the sexes into two distinct cultures, with sport deemed a male preserve. To retain some sense of control and identity, men went to great lengths to retain domination over both women and sport. Such improved opportunities as women gained in the 1920s and over the next several decades depended greatly upon changes in the 'minds and predisposition of men and women'. While their actual performances in sports should have demolished traditional stereotypes about feminine physical and emotional weaknesses, the usual response to successful women athletes was to question their gender identity. Achievements on the sports field of some post–1970 female athletes have forced a re-examination of what it means to be female and an athlete, but more powerful influences may have been the legitimation of sport as part of mass culture, and 'substantial redirection of thinking' regarding women on the part of both males and females.

This set of essays repairs omissions but only to a limited extent. Certainly it deals with sport as a source of social tension, as a means of both sexual antagonism and conciliation, as an illustration of both continuity and change in social life. Furthermore it demonstrates, to adapt Cunningham, that the history of sport is as much political as it is social. Power is frequently a central issue. But, of course, the work remains exploratory, tentative and incomplete. The topic is too large and the subject matter still too neglected to permit even an attempt at comprehensiveness. A great deal remains to be done. There is much still to learn about the relationship of women, sport, recreation and leisure not merely to political, social and cultural ideologies but to urban development, evolving work patterns, changing educational opportunities, public health improvements and social class fashions throughout the world. The status of women, relationships between the sexes, attitudes to child-rearing, are mirrored in the recreational, leisure and sporting opportunities available to women in society, past and present. It is hoped that this contribution to social historical studies will stimulate inquiry into such issues and progressively deepen our understanding of the place of women in the cultural heritage of modern society.

J.A.Mangan
Glasgow, 1986

Roberta J. Park
Berkeley, 1986

PART ONE

OVERVIEW

1

The Female Animal: Medical and Biological Views of Women and Their Role in Nineteenth-century America

Carroll Smith-Rosenberg and Charles Rosenberg

Since at least the time of Hippocrates and Aristotle, the roles assigned to women have attracted an elaborate body of medical and biological justification. This was especially true in the nineteenth century as the intellectual and emotional centrality of science increased steadily. Would-be scientific arguments were used in the rationalization and legitimization of almost every aspect of Victorian life, and with particular vehemence in those areas in which social change implied stress in existing social arrangements.

This essay is an attempt to outline some of the shapes assumed by the nineteenth-century debate over the ultimate bases for woman's domestic and childbearing role.[1] In form it resembles an exercise in the history of ideas; in intent it represents a hybrid with social and psychological history. Biological and medical views serve as a sampling device suggesting and illuminating patterns of social continuity, change and tension.

The relationships between social change and social stress are dismayingly complex and recalcitrant to both psychological theorists and to the historian's normal modes of analysis. In an attempt to gain insight into these relationships the authors have chosen an analytic approach based on the study of normative descriptions of the female role at a time of widespread social change; not surprisingly emotion-laden attempts to reassert and redefine this role constitute one response to the stress induced by such social change.

This approach was selected for a variety of reasons. Role definitions exist on a level of prescription beyond their embodiment in the individuality and behaviour of particular historical persons. They exist rather as a formally agreed set of characteristics understood by and acceptable to a significant proportion of the population. As formally agreed social values they are, moreover, retrievable from historical materials and thus subject to analysis. Such social role definitions, however, have a more than platonic reality; for they exist as parameters with which and against which individuals must either conform or define their deviance. When inappropriate to social, psychological, or biological reality such definitions can themselves engender anxiety, conflict, and demands for change.

During the nineteenth century, economic and social forces at work within Western Europe and the United States began to compromise traditional social roles. Some women at least began to question – and a few to challenge overtly – their constricted place in society. Naturally enough, men hopeful of preserving existing social relationships, and in some cases threatened themselves both as individuals and as members of particular social groups, employed medical and biological arguments to rationalize traditional sex roles as rooted inevitably and irreversibly in the prescriptions of anatomy and physiology. This essay examines the ideological attack mounted by prestigious and traditionally minded men against two of the ways in which women expressed their dissatisfaction and desire for change: women's demands for improved educational opportunities and their decision to resort to birth control and abortion. That much of this often emotionally charged debate was oblique and couched in would-be scientific and medical language and metaphor makes it even more significant; for few spokesmen could explicitly and consciously confront those changes which impinged upon the bases of their particular emotional adjustment.

The Victorian woman's ideal social characteristics – nurturance, intuitive morality, domesticity, passivity and affection – were all assumed to have a deeply rooted biological basis. These medical and scientific arguments formed an ideological system rigid in its support of tradition, yet infinitely flexible in the particular mechanisms which could be made to explain and legitimate woman's role.

Woman, nineteenth-century medical orthodoxy insisted, was starkly different from the male of the species. Physically, she was frailer, her skull smaller, her muscles more delicate. Even more striking was the difference between the nervous system of the two sexes. The female nervous system was finer, 'more irritable', prone to over-stimulation and resulting exhaustion. 'The female sex,' as one physician explained in 1827,

> is far more sensitive and susceptible than the male, and extremely liable to those distressing affections which for want of some better term, have been denominated nervous, and which consist chiefly in painful affections of the head, heart, side, and indeed, of almost every part of the system.[2]

'The nerves themselves,' another physician concurred a generation later, 'are smaller, and of a more delicate structure. They are endowed with greater sensibility, and, of course, are liable to more frequent and stronger impressions from external agents or mental influences.'[3] Few if any questioned the assumption that in males the intellectual propensities of the brain dominated, while the female's nervous system and emotions prevailed over her conscious and rational faculties. Thus it was only natural, indeed inevitable, that women should be expected and permitted to display more affect than men; it was inherent in their very being.

Physicians saw woman as the product and prisoner of her reproductive system. It was the ineluctable basis of her social role and behavioural characteristics, the cause of her most common ailments; woman's uterus and ovaries controlled her body and behaviour from puberty to menopause. The male reproductive system, male physicians assured, exerted no parallel degree of control over man's body. Charles D. Meigs, a prominent Philadelphia gynaecologist, stated with assurance in 1847 that a woman is 'a moral, a sexual, a germiferous, gestative and parturient creature'.[4] It was, another physician explained in 1870, 'as if the Almighty, in creating the female sex, had taken the uterus and built up a woman around it'.[5] A wise deity had designed woman as keeper of the hearth, as breeder and rearer of children.

Medical wisdom easily supplied hypothetical mechanisms to explain the interconnection between the female's organs of generation and the functioning of her other organs. The uterus, it was assumed, was connected to the central nervous system; shocks to the nervous system might alter the reproductive cycle – might even mark the gestating foetus – while changes in the reproductive cycle shaped emotional states. This intimate and hypothetical link between ovaries, uterus, and nervous system was the logical basis for the 'reflex irritation' model of disease causation so popular in middle and late nineteenth-century medical texts and monographs on psychiatry and gynaecology. Any imbalance, exhaustion, infection or other disorders of the reproductive organs could cause pathological reactions in parts of the body seemingly remote.[6] Doctors connected not only the paralyses and headaches of the hysteric to uterine disease but also ailments in virtually every part of the body. 'These diseases,' one physician explained, 'will be found, on due investigation, to be in reality, no disease at all, but merely the sympathetic reaction or the symptoms of one disease, namely, a disease of the womb.'[7]

Yet despite the commonsensical view that many such ailments resulted from childbearing, physicians often contended that far greater difficulties could be expected in childless women. Motherhood was woman's normal destiny, and those females who thwarted the promise immanent in their body's design must expect to suffer. The maiden lady, many physicians argued, was fated to a greater incidence of both physical and emotional disease than her married sisters and to a shorter life-span.[8] Her nervous system was placed under constant pressure, and her unfulfilled reproductive organs – especially at menopause – were prone to cancer and other degenerative ills.

Woman was thus peculiarly the creature of her internal organs, of tidal forces she could not consciously control. Ovulation, the physical and emotional changes of pregnancy, even sexual desire itself were determined by internal physiological processes beyond the control or even the awareness of her conscious volition.[9] All women were prisoners of the cyclical aspects of their bodies, of the great reproductive cycle bounded by puberty and menopause, and by the shorter but recurrent cycles of childbearing and menstruation. All shaped her personality, her social role, her intellectual abilities and limitations; all presented as well possibly 'critical' moments in her development, possible turning points in the establishment – or deterioration – of future physical and mental health. As the president of the American Gynecological Society stated in 1900: 'Many a young life is battered and forever crippled in the breakers of puberty; if it crosses these unharmed and is not dashed to pieces on the rock of childbirth, it may still ground on the ever-recurring shallows of menstruation, and lastly, upon the final bar of the menopause ere protection is found in the unruffled waters of the harbour beyond the reach of sexual storms.'[10]

Woman's physiology and anatomy, physicians habitually argued, oriented her towards an 'inner' view of herself and her worldly sphere. (Logically enough, nineteenth-century views of heredity often assumed that the father was responsible for a child's external musculature and skeletal development, the mother for the internal viscera, the father for analytical abilities, the mother for emotions and piety.[11]) Their secret internal organs, women were told, determined their behaviour; their concerns lay inevitably within the home.[12] In a passage strikingly reminiscent of some mid-twentieth-century writings, a physician in 1869 depicted an idealized female world, rooted in the female reproductive system, sharply limited socially and intellectually, yet offering women covert and manipulative modes of exercising power:

> Mentally, socially, spiritually, she is more interior than man. She herself is an interior part of man, and her love and life are always something interior and incomprehensible to him. . . . Woman is

to deal with domestic affections and uses, not with philosophies and sciences. . . . She is priest, not king. The house, the chamber, the closet, are the centres of her social life and power, as surely as the sun is the centre of the solar system. . . . Another proof of the interiority of woman, is the wonderful secretiveness and power of dissimulation which she possesses. . . . Woman's secrecy is not cunning; her dissimulation is not fraud. They are intuitions or spiritual perceptions, full of tact and wisdom, leading her to conceal or reveal, to speak or be silent, to do or not to do, exactly at the right time and in the right place.[13]

The image granted women in these hypothetical designs was remarkably consistent with the social role traditionally allotted them. The instincts connected with ovulation made her by nature gentle, affectionate, and nurturant. Weaker in body, confined by menstruation and pregnancy, she was both physically and economically dependent upon the stronger, more forceful male, to whom she necessarily looked up with admiration and devotion.

Such stylized formulae embodied, however, a characteristic yet entirely functional ambiguity. The Victorian woman was more spiritual than man, yet less intellectual, closer to the divine, yet prisoner of her most animal characteristics, more moral than man, yet less in control of her very morality. While the sentimental poets placed woman among the angels and doctors praised the transcendent calling of her reproductive system, social taboos made woman ashamed of menstruation, embarrassed and withdrawn during pregnancy, self-conscious and purposeless during and after menopause. Her body, which so inexorably defined her personality and limited her role, appeared to woman often degrading and confining.[14] The very romantic rhetoric which tended to suffocate nineteenth-century discussions of femininity only underlined with irony the distance between behavioural reality and the forms of conventional ideology.

The nature of the formalistic scheme implied as well a relationship between the fulfilling of its true calling and ultimate social health. A woman who lived 'unphysiologically' – and she could do so by reading or studying in excess, by wearing improper clothing, by long hours of factory work, or by a sedentary, luxurious life – could produce only weak and degenerate offspring. Until the twentieth century, it was almost universally assumed that acquired characteristics in the form of damage from disease and improper life-styles in parents would be transmitted through heredity; a nervous and debilitated mother could have only nervous, dyspeptic, and undersized children.[15] Thus appropriate female behaviour was sanctioned not only by traditional injunctions against the avoidance of individual sin in the form of inappropriate and thus unnatural modes of life but also by the higher duty of protecting the transcendent good of social health, which could be maintained only through the continued production of healthy children. Such arguments were to be invoked with increasing frequency as the nineteenth century progressed.

In mid-nineteenth-century America it was apparent that women – or at least some of them – were growing dissatisfied with traditional roles. American society in mid-nineteenth century was committed – at least formally – to egalitarian democracy and evangelical piety. It was thus a society which presumably valued individualism, social and economic mobility, and free will. At the same time it was a society experiencing rapid economic growth, one in which an increasing number of families could think of themselves as middle class and could seek a life-style appropriate to that station. At least some middle-class women, freed economically from the day-to-day struggle for subsistence, found in these values a motivation and rationale for expanding their roles into areas outside the home. In the Jacksonian crusades for piety, for temperance, for abolition, and in pioneering efforts to aid the urban poor, women played a prominent role, a role clearly outside the confines of the home. Women began as well to demand improved educational opportunities – even admission to colleges and medical schools. A far greater number began, though more covertly, to see family limitation as a necessity if they would preserve health, status, economic security, and individual autonomy.

Only a handful of nineteenth-century American women made a commitment to overt feminism and to the insecurity and hostility such a commitment implied. But humanitarian reform, education, and birth control were all issues which presented themselves as real alternatives to every respectable churchgoing American woman.[16] Contemporary medical and biological arguments identified, reflected, and helped to eliminate two of these threats to traditional role definitions: demands by women for higher education and family limitation.

Since the beginnings of the nineteenth century, American physicians and social commentators generally had feared that American women were physically inferior to their English and Continental sisters. The young women of the urban middle and upper classes seemed in particular less vigorous, more nervous than either their own grandmothers or European contemporaries. Concern among physicians, educators, and publicists over the physical deterioration of American womanhood grew steadily during the nineteenth century and reached a high point in its last third.

Many physicians were convinced that education was a major factor in bringing about this deterioration, especially education during puberty and adolescence. It was during these years that the female reproductive system matured, and it was this process of maturation that determined the quality of the children whom American women would ultimately bear. During puberty, orthodox medical doctrine insisted, a girl's vital energies must be devoted to development of the reproductive organs. Physicians saw the body as a closed system possessing only a limited amount of vital force; energy expended in one area was necessarily removed from another. The girl who curtailed brain work during puberty could devote her body's full energy to the optimum development of its reproductive capacities. A young woman, however, who consumed her vital force in intellectual activities was necessarily diverting these energies from the achievement of true womanhood. She would become weak and nervous, perhaps sterile, or more commonly, and in a sense more dangerously for society, capable of bearing only sickly and neurotic children – children able to produce only feebler and more degenerate versions of themselves.[17] The brain and ovary could not develop at the same time. Society, mid-century physicians warned, must protect the higher good of racial health by avoiding situations in which adolescent girls taxed their intellectual faculties in academic competition. 'Why,' as one physician pointedly asked, 'spoil a good mother by making an ordinary grammarian?'[18]

Yet where did America's daughters spend these years of puberty and adolescence, doctors asked, especially the daughters of the nation's most virtuous and successful middle-class families? They spent these years in schools; they sat for long hours each day bending over desks, reading thick books, competing with boys for honours. Their health and that of their future children would be inevitably marked by the consequences of such unnatural modes of life.[19] If such evils resulted from secondary education, even more dramatically unwholesome was the influence of higher education upon the health of those few women intrepid enough to undertake it. Yet their numbers increased steadily, especially after a few women's colleges were established in the East and state universities in the Midwest and Pacific Coast began cautiously to accept coeducation. Women could now, critics agonized, spend the entire period between the beginning of menstruation and the maturation of their ovarian systems in nerve-draining study. Their adolescence, as one doctor pointed out, contrasted sadly with those experienced by healthier, more fruitful forebears: 'Our great-grandmothers got their schooling during the winter months and let their brains lie fallow for the rest of the year. They knew less about Euclid and the classics than they did about housekeeping and housework. But they made good wives and mothers, and bore and nursed sturdy sons and buxom daughters and plenty of them at that.'[20]

Constant competition among themselves and with the physically stronger males disarranged the coed's nervous system, leaving her anxious, prey to hysteria and neurasthenia. One gynaecologist complained as late as 1901:

> the nervous force, so necessary at puberty for the establishment of the menstrual function, is wasted on what may be compared as trifles to perfect health, for what use are they without health? The poor sufferer only adds another to the great army of neurasthenic and sexual incompetents, which furnish neurologists and gynecologists with so much of their material . . . bright eyes have been dulled by the brain-fag and sweet temper transformed into irritability, crossness and hysteria, while the womanhood of the land is deteriorating physically.
>
> She may be highly cultured and accomplished and shine in society, but her future husband will discover too late that he has married a large outfit of headaches, backaches and spine aches, instead of a woman fitted to take up the duties of life.[21]

Such speculations exerted a strong influence upon educators, even those connected with institutions which admitted women. The state universities, for example, often prescribed a lighter course load for females or refused to permit women admission to regular degree programmes. 'Every physiologist is well aware,' the Regents of the University of Wisconsin explained in 1877, 'that at stated times, nature makes a great demand upon the energies of early womanhood and that at these times great caution must be exercised lest injury be done. . . . Education is greatly to be desired,' the Regents concluded:

> but it is better that the future matrons of the state should be without a University training than that it should be produced at the fearful expense of ruined health; better that the future mothers of the state should be robust, hearty, healthy women, than that, by over study, they entail upon their descendants the germs of disease.[22]

This fear for succeeding generations born of educated women was widespread. 'We want to have body as well as mind,' one commentator noted, 'otherwise the degeneration of the race is inevitable.'[23] Such transcendent responsibilities made the individual woman's personal ambitions seem trivial indeed.

One of the remedies suggested by both educators and physicians lay in tempering the intensely intellectualistic quality of American education with a restorative emphasis on physical education. Significantly, health reformers' demands for women's physical education were ordinarily justified not in terms of freeing the middle-class woman from traditional restrictions on bodily movement, but rather as upgrading her ultimate maternal capacities. Several would-be physiological reformers called indeed for active participation in house-cleaning as an ideal mode of physical culture for the servant-coddled American girl. Bedmaking, clothes scrubbing, sweeping and scouring provided a varied and highly appropriate regimen.[24]

Late nineteenth-century women physicians, as might have been expected, failed ordinarily to share the alarm of their male colleagues when contemplating the dangers of coeducation. No one, a female physician commented sardonically, worked harder or in unhealthier conditions than the washerwoman; yet, would-be saviours of American womanhood did not inveigh against this abuse – washing, after all, was appropriate work for women. Women doctors often did agree with the general observation that their sisters were too frequently weak and unhealthy; however, they blamed not education or social activism but artificialities of dress and slavery to fashion, aspects of the middle-class woman's life-style which they found particularly demeaning. 'The fact is that girls and women can bear study,' Alice Stockham explained, 'but they cannot bear compressed viscera, tortured stomachs and displaced uterus', the results of fashionable clothing and an equally fashionable sedentary life. Another woman physician, Sarah Stevenson, wrote in a similar vein: '"How do I look?" is the everlasting story from the beginning to the end of woman's life. Looks, not books, are the murderers of American women.'[25]

Even more significant than this controversy over woman's education was a parallel debate focusing on the questions of birth control and abortion. These issues affected not simply a small percentage of middle- and upper-middle-class women, but all men and women. It is one of the great and still largely unstudied realities of nineteenth-century social history. Every married woman was immediately affected by the realities of childbearing and child-rearing. Though birth control and abortion had been practised, discussed – and reprobated – for centuries, the mid-nineteenth century saw a dramatic increase in concern among spokesmen for the ministry and medical profession.[26]

Particularly alarming was the casualness, doctors charged, with which seemingly respectable wives and mothers contemplated and undertook abortions, and how routinely they practised birth control. One prominent New York gynaecologist complained in 1874 that well-dressed women walked into his consultation room and asked for abortions as casually as they would for a cut of beefsteak at their butcher.[27] In 1857, the American Medical Association nominated a special committee to report on the problem; then appointed another in the 1870s; between these dates and especially in the late 1860s, medical societies throughout the country passed resolutions attacking the prevalence of abortion and birth control and condemning physicians who performed and condoned such illicit practices. Nevertheless, abortions could in the 1870s be obtained in Boston and New York for as little as ten dollars, while abortifacients could be purchased more cheaply or through the mail. Even the smallest villages and rural areas provided a market for the abortionist's services; women often aborted any pregnancy which occurred in the first few years of marriage. The Michigan Board of Health estimated in 1898 that one third of all the state's pregnancies ended in abortion. From 70 to 80 per cent of these were secured, the board contended, by prosperous and otherwise respectable married women who could not offer even the unmarried mother's 'excuse of shame'.[28] By the 1880s, English medical moralists could refer to birth control as the 'American sin' and warn against England's women following in the path of America's faithless wives.[29]

So general a phenomenon demands explanation. The only serious attempts to explain the prevalence of birth control in this period have emphasized the economic motivations of those practising it – the need in an increasingly urban, industrial and bureaucratized society to limit numbers of children so as to provide security, education and inheritance for those already brought into the world. As the nineteenth century progressed, it has been argued, definitions of appropriate middle-class life-styles dictated a more and more expansive pattern of consumption, a pattern – especially in an era of recurring economic instability – particularly threatening to those large numbers of Americans only precariously members of the secure economic classes. The need to limit offspring was a necessity if family status was to be maintained.[30]

Other aspects of nineteenth-century birth control have received much less historical attention. One of these needs only to be mentioned for it poses no interpretative complexities; this was the frequency with which childbirth meant for women pain and often lingering incapacity. Death from childbirth, torn cervices, fistulae, prolapsed uteri were widespread 'female complaints' in a period when gynaecological practice was still relatively primitive and pregnancy every few years common indeed. John Humphrey Noyes, perhaps the best-known advocate of family planning in nineteenth-century America, explained poignantly why he and his wife had decided to practise birth control in the 1840s:

> The [decision] was occasioned and even forced upon me by very sorrowful experiences. In the course of six years my wife went through the agonies of five births. Four of them were premature. Only one child lived. . . . After our last disappointment, I pledged my word to my wife that I would never again expose her to such fruitless suffering. . . .[31]

The Noyeses' experience was duplicated in many homes. Young women were simply terrified of having children.[32]

Such fears, of course, were not peculiar to nineteenth-century America. The dangers of disability and death consequent upon childbirth extended back to the beginning of time, as did the anxiety and depression so frequently associated with pregnancy. What might be suggested, however, was that economic and technological changes in society added new parameters to the age-old experience. Family limitation for economic and social reasons now appeared more desirable to a growing number of husbands; it was, perhaps, also, more technically feasible. Consequently married women could begin to consider, probably for the first time, alternative life-styles to that of multiple pregnancies extending over a third of their lives. Women could begin to view the pain and bodily injury which resulted from such pregnancies not simply as a condition to be borne with fatalism and passivity, but as a situation that could be avoided. It is quite probable, therefore, that, in this new social context, increased anxiety and depression would result once a woman, in part at least voluntarily, became pregnant. Certainly, it could be argued, such fears must have altered women's attitudes towards sexual relations generally. Indeed the decision to practise birth control must necessarily have held more than economic and status implications for the family; it must have become an element in the fabric of every marriage's particular psycho-sexual reality.[33]

A third and even more ambiguous aspect of the birth control controversy in nineteenth-century America relates to the way in which attitudes towards contraception and abortion reflected role conflict within the family. Again and again, from the 1840s on, defenders of family planning – including individuals as varied and idealistic as Noyes and Stockham, on the one hand, and assorted quack doctors and peddlers of abortifacients, on the other – justified their activities not in economic terms, but under the rubric of providing women with liberty and autonomy. Woman, they argued with remarkable unanimity, must control her own body; without this she was a slave not only to the sexual impulses of her husband but also to endless childbearing and rearing. 'Woman's equality in all the relations of life', a New York physician wrote in 1866, 'implies her absolute supremacy in the sexual relation. . . . it is her absolute and indefeasible right to determine when she will and when she will not be exposed to pregnancy.' 'God and Nature,' another physician urged, 'have given to the female the complete control of her own person, so far as sexual congress and reproduction are concerned.'[34] The assumption of all these writers was clear and unqualified: women, if free to do so, would choose to have sexual relations less frequently, and to have far fewer pregnancies.

Implied in these arguments as well were differences as to the nature and function of sexual intercourse. Was its principal and exclusively justifiable function, as conservative physicians and clergymen argued, the procreation of children, or could it be justified as an act of love, of tenderness between individuals? Noyes argued that the sexual organs had a social, amative function separable from their reproductive function. Sex was justifiable as an essential and irreplaceable form of human affection; no man could demand this act unless it was freely given.[35] Nor could it be freely given in many cases unless effective modes of birth control were available to assuage the woman's anxieties. A man's wife was not his chattel, her individuality to be violated at will, and forced – ultimately – to bear unwanted and thus almost certainly unhealthy children.

Significantly, defenders of women's right to limit childbearing employed many of the same arguments used by conservatives to attack women's activities outside the home; all those baleful hereditary consequences threatened by over-education were seen by birth control advocates as resulting from the bearing of children by women unwilling and unfit for the task, their vital energies depleted by excessive childbearing. A child, they argued, carried to term by a woman who desired only its death could not develop normally; such children proved inevitably a source of physical and emotional degeneracy. Were women relieved from such accustomed pressures, they could produce fewer but better offspring.[36]

Many concerned mid-nineteenth-century physicians, clergymen, and journalists failed to accept such arguments. They emphasized instead the unnatural and thus necessarily deleterious character of any and all methods of birth control and abortion. Even coitus interruptus, obviously the most common mode of birth control in this period, was attacked routinely as a source of mental illness, nervous tension and even cancer. This was easily demonstrated. Sex, like all aspects of human bodily activity, involved an exchange of nervous energy; without the discharge of such accumulated energies in the male orgasm and the soothing presence of the male semen 'bathing the female reproductive organs', the female partner could never, the reassuring logic ran, find true fulfilment. The nervous force accumulated and concentrated in sexual excitement would build up dangerous levels of undischarged energy, leading ultimately to a progressive decay in the unfortunate women's physical and mental health. Physicians warned repeatedly that condoms and diaphragms – when the latter became available after mid-century – could cause an even more startlingly varied assortment of ills. In addition to the mechanical irritation they promoted, artificial methods of birth control increased the lustful impulse in both partners, leading inevitably to sexual excess. The resultant nervous exhaustion induced gynaecological lesions, and then through 'reflex irritation' caused such ills as loss of memory, insanity, heart disease, and even 'the most repulsive nymphomania'.[37]

Conservative physicians similarly denounced the widespread practice of inserting sponges impregnated with supposedly spermicidal chemicals into the vagina immediately before or after intercourse. Such practices, they warned, guaranteed pelvic injury, perhaps sterility. Even if a woman seemed in good health despite a history of practising birth control, a Delaware physician explained in 1873 that '. . . as soon as this vigor commences to decline . . . about the fortieth year, the disease [cancer] grows as the energies fail – the cancerous fangs penetrating deeper and deeper until, after excruciating suffering, the writhing victim is yielded up to its terrible embrace'.[38] Most importantly, this argument followed, habitual attempts at contraception meant – even if successful – a mother permanently injured and unable to bear healthy children. If unsuccessful, the children resulting from such unnatural matings would be inevitably weakened. And if such grave ills resulted from the practice of birth control, the physical consequences of abortion were even more dramatic and immediate.[39]

Physicians often felt little hesitation in expressing what seems to the historian a suspiciously disproportionate resentment towards such unnatural females. Unnatural was of course the operational word; for woman's presumed maternal instinct made her primarily responsible for decisions in regard to childbearing.[40] So frequent was this habitual accusation that some medical authors had to caution against placing the entire weight of blame for birth control and abortion upon the woman; men, they reminded, played an important role in most such decisions.[41] In 1871, for example, the American Medical Association Committee on Criminal Abortion described women who patronized abortionists in terms which conjured up fantasies of violence and punishment:

> She becomes unmindful of the course marked out for her by Providence, she overlooks the duties imposed on her by the marriage contract. She yields to the pleasures – but shrinks from the pains and responsibilities of maternity; and, destitute of all delicacy and refinement, resigns herself, body and soul, into the hands of unscrupulous and wicked men. Let not the husband of such a wife flatter himself that he possesses her affection. Nor can she in turn ever merit even the respect of a virtuous husband. She sinks into old age like a withered tree, stripped of its foliage; with the stain of blood upon her soul, she dies without the hand of affection to smooth her pillow.[42]

The frequency with which attacks on family limitation in mid-nineteenth-century America were accompanied by polemics against expanded roles for the middle-class woman indicates with unmistakable clarity something of one of the motives structuring such jeremiads. Family limitation necessarily added a significant variable within conjugal relationships generally; its successful practice implied potential access for women to new roles and a new autonomy.

Nowhere is this hostility toward women and the desire to inculcate guilt over women's desire to avoid pregnancy more strikingly illustrated than in the warnings of 'race suicide' so increasingly fashionable in the late nineteenth century. A woman's willingness and capacity to bear children was a duty she owed not only to God and husband but to her 'race' as well.[43] In the second half of the nineteenth century, articulate Americans forced to evaluate and come to emotional terms with social change became, like many of their European contemporaries, attracted to a world view which saw racial identity and racial conflict as fundamental. And within these categories, birthrates became all-important indices to national vigour and thus social health.

In 1860 and again in 1870, Massachusetts census returns began to indicate that the foreign-born had a considerably higher birthrate than that of native Americans. Indeed, the more affluent and educated a family, the fewer children it seemed to produce. Such statistics indicated that native Americans in the Bay State were not even reproducing themselves. The social consequences seemed ominous indeed.

The Irish, though barely one quarter of the Massachusetts population, produced more than half of the state's children. 'It is perfectly clear,' a Boston clergyman contended in 1884, 'that without a radical change in the religious ideas, education, habits, and customs of the natives, the present population and their descendants will not rule that state a single generation.'[44] A few years earlier a well-known New England physician, pointing to America's still largely unsettled western territories, had asked: 'Shall they be filled by our own children or by those of aliens? This is a question that our own women must answer; upon their loins depends the future destiny of the nation.' Native-born American women had failed themselves as individuals and society as mothers of the Anglo-Saxon race. If matters continued for another half century in the same manner, 'the wives who are to be mothers in our republic must be drawn from trans-Atlantic homes. The Sons of the New World will have to re-act, on a magnificent scale, the old story of unwived Rome and the Sabines.'[45]

Such arguments have received a goodly amount of historical attention, especially as they figured in the late-nineteenth and early twentieth centuries as part of the contemporary rationale for immigration restriction.[46] Historians have interpreted the race suicide argument in several fashions. As an incident in a general Western acceptance of racism, it has been seen as product of a growing alienation of the older middle and upper classes in the face of industrialization, urbanization and bureaucratization of society. More specifically, some American historians have seen these race suicide arguments as rooted in the fears and insecurities of a traditionally dominant middle class as it perceived new and threatening social realities.

Whether or not historians care to accept some version of this interpretation – and certainly such motivational elements seem to be suggested in the rhetorical formulae employed by many of those bemoaning the failure of American Protestants to reproduce in adequate numbers – it ignores another element crucial to the logical and emotional fabric of these arguments. This is the explicit charge of female sexual failure. To a significant extent, contemporaries saw the problem as in large measure woman's responsibility; it was America's potential mothers, not its fathers, who were primarily responsible for the impending social cataclysm. Race suicide seemed a problem in social gynaecology.

Though fathers played a necessary role in procreation, medical opinion emphasized that it was the mother's constitution and reproductive capacity which most directly shaped her offspring's physical, mental and emotional attributes. And any unhealthy mode of life – anything in short which seemed undesirable to contemporary medical moralists, including both education and birth control – might result in a woman becoming sterile or capable of bearing only stunted offspring. Men, it was conceded, were subject to vices even more debilitating, but the effects of male sin and imprudence were, physicians felt, 'to a greater extent confined to adult life; and consequently do not, to the same extent, impair the vitality of our race or threaten its physical destruction'. Women's violation of physiological laws implied disaster to 'the unborn of both sexes'.[47]

Though such social critics tended to agree that woman was at fault, they expressed some difference of opinion as to the nature of her guilt. A few felt that lower birthrates could be attributed simply to the conscious and culpable decision of American women to curtail family size. Other physicians and social commentators, while admitting that many women felt little desire for children, saw the roots of the problem in somewhat different – and perhaps even more apocalyptic – terms. It was not, they feared, simply the conscious practice of family limitation which resulted in small families; rather the increasingly unnatural life-style of the 'modern American woman' had undermined her reproductive capacities so that even when she would, she could not bear adequate numbers of healthy children. Only if American women returned to the simpler life-styles of the eighteenth and early nineteenth centuries could the race hope to regain its former vitality; women must from childhood see their role as that of robust and self-sacrificing mothers. If not, their own degeneration and that of the race was inevitable.

Why the persistence and intensity of this masculine hostility, of its recurring echoes of conflict, rancour and moral outrage? There are at least several possible, though by no means exclusive, explanations. One centres on the hostility implied and engendered by the sexual deprivation – especially for the male – implicit in many of the modes of birth control employed at this time. One might, for example, speculate – as Oscar Handlin did some years ago – that such repressed middle-class sexual energies were channelled into a xenophobic hostility towards immigrants and blacks and projected into fantasies incorporating the enviable and fully expressed sexuality of these alien groups.[48] A similar model could be applied to men's attitudes towards women as well; social, economic and sexual tensions which beset late nineteenth-century American men might well have caused them to express their anxieties and frustrations in terms of hostility towards the middle-class female.[49]

Such interpretations are, however, as treacherous as they are inviting. Obviously, the would-be scientific formulations outlined here mirror something of *post-bellum* social and psychic reality. Certainly some middle-class men in the late-nineteenth century had personality needs – sexual inadequacies or problems of status identification – which made traditional definitions of gender roles functional to them. The hostility, even the violent imagery expressed towards women who chose to limit the number of children they bore indicates a significant personal and emotional involvement on the part of the male author. Some women, moreover, obviously used the mechanisms of birth control and, not infrequently, sexual rejection as role-sanctioned building blocks in the fashioning of their particular adjustment. Their real and psychic gains were numerous: surcease from fear and pain, greater leisure, a socially acceptable way of expressing hostility, and a means of maintaining some autonomy and privacy in a life which society demanded be devoted wholeheartedly to the care and nurturance of husband and children. Beyond such statements, however, matters become quite conjectural. At this moment in the development of both historical methodology and psychological theory great caution must be exercised in the development of such hypotheses – especially since the historians of gender and sexual behaviour have at their disposal data which from a psychodynamic point of view are at best fragmentary and suggestive.[50]

What the nineteenth-century social historian can hope to study with a greater degree of certainty, however, is the way in which social change both caused and reflected tensions surrounding formal definitions of gender roles. Obviously, individuals as individuals at all times and in all cultures have experienced varying degrees of difficulty in assimilating the prescriptions of expected role behaviour. When such discontinuities begin to affect comparatively large numbers and become sufficiently overt as to evoke a marked ideological response one can then speak with assurance of having located fundamental cultural tension.[51]

Students of nineteenth-century American and Western European society have long been aware of the desire of a growing number of women for a choice among roles different from the traditional one of mother and housekeeper. It was a theme of Henry James, Henrik Ibsen, and a host of other, perhaps more representative if less talented, writers. Women's demands ranged from that of equal pay for equal work and equal education for equal intelligence to more covert demands for abortion, birth control information and sexual autonomy within the marriage relationship. Their demands paralleled and were in large part dependent upon fundamental social and economic developments. Technological innovation and economic growth, changed patterns of income distribution, population concentrations, demographic changes in terms of life expectancy and fertility all affected women's behaviour and needs. Fewer women married; many were numbered among the urban poor. Such women had to become self-supporting and at the same time deal with the changed self-image that self-support necessitated. Those women who married generally did so later, had fewer children, and lived far beyond the birth of their youngest child. At the same time ideological developments began to encourage both men and women to aspire to increased independence and self-fulfilment. All these factors interacted to create new ambitions and new options for American women. In a universe of varying personalities and changing economic realities, it was inevitable that some women at least would – overtly or covertly – be attracted by such options and that a goodly number of men would find such choices unacceptable. Certainly for the women who did so the normative role of home-bound nurturant and passive woman was no longer appropriate or functional, but became a source of conflict and anxiety.

It was inevitable as well that many men, similarly faced with a rapidly changing society, would seek in domestic peace and constancy a sense of the continuity and security so difficult to find elsewhere in their society. They would – at the very least – expect their wives, their daughters, and their family relationships generally to remain unaltered. When their female dependants seemed ill-disposed to do so, such men responded with a harshness sanctioned increasingly by the new gods of science.

NOTES

This article was originally published in the *Journal of American History* 60 (September 1973), 332–56. The Editors and publishers are grateful for permission to reprint it here.

1. For historical studies of women's role and ideological responses to it in nineteenth-century America, see William L. O'Neill, *Everyone was Brave: A History of Feminism in America* (Chicago, 1969); William Wasserstrom, *Heiress of all the Ages: Sex and Sentiment in the Victorian Tradition* (Minneapolis, 1959); Eleanor Flexner, *Century of Struggle: The Woman's Rights Movement in the United States* (New York, 1968); Aileen S. Kraditor, *The Ideas of the Woman Suffrage Movement, 1890–1920* (New York, 1965). For studies emphasizing the interaction between social change and sex role conflict see, Carroll Smith Rosenberg, 'Beauty, the Beast and the Militant Woman: A Case Study in Sex Roles and Social Stress in Jacksonian America', *American Quarterly*, XXIII (Oct. 1971), 562–84; Carroll Smith Rosenberg, 'The Hysterical Woman: Sex Roles and Role Conflict in 19th-Century America', *Social Research*, XXXIX (Winter, 1972), 652–78. The problem of sexuality in the English-speaking world has been a

particular subject of historical concern. Among the more important, if diverse, attempts to deal with this problem are Peter T. Cominos, 'Late-Victorian Sexual Respectability and the Social System', *International Review of Social History*, VIII (1963), 18–48, 216–50; Stephen Nissenbaum, 'Careful Love: Sylvester Graham and the Emergence of Victorian Sexual Theory in America, 1830–1840' (doctoral dissertation, University of Wisconsin, 1968); Graham Barker-Benfield, 'The Horrors of the Half Known Life: Aspects of the Exploitation of Women by Men' (doctoral dissertation, University of California, Los Angeles, 1968); Nathan G. Hale, Jr., *Freud and the Americans: The Beginnings of Psychoanalysis in the United States, 1876–1917* (New York, 1971), pp.24–46; David M. Kennedy, *Birth Control in America: The Career of Margaret Sanger* (New Haven, 1970), pp.36–71; Steven Marcus, *The Other Victorians: A Study of Sexuality and Pornography in Mid-Nineteenth-Century England* (New York, 1966). See also Charles E. Rosenberg, 'Sexuality, Class and Role in 19th-Century America', *American Quarterly*, XXV (May 1973), 131–54.

2. Marshall Hall, *Commentaries on some of the more important of the Diseases of Females*, in three parts (London, 1827), 2. Although this discussion centres on the nineteenth century, it must be understood that these formulations had a far longer pedigree.

3. Stephen Tracy, *The Mother and her Offspring* (New York, 1860), p.xv; William Goodell, *Lessons in Gynecology* (Philadelphia, 1879), 332; William B. Carpenter, *Principles of Human Physiology: With Their Chief Applications to Pathology, Hygiene, and Forensic Medicine* (4th ed., Philadelphia, 1850), 727. In mid-nineteenth century many of these traditional views of woman's peculiar physiological characteristics were restated in terms of the currently fashionable phrenology. For example, see Thomas L. Nichols, *Woman, in All Ages and Nations: A Complete and Authentic History of the Manners and Customs, Character and Condition of the Female Sex in Civilized and Savage Countries, from the Earliest Ages to the Present Time* (New York, c. 1849), p.xi.

4. Charles D. Meigs, *Lecture on Some of the Distinctive Characteristics of the Female. Delivered before the Class of the Jefferson Medical College, January 5, 1847* (Philadelphia, 1847), p.5.

5. M.L.Holbrook, *Parturition without Pain: A Code of Directions for Escaping from the Primal Curse* (New York, 1882), pp.14–15. See also Edward H. Dixon, *Woman, and her Diseases, from the Cradle to the Grave: Adapted Exclusively to her Instruction in the Physiology of her System, and all the Diseases of her Critical Periods* (New York, 1846), p.17; M.K. Hard, *Woman's Medical Guide: Being a Complete Review of the Peculiarities of the Female Constitution and the Derangements to which it is Subject. With a Description of Simple yet Certain Means for their Cure* (Mt. Vernon, Ohio, 1848), p.11.

6. In the hypothetical pathologies of these generations, the blood was often made to serve the same function as that of the nerves; it could cause general ills to have local manifestations and effect systemic changes based on local lesions. By mid-century, moreover, physicians had come to understand that only the blood supply connected the gestating mother to her child.

7. M.E. Dirix, *Woman's Complete Guide to Health* (New York, 1869), p.24. So fashionable were such models in the late-nineteenth century that America's leading gynaecologist in the opening years of the present century despaired of trying to dispel such exaggerated notions from his patients' minds. 'It is difficult,' he explained, 'even for a healthy girl to rid her mind of constant impending evil from the uterus and ovaries, so prevalent is the idea that woman's ills are mainly "reflexes" from the pelvic organs.' Gynaecological therapy was the treatment of choice for a myriad of symptoms. Howard A. Kelly, *Medical Gynecology* (New York, 1908), p.73.

8. [Dr. Porter,] *Book of Men, Women, and Babies. The Laws of God applied to Obtaining, Rearing, and Developing the Natural, Healthful, and Beautiful in Humanity* (New York, 1855), p.56; Tracy, *Mother and Offspring*, xxiii; H.S. Pomeroy, *The Ethics of Marriage* (New York, 1888), p.78.

9. On the involuntary quality of female sexuality, see Alexander J.C. Skene, *Education and Culture as Related to the Health and Diseases of Women* (Detroit, 1889), p.22.

10. George Engelmann, *The American Girl of To-Day: Modern Education and Functional Health* (Washington, 1900), pp.9–10.

11. Alexander Harvey, 'On the Relative Influence of the Male and Female Parents in the Reproduction of the Animal Species', *Monthly Journal of Medical Science*, XIX (Aug. 1854), 108–18; M.A. Pallen, 'Heritage, or Hereditary Transmission', *St. Louis Medical & Surgical Journal*, XIV (Nov. 1856), 495. William Warren Potter, *How Should Girls be Educated? A Public Health Problem for Mothers, Educators, and Physicians* (Philadelphia, 1891), p.9.

12. As one clerical analyst explained, 'All the spare force of nature is concerned in this interior nutritive system, unfitting and disinclining the woman for strenuous muscular and mental enterprise, while providing for the shelter and nourishment of offspring throughout protracted periods of embryo and infancy.' William C. Conant, 'Sex in Nature and Society,' *Baptist Quarterly*, IV (April 1870), 183.

13. William H. Holcombe, *The Sexes here and hereafter* (Philadelphia, 1869), pp.201–02. William Holcombe was a Swedenborgian, and these contrasting views of the masculine and feminine also reflect New Church doctrines.

14. In pregnancy many middle-class women 'sought to hide their imagined shame as long as possible', by tightening corsets and then remaining indoors, shunning even the best of friends – certainly never discussing the impending event. Henry B. Hemenway, *Healthful Womanhood and Childhood: Plain Talks to Non-Professional Readers* (Evanston, Ill., 1894); Elizabeth Evans, *The Abuse of Maternity* (Philadelphia, 1875), pp.28–9.

15. For a brief summary of late nineteenth-century assumptions in regard to human genetics, see Charles E. Rosenberg, 'Factors in the Development of Genetics in the United States: Some Suggestions', *Journal of the History of Medicine*, XXII (Jan. 1967), 31–3.

16. Since both male and female were ordinarily involved in decisions to practise birth control, the cases are not strictly analogous. Both, however, illustrate areas of social conflict organized about stress on traditional role characteristics. This discussion emphasizes only those aspects of the birth control debate which placed responsibility on the woman. Commentators did indeed differ in such emphases; in regard to abortion, however, writers of every religious and ideological persuasion agreed in seeing the matter as woman's responsibility.

17. 'The results,' as Edward H. Clarke put it in his widely discussed polemic on the subject, 'are monstrous brains and puny bodies; abnormally active cerebration, and abnormally weak digestion; flowing thought and constipated bowels; lofty aspirations and neuralgic sensations. . . .' Edward H. Clarke, *Sex in Education: Or, a Fair Chance for Girls* (Boston, 1873), 41. Thomas A. Emmett, in his widely used textbook of gynaecology, warned in 1879 that girls of the better classes should spend the year before and two years after puberty at rest. 'Each menstrual period should be passed in the recumbent position until her system becomes accustomed to the new order of life.' Thomas Addis Emmett, *The Principles and Practice of Gynecology* (Philadelphia, 1879), p. 21.

18. T.S. Clouston, *Female Education from a Medical Point of View* (Edinburgh, 1882), p.20; Potter, *How Should Girls be Educated?* p.9.

19. The baleful hereditary effects of woman's secondary education served as a frequent sanction against this unnatural activity. Lawrence Irwell, 'The Competition of the Sexes and its Results', *American Medico-Surgical Bulletin*, X (Sept. 19, 1896), 319–20. All the doyens of American gynaecology in the late-nineteenth century – Emmett, J. Marion Sims, T. Gaillard Thomas, Charles D. Meigs, William Goodell, and Mitchell – shared the conviction that higher education and excessive development of the nervous system might interfere with woman's proper performance of her maternal functions.

20. William Goodell, *Lessons in Gynecology* (Philadelphia, 1879), p.353.

21. William Edgar Darnall, 'The Pubescent Schoolgirl', *American Gynecological & Obstetrical Journal*, XVIII (June 1901), 1490.

22. Board of Regents, University of Wisconsin, *Annual Report, for the Year Ending, September 30, 1877* (Madison, 1877), p.45.

23. Clouston, *Female Education*, p.19.

24. James E. Reeves, *The Physical and Moral Causes of Bad Health in American Women* (Wheeling, W.Va., 1875), p.28; John Ellis, *Deterioration of the Puritan Stock and its Causes* (New York, 1884), p.7; George Everett, *Health Fragments or, Steps Toward a True Life: Embracing Health, Digestion, Disease, and the Science of the Reproductive Organs*)New York, 1874), p.37; Nathan Allen, 'The Law of Human Increase; Or Population based on Physiology and Psychology', *Quarterly Journal of Psychological Medicine*, II (April 1868), 231; Nathan Allen, 'The New England Family', *New Englander* (March 1882), 9–10; Pye Henry Chavasse, *Advice to a Wife on the Management of her Own Health. And on the Treatment of Some of the Complaints Incidental to Pregnancy, Labour and Suckling with an Introductory Chapter especially Addressed to a Young Wife* (New York, 1886), pp.73–5.

25, Sarah H. Stevenson, *The Physiology of Woman, Embracing Girlhood, Maternity and Mature Age* (2nd ed., Chicago, 1881), p.68, 77; Alice Stockham, *Tokology: A Book for Every Woman* (rev.ed., Chicago, 1887), p.257. Sarah H. Stevenson noted acidly that 'the unerring instincts of woman have been an eloquent theme for those who do not know what they are talking about.' Stevenson, *Physiology of Woman*, p.79. The dress reform movement held, of course, far more significant implications than one would gather from the usually whimsical attitude with which it is normally approached; clothes were very much a part of woman's role. Health reformers, often critical as well of the medical establishment whose arguments we have – essentially – been describing, were often sympathetic to women's claims that not too much, but too little, mental stimulation was the cause of their ills, especially psychological ones. M.L.Holbrook, *Hygiene of the Brain and Nerves and the Cure of Nervousness* (New York, 1878), pp.63–64, 122–23; James C. Jackson, *American Womanhood: Its Peculiarities and Necessities* (Dansville, N.Y., 1870), pp.127–31.

26. For documentation of the progressive drop in the white American birth rate during the nineteenth century, and some possible reasons for this phenomenon, see Yasukichi Yasuba, *Birth Rates of the White Population in the United States, 1800–1860: An Economic Study* (Baltimore, 1962); J. Potter, 'American Population in the Early National Period', Paul Deprez (ed.), *Proceedings of Section V of the Fourth Congress of the International Economic History Association* (Winnipeg, Canada, 1970), pp.55–69. For a more general background to this trend, see A.M. Carr-Saunders, *World Population: Past Growth and Present Trends* (London, 1936).

27. A.K.Gardner, *Conjugal Sins against the Laws of Life and Health* (New York, 1874), p.131. H.R. Storer of Boston was probably the most prominent and widely read critic of such 'conjugal sins'. Abortion had in particular been discussed and attacked since early in the century, though it was not until the postbellum years that it became a widespread concern of moral reformers. Alexander Draper, *Observations on Abortion. With an Account of the Means both Medicinal and Mechanical, Employed to Produce that Effect . . .* (Philadelphia, 1839); Hugh L. Hodge, *On Criminal Abortion; A Lecture* (Philadelphia, 1854). Advocates of birth control routinely used the dangers and prevalence of abortion as one argument justifying their cause.

28. *Report of the Suffolk District Medical Society On Criminal Abortion and Ordered Printed . . . May 9, [1857]* (Boston, 1857), p.2. The report was almost certainly written by Storer. The Michigan report is summarized in William D. Haggard, *Abortion: Accidental, Essential, Criminal.* Address before the Nashville Academy of Medicine, Aug. 4, 1898 (Nashville, Tenn., 1898), p.10. For samples of contemporary descriptions of prevalence, cheapness, and other aspects of abortion and birth control in the period, see Ely Van De Warker, *The Detection of Criminal Abortion, and a Study of Foeticidal Drugs* (Boston, 1872); Evans, *Abuse of Maternity*: Horatio R. Storer, *Why Not? A Book for Every Woman* (2nd ed., Boston, 1868); [N.F. Cook,] *Satan in Society: By A Physician* (Cincinnati, 1876); Discussion, *Transactions of the Homeopathic Medical Society of New York*, IV (1866), 9–10; H.R. Storer and F.F. Hears, *Criminal Abortion* (Boston, 1868); H.C. Ghent, 'Criminal Abortion, or Foeticide', *Transactions of the Texas State Medical Association at the Annual Session 1888–89* (1888–1889), 119–46: Hugh Hodge, *Foeticide, or Criminal Abortion: A Lecture Introductory to the Course on Obstetrics, and Diseases of Women and Children. University of*

Pennsylvania (Philadelphia, 1869), pp.3–10. Much of the medical discussion centred on the need to convince women that the traditional view that abortion was no crime if performed before quickening was false and immoral, and to pass and enforce laws and medical society proscriptions against abortionists.

29. Compare the warning of Pomeroy, *Ethics of Marriage*, v, p.6, with the editorial, 'A Conviction for Criminal Abortion', *Boston Medical & Surgical Journal*, CVI (Jan. 5, 1882), 18–19. It is significant that discussions of birth control in the United States always emphasized the role and motivations of middle-class women and men; in England, following the canon of the traditional Malthusian debate, the working class and its needs played a far more prominent role. Not until late in the century did American birth control advocates tend to concern themselves with the needs and welfare of the working population. It is significant as well that English birth control advocates often used the prevalence of infanticide as an argument for birth control; in America this was rarely discussed. And one doubts if the actual incidence of infanticide was substantially greater in London than New York.

30. For a guide to literature on birth control in nineteenth-century America, see Norman Himes, *Medical History of Contraception* (Baltimore, 1936). See also J.A. Banks, *Prosperity and Parenthood: A Study of Family Planning among the Victorian Middle Classes* (London, 1954), and J.A. and Olive Banks, *Feminism and Family Planning in Victorian Englan* (Liverpool, 1964); Margaret Hewitt, *Wives and Mothers in Victorian Industry* (London, c.1958). For the twentieth century, see David M. Kennedy, *Birth Control in America*.

31. John Humphrey Noyes, *Male Continence* (Oneida, N.Y., 1872), pp.10–11.

32. It is not surprising that the design for a proto-diaphragm patented as early as 1846 should have been called 'The Wife's Protector'. J.B. Beers, 'Instrument to Prevent Conception, Patented Aug. 28th, 1846', design and drawings (Historical Collections, Library of the College of Physicians of Philadelphia).

33. In some marriages, for example, even if the male had consciously chosen, indeed urged, the practice of birth control, he was effectively deprived of a dimension of sexual pleasure and of the numerous children which served as tangible and traditional symbols of masculinity as well as the control over his wife which the existence of such children implied. In some marriages, however, birth control might well have brought greater sexual fulfilment because it reduced the anxiety of the female partner. Throughout the nineteenth century withdrawal was almost certainly the most common form of birth control. One author described it as a practice so universal that it may well be termed a national vice, so common that it is unblushingly acknowledged by its perpetrators, for the commission of which the husband is even eulogized by his wife'. [Cook,] *Satan in Society*, p.152. One English advocate of birth control was candid enough to argue that 'the real objection underlying the opposition, though it is not openly expressed, is the idea of the deprivation of pleasure supposed to be involved.' Austin Holyyoake, *Large or Small Families* (London, 1892)p.11.

34. R.T.Trall, *Sexual Physiology: A Scientific and Popular Exposition of the Fundamental Problems in Sociology* (New York, 1866), p.xi, 202. As women awoke to a realization of their own 'individuality', as a birth control advocate explained it in the 1880s, they would rebel against such 'enforced maternity'. E.B. Foote, Jr., *The Radical Remedy in Social Science: Or, Borning Better Babies* (New York, 1886), p.132. See also Stevenson, *Physiology of Women*, p.91; T.L.Nichols, *Esoteric Anthropology* (New York, 1824); E.H.Heywood, *Cupid's Yokes: Or, the Binding Force of Conjugal Life* (Princeton, MA., 1877); Stockham, *Tokology*, p.250; Alice Stockholm, *Karezza: Ethics of Marriage* (Chicago, 1896); E.B.Foote, *Medical Commonsense Applied to the Causes, Prevention and Cure of Chronic Diseases and Unhappiness in Marriage* (New York, 1864), p. 365; J.Soule, *Science of Reproduction and Reproductive Control. The Necessity of Some Abstaining from Having Children. The Duty of all to Limit their Families According to their Circumstances Demonstrated. Effects of Continence Effects of Self-pollution — Abusive Practices. Seminal Secretion – Its Connection with Life. With all the Different Modes of Preventing Conception, and the Philosophy of Each* (n.p., 1856), p.37; L.B. Chandler, *The Divineness of Marriage* (New York, 1872). To

the radical feminist Tennie C. Claflin, man's right to impose his sexual desires upon woman was the issue underlying all opposition to women's suffrage and the expansion of woman's role. Tennie C. Claflin, *Constitutional Equality: A Right of Woman: Or a Consideration of the Various Relations Which She Sustains as a Necessary Part of the Body of Society and Humanity; With Her Duties to Herself – together with a Review of the Constitution of the United States, Showing that the Right to Vote Is Guaranteed to All Citizens. Also a Review of the Rights of Children* (New York, 1871), p.63. Particularly striking are the letters from women desiring birth control information. Margaret Sanger, *Motherhood in Bondage* (New York, 1928); E.B.Foote, Jr., *Radical Remedy*, pp.114–20; Henry C. Wright, *The Unwelcome Child; or, the Crime of an Undesigned and Undesired Maternity* (Boston, 1858). This distinction between economic, 'physical', and role consideration, is, quite obviously, justifiable only for the sake of analysis; these considerations must have coexisted within each family in particular configuration.

35. Noyes, *Male Continence*, p.16; Frederick Hollick, *The Marriage Guide, Or Natural History of Generation; A Private Instructor for Married Persons and Those About to Marry, Both Male and Female* (New York, c. 1860), p.348; Trall, *Sexual Physiology*, pp.205–06.

36. Indeed, in these post-Darwinian years it was possible for at least one health reformer to argue that smaller families were a sign of that higher nervous evolution which accompanied civilization. [M.L. Holbrook,] *Marriage and Parentage* (New York, 1882). For the eugenic virtues of fewer but better children, see E.R. Shepherd, *For Girls: A Special Physiology: Being a Supplement to the Study of General Physiology. Twentieth Edition* (Chicago, 1887), p.213; M.L.Griffith, *Ante-Natal Infanticide* (n.p. [1889]), p.8.

37. See Louis François Etienne Bergeret (trans. P. de Marmon), *The Preventive Obstacle: Or Conjugal Onanism,* (New York, 1870); C.H.F. Routh, *Moral and Physical Evils Likely to Follow if Practices Intended to Act as Checks to Population be not Strongly Discouraged and Condemned* (2nd ed., London, 1879), p.13; Goodell, *Lessons in Gynecology*, pp.371, 374; Thomas Hersey, *The Midwife's Practical Directory; Or Woman's Confidential Friend: Comprising, Extensive Remarks on the Various Casualties and Forms of Diseases Preceding, Attending and Following the Period of Gestation, with appendix* (2nd ed., Baltimore, 1836), p.80; William H. Walling, *Sexology* (Philadelphia, 1902), p.79.

38. J.R.Black, *The Ten Laws of Health; Or, How Disease Is Produced and Can Be Prevented* (Philadelphia, 1873), p.251. See also C.A. Greene, *Build Well. The Basis of Individual, Home, and National Elevation. Plain Truths Relating to the Obligations of Marriage and Parentage* (Boston, c. 1885), p.99; E.P. LeProhon, *Voluntary Abortion, or Fashionable Prostitution, with Some Remarks upon the Operation of Craniotomy* (Portland, ME, 1867), p.15; M. Solis-Cohen, *Girl, Wife and Mother* (Philadelphia, 1911), p.213.

39. There is an instructive analogy between these ponderously mechanistic sanctions against birth control and abortion and the psychodynamic arguments against abortion used so frequently in the twentieth century; both served precisely the same social function. In both cases, the assumption of woman's childbearing destiny provided the logical basis against which a denial of this calling produced sickness, in the nineteenth century through physiological, and ultimately, pathological processes – in the twentieth century through guilt and psychological but again, ultimately, pathological processes.

40. A.K. Gardner, for example, confessed sympathy for the seduced and abandoned patron of the abortionist, 'but for the married shirk, who disregards her divinely-ordained duty, we have nothing but contempt. . . .' Gardner, *Conjugal Sins*, p.112. See also E. Frank Howe, *Sermon on Ante-Natal Infanticide delivered at the Congregational Church in Terre Haute, on Sunday Morning, March 28, 1869* (Terre Haute, IN, 1869); J.H. Tilden, *Cursed before Birth* (Denver, c. 1895); J.M. Toner, *Maternal Instinct, or Love* (Baltimore, 1864), p.91.

41. It must be emphasized that this is but one theme in a complex debate surrounding the issue of birth control and sexuality. A group of more evangelically oriented health

reformers tended to emphasize instead the responsibility of the 'overgrown, abnormally developed and wrongly directed amativeness of the man' and to see the woman as victim. John Cowan, Henry C. Wright, and Dio Lewis were widely read exemplars of this point of view. This group shared a number of assumptions and presumably psychological needs, and represents a somewhat distinct interpretive task. John Cowan, *The Science of A New Life* (New York, 1874), p.275.

42. W.L. Atlee and D.A. O'Donnell, 'Report of the Committee on Criminal Abortion', *Transactions of the American Medical Association*, XXII (1871), p.241.

43. The most tireless advocate of these views was Nathan Allen, a Lowell, Massachusetts, physician and health reformer. Nathan Allen, 'The Law of Human Increase; Or Population based on Physiology and Psychology', *Quarterly Journal Psychological Medicine*, II (April 1868), 209–66; Nathan Allen, *Changes in New England Population, Read at the Meeting of the American Social Science Association, Saratoga, September 6, 1877* (Lowell, 1877); Nathan Allen, 'The Physiological Laws of Human Increase', *Transactions of the American Medical Association*, XXI (1870), 381–407; Nathan Allen, 'Physical Degeneracy', *Journal of Psychological Medicine*, IV (Oct. 1870),725–64; Nathan Allen, 'The Normal Standard of Woman for Propagation', *American Journal of Obstetrics*, IX (April 1876), 1–39.

44. Ellis, *Deterioration of Puritan Stock*, p.3; Storer, *Why Not?* p.85.

45. Clarke, *Sex in Education*, p.63. For similar warnings, see Henry Gibbons, *On Feticide* (San Francisco, 1878), p.4; Charles Buckingham, *The Proper Treatment of Children, Medical or Medicinal* (Boston, 1873), p.15; Edward Jenks, 'The Education of Girls from a Medical Stand-Point', *Transactions of the Michigan State Medical Society*, XIII (1889), 52–62; Paul Paquin, *The Supreme Passions of Man* (Battle Creek, Mi., 1891), p.76.

46. These arguments, first formulated in the 1860s, had become clichés in medical and reformist circles by the 1880s. See Barbara Miller Solomon, *Ancestors and Immigrants: A Changing New England Tradition* (Cambridge, MA, 1956); John Higham, *Strangers in the Land; Patterns of American Nativism, 1860–1925* (New Brunswick, NJ, 1955). Such arguments exhibited a growing consciousness of class as well as of ethnic sensitivity; it was the better-educated and more sensitive members of society, anti-Malthusians began to argue, who would curtail their progeny, while the uneducated and coarse would hardly change their habits. H.S. Pomeroy, *Is Man Too Prolific? The So-Called Malthusian Idea* (London, 1891), pp.57–58.

47. Ellis, *Deterioration of Puritan Stock*, p.10.

48. Oscar Handlin, *Race and Nationality in American Life* (5th ed., Boston, 1957), pp.139–66.

49. One might postulate a more traditionally psychodynamic explanatory model, one which would see the arguments described as a male defence against their own consciousness of sexual inadequacy or ambivalence or of their own unconscious fears of female sexual powers. These emphases are quite distinct. The first – though it also assumes the reality of individual psychic mechanisms such as repression and projection – is tied very much to the circumstances of a particular generation, to social location, and to social perception. The second kind of explanation is more general, time-free, and based on a presumably ever-recurring male fear of female sexuality and its challenge to the capacity of particular individuals to act and live an appropriate male role. For the literature on this problem, see Wolfgang Lederer, *The Fear of Women* (New York, 1968).

50. At this time, moreover, most psychiatric clinicians and theoreticians would agree that no model exists to extend the insights gained from individual psychodynamics to the behaviour of larger social groups such as national populations or social classes.

51. Most societies provide alternative roles to accommodate the needs of personality variants – as, for example, the shaman role in certain Siberian tribes or the accepted man-woman homosexual of certain American Indian tribes. In the nineteenth-century English-speaking world such roles as that of the religious enthusiast and the chronic female invalid or hysteric may well have provided such modalities. But a period of peculiarly rapid or widespread social change can make even such available role

alternatives inadequate mechanisms of adjustment for many individuals. Others in the same society may respond to the same pressures of change by demanding an undeviating acceptance of traditional role prescriptions and refusing to accept the legitimacy of such cultural variants. The role of the hysterical woman in late nineteenth-century America suggests many of the problems inherent in creating such alternative social roles. While offering both an escape from the everyday duties of wife and mother, and an opportunity for the display of covert hostility and aggression, this role inflicted great bodily (though non-organic) pain, provided no really new role or interest, and perpetuated – even increased – the patient's dependence on traditional role characteristics, especially that of passivity. The reaction of society, as suggested by the writings of most male physicians, can be described as at best an unstable compromise between patronizing tolerance and violent anger. See Carroll Smith Rosenberg, 'The Hysterical Woman: Sex Roles and Role Conflict in 19th-Century America', pp.652–78. For useful discussions of hysteria and neurasthenia, see Ilza Veith, *Hysteria: The History of a Disease* (Chicago, 1965); Henri F. Ellenberger, *The Discovery of the Unconscious: The History and Evolution of Dynamic Psychiatry* (New York, 1970); Charles E. Rosenberg, 'The Place of George M. Beard in Nineteenth-Century Psychiatry', *Bulletin of the History of Medicine*, XXXVI (May–June 1962), 245–59; John S. Haller, Jr., 'Neurasthenia: The Medical Profession and the "New Woman" of Late Nineteenth-Century', *New York State Journal of Medicine*, LXXI (Feb. 15, 1971), 473–82. Esther Fischer-Homberger has recently argued that these diagnostic categories masked an endemic male-female conflict: 'Hysterie und Mysogynie – ein Aspekt der Hysteriegeschichte', *Gesnerus*, XXVI (1969), 117-27.

2

The Feminist Physique: Physical Education and the Medicalization of Women's Education

Paul Atkinson

The following study does not claim to present new archival research on physical education for women. Rather, it is an attempt to reconsider aspects of our present knowledge and to offer a sociological account of the surveillance and control of women's bodies. It is argued that the measurement and monitoring of health and physique were incorporated into a powerful armamentarium of physical and social regulation. The weapons were double-edged. Physical education and measurement were powerful elements in the feminist reformers' struggle for academic education for women. They also added to the strictures of conformity and control within which women educators in Britain and the United States were forced to manoeuvre. The 'feminist physique' was both symbolic and instrumental in the contested domain of women's physical and intellectual well-being. The major sources drawn on for this contribution are the histories of women's educational institutions, the autobiographies and biographies of the reformers, and the growing number of secondary sources in this important area of feminist history.[1]

THE GREEK IDEAL

In 1893 the World's Fair was held in Chicago. Sara Burstall, headmistress of the Manchester High School for Girls, writing on the state of women's education in 1894, was impressed by reports of one specific artefact displayed there. Quoting an eye-witness report she described an 'interesting artistic exhibit' as follows:

> The girl's figure is said to be typically feminine; the sculptor thinks it nearer the Greek ideal than the man's; it will probably not suffer in comparison with that of the girl who has not had a college education, although as there are no measurements for

her, the comparison is not easy to make. 'The essential point is that it is fairly healthful, fairly attractive, and, above all, thoroughly womanly . . . This being the case, nature and the gymnastic teachers will provide for all the rest'.[2]

What was this interesting exhibit? It was the statue of a young woman which was paired with a male counterpart. It had been made to the average measurements of young women students in higher education. The statistics for the male and female representations had been compiled by Dr Dudley Sargent and his collaborators, in gymnasia in Cambridge, Massachusetts, for the students of Harvard and Harvard Annex.[3] Sargent's measurements and the sculptor's realization of them produced an idealization – an icon – of the educated young lady in late nineteenth-century America. It embodied a number of themes of profound significance in the establishment and consolidation of educational provision for women. They were of equal importance in Britain and the United States. They were: full-time, academic education; health and fitness; gymnastics and physical training; femininity. The creation of the statue had been made possible by the collection of measurements of students' physique.

> A . . . contrast may be obtained by placing a cast of the Venus de Medicis beside any young woman who, by the diligent employment of stays, has succeeded in converting the form that the Creator bestowed on her, into one which she in her wisdom deems more beautiful . . . The statue of the Venus exhibits the natural shape, which is recognized by artists and persons of cultivated taste as the most beautiful which the female figure can assume: accordingly it is aimed at in all the finest statues of ancient and modern times. Misled, however, by ignorance, and a false and most preposterous taste, women of fashion and their countless flocks of imitators, down even to the lowest ranks of life, have gradually come to regard a narrow or spider-waist as an ornament worthy of attainment at any cost or sacrifice.[4]

The World's Fair exhibit was concrete testimony to the fact that the modern educated women it represented had – if not quite attaining the classical ideal – at least escaped the anatomical consequences of high fashion. In doing so, her champions would have insisted, she would also have escaped the deformities and invalidism which had been the lot of former generations.[5] The 'modern' woman of the late twentieth century is not the only one to have been offered the image and ideal of a physically cultivated body. For the 'modern' women of just 100 years ago could also aspire to an improved physique through work in the gymnasium. For her it was part and parcel of the social construction of new canons of female aspiration and achievement. The measurements, models and the Greek ideal represented the possibility of a restoration to the 'natural' perfection of form and function.

The collection of measurements such as those furnished by Sargent was an important task for the pioneers of women's education, and was a valuable source of ammunition for feminists' rebuttals of their critics. Moreover, it was part of a vigorous programme to monitor the well-being and progress of individual women and girls, and to evaluate the success of schools and colleges for women. The debates concerning women's education were often couched in physiological and medical terms, and the advocates of women's education themselves became highly conscious of physique and physiology.[6]

It was, for instance, thoroughly in keeping with this spirit that students of Madame Bergman-Österberg at her Hampstead Physical Training College (later Dartford College) in the 1890s should have attended the Anthropometrical Laboratory at the South Kensington Museum. Under the direction of Francis Galton, they produced the profile of the 'average student'.[7]

TABLE 1

THE 'AVERAGE STUDENT'

Age	21 years 2½ months
Head length	7.31 inches
Head breadth	5.73 inches
Height standing	64.49 inches
Height sitting	33.97 inches
Span of arms	63.93 inches
Weight	123.01 lbs
Grasp, left	56.5 lb.
Grasp, right	59.71 lb.
Lung capacity	184.42 cu. in.
Reaction to sight in hundredths of seconds	18.32
Reaction to sound in hundredths of seconds	14.75
Measurement across chest, armpit to armpit	
Inflated	14.64 in.
Uninflated	14.00 in.
Measurement around lower ribs	
Inflated	29.62 in.
Uninflated	27.88 in.
Colour sense	Normal
Hearing	Normal

Now these figures are not especially important in themselves, but are aptly illustrative of the sort of measurements that were being made of young women attending many institutions. Of course, at the Physical Training College, it was understandable that the curriculum should include some reference to such matters (the students annually took the Anatomy and Hygiene examinations at the Museum's Laboratory). But such interest in measurement and physique was by no means confined to training colleges for teachers of physical education. It was of vital concern to women's educational institutions generally: the schools and colleges where Madame Bergman-Österberg's students were to practise as physical education teachers took such matters very much to heart. The products of the training colleges were to have a major role in monitoring the physique and health of the young women and girls receiving full-time education in schools and colleges. The teacher of physical education was part of a powerful coalition of professionals in the educational arena who co-operated in the close surveillance of students' physical performance and well-being.

Such surveillance was a central concern in schools and colleges in Britain and America in the final quarter of the nineteenth century and the early years of this. From relatively informal and *ad hoc* beginnings, it developed into a highly developed regime of 'medical inspection'. This emphasis on health and physique was fostered in the departments of physical education which were a major feature of institutions for women's education. Indeed, the medical and gymnastic were part and parcel of the same movement in women's education, and were of major significance in the ideological disputes surrounding the foundation of schools and colleges to provide academically sound education for young ladies. Such a movement among educationalists was a self-conscious response to medical opposition to the aspirations of feminist pioneers.

THE EDUCATION OF WOMEN: OPPOSITION AND RESPONSE

The medical opposition to women's education has now been widely documented and will not be elaborated on here. The essence of the argument can be summarized fairly straightforwardly. The nub of the matter was a physiological principle which was widely believed and deployed by scientists and medical practitioners. The principle in question was 'the conservation of energy'. It postulated that within any given system or organization there is only a fixed amount of energy available to be expended. Undue exertion would constitute a drain on the energy reserves, which would have to be replenished by a suitable period of rest and replenishment. Furthermore, the internal economy of fixed energy reserves would mean that undue exertion by any part of the organism would necessary deplete the reserves of energy available to other organs. The imagery of an economic model, or balance sheet, was quite explicitly drawn on by some authors who promoted such a view. Herbert Spencer,[8] for one, declared Nature to be a 'strict accountant' and Maudsley, the leading British medical opponent of women's education, enunciated the principle most clearly:

> Let it be considered that the period of the real educational strain will commence about the time when, by the development of the sexual system, a great revolution takes place in the body and mind, and an extra-ordinary expenditure of vital energy is made, and will continue through those years after puberty when, by the establishment of periodical functions, a regularly recurring demand is made upon the resources of a constitution that is going through the final stages of its growth and development. The energy of a human body being a definite and not inexhaustible quantity, can it bear, without injury, an excessive mental drain as well as the natural physical drain which is so great at that time? . . . When nature spends in one direction, she must economise in another direction.[9]

Clearly this argument could apply to the education of boys and girls, but it was given special force in relation to the latter. As is mentioned in the above quote from Maudsley, it was widely argued that the physiological demands of secondary sexual development among girls placed an extraordinary demand upon reserves of vital energy. The maturation of the reproductive organs and the onset of menstruation required, as it were, the full concentration of the body's resources. The diversion of energy from physical development to mental exertion in schools would, it was argued, damage girls' development and lead to serious long-term impairment of health and fertility.

The economic argument for the conservation of energy was applied to men and boys but in a rather different guise. In that context it related to what Barker-Benfield has referred to as the 'spermatic economy'.[10] The dangerous expenditure of vital energy for boys would be occasioned by masturbation – and for men the danger of too-frequent copulation was added. Such over-expenditure would result in mental and moral degeneration – resulting in nervous exhaustion and, ultimately, in lunacy.

There was, therefore, an asymmetry in the implications drawn from the conservation of energy principle. Provided they abstained from abnormal or excessive physical expenditure, then males could undertake mental exertion with no danger to their constitution. Females, on the other hand, could engage in intellectual activities only at the expense of their health. While there is no doubt that the medical arguments gave a special force to anti-feminist reaction in nineteenth-century Britain and America, it would be quite wrong to assume that they were concocted *ad hoc* to serve the opponents of educational reform.

The principles on which the physiologists' and clinicians' arguments were based were well-established fundamentals of natural science and philosophy. They *were* used to express cultural preoccupations, and they *were* 'sexist' in their implications, but they were in no sense derived specifically from sexist assumptions.

The principle of energy conservation was formulated by a number of natural scientists – Mayer, Joule, Colding and, most prominently, Helmholtz. Earlier principles based on the notion of 'force' were reformulated in terms of 'energy' in the 1840s, in what Kuhn describes as an example of simultaneous discovery.[11] Cohen suggests that the impact and significance of the idea in nineteenth-century natural science derived from the fact that the principles of conservation had 'wide applications and far-reaching results'.[12] Elkana's extensive treatment of the topic shows how mechanical and physiological conceptions of 'force', 'heat', 'work' and 'energy' became fused in the mathematical formulation of the laws of thermodynamics. The principle of energy conservation rapidly became 'one of the most fundamental principles in all natural science'.[13] It appeared not only in the technical scientific literature, but also in more popular books and periodicals. Through Spencer's work (which explicitly drew on the convergences of natural science, biology and sociology) the idea became firmly entrenched in popular science, and the tenets of Social Darwinism. Rosenberg aptly summarizes how the ideas contributed to the medical arguments concerning women's social and biological functions:

> Doctors had often asserted that any affliction of the uterus could affect a woman's mental attitude, but with the aid of recent work in physics, neurophysiology, and technology, Clarke explicitly linked the physiological demands of an academic education to the reproductive impairment of the nation's future mothers. The work of Hermann von Helmholtz in thermodynamics and Herbert Spencer in sociology suggested that all physical systems, including the body, were subject to the principle of conservation of energy, and that force expended in one function would not be available to any other.[14]

There was, indeed, a continuous dialectic and cross-fertilization between metaphors of the natural and metaphors of society: medical discourse was a particularly powerful medium in which the social and the biological were compounded. But the concerns and moral panics which were encoded into the language of medicine were more generic, and concerned with social issues which went well beyond the establishment of academies for upper- and upper-middle-class girls and women.

The dangers of 'nervous' depletion and attendant disorders were believed to be widespread in Victorian and Edwardian society. They threatened men and women of the cultivated classes in particular. It was, as Haller and Haller have dubbed it, a 'nervous century', and many physicians of the late nineteenth century recognised *neurasthenia* as one of the besetting maladies of modern civilization: the disease label itself was first coined in the 1860s. Some observers, indeed, almost welcomed it as the necessary concomitant of social progress. The over-excitement and stimulation of modern (especially urban) everyday life placed too great a demand on the body's finite stock of nervous energy.

For both men and women, neurasthenia became a 'subtle self-flattery', and a 'deluge' of neurasthenic men and women took themselves from treatment to treatment across Europe and the United States,

> tasting every drug from bromide to opium, wearing plates on their feet and magnetic belts around their waists and foreheads, converting to Christian Science, going on 'nerve food' diets, and trying innumerable quack devices to alleviate the suffering they endured for the sake of progress.[15]

While men were at risk of such nervous exhaustion, women of the better classes were especially vulnerable, it was believed. And none more so than the 'new' woman who took on roles and exertions beyond the supposedly traditional domestic sphere. 'Neurasthenia' became a fashionable disease in many quarters, adopted as a manifestation of increased 'cultivation' and intellectual activity.

This depletion of nervous energy and of physical development among the educated classes of womanhood spelled an obvious and pressing danger for medical commentators. It was inevitable that such women were decreasingly capable of fulfilling their primary role (both in Nature and in society). That is, they would be progressively unable to conceive, bear and rear children.

American and European observers, both from within and beyond the medical profession, voiced the anxiety that the average number of children born to women of the upper classes was falling. The lower orders were likely to outbreed their betters, to the ultimate detriment of the 'race'. In the United States, this argument was coupled with the issue of immigration. The 'old' American family of the white Anglo-Saxon Protestant stock (in New England, for instance) was threatened with extinction as its young women experienced the dubious privileges of emancipation. They would be swamped by the physically more robust and more fecund immigrants of peasant stock (Italians, Poles, Irish and the like).[16]

There were, then, powerful arguments which were mobilized against those feminist pioneers who attempted to make academically-based education for women available. The individual woman was threatened with a decline in her health. The medical opponents of reform frequently included case histories of young women who had, they claimed, suffered damage at the hands of over-demanding educational institutions. Clarke and Maudsley, for example, illustrated their polemics with detailed case histories of young women who, they claimed, had been severely damaged by the undue demands of academic work. Their maladies included dysmenorrhoea and amenorrhoea, hysteria and debility. Their accounts were remarkable for the frankness with which gynaecological disorders were discussed in publications intended to reach a mass audience. (The authors reporting such case histories from their own clinical practice seem to have been more reticent over the treatments they prescribed or their own rate of cure.)

It was against this background of debate and opposition that physical education took root in women's schools and colleges. The gymnasium became a key feature of the school's physical resources, and the teacher of physical education a key member of staff. It was part of a conscious response on the part of the pioneers. They were in no position to ignore their medically-informed opponents, and although Elizabeth Garrett Anderson wrote a refutation of the Clarke/Maudsley thesis,[17] the issue of health and fitness had to be taken seriously. Indeed, many nineteenth-century principals and headmistresses were at pains to emphasize their own concern for their students' health.

The teachers of gymnastics had a key role to play in the monitoring and promotion of physical vigour – and in the detection and treatment of weakness or disorders. Often they worked in close collaboration with the physician appointed as medical adviser to the school. Burstall's 1894 survey of educational institutions in the United States revealed as much. She noted that important precursors to the movement were provided by German immigrants' enthusiasm for gymnastics, and the adoption of drill, which had originally been promoted in boys' schools during the Civil War. The special impetus in girls' education derived, however, from

> the change in the ways of living, consequent upon the growth of towns and of wealth, which has brought about a condition of high nervous tension, injurious to both sexes, but especially affecting women.[18]

The system of exercise devised by Dio Lewis had been adopted by many institutions. A renewed emphasis came in 1879 with the establishment of a gymnasium at Harvard, under the direction of Dr Sargent (from the Yale Medical School) and the creation of a special gymnasium in Cambridge for the training of female students of the Harvard Annex.

Dr Sargent's regime was based upon a diagnostic and therapeutic approach. Treatment was prescribed on an individual basis, and appliances used to strengthen particular parts of the body. (*Plus ça change*: the descriptions of Dr Sargent's system sound quite similar to the 'studios' and 'spas' with their 'Nautilus' equipment, to be found in Cambridge, Boston and other American cities just 100 years later.) It was a major part of Sargent's system that regular measurements of the students were taken: indeed, the World's Fair models were based on the measurements taken from Harvard and Harvard Annex students.[19]

Typical of provision of gymnastics in the United States – though perhaps unusually lavish – was the facility established at Vassar. The Calisthenium, housing the gymnasium and a riding school, was an imposing architectural feature of the college: it was opened in 1866 in the second year of the college's existence. The first Vassar College Catalog stated:

> The Gymnasium will be furnished with every variety of apparatus required to make it attractive and useful, and placed under the direction of an experienced and successful lady instructor. The system of light gymnastics, as perfected by Dr Dio Lewis, will be taught to all the College without extra charge, and all possible encouragement given to healthful feminine sports in the open air. Each student is required to provide herself with a light and easy-fitting dress adapted to these exercises.[20]

Similar emphasis on physical activity were to be found in other American foundations. A gymnasium was built at Mount Holyoke; Smith and Wellesley laid a similar stress on health and physical education. The Wellesley Calendar gives evidence of the collaboration between gymnasium teachers and medical advisers.

The physicians with the director of the gymnasium, the physical examiner, and the professor of education, constitute a Board of Health, under whose direction the students are examined on admission to the College . . . From the records of these examinations the exercises in the gymnasium are adapted to meet the special wants of each student.[21]

In the same fashion, Smith had a resident physician with overall responsibility for the physical education. Students were examined, and had a regime of exercises individually prescribed. Bryn Mawr too had a gymnasium equipped with Dr Sargent's apparatus. Here, students were required to undergo half-yearly examinations, as well as having a physical examination before admission.

The first 'system' to be introduced at various American colleges was that pioneered by Dio Lewis, who was influential in the promotion of physical training in the cause of female health and education in the United States. At his Family School for Young Ladies in Lexington, health was a primary objective. In the Prospectus for 1866 it was explained that:

American girls, especially of the higher classes, are too often pale, nervous and fragile, with stooping shoulders, weak spines and narrow chests. In studying under the ordinary systems of education, such girls imperil their chances of health, compromise their enjoyment of life, and often break down in the midst of their labours;[22]

Lewis was concerned, by contrast, to promote 'strength, endurance and grace' among his students. In order to do so he instituted the following regime:

1. Regular and thorough instruction in anatomy and physiology and frequent lectures on practical hygiene; and attention to pupils' personal habits.
2. Two to four half-hour sessions each day of gymnastics, including the prescription of Swedish movement for students needing special treatment.
3. Plain and nutritious food.
4. Fixed hours for rising and retiring.
5. Baths, warm and cold.
6. Regular walks, morning and evening – weather permitting.
7. Dress designed on 'physiological' principles, which would protect but not restrict the body.

As physical education developed, American schools fostered a number of different systems. As well as that of Dio Lewis, there was a system developed by Delsarte, that of Sargent, and the Swedish system as modified by Per Ling. The latter, for example, was introduced at the Boston Normal School in 1893, for the instruction of men and women.

It was the Swedish system which became firmly established in Britain, and – as in the United States – such gymnastic exercise was closely linked with the medical inspection and monitoring of students. Indeed, observers such as Sara Burstall tended to argue that Britain was even more enlightened and 'advanced' in that respect.

The background of medical opinion in Britain paralleled that of American commentators. The most widely distributed and debated polemic – by Maudsley – was extremely derivative of Clarke's pamphlet. Likewise, an emphasis on women's health and fitness was characteristic of many of the high schools and colleges which were founded in the second half of the nineteenth century.

In her survey of private schools for young ladies in Britain, Burstall found that the great majority had some system for medical inspection coupled with physical education. It was customary to carry out a physical examination on pupils on admission and at regular intervals.

> In the days when feminine weakness and physical delicacy were thought to be womanly charms such a standard needed to be set up. The teaching of hygiene, and the inclusion in the curriculum of regular formal physical training by gymnastic exercises were marked characteristics of the high schools from their very beginning, as was also very careful supervision of the school buildings and equipment, and of the physical condition of the pupils. Regular medical inspection by a school doctor began almost as soon as there were women doctors qualified to carry out such inspections.[23]

On the basis of such medical and gymnastic inspection, physical weaknesses were identified and appropriate remedial exercises prescribed:

> The medical woman will sometimes find it necessary to inspect a child term after term, and it is not infrequent for heads and assistant mistresses to send special girls for inspection, because of some difficulty that has arisen in work or discipline. The present writer would wish to have the medical inspector's opinion about the girl in every serious case that comes before her. It is, indeed, often found that idleness and bad work are connected with some physical condition.[24]

Medical inspection coupled with gymnastics was begun at the North London Collegiate School, under the headship of Frances Buss, in 1881, for instance.[25] There gymnastic exercise was under the general direction of a school doctor. Medical records were compiled as a matter of course, and there was a close relationship between academic work and physical work. At the North London Collegiate, as at comparable British schools, medical records were kept on the girls, and details of physique. Remarks such as the following, from anonymous headmistresses, are testimony of the importance attached to medical inspection and gymnastics.

> In two forms the intellectual work was found in one session to be below the proper standard: a study of the cards for the individual girls showed that the average weight was below what it had been in those forms the previous session, when the work was good. Inspection of the forms in the gymnasium showed lack of power of co-ordination and quick response. Consultation took place with the head, the number of subjects taught and the amount of homework was cut down, more drill lessons were given, letters were sent home asking mothers to send the girls to bed early and to see they ate well of simple nourishing food. In a term the work and the average and the maximum percentage of marks, as well as the pupils' vigour, rose in a most satisfactory way.
> I consider this inspection essential as it makes me aware of the physical as well as intellectual capacity of each pupil, and her time-table can be regulated accordingly. In the case of a delicate girl work can be somewhat minimized, until her health is normal. Where advised by an inspectress, special private remedial exercises are given, and these have been very useful in numberless cases where otherwise temporary muscular weakness might lead to permanent delicacy.[26]

Such a combination of physical education and medical supervision was taken especially seriously at St Leonards School. There Louisa Lumsden – the first head teacher – turned the stables into a gymnasium, and introduced gymnastic dress. There too, Jane Frances Dove contributed to an ethos which made St Leonards a leading exemplar in physical education (and made herself a leading expert on the topic). In one of the most widely cited essays, she drew on her experience of St Leonards School and its medical records. She tabulated the measurements from St Leonards (see Table 2 below) and expressed the hope that the Anthropometric Society would organise a wider survey of young women and girls. The tabulated results at St Leonards were used as a yardstick whereby individual girls' physical and mental development could be monitored.

> If . . . a growing girl did not increase in weight during a year, and was lighter than the average for her age, and height, then it would be high time to send for the doctor and have her thoroughly overhauled. On the other hand, if a girl was found to be persistently idle and inattentive, although apparently in good health, on consulting the weight book it would normally be found that she was underweight for her age, and a cure was easily affected by cutting off some of her work, giving her extra nourishment and more time for exercise in the open air.[27]

TABLE 2

ANTHROPOMETRIC RECORDS FROM ST LEONARDS SCHOOL

| Age | Height | | Weight | | | No of |
	ft.	ins.	st.	lb.	oz.	observations
9–10	4	3.38	4	4	10	22
10–11	4	5.763	4	12	14	36
11–12	4	8.403	5	6	6	49
12–13	4	11.509	6	5	1	81
13–14	5	1.639	7	2	2	218
14–15	5	3.128	7	12	3	490
15–16	5	3.972	8	6	0	737
16–17	5	4.451	8	11	6	870
17–18	5	4.666	9	1	7	627
18–19	5	4.804	9	4	10	242
19–20	5	5.267	9	5	6	51

In the collection of medical records and statistics, and in the monitoring of health and exercise, there was thus a powerful coalition in the schools. The headteacher, form teacher, school doctor and teacher of gymnastics could collaborate in the close surveillance of young women's bodies and minds. Physique, physiology, intellect and moral quality were held to exercise mutual influence.

Mills College (in California) provides a pertinent example, which reflects the concern with *weight*. In a manner alien to more modern sensibilities, the women charged with the care of girls were primarily preoccupied with avoiding frailty. The female stereotype they sought to avoid was the slender, pale, sickly neurasthenic: hence the desire to promote a more robust physique. Of Mills College we are told that the students themselves proudly reported weight gain.

The number of pounds gained during this year was over fourteen hundred. One young lady has gained twenty-five pounds in six months . . . The class of 1873 boasted a combined weight of 'a clear two thousand three hundred seventy-five and a quarter pounds' as its 'social-scale' and its combined height as 'ninety-eight feet and ten inches . . .' of 'perfect woman, nobly featured . . .'[28]

The collection and publication of statistics on health and physique was continued and became a major feature of women's educational institutions:

In many schools periodical examinations of backbones, and ankles and eyesight are made. Records are kept, skilled and scientific physical training is carried out. Nothing is neglected which can serve to make the body straight and strong and to develop perfectly in all its powers. The benefit to the present generation of girls of the skilled care and training of their bodies cannot be exaggerated.[29]

As the first generation of women graduated from institutions of higher education in Britain and the United States, medical inspection was followed up by surveys of the reported health of graduates and alumnae. Continued concern and vigilance were necessary on the feminists' part: despite the evident success of women's schools and colleges, medically-informed opposition to their work remained current for several decades. It was therefore imperative that the benefits of mental and physical exertion be demonstrated.

One of the most widely quoted of such surveys was conducted by the Association of College Alumnae in 1885, and published by the Massachusetts Bureau of Labor Statistics.[30] It was based on a questionnaire sent out to 1,290 women graduates of 12 colleges and universities. Of the 705 who returned completed replies, 138 women

TABLE 3

ASSOCIATION OF COLLEGE ALUMNAE SURVEY RESULTS

	% in excellent or good health	% in fair health	% in poor or bad health or dead
On entering College	78.16	1.98	19.86
During College	74.89	7.80	17.31
Present	77.87	5.11	17.02

(19.6 per cent) reported deterioration in their health while at college, 418 (59.3 per cent) reported no change, and 149 (21.1 per cent) reported that their state of health had improved. Table 3 shows the women's reported state of health.

The responses were analysed in order to examine the possible effects of study habits on the women's health. It was found that 199 (28.2 per cent) had worked 'severely' – of whom 20 per cent enjoyed 'poor' health; 438 (62.1 per cent) worked 'moderately – of whom 15 per cent were in 'poor' health. The authors of the report concluded that *worry* was 'the most potent of all the predisposing causes of disease among these students' and of those who reported no worries over their studies or personal affairs, 92 per cent were in fair or good health.

John Dewey worked on the data of the survey, and he concluded that 'They certainly bear out the conclusions drawn regarding the uninjurious effect of collegiate study', although he was unhappy that the survey had not adequately investigated the environment of the college, and he appeared still to have reservations about women's colleges:

> It has long been a commonplace of vital science that intellectual pursuits for men *per se* are healthy. The questions which need solution are: What conditions prevent their being equally healthy for women, the exact part played by each factor, and how far it is removable?[31]

The survey by the Association of College Alumnae inspired a similar study of Oxford and Cambridge women, reported by Mrs Henry Sidgwick.[32] As an additional comparison group, the British students' sisters who had not attended college were also surveyed. The sister nearest in age was selected, or, failing a sister, a cousin of similar age who had not attended college. In all, responses from 566 English students were gathered and from 450 sisters or cousins. Relevant figures from the survey are given in Table 4.

Of the 328 students who had attended college for three years or more, 78 (20.7 per cent) reported a deterioration in health, of whom 65 showed 'slight' deterioration and only eight 'more serious'; 51 (15.5 per cent) reported an improvement and 199 (60.7 per cent) reported 'no change'. Hayes, in summarizing and commenting on the survey results, concluded that the

> . . . temporary falling off during college life of about five per cent in good health, compared with either health at entering or present health, to some extent depends on illness or other things

TABLE 4

SURVEY OF OXFORD AND CAMBRIDGE STUDENTS: PERCENTAGE OF
RESPONDENTS REPORTING 'EXCELLENT' OR 'GOOD' HEALTH

	Students	'Sisters'
3–8 years of age	71.5	64.7
8–14 years of age	67.1	63.5
14–18 years of age	62.0	56.3
At entering college life	68.2	—
During college life		
(sisters 18–21 years)	63.1	58.5
Present health	68.0	59.3
N =	566	450

occurring accidentally during the college course, and to some
extent to probably due to the relaxing climate of our universities;
but it is also partly caused by overwork and want of attention to
well-known rules of health, and to this extent both could and
ought to be prevented by reasonable care on the part of the
students themselves.[33]

In other words, while the figures did not bear out fears of widespread
disability as the outcome of college work, there was no cause for
complacency; vigilance and concern were needed.

CONCLUSION:
NATURE, CULTURE AND DOUBLE CONFORMITY

The development of physical education in parallel with medical
inspection was therefore firmly grounded in debates over women's
capacity to withstand the rigours of intellectual effort. The feminist
pioneers of educational reform took medical opposition to heart, and
their collective response to it became thoroughly characteristic of the
ethos and organization of school life.

The arguments concerning female physical and mental functioning,
and the feminist response, rested on competing definitions of the
boundaries of Nature and Culture. The dominant model, articulated
by men like Clarke and Maudsley, treated Nature and Culture as
opposed categories which were paralleled by a duality between the
sexes, and a corresponding duality between their respective social
spheres. Women were 'beneath' culture, imprisoned in their natural,

physiological limitations. Should a woman seek to escape from her naturally ordained social position, then nature would exact retribution in the form of ever greater weakness. The woman who sought, consciously or unconsciously, to undermine the cultural order would find her own physical order destroyed in the process.

Confronted with such a model, the would-be reformers were forced to seek some alternative position. The introduction of physical education provided them with what they needed. They acknowledged their physical weakness, but refused to attribute it to the immutable laws of nature. Rather, they saw its origins as cultural. They emphasized that women were sick, not because of inherent frailty, or the peculiarities of the reproductive organs, but from a lack of healthy occupation, from boredom, lack of fresh air and exercise, the unhealthy dictates of dress fashion and so on. Hence they achieved some reconciliation between the dominant Nature/Culture opposition by recourse to their programmes of physical training, which treated the female body as a field for cultural intervention, rather than as a passive field of naturally determined processes (and suffering). Through such schooling they attempted to redefine themselves as potentially fit for entry to the masculine, cultural domain.

The feminist response in this context highlights a recurrent feature of nineteenth-century feminism. In attempting to achieve their reforms, the feminist reformers were forced to manoeuvre within very narrow limits. In order to preserve their credibility they were not able simply to reject the predominant conceptual schemes of Victorian society, even if they had been able to conceptualize such radical transformations anyway. Rather than turn the world upside down, they had to modify the existing cultural categories in order to find some leeway for themselves. But in the course of such manoeuvres, the women often constructed new straitjackets for themselves. In the girls' schools, their reliance on physical education turned the medicalized arguments of the opponents of reform.

At the same time, the introduction of physical education in combination with medical inspection created an especially strong form of discipline and control over young ladies' bodies. It has been shown that the twin aims of ladylike decorum and academic attainments subjected women's education to the demands of 'double conformity'.[34] To this was added the discipline and detailed surveillance of the body. The individual body was inspected for any weakness or deformity, and any necessary correction imposed. Likewise, successive cohorts were subjected to scrutiny and measurement. The anthropometry discussed above was but part of a more general preoccupation with the ordering, discipline and control of women's bodies. Accounts of daily life and work in training colleges for women's physical education indicate that the control exercised over students was strict, and that physical control and social control were equated – symbolically and practically. The graduates of such training colleges took such an ethos into the schools where they practised and made a major contribution to their emergent character. The resulting inspection and supervision of girls' schooling generated a new form of medicalized ideology and social control.

NOTES

1. Sources consulted which include reference to physical education and physique include, for Britain: Violet Mary MacPherson, *The Story of St Anne's, Abbots Bromley 1874–1924* (Shrewsbury, 1925); Joyce Godber and Isabel Hutchins, *A Century of Challenge: Bedford High School 1882 to 1982* (Bedford 1982); Janet Whitcut, *Edgbaston High School 1876–1976* (Birmingham, 1976); Winifred I Vardy (ed.), *King Edward VI High School for Girls Birmingham 1883–1925* (Birmingham, 1928); Constance M. Broadway and Esther I. Buss, *The History of the School* [Bedford Girls' Modern School], (Bedford, 1982); Dorothy E. de Zouche, *Roedean School 1885–1955*, (Brighton 1955); *Colston's Girls' School Jubilee 1891–1941* (Bristol, n.d.); F. Cecily Steadman, *In the Days of Miss Beale* (London, 1931); M.G. Shaw, *Redland High School* (Bristol, 1932); E.J.Atkinson, *A School Remembered* (Ipswich, 1980); Kathleen Davies, *Polam Hall: Story of a School* (Darlington, 1981); Susan Hicklin, *Polished Corners, 1878–1978* (London, 1978); E.B. Godwin (ed.), *The Story of the Mary Datchelor School 1877–1977* (London, 1977); R.M. Scrimgeour (ed.), *North London Collegiate School 1850–1960* (London, 1950); V.E. Stack (ed.), *Oxford High School 1875–1960* (Oxford, 1963); Hazel Bates and Anne A.M. Wells, *A History of Shrewsbury High School 1885–1960* (Shrewsbury, 1962); *Sherborne School for Girls 1899–1949* (Sherborne, 1949); Valentine Noake, *History of the Alice Ottley School Worcester* (Worcester, 1952); Elsie Bowerman, *Stands There a School: Memories of Dame Frances Dove* (Wycombe Abbey, n.d.); B.W. Welsh, *After the Dawn: A Record of the Pioneer Work in Edinburgh for the Higher Education of Women* (Edinburgh, 1939); Julia M. Grant, Katherine H. McCutcheon and Ethel F. Sanders (eds.), *St Leonards School 1877–1927* (London, 1927). For the United States, reliance has been made primarily on secondary sources listed in the notes below.
   For general discussions of the history of physical education in women's schools and colleges, see: Paul Atkinson, 'Fitness, Feminism and Schooling' in S. Delamont and L. Duffin (eds.) *The Nineteenth Century Woman: Her Cultural and Physical World* (London, 1978); Sheila Fletcher, *Women First: The Female Tradition in English Physical Education 1880–1980* (London, 1984); Jennifer A. Hargreaves, *Playing Like Gentlemen While Behaving Like Ladies: The Social Significance of Physical Activity for Females in Late Nineteenth and Early Twentieth Century Britain* (unpublished M A dissertation, University of London Institute of Education, 1979); see also pp. 130–44 below.
2. Sara Burstall, *The Education of Girls in the United States* (London, 1894) p. 150.
3. For examples of Sargent's anthropometric work, see: Dudley A. Sargent, 'The Physical Proportions of the Typical Man', *Scribner's* II (July 1887), 3–17; idem, 'The Physical Development of Women', *Scribner's* V (February 1889), 172–85.
4. Andrew Combe, *Principles of Physiology Applied to the Preservation of Health and to the Development of Physical Education* (London, 14th edn., 1852) p. 182.

5. For a general review of female invalidism, see Lorna Duffin, 'The Conspicuous Consumptive: Woman as an Invalid', in S. Delamont and L. Duffin (eds.), *The Nineteenth Century Woman: Her Cultural and Physical World*, (London, 1978), pp. 26–56.

6. See John N. Burstyn, *Victorian Education and the Ideal of Womanhood* (London, 1980) and 'Educators' Response to Scientific and Medical Studies of Women in England 1860–1900', in S. Acker and D.W. Piper (eds.), *Is Higher Education Fair to Women?* (Guildford, 1984), pp. 65–80; 'Education and Sex: The Medical Case Against Higher Education for Women in England, 1870–1900, *Proceedings of the American Philosophical Society*, 117, 2, (1973), 79–89. The most widely cited sources of medical opposition were, in the United States, Edward Clarke, *Sex in Education, or, A Fair Chance for the Girls* (Boston, 1873) and, in Britain, Henry Maudsley, 'Sex in Mind and Education', *Fortnightly Review*, 14 (1874), 466–83. Feminist responses included: Julia Ward Howe (ed.), *Sex and Education: A Reply to Dr E.H. Clarke's 'Sex in Education'* (Boston, 1874); Eliza Duffey, *No Sex in Education: Or, An Equal Chance for Both Girls and Boys* (Philadelphia, 1874); Elizabeth Garrett Anderson, 'Sex in Mind and Education: A Reply', *Fortnightly Review*, 15 (1874), 582–94. For a useful source illustrating the extent to which this and similar debates on the biological determination of women's status entered into popular science, see Louise Michele Newman (ed.), *Men's Ideas/Women's Realities: Popular Science, 1870–1915* (Oxford, 1985). Newman (pp. 66–7) shows that *Popular Science Monthly* alone carried 32 articles on the 'evils of education' between 1874 and 1913. It contained many more on more general themes relating to biological determinism.

7. Jonathan May, *Madame Bergman-Österberg* (London, 1969), p. 56.

8. Herbert Spencer, *Education: Intellectual, Moral and Physical* (London, 1911), p. 144.

9. Henry Maudsley, 'Sex in Mind and in Education', *Fortnightly Review* (1874), 467.

10. Ben Barker-Benfield, 'The Spermatic Economy: A Nineteenth-Century View of Sexuality', *Feminist Studies*, 1(Summer 1972), 45–74.

11. Thomas S. Kuhn, 'Energy Conservation as an Example of Simultaneous Discovery', in M. Clagett (ed.), *Critical Problems in the History of Science* (Madison, 1962), pp. 321–56.

12. I. Bernard Cohen, 'Conservation and the Concept of Electric Charge: An Aspect of Philosophy in Relation to Physics in the Nineteenth Century', in M. Clagett (ed.), *Critical Problems in the History of Science* (Madison, 1962), pp. 357–83.

13. Yehuda Elkana, *The Discovery of the Conservation of Energy* (London, 1974).

14. Rosalind Rosenberg, *Beyond Separate Spheres: Intellectual Roots of Modern Feminism* (New Haven, 1982), p. 9.

15. J.S. Haller and R.M. Haller, *The Physician and Sexuality in Victorian America* (Urbana, 1974), p. 26.

16. These arguments are summarized in Carol Dyhouse, 'Social Darwinistic Ideas and the Development of Women's Education in England 1880–1920', *History of Education*, 5, 1 (1976), 41–58.

17. Elizabeth Garrett Anderson, 'Sex in Mind and Education: A Reply', *Fortnightly Review*, 15 (1874), 582–94.

18. Burstall, *The Education of Girls in the United States*, p. 148.

19. Roberta J. Park, 'Sport, Gender and Society in a Transatlantic Victorian Perspective', *British Journal of Sports History*, 2, 1 (1985), 5–28: see below, pp. 58–93.

20. Quoted in Thomas Woody, *A History of Women's Education in the United States* (New York, 1926), p. 118. See also Helen Lefkowitz Horowitz, *Alma Mater: Design and Experience in the Women's Colleges from Their Nineteenth-Century Beginnings to the 1930s* (New York, 1984), p. 36.

21. Quoted in Burstall, *The Education of Girls in the United States*, p. 153.

22. Quoted in Woody, *Women's Education in the United States*, p. 115.

23. Sara Burstall, *English High Schools for Girls: Their Aims, Organisation, and Management* (London, 1907), p. 90.

24. Sara Burstall, 'Medical Inspection', in Sara Burstall and M.A. Douglas (eds.), *Public Schools for Girls* (London, 1911), p. 224.

25. K.M.Reynolds, 'The School and its Place in Girls' Education', in R.M. Scrimgeour (ed.), *The North London Collegiate School 1850–1950* (London, 1950), p. 121.
26. Burstall, 'Medical Inspection', pp. 224–25.
27. Jane Frances Dove, 'Cultivation of the Body', in Dorothea Beale, Lucy Soulsby and Jane Frances Dove, *Work and Play in Girls' Schools* (London, 1898), p. 416.
28. Rosalind A. Keep, *Four Score and Ten Years: A History of Mills College* (California, 1946), p. 81.
29. F. Gadesden, 'The Education of Girls and the Development of Girls' High Schools', in R.D. Roberts (ed.), *Education in the Nineteenth Century* (Cambridge, 1901), p. 101.
30. Massachusetts Bureau of Labor Statistics, *Health Statistics of Female College Graduates* (Boston 1885); see also Willystine Goodsell, *The Education of Women: Its Social Background and its Problems* (New York, 1923), p. 84 ff.
31. Cited in Goodsell, *The Education of Women*, p. 88.
32. Mrs Henry (Eleanor) Sidgwick, *Health Statistics of Women Students of Cambridge and Oxford and of their Sisters* (Cambridge, 1890). A digest of these statistics was also published by Alice Hayes, 'Health of Women Students in England', *Education*, January 1891, 284–93; they are also cited extensively by Goodsell.
33. Hayes, 'Health of Women Students'.
34. S. Delamont, 'The Contradictions in Ladies' Education', in S. Delamont and L. Duffin (eds.), *The Nineteenth Century Woman: Her Cultural and Physical World* (London, 1978).

3

Sport, Gender and Society in a Transatlantic Victorian Perspective

Roberta J. Park

This chapter attempts to cast some further light on nineteenth- and early twentieth-century concepts of sport and gender, specifically in a transatlantic Anglo-American perspective. The focus is upon 'middle class' constructs and the involvement of women. Considerable attention is also given to men and sport, as modern sport has been defined and dominated by the male model. Moreover, the notion of gender makes little sense in human societies unless 'male' and 'female' are compared and contrasted. The word 'sport' is used as an inclusive category term to comprehend a diversity of physical activities which, in the eyes of participants and commentators, were intended to improve one's physical, mental, and/or moral health, as well as those events which range from simple recreative pursuits of a physical nature to highly organized agonistic contests. One other point: Americans were not always very precise in their use of the term 'British', often using it when they meant only the English. In general, I have followed the conventions of the nineteenth-century American press.

The title of the chapter makes it clear that these phenomena are considered in a 'transatlantic' context. The vector arrow points westward from Great Britain to the United States. The antecedents of American forms of sports – and the values associated with them, at least initially – came from Great Britain, especially from England. Nineteenth-century American concepts of proper gender role, particularly among the middle and upper classes, were also derived substantially from 'English' models. With relatively few exceptions, the predominant sports in America at the end of the nineteenth century had crossed the Atlantic with British immigrants and visitors. Basketball, a game devised for young men at the Springfield, Massachusetts, YMCA Training School by James Naismith in 1891, soon became popular with college women. Baseball, touted as early as 1869 as America's 'national game' had evolved from rounders. Gridiron football, the major intercollegiate sport, had been manufactured by college students and their professional coaches from rugby in the 1880s and 1890s. Tennis, golf, croquet, crew, track athletics, and field hockey – the last always more popular with American women than men – had all been introduced from Britain, as had horse-racing, cricket, cock-fighting, and boxing in the 1700s. Callisthenic exercises and gymnastic programmes, on the other hand, were more likely to trace their antecedents to German and Scandinavian immigrants, although even some forms of these had come by way of England.[1]

The forms which sporting and recreative activities took helped to define and reinforce prevailing concepts of *gender*. In fact, in the decades following the American Civil War (1861–1865), organized sport and various forms of vigorous physical activity became major vehicles for defining and acting out male gender roles.[2] This was true whether one participated, watched, discussed, read about or wrote about sport. On both sides of the Atlantic, nineteenth-century sport came to be forcefully and graphically depicted as the 'natural' province of males; hence, sport contributed substantially to establishing and maintaining ideologies about the proper sphere of women.

In the Western world, as several recent commentators have noted, there has been a tendency to describe natural and social phenomena in terms of oppositional characteristics. The world is dichotomized and two opposed terms mutually define each other. Debates about sex and sex roles during the nineteenth century hinged on the ways in which sexual boundaries might become blurred.[3] To be sure, this categorization, and the assumptions which underlay it, was largely a 'middle-class' construct: but as the middle class increasingly became the arbiters of right conduct, it also affected, in varying degrees, others in society. There were, of course, large numbers of men and women who did not share the same lived experience and hold the same values. Disraeli had remarked on 'the Two Cultures' in 1845 and, as Trachtenberg has pointed out, by the 1890s, most middle-class Americans had no idea how 'the other half' lived. The sporting scenes depicted in the *National Police Gazette* after Belfast-born Richard Kyle Fox took over the moribund publication convey quite a different concept of women from the more cultured press. According to Fox, who was ever prone to exaggeration, American women were playing baseball in the 1870s, and were wrestlers, boxers, balloonists and performing gymnasts. Moreover, pioneer farm and ranch women often found it necessary to perform work similar to that of their men folk, and a few were ranch *owners*, totally responsible for overseeing enormous herds of cattle. On the frontier, women might fish, hunt, engage in camping and go hiking. Some, like Annie Oakley, became trick-shooting or rodeo stars.[4]

As Daniel Walker Howe has pointed out in *Victorian America*: 'Using the name of a foreign monarch to describe an aspect of a country's history implies some relationship between the two countries'.[5] Indeed, a close connection between Great Britain and the United States existed in the nineteenth century, especially in the period preceding the Civil War. Colonial (i.e. eighteenth-century) literary, artistic, political, and legal forms, as well as colonial sport, reflected their British antecedents. Continued influence was reinforced by a shared language. Until the 1850s a very large percentage of what Americans read was of British origin, and because foreign works were not protected by international copyright laws until 1892, American publishers could, and did, routinely pirate the works of popular authors. *Harper's Monthly Magazine*, established in 1850 to appeal to a broad American readership, flatly declared: 'The magazine will transfer to its pages as rapidly as they may be issued all the continuous tales of Dickens, Bulwer, Croly, Lever, Warren and other distinguished contributors to British periodicals. . .' .[6] E.L. Godkin's *The Nation*, intended by its editor to be an American version of *The Spectator*, routinely included commentaries on British events well into the twentieth century. Sports-minded Americans before the Civil War era often read more about English sport than they did of their own. *Bell's Life in London* and the *English Sporting Magazine*, for example, served as models for American publishers.[7]

Of all the books available to readers in America in 1858, only *Little Dorrit* sold more copies than *Tom Brown's School Days*. In 1893 Selwin Tait and Sons, New York publishers, surveyed major libraries to determine which books circulated most frequently. A list of 170 titles, headed by *David Copperfield*, included *Ivanhoe, Vanity Fair, Jane Eyre, John Halifax-Gentleman, The Mill on the Floss, Tom Brown's School Days* and Kingsley's *Hypatia* among the top 25.[8] Hughes' stories were instrumental in establishing sport in the school story genre which developed in America in the 1880s and 1890s. Frank Merriwell's and Ralph Barbour's young athletic heroes shared a number of physical and moral virtues with Tom Brown at both Rugby and Oxford – as did figures like Lester Chadwick's Phil Clinton – even as they conveyed to the reader a plethora of 'Yankee' values. American versions of manuals such as *The Boys Own Book: A Complete Encyclopedia of All the Diversions, Athletic, Scientific and Recreational* were available, and a 1880s London edition of *Cassell's Complete Book of Sports and Pastimes* included sections on LaCrosse and Baseball, undoubtedly to increase its attractiveness in North

America. Influential books such as *Football* (1896) by Walter Camp and Lorin F. Deland included commentaries about English public school rugby and other British games. Several New England elite preparatory schools, such as, for example, Worcester Academy, Groton, and St Paul's, were patterned after English public schools and imported much of their game-playing ethos from them.[9]

During the nineteenth century American concepts of manliness changed. So, too, did the concept of the ideal woman. Anthony Rotundo has recently described this major shift in middle-class ideals of manhood from a standard ' . . . rooted in the life of the community and qualities of a man's soul to a standard of manhood based on individual achievement and the male body'.[10] These new values could be seen, in part, in the rapid rise of interest in intercollegiate athletics, the out-of-doors movement, and the anthropometry craze of the 1880s and 1890s. They could also be seen in growing anxieties about masturbation, impotence, illness, and a feebleness in the American (read middle-class Anglo-Saxon American) race.[11] Dr Charles Woodhall Eaton's *Things a Young Man Should Know: A Manual of the Anatomy, Physiology and Hygiene of the Sexual System* (1884), one of several such works published in the middle of the century, drew substantially upon Archibald Maclaren's *A System of Physical Education* (1865) for its recommendations on exercise. Similar manuals for girls combined suggestions about health, proper dress, physiological function, 'self-abuse' (masturbation), and physical exercise. *Vigorous* exercise, it was believed, could do much to transform boys into 'manly' men. *Mild* exercise was intended primarily to turn inherently weak girls into 'fit' mothers. By the last decade of the century, however, several of the more traditional values were being questioned. Among the prominent features of the 'reorientation of American culture' in the 1890s, John Higham has argued, was an ' . . . urge to be young, masculine and adventurous'. It was also in the 1890s that the concept of the 'New Woman' emerged and college-educated and upper-class women, in particular, began to engage in organized sporting activities.[12]

Many women in Colonial America had owned and run taverns; some were printers, and a few had been carpenters and blacksmiths. Even within those families which were quite well off, colonial women were expected to balance femininity with a certain amount of robustness. For reasons which are still not entirely clear – but which certainly seem to be related to more routinized work patterns, a growing materialism and competitiveness in commerce and business, and a perceived need among the rising entrepreneurial class to define and legitimate its status – ideas about woman's proper sphere had begun to change in the early 1800s. Her range of activity and influence was increasingly confined to the home at the same time that her body was encased in whalebone corsets and layers of clothing which covered her from throat to floor. Her physiology, dominated by the reproductive function, confined her to an entirely 'separate sphere'. By the middle years of the nineteenth century the tradition that women had useful work to perform had given way to newer ideals of grace and ornament, at least for those families which could afford such life styles. The leisured woman, unsullied by toil, well but modestly dressed, became a visual symbol of the success of the household, giving status to its male head.[13] Mary Kelley has provided a perceptive portrait of the type of life which was open to middle-class women in the United States in her study of best-selling American 'literary domestics', those female writers whose enormously popular, saccharine novels made them well-known *public* figures, even though their private lives may have been circumscribed by convention:

> That any of these nineteenth century [literary] women came to have this semblance of male status was a strange development indeed. Women were isolated from and generally denied participation in their country's public life. . . . Unlike a male, a female's person was to be shielded from public scrutiny. Neither her ego nor her intellect was cultivated for future public vocation. . . . Even her exercise of moral, social, or personal influence was to be indirect, subtle, and symbolic. Her voice was to be soft, subdued, and soothing. In essence, hers was to remain an invisible presence.[14]

I

Middle-class Victorian concepts of woman were remarkably similar on both sides of the Atlantic. Much of the reason for this may be accounted for by the fact that both countries were experiencing the same types of technological changes. Similarities in ideas concerning women were also perpetuated by a continued contact between the two countries. British novels about women were popular in America. Authors such as Dickens, Charlotte Brontë, and Elizabeth Gaskell served as models for the American 'literary domestics', whose novels greatly outsold those of their male contemporaries, leading Nathaniel Hawthorne to fulminate: 'America is now wholly given over to a d----d lot of scribbling women . . .'. American ideas also sometimes flowed eastward; three different dramatizations of Mrs E.D.E.N. Southworth's *The Hidden Hand*, for example, played simultaneously in London in the 1850s.[15] But it is doubtful that American values had anything like the same impact on British culture.

Middle-class Americans were also familiar with much of the Victorian British health reform literature, drawing upon it for many of their pamphlets and manuals. They also expressed their own concerns in a wide assortment of journals and periodicals. Vegetarians, Grahamites, hydropathists, phrenologists, and advocates of exercise systems bombarded the public with their ideas. An anxiety that Americans were physically inferior to their English contemporaries, apparent in literary, educational, religious, and popular journals before the Civil War, became even more evident in the 1870s.[16] By the 1890s, however, Americans were asserting that they were the world's foremost nation, and that they were physically and technologically, if not intellectually and morally, superior to everyone. Sport – that is, male sport – was frequently used in an effort to establish and give weight to this presumption of superiority.

The messages were often highly contradictory, however, with the same journal first proclaiming that a new and better breed of men was being developed in the land of boundless opportunity, then lamenting that an overabundance of work and a singleminded dedication to getting ahead was weakening the American race. In general, the tendency was to assume repeatedly that English girls and women were physically superior to American women. *Graham's Journal of Health and Longevity*, for example, declared in 1838: ' . . . English girls, it is well known, walk five or six miles with ease. They do not reason, as our girls do, that to be pretty and "interesting", they must be livid, pale and consumptive. . .'.[17] The *Massachusetts Teacher* in 1856 proclaimed:

> It is . . . a palpable fact, that the girlhood of our countrywomen does not have those advantages for full development of the physical nature which English customs have long since established. The English girl spends one half of her waking hours in physical amusements. . . . She rides, walks, drives, rows upon the water, runs, dances, plays, sings, jumps the rope, throws the ball, hurls the quoit, draws the bow, keeps up the shuttlecock. . . .[18]

Hours at Home in 1865 discussed 'National Characteristics' claiming that the American educational system, the most open in the world, had fallen far short ' . . . of the public schools of England, which have done so much toward making England the power that she is. An English lad is a trained boxer, a cricketer, an oarsman, and so learns muscular control and mastery . . .'.[19] *Lippincott's Magazine* in 1868 found that the great schools and universities of England provided ' . . . a training toward true manliness . . . a tone of honor, liberality without prodigality . . . and a superb physical development which produces a type of manly and accomplished gentlemen such as are found, as a class, nowhere else'.[20] Comments such as these appeared frequently in literary journals, and often in educational journals, while the popular press was more intent on portraying a more rugged male 'Yankee' demeanour in sports.

No American in the middle decades of the nineteenth century was as constant and impassioned a spokesman for the cause of 'manly exercise' as was Thomas Wentworth Higginson, aptly called America's prophet of 'muscular Christianity'.[21] Higginson also believed in greater opportunities for women, and in 1862 he discussed the relative poor health of American girls and the benefits they might derive from gymnastic exercises, concluding that England '. . . furnish[ed] the representative types of vigorous womanhood'.[22] Catharine Beecher's extremely popular *Physiology and Calisthenics for Schools and Families* (1856), a work which had a considerable impact on education for women as well as on ideas regarding physical education, informed its readers: 'In this nation it is rare to see a married woman of thirty or forty, especially in the more wealthy classes, who retains the fullness of person and the freshness of complexion that mark good health. But in England, almost all women are in full perfection of womanhood at that period of life'.[23] While vast numbers of British girls and women might have had cause to dispute the contentions of American commentators, what is of consequence is that many Americans *believed* that British men and women were healthier, more physically active, more prone to take out-of-door exercise, and, it was usually feared, superior beings.

Dickens, Anthony Trollope, Harriet Martineau, Lyell, Matthew Arnold, Spencer, Huxley, Kingsley, Hughes and Kipling were but a few of the many British and other European visitors who made one or more tours of the United States in the nineteenth century. Most foreign observers were convinced that American men paid their women an exaggerated chivalry, and suggested that perhaps it was to compensate for '. . . the fact that the female was not [really] granted equality . . .' in a nation which boasted of being egalitarian. Most doubted that American women deserved the elevated status accorded them.[24] They also found objectionable the American fascination with youth and the tendency to early marriage. By the 1880s, however, a new message began to be heard. In his popular and well-received *The American Commonwealth* (1888), James Bryce concluded that America's progress owed much to the contributions of its women, and David Macrae found on his visit in 1898 that the women seemed stronger and better developed than he had observed 30 years earlier.

Kipling, who married one, found American women superior to their English counterparts in their ability to think and talk; and almost everyone was convinced that American women were superior to American men. It must be remembered, however, that the types of women with whom foreign visitors came into contact were almost certainly not as representative as the men. In general, they were the better educated, wealthier women, and likely to possess at least a few of the social graces which could make a cultured visitor feel that some semblance of civilization had finally come to this barbarous country.[25]

Before the 1860s, organized sport was embryonic in the United States. Cricket teams were forever forming and disbanding, baseball was an evolving game, and college sports were desultory affairs frowned upon by faculty and administrators. The Harvard–Yale Regatta of 1852 marked the nation's first 'official' intercollegiate athletic contest.[26] Even such rudimentary forms of sport for women would have been unthinkable, given prevailing Victorian standards. Callisthenic exercise and simple recreations, however, were another matter. Sara Josepha Hale, who edited *Godey's Lady's Book* for nearly 40 years, advocated somewhat increased participation in physical activity for girls, using the authority of contemporary physicians to legitimize her claims. A spate of periodicals, of which the *Journal of Health and Longevity* was one example, urged dietary reform, callisthenic exercises, the 'water cure', outdoor amusements and physical education for girls and women, as well as for boys and men. Dr R.T. Trall's *The Illustrated Family Gymnasium*, first published in New York in 1857, for example, contained numerous diagrams taken from Walker's *Manly Exercises* (1834), and included a variety of callisthenic and vocal exercises for girls. On the eve of the Civil War Dioclesian Lewis opened his New Gymnasium for Ladies, Gentlemen and Children and began publication of his *Boston Journal of Physical Culture*. Lewis gave considerable attention to the physical training of females, and in 1861 established a Normal Institute for Physical Education which sought to train both 'ladies and gentlemen' to teach gymnastics. The benefits of healthful exercise in the formation of proper female virtue, and as preparation for the important duties of motherhood were frequently stressed. The majority of the advice was similar to that offered by Margaret Coxe in *Young Lady's Companion* (1842): women needed proper physical education because it was their Christian duty to raise physically healthy and morally sound children.[27] A few early women's rights advocates, however, saw in physical education a means to emancipation and self-fulfilment.

Elizabeth Cady Stanton related that her lifelong crusade for

'women's rights' was given added impetus when she and Lucretia
Mott were refused seats on the main floor at the 1840 London World
Anti-Slavery Convention. Of all the pre-Civil War female women's
rights advocates, Stanton was most convinced that vigorous physical
activity and a stronger and healthier body were vital to the
advancement of women. Writing for *The Lily*, a newspaper founded
by Amelia Bloomer and dedicated to women's issues, Stanton
rejected 'man's claim to physical superiority', stating: 'We cannot say
what the woman might be physically, if the girl were allowed all the
freedom of the boy, in romping, swimming, climbing and playing
ball . . .'.[28] Such hoydenish activities could help women to become
intelligent and self-reliant. It was for this reason, far more than
because healthy women would be better mothers, that Stanton
continually insisted that girls and women should have improved
physical education. Dress reform, admission to schools which could
prepare them for law, medicine and divinity (the 'male professions'),
and an adequate 'physical education' were central issues in the
pre-Civil War women's rights movement. Stanton and several others
began to wear a slightly shortened skirt and pantaloons, ultimately
referred to as 'bloomers', after Mrs Bloomer, whose paper pressed
the dress reform issue. This costume was repeatedly criticized in the
male-dominated general press, which pictured those who wore it
smoking cigars, entering saloons, and abandoning their child-rearing
duties. In the end, even Stanton gave it up, agreeing that the
antagonism which dress reform had aroused was impeding other
efforts to improve the condition of women. The costume did come to
be accepted, however, as appropriate for women to wear when they
took exercises in the gymnasium, and it was clearly advocated in the
early 1860s in Dio Lewis' popular book *New Gymnastics*.[29]

II

The Civil War marks an important watershed in American history.
The agonizing dislocations of the sectional strife had forced the nation
to grow from 'infancy' to 'adulthood' – or at least to 'adolescence'. In
the last three decades of the century industry and technology
developed rapidly, affecting the entire nation. The move to
medium-sized towns and large cities, which had begun as a trickle in
the 1850s, reached major proportions by the late 1870s, creating as
Robert Wiebe has maintained in *The Search for Order* a revolution in
values and the creation of a new middle class whose ambition was to
'. . . fulfill its destiny through bureaucratic means'.[30] The populations
of many rampantly growing cities were swollen by hordes of

immigrants. Whereas the majority of newcomers had initially come from Britain, Germany, and less frequently, Scandinavia, by 1890, immigrants from Central and Southern Europe comprised the largest percentage of the new arrivals. Attitudes regarding what constituted the *ideal* man changed, as did attitudes concerning the *ideal* woman. By the 1890s, among the better educated, in particular, Victorian womanly virtues were being challenged by those of 'the New Woman'; there was much ambivalence, however, even among those who subscribed to more equity for women. Characteristics which this 'New Woman' embodied included independent spirit and athletic zeal: 'She rode a bicycle, played tennis or golf, showed six inches of stocking beneath her skirts, and loosened her corsets'. The New Woman wanted '. . . to belong to the human race, not the ladies' aid society to the human race'.[31] While these values were by no means uniform across the geographic United States, or among the various populations which made up the highly pluralistic society at the end of the nineteenth century, the fact that they predominated among those who were in a position to influence institutions and attitudes gave them an especially potent force.

For women to have increased opportunities in sport, attitudes towards both the female sex and towards sport, in general, had to change. Two articles which appeared at the end of the decade of the 1860s reflect newly emerging American attitudes towards leisure and sport. In 1867 the *New Englander* reported: 'The number and variety of the papers on the subject of Amusements which have [recently] appeared . . . indicate that this theme is one which demands a new discussion, if not a change of position'.[32] *The Nation* flatly stated in 1869: 'The taste for athletic sports in America is not over fifteen years old. It is only within the last ten or twelve years that it can be said to have found a firm foothold in the colleges'.[33] This rapid rise of organized sport in the last three decades of the nineteenth century, a phenomenon which has now received the attention of numerous historians, was accompanied by a clear shift in attitudes towards games-playing, as well as towards the body.[34]

Numerous British sportsmen and sports teams visited the United States in the nineteenth century, routinely demonstrating their athletic superiority well into the 1880s. Earlier visits usually received cordial treatment in the press. *Harper's Weekly* for 15 October 1859, for example, discussed a series of cricket matches between an All England Eleven and a United States Twenty-Two, noting that the superiority of the English was to be expected as in America,

the importance of athletic exercises is only beginning to be

understood. Men of thirty can remember well that, when they
were at school, proficiency in the athletic games of the
play-ground was regarded rather as a drawback. . . . Bank
clerks, young merchants, mercantile aspirants, all seemed to
think time devoted to manly exercise wasted . . .[35]

However, the author concluded: 'Another twenty years, and no doubt
our people will be as devoted to athletic exercises as the English. The
results on the American frame will surprise physiologists'.[36] By the
last decades of the century Americans, indeed, had taken to athletic
sports with a vengeance, converting most of them into models which
were highly visible, businesslike, professional and thoroughly infused
with pragmatic Yankee values. This tendency was criticized in the
British press and also by numerous Americans who preferred what
might be called an idealized interpretation of 'muscular Christianity'
and English schoolboy sport. The conflict between the two views
became intense in the 1890s and early 1900s, especially in
intercollegiate athletics and with regard to programmes like many of
those conducted by the Amateur Athletic Union.[37]

   In 1854 Theodore Parker, New England Unitarian minister, had
declared: 'America was settled by two very different classes of men,
one animated by moral and religious motives, coming to realize an
idea; the other animated by only commercial ideas. . . .'[38] There was
a certain aptness, albeit exaggeration, to Parker's remark – one which
was increasingly reflected in American attitudes concerning vigorous
exercise, physical education, sport, and ultimately, intercollegiate
athletics. Foreign commentators from de Tocqueville onwards had
remarked on the materialistic bent of American society, and
Americans themselves had often noted their countrymen's preoccupation with getting ahead. The framers of the Constitution had
endeavoured to eliminate two dominant features of European
tradition – a state religion and a hereditary aristocracy. All free-born
men in Colonial America were to be ensured certain inalienable
rights. (It is doubtful whether the intention was to extend the same
rights to women.) Although the ideology might hold that all men were
possessed of certain basic inalienable rights, it was clear that they were
not all equally endowed with the same aptitudes. Thomas Jefferson
had argued in the late eighteenth century that the most able
individuals must be permitted to rise to positions of leadership if the
nation was to survive. A 'natural aristocracy' based upon talent and
ability, rather than some artificial distinction of rank or class, was to
be encouraged.[39] It was not too great a step from the concept of a
Natural Aristocracy to the American belief in the Self-Made Man

which gained widespread popularity in the 1820s. The reality, of course, fell far short of the ideal (it was easier, for example, to be 'self-made' if one were Protestant and Anglo-Saxon), yet in a country which was rich with natural resources and where land was either free or inexpensive, one could move into the unsettled stretches of the Ohio Valley and on towards the Far West. Grit and hard work *could* help one advance! By the 1890s, however, such opportunities for free land had virtually disappeared, and vast numbers of Americans, especially blacks, the Irish and those whose native language was not English, found their opportunities limited largely to the more menial jobs in large cities.

Throughout the century, however, the belief that hard work, more than talent, provided the surest avenue to success was widespread, even if the reality fell short of the ideal. And nineteenth-century Americans placed a premium on useful labour. In his prize-winning study of the work ethic in industrial America, Daniel T. Rodgers has described how a new world of mills, factories, massed wage-earners, machinery and sub-divided labour in the mid-1800s changed both the nature of the work which Americans did and their ideas about it. Hours of employment decreased in the 1870s and more 'free' time became available. Increasingly this leisure was turned to activities which were as arduous as work and were carried out at the frenetic pace of the market-place: 'The doctrine of the industrious life pervaded churches and children's storybooks, editorial columns and the stump rhetoric of politics. . . . Theodore Roosevelt caught its tenor in his thundering insistence that only the strenuous life was worth living. . .'.[40] *Action*, and quantitatively measured success, in business, in daily life and in leisure pursuits, had become an American preoccupation by the last decades of the nineteenth century.

Both social scientists and historians have drawn attention to various relationships which developed between business, concepts of work, and the dominant forms of sport which arose in the late Victorian period. Gelber, for example, recently examined the '. . . relationships between nineteenth century business society and baseball, and the bachelor subculture of which baseball was such an important part'.[41] Analysing arguments which favour the *compensatory* theory of sports and arguments which support the *congruence* theory of sport, Gelber concluded that baseball was popular because underneath such superficial differences as the pastoral-appearing parks in which it was played and the lack of clock-defined playing periods, baseball had a deep correspondence with men's everyday work experiences. The *Metropolitan* declared in 1883 that men took the same '. . . delight in exercising the physical and mental powers . . .

over a game of baseball . . .' as a ' . . . workman takes in laying bricks handsomely . . .'.[42] A similar observation was made by the coach of the Harvard University football team to the president of the University of California in 1906 when Berkeley was about to abandon gridiron football and take up English rugby in rejection of the professionalism and commercialism which had come to characterize the American game. Harvard's coach, William Reid, Jr., was convinced that rugby would never appeal to the American boy because it lacked precision and science.[43]

III

It is only recently that we have begun to understand that sports are cultural artifacts, and as such are very likely to reflect the dominant social structures and salient values of the societies in which they exist. Games are filled with symbolism: and, as extended performative systems, they can sometimes become complex and elaborate statements about cultures. This has been powerfully illustrated by anthropological works such as Clifford Geertz's influential paper on the Balinese cockfight and by G. Whitney Azoy's study of *buzkashi* as a game of power in Afghanistan. More recently, John MacAloon has built upon Victor Turner's rich insights concerning 'social dramas' – and Gregory Bateson's and Erving Goffman's work on the 'framing of experience' – and analysed the origins of the modern Olympic Games. MacAloon's work forces us to recognize that these types of cultural performances are constituted of far more than the athletic contest, which is usually embedded in ritual, festival and spectacle frames. This is especially the case in highly elaborated forms such as the Olympics, American football's Super Bowl, the Oxford – Cambridge boat race, World Cup soccer matches, baseball's 'World' Series, and similar events.[44] These types of multi-layered performances were on the ascendancy in the late nineteenth century.

In *The End of American Innocence* Henry May depicted pre-First World War American society as a triptych. On the left were the advocates of progress whose dispositions and aspirations were embodied in men like Theodore Roosevelt. These were the men who had built great steel companies, oil monopolies and financial empires: those who saw the United States replacing Great Britain as the international power broker. They were the types of men whom Frank Norris portrayed in his novel *A Man's Woman*: '. . . great, strong, harsh, brutal men – men with purpose who let nothing, nothing stand in their way'.[45] Here, too, were the ambitious, energetic social reformers, men like Jacob Riis and Lester Ward, '. . . ruthless in their zeal for human advancement'.[46] On the right, and smaller, panel, were the 'custodians' of a culture which was largely founded in Anglo-Saxon traditions and values: men like Harvard's president Charles William Eliot, who revered America b the)und it mortifying that in their games Americans were morally inferior to the English. The present and the future, May concluded, belonged to those on the left hand panel. This was as true for athletics as it was for politics, business, industry and a whole range of other endeavours.

In late April 1898 the United States had declared war on Spain over the issue of Cuban independence. The 'Splendid Little War'[47] was over all too soon for those who, like Theodore Roosevelt, revelled in the cult of the 'strenuous life'.[48] What war could not provide, perhaps sports could. The litany of strenuosity issued from the pages of an astonishing assortment of journals and periodicals on the eve of the twentieth century. Of all the sports, football became the most martial, and within the college ranks, the most popular. It was touted as the game which exemplified all the qualities of the best of American manhood. It was also the game which most encapsulated, in multiple layers of performative frames, the salient values of American society.

By the 1890s America had clearly become desirous of assuming the position of the leading sporting nation in the world. In 1894 W.H. Grenfell reported the results of the first international intercollegiate track meeting – between Oxford and Yale – in the *Fortnightly Review*. Although Yale had lost the match 3½ events to 5½ events, the American team members were praised for their deportment. The visitors, the author asserted, had done a great deal to '. . . draw two great portions of the Anglo-Saxon race closer together . . .'.[49] Most Americans, however, were not very disposed to place comradeship or common ancestral origins (real or assumed) above victory in athletics. At the Penn Relays of 1895, American athletes were victorious over the London Athletic Club, and did not hesitate to proclaim their superiority. Of these contests, the satirical London *Weekly Sun* declared: ' "Rule Britannia" is but the last despairing wail of a played out race. We are no longer athletically or nautically supreme; indeed we are very small beer'. In the same year Lord Dunraven refused to race his *Valkyrie II* against *Defender* because of a dispute with American yachting officials.[50] In a panegyric to American athletics written in 1901, James E. Sullivan, President of the Amateur Athletic Union, boasted that although in 1875 all the holders of amateur records in running and walking events had been English, Irish, or Scottish, Americans now held nine-tenths of the records. Moreover, Sullivan maintained, it was the Americans who had won nearly all the significant prizes at the 1900 Olympic Games.[51] He neglected to point out, however, that outside of the admittedly important track and field competitions, Americans had won only one other medal – third place in 'game shooting' – at these Games.[52] Victory was sweet, but it was most sweet when the nation which had given the world 'sport' was the one which the Yankees defeated.

In 1895 American college crews had begun to attend the Henley Regatta. Bent upon demonstrating their rowing superiority, they followed practices similar to those which most American crews used at home. Charles Courtney, the professional coach from Cornell University, was criticized by the British for holding work-like training regimens and keeping his athletes away from other competitors. Things had become so bad in 1901, following the visit of a University of Pennsylvania crew, that the stewards served notice that henceforth American crews wishing to compete at Henley would have to leave their salaried instructors at home. In reporting on the different attitudes of the two countries towards athletics, and the British assertion that American teams were only likely to venture abroad if they were sure of victory (a reaction to the 1904 Harvard/Yale – Oxford/Cambridge track meet), Ralph D. Paine, a regular contributor to Casper Whitney's elite *Outdoor Magazine*, observed: 'Our army of professional coaches and trainers, and the almost incredible cost of intercollegiate sport, have helped to feed the suspicions of the British onlooker'.[53] The *Quarterly Review* in 1904 discussed a growing professional tendency in Britain and expressed alarm that American Rhodes scholars were beginning to pollute British university sport with their single-minded attitudes towards winning:

> A subtle influence from abroad will shortly be felt in one of these ancient strongholds of fair-play. . . . Mr Eugene L. Lehmann of New York City, who graduated from Yale in 1902, was chosen as a Rhodes scholar for Oxford at the age of twenty-two. . . . Already American athletes have proved their value as Oxford undergraduates at the Queen's Club meeting. It is not unlikely that several of the Rhodes scholars will be first-rate athletes too. . . . Shall we have to congratulate an English Cambridge on standing unaided in the encounter, or to discount her rival's victories by the fact of alien assistance?[54]

Crew, track, baseball, and gridiron football were then, and still are, the major American intercollegiate sports. Although each had its devoted followers, no sport was as popular as football. Few universities or colleges in the late nineteenth century, no matter how small, failed to have a team. Each institution also quickly secured an arch rival, an attempt at emulation of the Harvard–Yale rivalry, which in its turn was patterned on an American conception of the Oxford–Cambridge athletic rivalry. Alumni returned to their campuses each year for the annual renewal of the football spectacular – or, perhaps, for the regatta, if the college had a crew. It became widely believed that a victory for *alma mater* would be rewarded by financial offerings, in the form of alumni donations to the college, from the now-satisfied members of the extended family. At institutions with prestigious athletic teams, income from football could and did sometimes support the entire athletic programme and even physical education classes in the years before the First World War. The average receipts for the Harvard University football team, for example, were $18,964.43 for the years 1891–94; for 1899–1902 these receipts averaged $52,345.64 yearly.[55]

These 'big games' rapidly became elaborate ramified cultural performances. For several days before the event frenetic activities were held at the campuses of the two protagonists. At rallies the student-body was exhorted to assist its team's efforts to defeat the enemy on the day of the battle. On the day of the contest songs, school colours, cheering sections, mascots, banners, and a host of other devices helped to intensify the cultural messages which were being enacted on the playing field. The contest itself incorporated a number of salient turn-of-century American values, two of the most important being, an assumption of equality, and a celebration of rank. While it was assumed that both teams started off even, and that the codified playing-rules set the conditions whereby a fundamental equality would be insured, it was also clear that effort, ability and teamwork usually enabled one to prevail. Egalitarianism spoke to the ideals upon which the country had been founded, while effort and achievement echoed the Jeffersonian ideal of a Natural Aristocracy. (The Jacksonian Self-Made Man incorporated both.) The teamwork and intense specialized training needed to prevail in games such as football also clearly reflected the commercial, competitive dictates of the new corporate-industrial order.[56] (There could also be muted statements that one must have a modicum of 'luck', a message which also formed the core of the Horatio Alger success stories which were popular at the end of the century.)[57]

Football also literally 'embodied' another concept which had increasingly troubled many Americans ever since Spencer's *Education: Intellectual, Moral and Physical* (1862) and Darwin's books, especially *The Descent of Man* (1871), had engendered a host of evolutionary controversies. The movement, which came to be known as 'Social Darwinism', has now received considerable attention from social scientists and historians on both sides of the Atlantic. Many contemporary tendencies were caught up in and expounded under the rubric of evolutionary and hereditarian theories. The concepts of 'struggle' and 'survival of the most fit' articulated well with already existing notions of competition, merited success and deserved failure.[58] Commentators increasingly began to draw parallels between the college athlete and the type of man most likely to ensure the future success of the nation. In 1879 Lloyd S. Bryce's article 'A Plea for Sport' appeared in the *North American Review*. Borrowing from Darwinian biological theory – and using this to buttress his own notions of how societies should be ordered – Bryce sought to show why it was necessary for every educational establishment in the United States to provide ample outdoor facilities where the youth of the nation might acquire not only ' . . . muscular vigor, but the manly virtues of truth, honor and fair play'. In an accompanying argument which smacked of elitism, he advocated healthful exercise both for those destined to lead society and for the urban poor. The former needed physical, intellectual, and moral vigour in order to lead. The latter were to learn through games that what a man achieves is a result of industry and self-control and thereby become reconciled to their lot.[59]

Increasingly varsity athletes were depicted as men who possessed those qualities which the American nation most needed: leadership; executive power; perseverance; determination; courage; virility. Arms akimbo, in the battledress of sport, they were living portrayals of captains of industry or of Commodore Dewey in Manila Harbor. At the same time, however, athletes were expected to develop 'a faithful obedience to authority'. In December 1892 the Chicago *Graphic* declared: 'Football is typical of all that is heroic in American sport'. The *Saturday Evening Post*, three months after the short-lived Spanish–American War, asserted: 'The capacity to take hard knocks which belongs to a successful football player is usually associated with the qualities that would enable a man to lead a charge up San Juan Hill . . .'.[60] The jingoism was unmistakable. While a Rough Rider was not identical to a member of the immortal 'Light Brigade', each was infused with physical stamina, virile masculinity, and manly courage – or so the ideology proclaimed. Each soldier was doing good work for his country, just as the athlete was doing 'good work' for his school. Young, strong, courageous, competent, the athlete was the idealized hope of the future: imperialistically, economically, socially *and* biologically. In an age which believed in the possibility of the inheritance of *acquired* characteristics, the athlete was the image of the ideal sire. It is more than chance that many who advocated vigorous athletics were also active in early twentieth-century eugenics movements.[61]

Many of the more important features of evolutionary and hereditarian theorizing were also caught up in the anthropometry movement which developed on both sides of the Atlantic. Francis Galton's growth studies had a substantial influence on American anthropometricists, and his *Hereditary Genius* (1879) greatly influenced the eugenics movement. Galton and Charles Roberts were made Honorary Members of the American Association for the Advancement of Physical Education (AAAPE) shortly after that organization was founded in 1885. The field of physical education saw itself as one of the most important of the age for studying and solving problems of great value to the human race, and it has always had a strong reformist orientation. Edward L. Hitchcock, the first president of the AAAPE, had begun to collect anthropometric measures of male students at Amherst College in the 1860s. In his 1887 annual address before the AAAPE, Hitchcock declared that educators needed information about the proper and normal proportions of the body so that they might ' . . . develop the most perfect type of man and woman in body, soul and spirit'.[62] At the 1890 AAAPE convention Luther Halsey Gulick, medical doctor, physical educator, YMCA leader, and future officer of the Playground Association of America, insisted that the profession of physical education offered a fundamental means for building the nation '. . . as it works to develop a superior race'.[63]

No American physical educator in the late 1800s was as ardent an anthropometrist as Dudley Allen Sargent, M.D., Director of the Hemenway Gymnasium at Harvard University. Between 1887 and 1889 Sargent published a three-part series in *Scribner's Magazine* on the physical development of the 'typical man', 'women', and 'the athlete'.[64] The anthropometric movement was preoccupied with ideal *forms*, statistical abstractions derived from scores of measurements of the length and girth of various body segments of thousands of individuals. Based on these, individual measurements were judged to be deficient in certain attributes, and students were required to engage in gymnastic programmes devised to correct whatever measurements were deemed inferior. Male athletes constituted a separate – and elevated – group, with special sub-categories rapidly developed for each of the various sports. A man was now defined not only by what he accomplished; he was also given identity and status on the basis of his morphology. Similar measurements were also applied to female students, and few American college women and men in the decades between 1890 and the First World War were not subjected to various batteries of anatomical measurements. Dr Delphine Hanna compiled anthropometric tables from the measurements of 1600 women students at Oberlin College in 1893, and Dr Claes Enebuske's intensive study of the strength, endurance and skill improvements of 26 female students at the Boston Normal School of Gymnastics was published in the 1892 *Proceedings* of the American Association for the Advancement of Physical Education. Reflecting nineteenth-century reasoning, Enebuske argued that ' . . . a sound, healthy, and shapely body . . .' benefited a woman's posterity, and maintained that schoolgirls needed to develop sufficient strength to support their 'brain-work'.[65]

Strenuousness, vigour, action and similar concepts were used by many Americans to define 'maleness' in the last decades of the nineteenth century. So was bodily form which was also used to define 'female'. Some authors went so far as to calculate 'physical laws' for the ideal male and female. In 1884 Mrs E.R. Shepherd informed her readers that 'a woman's waist should be two-fifths of her height. . . . Beauty in the figure of a man and beauty in the figure of a woman has each its own and separate standard'. A host of strength manuals, of which William Blakie's popular *How to Get Strong and How to Stay So* (1879) was a popular example, extolled the vitures of muscular power and a well-proportioned male body. Dedicated to Archibald Maclaren, the director of the Oxford Gymnasium, Blakie's book urged American girls and women, as well as American males, to engage in vigorous exercise as did their British and European counterparts. In an effort to assuage any concerns about the development of ' . . . hard and knotted muscles' among women, Blakie pointed out that Venus and Juno had taken exercise but retained the classical beauty of female form.[66]

IV

Higher education and athletic sport were both instrumental in the transformation of American concepts regarding the feminine ideal in the late 1800s. Traditional notions associated with the 'Cult of True Womanhood' continued to exist alongside the emerging model of the 'New Woman', and tensions between the two sets of values were often quite apparent. The belief that women and men were entirely dissimilar – a belief which had gained ascendancy in Victorian Britain and America – began to be slowly challenged by discoveries in physiology which disclosed that women might be quite like men in all save the reproductive function. Increasingly after 1890 the debate focused upon *where* the division between gender should be made, not whether or not there should be any division. Dr Lyman Sperry declared in his *Confidential Talks with Young Women* (1898): 'No microscope or other aid to study has revealed to the scientist any difference in the blood, the nerve or the muscle of the two sexes'. While it was not necessary for a woman to be a champion ' . . . at bat or oar . . .', trained muscles were important for grace, efficiency, and most importantly, to secure the sexual organs from ' . . . the nerve irritation and congestions . . . to which sedentary and idle women are so prone . . .'.[67]

Oberlin College in Oberlin, Ohio, had admitted 30 women students in 1833, but it was not until 1865 when Vassar College in Poughkeepsie, New York, opened that higher education began to be accessible to numbers of American women. From the beginning Vassar students were required to engage in callisthenic exercises. By 1877 they were permitted to substitute boating, gardening, walking or croquet, a diversion which had been imported from Britain in the 1860s and had enjoyed a flurry of interest among young middle-class Americans.[68] When Henry Durant opened Wellesley College near Boston in 1874, callisthenics and sports were a required part of the curriculum. Not able to find equipment for the new game of tennis, Durant sent to England for rackets and nets. Wellesley established academic standards comparable with those at Harvard, and served as a model for many of the other small elite eastern women's colleges which were founded in the late 1800s.[69] Wellesley College also became America's most influential and prestigious institution for training women college directors and instructors of physical education after 1909 when it merged with the Boston Normal School of Gymnastics. When women began to enter higher education a great deal of concern was expressed that intellectual study would result in breaking down their physical health. The required programmes of callisthenic exercises and simple forms of recreational activities were intended to enable them to become strong enough to withstand the rigours of 'brain work'. Many American men, and not a few women, were convinced that higher education would masculinize females and make them unfit mothers, thereby threatening the well-being of the nation. In 1872 Edward Clarke, M.D., a member of Harvard's Board of Overseers, was invited to address the New England Women's Club. To his listeners' surprise and dismay, Dr Clarke declared that a woman's unique physiology limited her capacity for education. He subsequently published these views in two works: *Sex in Education; Or a Fair Chance for the Girls* (1873) and *The Building of a Brain* (1874). Drawing selectively from Darwin, Spencer, Alexander Bain and Henry Maudsley, Clarke invoked the conservation of energy theory to insist that 'the muscles and the brain cannot function in the

best way at the same moment'.[70] Intellectual work could interfere
with women's reproductive function with disastrous consequences for
the individual – and for the nation.

In the late 1800s most Americans, even most feminists, accepted
the evolutionists' belief that men and women differed in their
physiology and psychology. Not so Elizabeth Cady Stanton, who had
already spent the majority of her 66 years as one of the nation's most
outspoken women's rights advocates. In 1882 she declared in the
widely circulated *North American Review*: ' . . . a girl's impulses seem
to be ever in conflict with custom. . . . Woman is now in the transition
period from the old to the new . . . all girls are not satisfied with the
amusements society has to offer . . . [and] statistics show that girls
taking a college course are more healthy than those who lead listless
lives . . .'.[71] It would be necessary, however, for women to
demonstrate that academic work did not either break their health or
make them unfit mothers before Victorian assumptions would begin
to be modified. And changes, when they did come, reflected the
tensions of the older and the newer concepts of woman. Slowly it was
realized that those college women who did marry produced healthy
children. Many college-educated women remained single, however,
finding a career plus marriage an impossible burden, or because they
preferred the personal freedom which a career offered. Statistics
showed, too, that college-educated families had fewer children, and
this fuelled the arguments of those who opposed higher education for
women.

The decades following the Civil War witnessed a rapid growth of
institutions of higher learning in America. The Morrill Land Grant
Act of 1862 provided the financial and legal basis for the large state
universities of the twentieth century. Numerous religious and
non-denominational colleges (many of short duration) were founded
in the decades between 1870–1910. It was also in the post-Civil War
decades that many of the nation's prestigious private universities were
established.

The state universities of the Mid- and Far-West and several
private institutions, such as for example the University of Chicago,
admitted women quite early, largely in order to bolster enrolments.
Those women who were admitted soon demonstrated that they could
do very well in academic work and that study did not cause their health
to break down. Although the majority trained for teaching and similar
service-oriented fields, many did exceptionally well in mathematics,
chemistry and other scientific studies. Colleges and universities
rapidly developed departments of physical education and engaged
medical doctors and gymnasium assistants to oversee the health of

their students and provide for them programmes of callisthenic and gymnastic exercises Initially sports were student-initiated extra-curricular activities, but by the 1890s these were increasingly brought under the control of the faculty. Whereas before 1900 most directors of physical culture or physical training (both terms were in use) at the coeducational universities were men – quite frequently medical doctors – by the early 1900s many of these institutions had established separate departments of physical education for women, often engaging a woman physician to examine female students and serve as the director of physical training for women.[72] Delphine Hanna, appointed Instructor of Physical Culture at Ohio's Oberlin College in 1885, and Director of the Women's Department in 1887, was a 1874 graduate of the State Normal School at Brockport, New York. She completed a year of work at Dudley Allen Sargent's Normal School of Physical Education in 1885 and received the medical degree from the University of Michigan in 1890. Although her most substantial contributions were to anthropometry, Dr Hanna did not neglect sports in the curriculum which she established for Oberlin's female students, giving particular attention to swimming, tennis, skating, cycling and hiking.[73]

The Women's College of Baltimore (which later assumed the name of its founder and became Goucher College) enrolled its first class in September 1888. When Daniel Coit Gilman, president of neighbour-ing Johns Hopkins University, delivered the inaugural address to Goucher's young women, he declared that the first of the seven things to be secured by a liberal education was ' . . . sound, healthy, active bodies'. Considerable attention was devoted to the health and physical well-being of Goucher students. A Department of Hygiene and Physical Training was established in 1891, headed by a woman physician who held the rank of full professor. The required programme was modelled on that of Stockholm's Royal Central Gymnastic Institute, but a variety of games rapidly became an important part of the total programme of physical activities. The first Professor of Physical Training, Lecturer in Human Anatomy and Physiology, and Director of the Gymnasium, Dr Alice T. Hall, had graduated from Wellesley College and the Women's Medical College of Pennsylvania. Before entering upon her new duties, she visited Vienna, Berlin, Zurich, Paris and Stockholm to study hygiene and physical training. Mathilda Wallin, a graduate of the Royal Central Gymnastic Institute, was appointed the first Gymnasium Assistant. Dr Lillian Welsh, also a graduate of the Women's Medical College of Pennsylvania, became Professor of Physical Training in 1894 – a post she held for over 30 years. In her reminiscences, she recalled that in the late 1800s Americans were: '. . . still in the midst of the discussion precipitated by Dr Clarke's book entitled *Sex in Education*. The reproductive organs in women were looked upon as the source of most of their ills. . .'. Dr Welsh, too, spent several months studying in Sweden and Germany, and also England, returning to her newly acquired duties ' . . . convinced that the Swedish system offered the best foundation for systematic formal gymnastics . . .' but to this should be added ' . . . the English zest for sports and athletics'.[74]

There can be little doubt that Dr Welsh visited Madame Bergman-Österberg's Physical Training College at Dartford Heath while she was in England. One of the first assistants she engaged was Miss Hanna Flyborg, a graduate of the Royal Central Gymnastic Institute and Dartford. (Until 1913 – with one exception who was apparently not up to Dr Welsh's high standards – all Assistants of Physical Training at Goucher College had been trained at one or the other of these institutions.) The English- and Swedish-trained assistants found the American girls to be 'soft' and unprepared to ' . . . undertake really vigorous exercise',[75] but sports soon became quite popular at Goucher. In their *History of Goucher College*, Knapp and Thomas state:

> In the fall of 1897, with the coming of a graduate [probably Flyborg] of an English athletic school as gymnasium instructor, hockey and golf were introduced. The call for hockey players brought so many volunteers – over eighty – that instead of one club which had been planned, there were three. The advent in 1899 of Miss Hillyard [from Dartford] as the new assistant in 'physical culture', whose special work it was to develop an interest in English out-of-door games, intensified the zest for hockey.[76]

The Boston Normal School of Gymnastics (BNSG), which became the Department of Hygiene and Physical Education, Wellesley College, in 1909, is the prototype for American women's college physical education and sport. The BNSG was founded in 1889 through the benefaction of Mary Hemenway, a Boston philanthropist, and the persistent efforts of Amy Morris Homans, who had directed Hemenway's projects since 1877. Its programme was modelled on that of Stockholm's Royal Central Institute of Gymnastics. At the time of its founding only four Normal (teacher-training) Schools of Physical Education existed in the United States: the Training School of the North American Turner Bund (1866); the Sargent School (1883); the Anderson School (1886); the YMCA Training School at Springfield, Massachusetts (1887). Homans served as director of the

BNSG/Department of Hygiene and Physical Education, Wellesley College, for 40 years. Early in her career she embarked on a successful mission of placing her graduates in positions as directors of programmes in colleges and universities across the United States, thereby ensuring the dissemination and perpetuation of the BNSG/ Wellesley College ideology. Homans called in professors from Harvard and doctors from the Harvard Medical School to instruct the students. Swedish gymnastics formed the core of the activity curriculum, but by the 1890s swimming, games, dancing, basketball, boating, tennis and athletics were also included. Field hockey was added in the early 1900s. On the walls of the Wellesley gymnasium were placards inscribed with the words: 'Her voice was ever soft, gentle and low; an Excellent thing in woman'. These lines from *King Lear* admirably convey Homans' philosophy. Although her graduates might be accomplished in gymnastic activities and sports, sound businesswomen and able administrators, they were never to forget that they were first and foremost *ladies*.[77]

American female collegiate physical education directors present an interesting and still not well-explored group. In order to succeed, they had to possess the same types of attributes as successful businessmen. Their stock in trade was games and callisthenics, the former, in particular, deemed to be substantially the province of males in the late nineteenth and early twentieth centuries. They were often among the few women on a college or university faculty which might include many men who were hostile to the idea of higher education for women. How were they able to succeed? In part, because they invoked either the Victorian feminine ideal or the Image of the New Woman, whichever the situation called for – and they learned to do this with consummate skill. Additionally, they endlessly insisted that only women, creatures who shared the same physiology, could know what was best for college girls. In coeducational institutions, the women's physical education department was a bastion which males were not encouraged to enter: an enclave within the broader campus much as the Victorian home had been a sheltered refuge in a competitive and male-dominated society. In the smaller sex-segregated women's colleges and within these separate departments of physical education, female directors usually ruled with iron, but not unkindly, fortitude.

V

It is somewhat more difficult to discern direct connections between Britain and the United States for women's sports than it is for men's sports in the late nineteenth century. For one thing far less was written about this by contemporaries. Also, historians to date have not provided extensive investigations and analyses, from which meaningful generalizations might be derived, of individual schools, clubs, or organizations which involved women and sport in the late 1800s and early 1900s. Some eastern girls' preparatory schools had principals and/or instructors from England, and English games mistresses were sometimes engaged to teach at various of the eastern women's colleges. Middle- and upper-class Americans had considerable opportunity to read about British customs, both in the popular press and in the more specialized sports-oriented periodicals. In the 1880s, 1890s and early 1900s a kind of 'Anglo-mania' existed among Americans who were aspiring to establish themselves as a socially superior group and much of the literature which this group prepared for and about itself reflects at least a superficial interest in things 'British'.

During the 1880s, as wealthy and 'comfortable' Americans sought ways to define and legitimize their elevated status in society, they created a variety of social clubs which were equipped with facilities for various sports, especially tennis and golf. Membership in an elite 'country club' was seen to be a visible symbol of achieved success. An article which appeared in *The Fortnightly Review* in 1894 entitled 'The American Sportswoman' conveyed with some accuracy the nature and extent of country club and athletic club sport for women which existed in the United States. Most country clubs, hunt clubs, tennis clubs and other sporting clubs had a ladies' department or affiliated memberships.[78] Beginning in 1887, a Ladies' National Tennis Championship was held each year at Philadelphia. According to one commentator, lawn tennis had been the only 'game' available to American women in 1889, although propriety also permitted them to ride, walk, row or 'play at mask and foil'. Discussing the emergence of tennis as a game for women at such places as the Philadelphia Cricket Club and the Staten Island Cricket and Baseball Club, the author noted: 'To enumerate and describe all of the clubs in the neighborhood of New York City which gladly welcome ladies to membership would be an almost endless task . . .'. None the less, he believed that '. . . the English girl plays lawn tennis much better than the American simply because she is physically her superior, and can more easily handle a racquet of adequate weight . . .'. Marion Jones, who lost the 1898 Ladies' tournament to Juliette Atkinson, spent part of 1900 in England, returning with renewed enthusiasm for the game thanks to her experiences with British women's tennis. Riding, in Hunt Clubs emulating the best English clubs, was considered *de*

PAST AND PRESENT.

IN THE SIXTIES.   IN THE SEVENTIES.

IN THE EIGHTIES.   IN THE NINETIES.

1. Fashions for the Victorian sportswoman (*Punch*, 18 July 1891

OUR LADIES' HOCKEY CLUB.

One of the Inferior Sex who volunteered to Umpire soon discovered his office was no sinecure.

2. Hockey became increasingly popular in the 1890s, though regarded as unladylike (*Punch*, 6 December 1899)

Ethel. "I HOPE BICYCLING WILL GO OUT OF FASHION BEFORE NEXT SEASON, I *DO* HATE BICYCLING SO!"
Maud. "SO DO I! BUT ONE *MUST*, YOU KNOW!"

3. Bicycling had become a craze for all who could afford it by the 1890s, despite the caption to this cartoon (Punch's Almanack for 1897)

rigueur 'among girls of the highest circles'. *Scribner's Magazine* declared that 'all England is a sort of country club', and likened American gentlemen who chased foxes to the English landed gentry. Golf was taken up by the fashionable set at Newport in the 1890s. In 1895 the first women's championship was held at the Meadowbrook Hunt Club under the auspices of the United States Golf Association. Books on the subject soon began to appear. Miss Rhona K. Adair, for three years English Open Champion and five years Irish Open Champion, provided the final chapter for the 1904 edition of Genevieve Hecker's *Golf for Women*. The author (Mrs Charles T. Stout), the 1901, 1902 and 1903 American National Woman Champion, described the game's rapid spread among women in England, Scotland and America, noting that women were now accepted on most golf courses in both countries. *The Book of Sport*, published in 1901 as a tribute to upper-class American sportsmen and sportswomen, contained numerous references to upper-class English sport and was patterned on similar British publications.[79]

Introduced into the United States from Britain in the early 1870s, bicycling had become a craze for all who could afford a machine by the 1890s. Many women joined clubs, and in some instances formed their own. When cycling became one of the principal types of outing for the middle classes – shopkeepers, tradesmen, mechanics and clerks – those upper-class women who cycled tended not to do so in public. As with so many of the physical activities in which women might engage in the 1890s and early 1900s, commentators attributed varied and sometimes conflicting benefits and dangers to exercise taken on the bicycle. The author of an article which appeared in *Physical Education*, the monthly journal of the International YMCA Training School, argued that cycling was an ideal form of exercise for women. The American college girl 'with a very highly organized nervous system . . . cannot work for any great length of time . . .'; cycling, however, would help by strengthening the participant. As cycling necessitated the use of large muscle groups (the legs), deep breathing, vigorous circulation and an erect posture, it was deemed an especially effective means of developing strength. Married women, it was held, might also benefit from the bicycle because it offered both exercise and a respite from the ceaseless toil of caring for their children.[80]

The bicycle required women to wear special clothing so that the skirt would not catch in the gears or wheels. Much has been said by historians about the roles which both sporting attire and games have performed in the emancipation of women from traditional Victorian constraints. This was also the feeling of contemporaries. In 1896 Sophia Foster Richardson, a graduate of Vassar College, addressed the Association of Collegiate Alumnae on 'Tendencies in Athletics for Girls in Colleges and Universities'. College women, Richardson pointed out, were now boating, doing gymnasium work, and playing tennis and basketball, all to their physical, intellectual and moral betterment. American women had finally begun to learn the advantages of those outdoor games which had traditionally been part of the English girl's education: 'At college [the English girl] plays hockey or hand polo, cricket, fives, and the games with which we are more familiar, for *at least* two hours a day . . .', Richardson maintained. 'Every American who studies at Cambridge adopts the work of her English friends, and ever afterward looks with compassion on the mistakes of her countrywomen'.[81]

Although it is clear that field hockey was played at Goucher College before 1900, Miss Constance M.K. Applebee is credited with introducing the game to the United States at the 1901 Harvard Summer School for Teachers, using ice hockey sticks and an indoor baseball for equipment. It was largely through her dedicated efforts that the game spread to women's colleges and women's physical education departments in co-educational institutions. For seven decades 'the Apple' was the revered, and feared, patroness of field hockey in America. It soon became a popular autumn sport in elite eastern women's colleges and at those institutions which engaged women physical educators who had studied at these colleges. In 1905 *Outing Magazine* reported on women's hockey, declaring: 'Certainly there is no game to test endurance, wind and agility of womankind, that can be compared with hockey as they play it in England. . . . A football player would not be blamed for dodging from the path of these headlong Amazons . . .'.[82] Because it was perceived to be an elite British schoolgirl sport, field hockey was frequently considered an acceptable, even desirable, albeit vigorous women's sport. It was, for example, quite permissible for a woman to run nearly an hour in a hockey match while it might be totally unacceptable for her to run in a track meet. Female hockey players might traverse the length of the 100 yard field but be confined to half or less of an 80 foot basketball court.

The reasons why hockey retained its respectability as a game for women while track, and even basketball, began to fall into disfavour with many women physical educators in the 1920s, have not yet been fully explored, but part of the explanation must be sought in the elite English origins which Americans associated with field hockey. Additionally, in America the game was confined almost exclusively to women. In her excellent study of games in late Victorian British girls' public schools, Kathleen McCrone has argued that at schools like

Roedean and St Leonards 'the introduction of new sports, like hockey, netball, and lacrosse, that did not carry the stigma of overt masculinity . . .' fostered the notion that at least some team games could be acceptable for girls and young women. Such sports, contemporaries claimed, did not require ' . . . physical contact, awkward positions, endurance and great strength'.[83] The same non-strenuous qualities in women's sports were also deemed extremely desirable by Americans: And these values persisted at least until the 1970s. The ideology was reinforced by the incessant proclamations of those women physical educators who established and supported professional organizations like the Committee on Women's Athletics of the American Physical Education Association and its various successor organizations, as well as by the images of women portrayed in the popular press.[84]

In 1898, Penelope Lawrence, one of the co-founders of Roedean, reported that the school's first eleven had been invited to play the Ladies' Colleges of Cambridge and Oxford. In words which would have warmed the hearts of supporters of America's burgeoning men's intercollegiate athletic programmes, Miss Lawrence declared, 'the matches of the first eleven do not alone ensure its prestige. . . .' The girls provided an inducement to the 'rank and file' and, therefore, merited their distinguised position. The players and the matches were deemed to be ' . . . a great stimulus to the *esprit de corps* of the school . . .'.[85] This ideology was even more powerfully expressed with regard to boys' and men's sports. On both sides of the Atlantic educators shared the belief that the presence of elite performers – especially in team games – could rouse the remainder of the student-body to emulate their participation; and that such teams were of great significance in developing a common spirit of school loyalty among students, faculty and alumni. J.A. Mangan has described the important functions which Old Boys' Clubs performed in maintaining links with former schools, noting that Uppinghamians in India even arranged for the school outfitter to supply them with cricket caps and other accoutrements. Writing for the *North American Review* in 1891, Joseph H. Sears declared football to be a strong positive force in the lives of college undergraduates for it taught wholesome restraint, the values of vigorous exercise, self-control and decisiveness. Although Sears did not explain how it was supposed to occur, students who 'merely stand and watch' were believed to benefit also. J. William White, Professor of Surgery and founder of the Department of Physical Education at the University of Pennsylvania, proclaimed the same benefits and much more for spectators in his defence of American football in 1905.[86]

There is some evidence that in women's colleges – and in some American high schools, especially in rural areas – the matches of distaff 'first teams' could be of consequence in developing the desired *esprit de corps*. Janice Beran has argued persuasively, for example, that girls' basketball in rural Iowa in the late 1800s/early 1900s was held in esteem by school administrators as well as by students and townspeople.[87] It would be a gross exaggeration, however, to imply that girls' and women's games attained a level of significance anywhere near that of boys' and men's games. In the larger coeducational institutions, in particular, the presence of highly visible and extremely popular male teams relegated women's sports to a role of insignificance. None the less, by the early twentieth century American college women were playing many of the games that male students were playing; and the intensity with which the women approached their sports could be fully equal to that of their male contemporaries.

Although James Naismith had created basketball as a winter game for young men, its appeal among college women was almost instantaneous. In October 1901 the Spalding's Athletic Library series published *Basket Ball for Women*, edited by Senda Berenson of Smith College in Northampton, Massachusetts. In her opening editorial, Berenson declared: '. . . directors of gymnasia for women saw at once that it was, perhaps, the game they were eagerly seeking', as it was interesting and had the potential to develop strength and physical endurance. Women graduates of physical training schools rapidly adopted and spread the game, and by 1901 it was referred as '. . . the most popular game that women play'. The game crossed the Atlantic in 1895, Madame Österberg introduced it, and it was soon converted into English netball. American commentators considered basketball particularly useful in teaching women self-control, physical and moral courage, and teamwork. This emphasis on teamwork and at least some physical ability reflects many of the changes which were associated with the New Woman at the turn of the century. Dr Luther Gulick, and early president of the American Association for the Advancement of Physical Education, observed that this was '. . . a time of great unrest in regard to the status of women', for they were beginning to enter '. . . many lines of work that hitherto have been carried on entirely by men'. If they were to succeed in these new endeavours, Gulick and others held, they would need both physical stamina and the type of teamwork and loyalty which it was assumed came naturally to men. Basketball was deemed an admirable game for teaching such qualities.[88]

With few exceptions, however, women played their sports away from the prying eyes of the public. Whereas the male sports model was intentionally a very public cultural performance, women's sporting events remained largely cloistered. Jennifer Hargreaves has concluded in her study of contradictory features of the formative years of women's sport in Britain that ' . . . by being insular, sportswomen did not constitute a challenge in their relationship with men'.[89] A similar phenomenon occurred across the Atlantic in the United States. An article which appeared in the *Cosmopolitan Magazine* in 1901 entitled 'A Girl's College Life' aptly reflects the collegiate experience of many early twentieth-century American women. College women, it was asserted, were serious (perhaps more serious) than college men because the majority of them were in college to prepare themselves to earn a livelihood. While it was not acceptable for these young women to engage in riotous behavior over an athletic victory, as the men often did, ' . . . the triumph of their class and colors [was] just as dear to them'. Within their own precincts these young women could be, and often were, extremely enthusiastic about their sports. It became customary in the early 1900s for each college to hold a 'Field Day' – later a 'Field Week' – to culminate the year's athletic work. On this *special* occasion a public display of athletic accomplishment was permitted. It was also permissible at these well-defined times to 'break previous records' and exalt and fête winners.[90] Once a year the newly emerging mould in which the New Woman and the Victorian Angel in the House were still bound together could be broken. But in athletic sport, one of the few remaining male bastions in twentieth-century America, it would not be until the 1970s that anything even beginning to resemble equality for the two sexes would become available.

NOTES

1. See, for example, John A. Lucas and Ronald A. Smith, *Saga of American Sport* (Philadelphia, 1978); William J. Baker, *Sports in the Modern World* (Totowa, NJ, 1982). See also M. Roth, *The Gymnastic Free Exercises of P.H. Ling, Arranged by H. Rothstein* (Boston, 1853). Dr Roth listed himself as Physician to the Institution for the Treatment of Deformities . . . in Old Cavendish St. For a more general discussion of the influence of Great Britain on the United States, see H.C. Allen, *The Anglo-American Relationship Since 1783* (London, 1959), II; see also Thomas Colley Grattan, *Civilized America* (London, 1859), Chapters II and III. Grattan had been H.B.M. Consul for the State of Massachusetts.
2. Far less has been done with this topic for American sport than has been done for English sport. For the United States there is little to compare, for example, with Norman Vance, 'The Ideal of Manliness', in B. Simon and I. Bradley (eds.), *The Victorian Public School* (Dublin, 1975), and nothing to compare with J.R. Honey, *Tom Brown's Universe: The Development of the English Public School in the Nineteenth Century* (New York, 1977) or J.A. Mangan, *Athleticism in the Victorian and Edwardian Public School* (Cambridge, 1981).

3. L.J. Jordanova, 'Natural Facts: A Historical Perspective on Science and Sexuality', in Carol MacCormack and Marilyn Strathern (eds.), *Nature, Culture and Gender* (Cambridge, 1980), pp. 42–4, and other papers therein.
4. Alan Trachtenberg, *The Incorporation of America: Culture and Society in the Gilded Age* (New York, 1982), Chapter V. See also such works as Gene Smith and Jayne Barry Smith (eds.), *The Police Gazette* (New York, 1972); Sandra L. Myres, *Westering Women and the Frontier Experience 1800–1915* (Albuquerque, NM, 1982), pp. 167–85; Mary Lou Remley, 'From Sidesaddle to Rodeo', *Journal of the West*, XVII (July 1978), 44–52.
5. Daniel Walker Howe (ed.), *Victorian America* (Philadelphia, 1976), p. 3.
6. *Harper's Monthly Magazine*, I (June 1850), 9.
7. See John Rickards Betts, *America's Sporting Heritage: 1850–1950* (Reading, MA, 1974), Chapter I; *passim*; Jennie Holliman, *American Sport, 1785 to 1835* (Durham, NC, 1931).
8. Hamilton W. Mabie, 'The Most Popular Novels in America', *The Forum*, XVI (1894), 508–16.
9. See Christian K. Messenger, *Sport and the Spirit of Play in American Fiction: Hawthorne to Faulkner* (New York, 1981); Walter Evans, 'The All-American Boys: A Study of Boy's Sports in Fiction', *Journal of Popular Culture*, VI (Spring 1972), 104–21; Ralph Henry Barbour, *For the Honor of the School: A Story of School Life and Intercollegiate Sport* (New York, 1900); idem, *The Crimson Sweater* (New York, 1905); Lester Chadwick, *A Quarter-Back's Pluck: A Story of College Football* (New York, 1910); Walter Camp and Lorin F. Deland, *Football* (Boston, 1896), especially pp. 1–17; *Cassell's Complete Book of Sports and Pastimes: Being A Compendium of Outdoor and Indoor Amusements* (London, 188[?]). See also Alex Bungaard, 'Tom Brown Abroad: Athletics in Selected New England Public [*sic*] [Private] Schools, 1850–1910', *Research Quarterly for Exercise and Sport*, Centennial Issue (April 1985), 28–37.
10. E.Anthony Rotundo, 'Body and Soul: Changing Ideals of American Middle Class Manhood, 1770–1920', *Journal of Social History*, XVI (Summer 1983), 23–38.
11. See, for example, Charles E. Rosenberg, 'Sexuality, Class, and Role', in Charles E. Rosenberg (ed.), *No Other Gods: On Science and American Social Thought* (Baltimore, 1978), pp. 71–88; S.G. Young, 'Are Americans Less Healthy Than Europeans?', *The Galaxy*, XIV (1872), 630–9; Edward Spencer, 'The Philosophy of Good Health', *Scribner's Monthly*, II (1871), 589–94; Charles Woodhall Eaton, *Things Young Men Should Know: A Manual of the Anatomy, Physiology and Hygiene of the Sexual System* (Des Moines, IA, 1884); Archibald Maclaren, *A System of Physical Education: Theoretical and Practical*, (Oxford, 2nd edn., 1865); [Mrs] E.R. Shepherd, *For Girls: A Special Physiology* (Chicago, 1884); Lyman B. Sperry, *Confidential Talks With Young Women* (Chicago, 1893).
12. John Higham, 'The Reorientation of American Culture in the 1890s', in John Higham (ed.), *Writing American History: Essays On Modern Scholarship* (Bloomington, IN, 1972), pp. 73–102.
13. See, for example, Nancy L. Struna, ' "Good Wives" and "Gardeners", Spinners and "Fearless Riders": Middling and Upper Rank Women in the Colonial Anglo-American Sporting Culture' (see below, pp. 235–55); Gerda Lerner, 'The Lady and the Mill Girl: Changes in the Status of Women in the Age of Jackson', in Jean E. Friedmand and William G. Shade (eds.) *Our American Sisters: Women in American Life and Thought* (Lexington, MA, 1982), pp. 183–95, and other papers therein; Mary P. Ryan, *Womanhood in America: From Colonial Times to the Present* (New York, 1983); Barbara Welter, *Divinity Convictions: The American Woman in the Nineteenth Century* (Athens, OH, 1976). Deborah Gorham, *The Victorian Girl and the Feminine Ideal* (Bloomington, IN, 1982) is concerned with the British context.
14. Mary Kelley, *Private Woman, Public Stage: Literary Domesticity in Nineteenth Century America* (New York, 1984), pp. 111–12; *passim*.
15. James D. Hart, *The Popular Book* (Berkeley, 1950), esp. Chapters VI, VII.
16. Ronald G. Walters, *American Reformers, 1815–1860* (New York, 1978), Chapter VII; Roberta J. Park, 'The Attitudes of Leading New England Transcendentalists Toward

Healthful Exercise, Active Recreations and Proper Care of the Body: 1830–1869',
Journal of Sport History, IV (Spring 1977), 34–50; [Oliver Wendell Holmes], *The
Autocrat of the Breakfast Table* (Boston, 1859); Thomas Wentworth Higginson,
'Barbarism and Civilization', *The Atlantic Monthly* VII (January 1861), 51–61; idem,
'Gymnastics', *The Atlantic Monthly*, VII (March 1861), 283–302. See also Bruce Haley,
The Healthy Body and Victorian Culture (Cambridge, MA, 1978).

17. 'Exercise of Females', *The Graham Journal of Health and Longevity*, II (August, 1838),
254.
18. 'Out of Door Amusements', *Massachusetts Teacher*, XII (1856), 564.
19. 'National Characteristics', *Hours at Home*, I (October, 1865), 544–8.
20. 'The Englishman As A Natural Curiosity', *Lippincott's Magazine*, II (October 1868),
441–7.
21. John A. Lucas, 'Thomas Wentworth Higginson: Early Apostle of Health and Fitness',
Journal of Health, Physical Education and Recreation, XLII (February 1971), 30–3.
22. Thomas Wentworth Higginson, 'The Health of Our Girls', *The Atlantic Monthly*, IX
(June 1862), 722–31.
23. Catharine E. Beecher, *Physiology and Calisthenics for Schools and Families* (New
York, 1856), p. 11.
24. 'On Some Peculiarities of Society in America', *The Transatlantic*, VII (February 1873),
206–18; Richard L. Rapson, *Britons View America: Travel Commentary, 1860–1935*
(Seattle, WA, 1971), pp. 106–12.
25. Rapson, *Britons View America*, pp. 113–19.
26. Foster Rhea Dulles, *A History of Recreation: America Learns to Play* (New York,
1965); Jennie Holliman, *American Sports*; Guy M. Lewis, 'America's First
Intercollegiate Sport: The Regattas From 1852 to 1875', *Research Quarterly*, XXXVIII
(December 1967), 637–48.
27. See Roberta J. Park, ' "Embodied Selves": The Rise and Development of Concern
for Physical Education, Active Games and Recreation for American Women,
1776–1865', *Journal of Sport History*, V (Summer 1978), 5–41; Sara Joseph Hale,
[Godey's] *Lady's Book, XXIII* (July 1841), 41–2; R.T. Trall, *The Illustrated Family
Gymnasium . . .* (New York, 1873). Trall's first edition appeared in 1857; *Boston
Journal of Physical Education*, I (June 1861), 128. Lewis was more progressive than
most of his contemporaries and refused to permit in his gymnasium any exercise in
which both the sexes could not 'simultaneously occupy themselves', p. 104.
28. Elizabeth Cady Stanton, 'Man Superior – Intellectually, Morally and Physically', *The
Lily*, II (April 1, 1850), 31; 'Improper Education of Women', *The Lily*, VII (April 1,
1855), 5.
29. Dio Lewis, *The New Gymnastics* (Boston, 1868); idem., 'New Gymnastics', [Barnard's]
American Journal of Education, XXVII (June 1862), 531–62.
30. Robert H. Wiebe, *The Search for Order, 1870–1920* (New York, 1967), p. 166. See also
Burton Bledstein, *The Culture of Professionalism: The Middle Class and the
Development of Higher Education in America* (New York, 1976).
31. Rosalind Rosenberg, *Beyond Separate Spheres: Intellectual Roots of Modern Feminism*
(New Haven, 1982), p. 54.
32. 'Amusements', *The New Englander*, L (July 1867), 399–424.
33. 'The Boat Race', *The Nation*, IX (2 September 1869), 187–9.
34. Benjamin G. Rader, *American Sports: From the Age of Folk Games to the Age of
Spectators* (Englewood Cliffs, NJ, 1983), Part II; Donald J. Mrozek, *Sport and
American Mentality, 1880–1910* (Knoxville, TN, 1983); Stephen Hardy, *How Boston
Played: Sport, Recreation and Community, 1865–1915* (Boston, 1982). More recently,
Melvin L. Adelman, *A Sporting Time: New York City and the Rise of Modern Athletics,
1820–1870* (Urbana, 1986) has argued that in New York 'modern' sport arose before
the Civil War.
35. 'The Cricket Mania', *Harper's Weekly* (15 October 1859), 658.
36. Ibid.
37. For contemporary commentary see, for example, Ralph D. Paine, 'The Spirit of School
and College Sport: American and English Rowing', *The Century Magazine*, LXX

(August 1905), 483–503; idem, 'The Spirit of School and College Sport: English and American Football', *The Century Magazine*, LXXI (September 1905), 99–116; 'The Future of Football', *The Nation* (20 November 1890), 395; Edwin H. Hall, 'Athletic Professionalism and Its Remedies', *The School Review*, XIII (December 1905), 758–88; 'Some Tendencies in Modern Sport', *The Quarterly Review*, CXCIX (1904), 127–52. The author of the last article was very concerned about a growing 'professionalism' in English sport.

38. Theodore Parker, 'Some Thoughts on the Progress of America and the Influence of Her Diverse Institutions', in *Additional Speeches, Addresses and Occasional Sermons* (Boston, 1855), II, p. 24.

39. John R. Howe, *From the Revolution Through the Age of Jackson: Innocence and Empire in the Young Republic* (Englewood Cliffs, NJ, 1976), Chapter I. See also, Richard D. Brown, *Modernization: The Transformation of American Life, 1600–1865* (New York, 1976).

40. Daniel T. Rodgers, *The Work Ethic in Industrial America: 1850–1920* (Chicago, 1974), pp. xiii–xiv, 7.

41. Quoted in Steven M. Gelber, 'Working At Playing: The Culture of the Workplace and the Rise of Baseball', *Journal of Social History*, XVI (Summer 1983), 3–22.

42. Ibid.

43. William T. Reid, Jr., letter to Benjamin Ide Wheeler, 9 March 1906 (Bancroft Library, University of California, 'Football Folder'). See also, Roberta J. Park, 'From Football to Rugby – And Back, 1906–1919: The University of California–Stanford University Response to the "Football Crisis" of 1905', *Journal of Sport History* XI (Winter 1984), 5–40.

44. Clifford Geertz, 'Deep Play: Notes on the Balinese Cockfight', *Daedalus*, CI (Winter 1972), 1–37; G. Whitney Azoy, *Buzkashi: Game and Power in Afghanistan* (Philadelphia, 1982); John J. MacAloon, *This Great Symbol: Pierre de Coubertin and the Origins of the Modern Olympic Games* (Chicago, 1981); idem, 'Olympic Games and the Theory of Spectacle in Modern Societies', in John J. MacAloon (ed.), *Rite, Drama, Festival, Spectacle: Rehearsals Toward a Theory of Cultural Performances* Philadelphia, 1984), pp. 241–80.

45. Henry May, *The End of American Innocence: A Study of the First Years of Our Own Time, 1912–1917* (Chicago, 1959).

46. Higham, 'Reorientation', 93.

47. See, for example, Gerald F. Linderman, *The Mirror of War: American Society and the Spanish-American War* (Ann Arbor, 1974), especially Chapter IV.

48. Theodore Roosevelt, *The Strenuous Life: Essays and Addresses* (New York, 1901), pp. 4–5; 8; J. William White, 'Football and Its Critics', *Outlook*, LXXXI (November 1905), 662–9. See, especially, the books and commentaries by Walter Camp, who was widely considered 'the authority' on football and amateur athletics at the turn of the century. One example is Walter Camp, *Walter Camp's Book on College Sports* (New York, 1893). See also Roberta J. Park, 'Boys Into Men – State Into Nation: *Rites of Passage* in Student Life and College Athletics, 1890–1915', in Brian Sutton-Smith and Diana Kelly-Byrne (eds.), *The Masks of Play* (New York, 1984), pp. 51–62.

49. W.H.Grenfell, 'Oxford v. Yale', *The Fortnightly Review*, LVI (1894), 368–82.

50. Quoted in Betts, *America's Sporting Heritage*, pp. 196–7; *San Francisco Bulletin*, 13 September 1895. For an amusing and informative account of America's first yachting challenge to Great Britain see John Dizikes, *Sportsmen and Gamesmen* (Boston, 1981), Chapter V.

51. James E. Sullivan, 'Athletics and the Stadium', *Cosmopolitan*, XXXI (September 1901), 501–8.

52. See, for example, William M. Henry, *An Approved History of the Olympic Games* (New York, 1948).

53. Paine, 'American and English Rowing', 481.

54. 'Some Tendencies of Modern Sport', 151–2.

55. See, for example, Clarence Deming, 'Athletics in College Life: The Money Power in College Athletics', *The Outlook*, LXXX (July 1905), 569–72. Deming accused Yale, his

alma mater, of being among the leaders of those colleges whose athletic programmes were excessively costly, and concluded that: 'The large riches that ever crave more in the outside world find their analogue in the college microcosm'. See also Thomas Wentworth Higginson, 'The Aristocracy of the Dollar', *The Atlantic Monthly*, XCIII (April 1904), 506–13; Ira N. Hollis, 'Athletic Sports', *President's Report: Harvard University, 1900–1902*, p. 127. In the early 1900s the muck-raking *McClure's Magazine* began a series of exposés of large corporations, monopolies, and men who had built vast financial empires, like John D. Rockefeller and Andrew Carnegie. See, for example, 'Miss Tarbell's New Series', *McClure's Magazine*, XXV (June 1905), 144.

56. See Robert J. Park, 'Morality Embodied: The College Athlete and American Views of Right Action and Success, 1870–1900', in *The University's Role in the Development of Sport: Past, Present and Future* (Edmonton, 1983), pp. 328–41.

57. Michael Zuckerman, 'The Nursery Tales of Horatio Alger', *American Quarterly*, XXIV (May 1972), 191–209.

58. See John G. Cawelti, *Apostles of the Self-Made Man: Changing Concepts of Success in America* (Chicago, 1965); Robert C. Bannister, *Social Darwinism: Science and Myth in Anglo-American Social Thought* (Philadelphia, 1979), pp. 3–33.

59. Lloyd S. Bryce, 'A Plea for Sport', *North American Review*, CXXVIII (1879), 511–25.

60. Quoted in Frank L. Mott, *A History of American Magazines, 1885–1905* (Cambridge, MA, 1957), IV, pp. 374–5.

61. See, for example, Mrozek, *Sport and American Mentality*; idem, 'Sport and the American Military: Diversion and Duty', *Research Quarterly for Exercise and Sport*, Centennial Issue (April 1985), 38–45, and my Introduction to that section, ibid., 25–7; Theodore Roosevelt, *The Rough Riders* (Philadelphia, 1903), Chapter I.

62. Edward L. Hitchcock and H.H. Seelye, *An Anthropometric Manual, Giving the Average and Mean Physical Measurements and Tests of Male College Students, and Methods of Securing Them* (Amherst, 1889), p. 4.

63. Luther H. Gulick, 'Physical Education: A New Profession', in *Proceedings of the American Association for the Advancement of Physical Education, 1890* (Ithaca, 1890), p. 65; see also Roberta J. Park, ' "Science", "Service", and the Professionalization of Physical Education: 1885–1905', *Research Quarterly for Exercise and Sport*, Centennial Issue (April 1985), 7–20.

64. Dudley A. Sargent, 'The Physical Proportions of the Typical Man', *Scribner's*, II (July 1887), 3–17; idem, 'The Physical Characteristics of the Athlete', *Scribner's*, II (November 1887), 541–61; idem, 'The Physical Development of Women', *Scribner's*, V (February 1889), 172–85.

65. See, *Publications of the American Statistical Association*, III, 1892–1893 (Boston, 1893), 138; Claes Enebuske, 'Some Measurable Results of Swedish Pedagogical Gymnastics,' *Proceedings of the American Association for the Advancement of Physical Education, 1892* (Springfield, 1893), 207–35.

66. Shepherd, *For Girls: A Special Physiology* . . . 67–76; William Blakie, *How to Get Strong and How to Stay So* (New York, 1879), 42–73.

67. Rosenberg, *Beyond Separate Spheres;* Lyman B. Sperry, *Confidential Talks with Young Women* (Chicago, 1898), 80–84.

68. Thomas Woody, *A History of Women's Education in the United States* (New York, 1929), II, pp. 98–136; Betty Spears and Richard A. Swanson, *History of Sport and Physical Activity in the United States* (Dubuque, IA 1978), pp. 124–7.

69. Betty Spears, 'The Influential Miss Homans', *Quest*, XXIX (Winter 1979), 46–57.

70. Edward Clarke, *Sex in Education; Or, A Fair Chance for the Girls* (Boston, 1873); idem, *The Building of a Brain* (Boston, 1874). See also T.S. Clouston, 'Women From a Medical Point of View', *Popular Science Monthly*, XXIV (December 1883), 214–28; 319–34.

71. Elizabeth Cady Stanton, 'The Health of American Women', *North American Review*, CCCXIII (December 1882), 510–17.

72. Sheila Fletcher's recently published *Women First: The Female Tradition in English Physical Education, 1880–1980* (London, 1984) should serve as a model for other studies of single-sex specialist colleges, or for women's physical education departments

within state and private universities in the United States. For a useful work which deals with women's collegiate education in selected New England colleges, see Roberta Frankfort, *Collegiate Women: Domesticity and Career in Turn-of-the-Century America* (New York, 1977).

73. Ellen W. Gerber, *Innovators and Institutions in Physical Education* (Philadelphia, 1971), pp. 325–31.
74. Extract from Inaugural Address Delivered by President D.C. Gilman, November 14, 1888 (Goucher College Archives); *Women's College of Baltimore Prospectus*, 1889 (Goucher College Archives); Lilian Welsh, *Reminiscences of Thirty Years in Baltimore* (Baltimore, 1925), pp. 114–29.
75. Welsh, *Reminiscences*, 120–1. While Dr Welsh, who hired these individuals, contends that the first instructor from Dartford was Miss Hillyard, *The Tenth Annual Program of the Woman's College of Baltimore* (1898) indicates that Hanna Gustava Flyborg, a graduate of the Physical Training College, Dartford Heath, Kent, England, and Eva Braun, a graduate of the Royal Central Gymnastic Institute, were the two Instructors in Physical Training, pp. 11, 46.
76. Anna H. Knipp and Thaddeus P. Thomas, *The History of Goucher College* (Baltimore, 1938), pp. 471–6, contend that Miss Hillyard introduced hockey to Goucher.
77. Spears, 'The Influential Miss Homans'; Spears and Swanson, *History of Sport*, pp. 175–7; Boston Normal School of Gymnastics, *Fourth Annual Catalogue of the Instructors, Students, and Graduates, With A Statement of the Course of Instruction, 1894–95* (Boston, 1895).
78. Robert Dunn, 'The Country Club: A National Expression – Where Woman Is Really Free', *Outing*, XLVII (November 1905), 160–73; Elizabeth C. Barney, 'American Sportswoman', *Fortnightly Review*, LXII (August 1894), 263–77; Mrs Burton Harrison, 'Henley Week', *Cosmopolitan*, XXIX (July 1900), 241–52. (Reflections of an American visitor on Henley, in general, and the Yale crew, in particular.)
79. Henry W. Slocum, Jr. 'Lawn Tennis As A Game for Women', *Outing*, XIV (July 1889), 289–300; William Patten (ed.), *The Book of Sport* (New York, 1901); John Brewster Dane, 'Jerome Park Racing Days', *Cosmopolitan*, XXX (February 1901), 346–55; Edward S. Martin, 'Country Clubs and Hunt Clubs in America', *Scribner's Magazine* XVIII (September 1895), 302–21; Genevieve Hecker, *Golf for Women* (New York, 1904), 11–23.
80. 'Bicycling for Women', *Physical Education*, 1 (July 1892), 83–5.
81. Sophia Foster Richardson, 'Tendencies in Athletics for Women in Colleges and Universities', *Popular Science Monthly*, L (February 1897), 517–26; Maria E. Ward, *Bicycling for Ladies* (New York, 1896).
82. 'Field Hockey As A Woman's Sport', *Outing*, XLV (January 1905), 475–9; Helen T. Mackey, *Field Hockey: An International Team Sport* (Englewood Cliffs, NJ, 1963), pp. 1–6.
83. Kathleen McCrone, 'Play Up! Play Up! and Play the Game!: Sport at the Late Victorian Girls' Public School', *Journal of British Studies*, XXIII, (Spring 1984), 106–34; see also below, pp. 97–129.
84. See, for example, Joan S. Hult, 'The Governance of Athletics for Girls and Women: Leadership by Women Physical Educators, 1899–1949', *Research Quarterly for Exercise and Sport*, Centennial Issue (April 1985), 64–77; Ellen Gerber, 'The Controlled Development of Collegiate Sport for Women, 1923–36', *Journal of Sport History*, II (Spring 1975), 1–28; Eline von Borries, *History and Function of the National Section on Women's Athletics* (Washington, 1941).
85. Penelope Lawrence, 'Games and Athletics in Secondary Schools for Girls', Great Britain, *Education Department, Special Reports on Educational Subjects*, II (1898), 145; see also McCrone, 'Play Up!'.
86. Mangan, *Athleticism*, 144–6; Joseph H. Sears, 'Foot-ball: Sport or Training', *North American Review*, LIII (1891), 750–3; White, 'Football and Its Critics', 662–9.
87. Janice A. Beran, 'Playing to the Right Drummer: Girls' Basketball in Iowa, 1893–1927', *Research Quarterly for Exercise and Sport*, Centennial Issue (April 1985), 78–85.

88. Senda Berenson, 'Editorial', *Basket Ball for Women: Spalding's Athletic Library*, October 1901, 5–7; Luther Gulick, 'The Psychological Effects of Basket Ball for Women', ibid, 11–14.
89. Jennifer A. Hargreaves, ' "Playing Like Gentlemen While Behaving Like Ladies": Contradictory Features of the Formative Years of Women's Sport', *British Journal of Sports History*, II (May 1985), 50; see also below, pp. 130–44.
90. L. Hart, 'A Girl's College Life', *Cosmopolitan*, XXXI (June 1901), 188–95; 'The First 100 Years: Goucher College', *The Goucher Quarterly*, LXII (Summer 1984), 4–7; see also several of the articles in Reet Howell (ed.), *Her Story in Sport: A Historical Anthology of Women in Sports* (West Point, 1982).

PART TWO

BRITISH PERSPECTIVES

4
Play up! Play up! And Play the Game! Sport at the Late Victorian Girls' Public Schools

Kathleen E. McCrone

An examination of Western society before the Victorian era, as it was represented in a variety of historical sources, reveals that the role of woman was defined largely by her child-bearing capacity and her status was derived from that of male relatives. Her natural sphere was a domestic world dominated by an often absent patriarch, and within it her physical and social functions were co-extensive. When she married she was, in effect, given permission by her father to surrender her body and its precious virginity to her husband, and henceforth to do her duty by satisfying his desires and bearing his children. Despite and because of their unique biology women were considered innately physically inferior to men, and that inferiority underlay fundamental presumptions of mental and social inferiority that were translated into masculine scepticism about women's abilities to secure independent action and partake in activities like sport hitherto monopolized by men.

Since members of both sexes were heirs of a common culture and shared ingrained assumptions about sex and gender roles, changes occurred neither easily nor rapidly. Indeed, they became substantial only as men and women went through a process of discovery under the impetus of the industrial revolution and the women's movement which demonstrated and provided experience of women's varied potential. As woman's sphere gradually widened, since suppositions about her physique were the most powerful factor controlling role and place, and since her exclusion from sport was deeply rooted in Western cultural traditions, physical barriers were among the last to fall. The invasion by women of the world of sport represented a critical breach in those barriers. Women's sport involved unprecedented physical activity and opportunities for physical liberation. It stood at the juncture of the transformation process, on the threshold between definitions of male and female and between women of the past and future; and it symbolized the manifest changes affecting not only women but the value orientations of society as a whole. It is thus disappointing that, although in recent years Victorianists have eagerly cultivated the fields of sport and women's history, they have produced surprisingly little relating the two areas.[1] Historians of women have virtually ignored the physical dimension of the struggle for female emancipation,[2] while historians of sport have reflected sport's traditional male orientation by neglecting the distaff side. As W.J. Baker noted recently, 'the history of British women in sports . . . stands high on the agenda of work to be done'.[3]

What limited material there is on women's sport history as such has tended to be produced by physical educators or amateurs such as former players and journalists whose methodology can only be described as narrative-descriptive.[4] A broad historical perspective permitting an exploration of the relationship between women's sport and social change is noticeably absent. Interpretation and analysis, if they exist at all, are usually limited to commonplace and uncritical observations about sport mirroring social attitudes to women and providing them with new opportunities for recreation and physical exercise. Such studies should not be denigrated, for when precious little has been known even of the facts of women's involvement in sport their revelation is certainly an important stage in the journey of discovery. However, if a truly meaningful and comprehensive picture is to be developed interpretative accounts are needed, which deal with such topics as power and control, motivation, the nature of participation, female sport's ambiguities and socially disruptive potential, its emancipating and restricting characteristics, and the interaction between feminism and female athleticism.[5]

Clearly, they should also consider the role played by sport in creating and reflecting tensions surrounding definitions of sex and gender roles;[6] for, as sociologists and anthropologists have demonstrated, sex differences constitute a significant basis for assigning status and functions in all societies, and sport is one of the institutions which most clearly reflects this. Sport is laden with rituals, symbols, and preconceptions that disseminate, affirm and reinforce a plethora of idealized social values, and hence it often acts as an effective mechanism of social control. In social systems dominated by men, such as that of Victorian England, a useful means of controlling women was a projection of the view that sport was essentially masculine, requiring physical and psychological attitudes and behaviour unnatural to women, and thus that it was beyond their proper sphere.[7]

I

In the face of powerful economic and social forces that were producing unprecedented change, stress and instability, traditional Victorians summoned all the power of custom, religion and science at their disposal in defence of existing social arrangements. They insisted that God and nature had imbued woman with qualities of mind and body that destined her for specific tasks, such as being man's helpmate, nurturing his children, and protecting the sanctity of his home. Their ideal woman was antithetical to sport.[8] Passive, gentle, emotional and delicate, she had neither the strength nor the inclination to undertake strenuous exercise and competitive games.

During the mid-nineteenth century, however, the same forces that produced the ideal also revealed its incompatability with reason and reality. They spawned a women's movement that raised questions about women's disabilities and constricted place in society and sought a partial redefinition of sex roles and the admission of women into spheres previously dominated by men.[9] One of these was sport. Unlike the fight for improved education, respectable employment, and legal and political rights, there was no organized campaign to promote women's sport, and its development was somewhat removed from the centers of controversy.[10] Nevertheless, as has been the case more recently, the entry of women into sporting activities was a significant part of the general movement for female emancipation and of its translation of demands for equity for women 'into demands for privileges and practices attendant to the male competitive model'.[11] While the circumstances of the Victorian period differed markedly from those at present, then as now the separation of the sexes in sport was based on the premise of women's inferiority. Then as now feminism acted as a catalyst that stimulated changes. Then as now, in counteracting the stereotype of female frailty, sportswomen reflected feminist hopes of diminishing the significance of sex differences, providing women with every opportunity to develop all their powers, and enabling them to gain control over their own lives and bodies.[12]

England had a long and distinguished sporting tradition, but women's place in it was peripheral and primarily passive. During the Middle Ages noble ladies hunted and hawked, sometimes in parties of their own and with considerable skill.[13] But over the centuries women of the middle and upper classes tended to become less physically active as their general status declined; and their education excluded exercise other than dancing instruction designed to produce graceful movement rather than health and strength.[14] Women's participation in sport, it must be noted, did not disappear completely. Some women of the landed classes continued to hunt and ride, and each century recorded unusual incidents involving sporting women of various ranks, such as horse and foot races, and football, boxing, golf and cricket matches. However, these activities were always considered exceptional and did nothing to compromise the view that sport was basically a man's business.[15]

During the late eighteenth century some of the proposals to improve female education offered by people like Erasmus Darwin, Catherine Macaulay Graham, Hannah More and Mary Wollstonecraft began to express a concern for women's health and to advocate therapeutic and preventive physical exercise.[16] These were followed, in the early nineteenth century, by a phethora of works advocating moderate and supervised programmes of exercise to improve female health and remedy what appeared to be an epidemic of postural defects. They usually conceded important physical differences between the sexes from the onset of puberty and were extremely cautious about the type of activity recommended, because of the need to preserve proprieties; and they were completely without a feminist perspective. But they were progressive at least insofar as they criticized the lack of exercise in girls' education and the standards of fashion and decorous behaviour that were making physical activity among women in polite society ever more difficult, and because they asserted that properly conceived exercises would in no way compromise femininity and gentility.[17]

By mid-century people like Herbert Spencer and Dr Elizabeth Blackwell, the first woman on the British Medical Register, had joined the fray. In 1859 Spencer attacked the misconceived ideal of womanhood that was responsible for the neglect of physical exercise in girls' schools, and asked why, if sporting behaviour among boys did not prevent their growing into gentlemen, play among girls should prevent their becoming ladies. Unfortunately, his interest in female physical exercise arose exclusively from his desire to ensure the production of healthy mothers who would protect England against racial degeneration, rather than from an advocacy of women's rights.[18] Dr Blackwell's views were more liberated, and in an early article written for the *English Woman's Journal* she made the perspicacious observation that 'bodies that can move in dignity, in grace, in airy lightness, or conscious strength, bodies erect and firm, energetic and active bodies that are truly sovereign in their presence, are expressions of a sovereign nature'.[19] In other words, the woman who controlled her body controlled her destiny.

Well into the century opinions about girls' need of exercise had little influence on educational practice. As the middle class grew in wealth and ambition, wives and daughters who emulated the admired ideal were increasingly regarded as a sign of respectability and success in business. Perceiving 'rude health' as unladylike and weakness as an indication of gentility and refinement, aspiring ladies eschewed vitality by cultivating a sedentary lifestyle and dressing in fashions that constricted their organs and inhibited movement.[20] Their education focused on polite accomplishments that were thought to improve marital chances rather than on sound intellectual and physical training which, it was feared, would do the opposite. The only exercise offered in the typical girls' school was taking a chaperoned walk, dancing, and gentle callisthenics, all of which were designed to produce a ladylike image rather than energy and strength.[21] Vigorous activities, including open-air games, were undreamed of.

II

Meanwhile, one of the most fascinating phenomena in Victorian social history was unfolding out of the demand by males of the rising middle class for recreational yet utilitarian physical activities to occupy the leisure time that was being produced by their growing affluence.[22] This was the development of a variety of institutionalized and well-defined team games for men and boys and the explosion in their popularity.

Its womb was the old boys' public schools and the new ones founded to accommodate the sons of ambitious professional and merchant families. Before the 1850s games-playing was an irregular feature of public-school life, but as schools multiplied in number and competitiveness the situation changed rapidly. By 1864 the Public Schools Commission could both admonish the increasing emphasis on games at the expense of book learning and applaud games as creators of health and manly virtues.[23] In *Athleticism in the Victorian and Edwardian Public School* J.A. Mangan reveals that the transition to games was not as rapid, smooth and complete as formerly thought, yet that by the end of the nineteenth century athleticism and its corollary, manliness, had become the hallmark of the acceptable public school.[24] The late Victorians came to regard manliness – the fusion of moral rectitude and physical robustness – as the most estimable masculine characteristic. They believed that games-playing best provided both an antidote to so-called 'brutal tendencies' and the moral training which produced the manly characteristics – endurance, self-reliance, discipline, courage, loyalty and rapid judgement – that were essential for success in the battle of life. On the other hand critics of the cult of athleticism realized that the physical and moral were not in fact identical. They appreciated only too well that games, and the plethora of rituals and symbols surrounding them, were insidious forms of social control whose ultimate ends were status and power. Games produced men imbued with an aggressive patriotism, men who were admirably suited for maintaining a static social and political system and for building an empire, but who were lacking in maturity, intellect, imagination and aesthetic sensibility.[25] Nevertheless, the emphasis on character to the disparagement of brains and the conviction that the nation owed its greatness to the manliness of its sons characterized the public schools to 1914.[26]

By passing through the proving ground of the public school games-playing became progressively more masculine. Manliness was a completely non-feminine concept that strengthened sport's male chauvinism by condemning effeminacy in men and female participation in so-called manly games. To the muscular Christian gentleman a woman's only role in sport was to watch and applaud. Yet the significance of games at the public schools to the education of women was considerable, for it was their curricula, organization and way of life that many reformers of female education sought to emulate, and at similar institutions for women of the same class that female sports made some of their first appearances.

Education was a particularly important arena for the working out of advances in the status of middle-class women as well as accommodating to prevailing stereotypes and social norms. Around the middle of the nineteenth century, partly as a result of a growing concern about the state of the nation's health in general and that of future mothers in particular and about the overall nature and quality of female education, somewhat more rational and varied exercise began to be allowed to growing girls. To the traditional crocodile walk and dancing lessons some schools added more energetic callisthenics, drill lessons supervised by NCOs from local regiments, or the musical gymnastic system of the American, Dio Lewis. But if their aim now included the improvement or maintenance of health, it still emphasized the production of graceful deportment rather than genuine physical fitness. Too many parents and teachers continued to believe 'that a girl was doing all that could be expected of her if she learned to keep her head up, her stomach in and her back straight'.[27] As late as 1868 the Schools Inquiry Commission complained that 'the important subject of bodily exercise for girls appears still to be imperfectly attended to' and that 'the want of systematic and well directed physical education is often the cause of failures in health and an impediment to study'.[28] Repeatedly noting the lack of playgrounds and provision for vigorous open-air exercise and games in girls' schools, it reported that an examination of 100 private girls' schools revealed 32 which provided nothing but a form of gentle callisthenics, while 60 offered only 'walking abroad, croquet and dancing'.[29]

Pioneer educational reformers like Frances Mary Buss and Dorothea Beale recognized the important conjunction between mental and physical development and sought to produce girls who were healthy as well as intelligent. However, they were well aware that the rigorous academic programmes they sought to introduce violated many tenets about the socialization of female adolescents, and thus would invoke strong criticism. If they were to succeed in the long run they would have to proceed cautiously in order to allay the fears of parents, who were extremely nervous about the deleterious effects which an academic education might have on their daughters, and would have found intolerable the added fear induced by the introduction of vigorous exercise. Hence, although they made sure their students got more exercise than was customary in the past, even the most advanced girls' schools continued to insist on impeccably ladylike behaviour. Within them the transition from gentle callisthenics and dancing to real physical education and competitive games was gradual and did not occur to any extent until the 1880s.[30]

III

Games entered girls' schools only with the first generation of college-educated women who had learned to appreciate them at Oxford and Cambridge. The founders of the women's university colleges believed that women had a right to develop their bodies as well as their minds, and they sought to keep students as fit as possible in order to prove that women could endure, without damage, the strain of solid learning.[31] This was of critical importance, for the most potent and durable argument against higher education for women was that maturing female minds and bodies were incapable of sustaining the hard labour required, and thus would be permanently damaged, to the detriment of future generations.

At issue was the very nature of woman and her physical and mental capacities. From time immemorial woman's biology had determined her destiny. This was especially true in the nineteenth century when the centrality of science increased steadily, and the authority of scientific arguments began to be applied to areas where change inflicted stress on existing social arrangements. There was no denying the important biological differences between males and females, but these were distorted and magnified by cultural norms used by scientists and medical doctors who invoked supposedly scientific justifications for traditional female functions and thus against the higher education of women.[32]

Such arguments were put particularly powerfully in the 1870s by two eminent physicians, Dr Edward Clarke of Harvard University and Dr Henry Maudsley of University College, London. Both insisted that the sexes' biological variations dictated significant differences in behaviour and roles. Females, they said, had only a limited amount of energy, the bulk of which during puberty was required for the development of the organs of reproduction. Normal puberty was equated with normal behaviour, and if women and girls behaved abnormally by acquiring a masculine type of education, their vital energy would be sapped and their health ruined. More specifically, the doctors predicted, they would lose their natural grace and gentility and be turned into coarse, imperfectly developed creatures who would produce degenerate offspring or none at all.[33]

Paradoxically, medical opinion was not at first particularly concerned about the potentially high energy demands of exercise, perhaps because there was still little exercise to worry about. In fact, it not only failed to invoke the constitutional overstrain theory, but actually supported limited amounts of exercise as a counterweight to the strain produced by serious study. Moderate and womanly exercise, it was argued, would benefit female health and thus improve the odds in favour of the production of healthy children. Only when women began to play vigorously and compete seriously were questions raised about the 'pelvic disturbances' that might result from falls and collisions, and warnings issued concerning the negative effects of strenuous games on hormones and reproduction.[34]

The Clarke–Maudsley thesis was widely held for years and, unchallenged, represented a potentially fatal blow to the ambitions of women in every direction except the domestic.[35] It could not help but influence educators who generally agreed with the doctors on the close connection between physical and mental development and on the need to protect students from overstrain. But whereas critics of higher education for women assumed that intellectual effort would deplete women's physical reserves, supporters began to suggest that differences in behaviour that were assumed to be natural were actually related far more closely to conformity to cultural norms than to absolute biological determinants.[36] As Jonathan Gathorne-Hardy points out, if one of the most potent arguments against girls receiving a decent education was that they were too weak, then, as well as proving they were not, new schools and colleges could take pains to make them stronger. This, he says, was at the root of most of the early games activities at girls' schools and colleges, and it dictated their form.[37]

It was certainly true of the Oxbridge women's colleges[38] and the public schools which fed into and were fed by them. At the former pioneer heads refused to compromise their principles and water down academic programmes. Instead they emphasized that increased physical fitness was an important corollary of intellectual success.[39] From the start students were encouraged to take exercise, and they responded enthusiastically.

Discretion was the watchword, however. The likes of Emily Davies, Anne Jemima Clough and Elizabeth Wordsworth knew only too well that the majority of university men viewed higher education as incompatible with the qualities of true womanhood and inseparable from dangerously revolutionary views on other subjects, and thus disapproved of the presence of even a few female students. Any inconvenience or offence caused by them was certain to provoke censure and jeopardize their chances of acceptance. Hence the authorities at the women's colleges insisted on discreet, inconspicuous and ladylike behaviour. Although students were adults every detail of their conduct was closely monitored for years, and exercise, while encouraged, was circumscribed.[40]

The story of the growth of sport at the women's university colleges is worthy of detailed study. For the time being, however, it is sufficient to note that, the dictates of conventional behaviour notwithstanding, facilities for sports were gradually provided, and on the initiative of both students and administrators the range of athletic activities became remarkably diverse. By 1914 the women's colleges at Oxford and Cambridge had an elaborate athletic structure. A complicated series of university, college, hall, and old students' clubs in a variety of sports selected teams, arranged practices and matches, obtained coaches, made rules, and awarded cups and colours; and there was a similarly complicated range of competition from the university level down through colleges, halls, years, and subjects of study. Enthusiasm for games and sports was not quite universal. Habits of play, being new to women, had to be learned, and the records indicate that it was sometimes difficult to persuade players to practise. However, the majority of students appear to have been involved either as participants or spectators in a range of athletic activities including tennis, golf, fives, racquets, croquet, fencing, swimming, boating, cycling, gymnastics, hockey, cricket and lacrosse. Athletes of distinction were major personages, and the attention of whole colleges appears to have been focused on the never-ending struggle with other colleges for athletic supremacy.

All things considered, the emergence of the female collegiate athlete created remarkably little controversy, probably because of the care taken not to violate behavioural rules, the generally inoffensive type of games played, the undoubted femininity of the players, and the fact that for years play was virtually invisible within the protected confines of college or private grounds, where it was completely separate from and no challenge to men's sport. Perhaps it was because sport was legitimated by its social value as a supposed builder of character, its apparent usefulness in curing the physical defects caused by study, and its value as a preventive measure when the female constitution proved equal to the strain of higher education. Perhaps it was because the dangers of athleticism were acknowledged and avoided, and because examination results revealed no incompatibility between games and academic success.[41] There was some controversy, of course, as was demonstrated by the ban by Lady Margaret Hall and Somerville on hockey and cricket in the mid-1880s and by the strict rules surrounding the riding of bicycles.[42] But on the whole the collegiate sportswoman appears to have been accepted as readily as the lady wrangler. And, it could be argued, her influence on spheres of education beyond the Cam and the Isis was in its own way almost as significant.

IV

Complementing the creation of university colleges for women was the foundation, during the second half of the nineteenth century, of a number of public schools for girls, which represented a sharp break with educational tradition in both goals and organization.[43] Their noble aim was to establish the intellectual capabilities of women by providing them with the same opportunities for academic development as were offered by the boys' public schools. Administrators felt that if girls were not to be relegated to a position of second best in perpetuity, girls' schools must resemble boys' in curricula and academic standards and in other respects as well, including the unlikely sphere of sports. Most educators remained committed to the view that men and women had different missions in life and to the preservation of Victorian values concerning family life and femininity, so the new schools, like the old, taught deportment and needlework and insisted on genteel behaviour.[44] But as far as possible curricula were modelled on those in boys' schools, the house system, with all its emphasis on conformity and scope for ideological indoctrination, was introduced, discipline and team spirit were lauded, and games were vigorously promoted.

The introduction of games was an extension of women's entry into the academic and physical context of the university world, for initially it was largely undertaken by Oxbridge-trained mistresses who had come to appreciate the value and pleasure of games while at college and who were eager to share them with their students.[45] Intellectual training was their first priority, but they also held the distinctly unconventional view that sporting activities incorporating both competition and play should be an intrinsic part of the educational life of girls as well as boys.[46] Their expectations of the benefits of participation in games were both high and varied. Games-playing, they insisted, would improve girls' health, relieve mental strain, stimulate study and aid discipline. Above all, it would impart valuable moral qualities, such as honour, loyalty, determination, resourcefulness and courage, that had previously been ascribed exclusively to males.[47]

An exception to this ethos was the Cheltenham Ladies' College, founded in 1853 to give the daughters of noblemen and gentlemen an education like that received by their brothers at the Cheltenham College for boys. Its principal from 1858 to 1906 was Dorothea Beale, one of the first and most famous reformers of female education. Through adaptation rather than imitation, Miss Beale aimed to furnish girls with a sound and balanced religious, intellectual and physical training in a manner that would magnify rather than threaten their womanhood.

Cheltenham's first prospectus listed callisthenic exercises, and under Miss Beale they remained an integral part of the curriculum.[48] In 1864 she reported to the Schools Inquiry Commission:

> The vigorous exercise which boys get from cricket, etc., must be supplied in the case of girls by walking and callisthenic exercises, skipping, etc. We have a room specially fitted up with swings, etc. It is to be wished that croquet could be abolished; it gives no proper exercise, induces colds, and places the body in a crooked posture. . . .[49]

About the same time she became concerned that students had insufficient opportunities for outdoor exercise, so despite parental protests she decided to terminate the school day at 12:55 p.m. Over the years Miss Beale endorsed the gradual improvement of exercise facilities. A larger callisthenic room was added in 1876. Callisthenics teachers were appointed, as, in 1890, was a woman trained in Swedish gymnastics who quickly replaced musical drill with the full Swedish system and persuaded Miss Beale to provide a gymnasium 'specially fitted with all the needful appliances'.[50] For years, however, Miss Beale refused to countenance games. She disliked competition for girls in any form, regarding it as incompatible with their unique emotional and intellectual needs and future family responsibilities, and games she particularly equated with masculinity and a loss of feminine gentleness and dignity of manner. It took all the persuasive powers of Louisa Lumsden, one of the Girton pioneers and classics mistress at Cheltenham, to get her even to allow a tennis court in the mid-1870s.[51]

The next concession did not come until 1890 when Miss Beale finally ordered the acquisition of a piece of ground for experimental use as a playing field, apparently convinced that the introduction of games in some form was inevitable. As students joyously took up rounders, cricket and hockey, and parents looked on with trepidation, she determined that games would develop in harmony with the general purposes of her school. Remaining true to her distrust of competition, she refused to allow matches against other schools for fear they would foster the emulation and over-strain she tried to avoid in the classroom.[52] She reported to the school council in 1893–94:

> The Physical Education is much advanced and many take lessons in the Swedish Gymnasium. . . . Our twenty-six tennis grounds and our new playground, give facilities for outdoor games which are much appreciated, but [she said] I am most anxious that our girls should not over-exert themselves, or become absorbed in athletic rivalries, and therefore we do not play against the other schools. I think it better for girls to learn to take an interest in botany, geology, etc., and to make country excursions.[53]

Miss Beale eventually came around to the view 'that the power of acting with others, or rapidly judging, is cultivated by the exercise of school games',[54] and keen competition was allowed between Cheltenham's various boarding houses. However, the principal frequently reasserted the prohibition against prizes and outside matches, so as to prevent games becoming the predominant interest and to protect against undue strain, fatigue and excitement. Only just before her death did she yield slightly and allow hockey matches against old Cheltonians and a local women's club.[55]

By the time Miss Beale died in 1906 Cheltenham had 26 tennis courts, two fives courts, a twelve-acre playground and a Swedish gymnasium, and its prospectus listed dancing, callisthenics, fencing, swimming, riding, and Swedish drill as providing exercise opportunities.[56] Games had not yet become as prominent as at other public schools. However, their gradual institution, despite Miss Beale's deeply rooted suspicions, indicates the inexorable growth of their influence and acceptance, and a pronounced change of attitude towards proper female behaviour during the late Victorian period.

Miss Beale's successor was Lilian M. Faithfull, an old Somervillian and all-round athlete, whose appointment was at least partly due to her presidency of the All-England Women's Hockey Association. Under Miss Faithfull, games were given much more encouragement. Trophies, colours and outside matches were introduced in hockey, tennis and cricket, and the roster of athletic activities was broadened to include badminton, netball and lacrosse. However, Miss Faithfull had the foresight to make certain that school and house teams did not occupy all the games mistresses' attention, when it was the ordinary girl who most needed encouragement and instruction.[57]

More typical of the girls' public school phenomenon were St Leonards School, St Andrews, and Roedean School, Brighton. St Leonards, which opened to a middle-class clientele in 1877, was the first school for girls to adopt many features of the boys' public school. Its original principal, Louisa Lumsden, late of Girton and Cheltenham, believed the harmonious development of the physical powers was essential to the development of character and intellect.[58] Hence games and physical training were made an integral part of the new school's educational system. At a time when a playground and gymnasium in a girls' school were as incongruous as sewing classes in boys' schools, both were provided despite initially cramped quarters. A drill mistress was appointed to the original staff, and students were allowed to play cricket, rounders, fives and goals, regardless of protests from townspeople against such 'masculine' activities.[59]

For the typically Victorian reason that her mother was ill and needed her at home, Miss Lumsden resigned in 1882 just before St Leonards removed to spacious new quarters. Her successor was Jane Frances Dove, another old Girtonian, who shared Miss Lumsden's views on the value of exercise – as the first prospectus issued under her aegis clearly indicated. 'St Leonards School', it said,

> is intended to provide for Girls from all parts of the United Kingdom an education which, while especially adapted to their requirements, is not less thorough than that given to their brothers at the great public schools . . . plenty of time for open-air exercise is given; and the use of the extensive playground is specially encouraged. . . . The playground is immediately attached and has well-drained gravel tennis courts, etc. There is good and safe bathing, and swimming forms one of

the chief recreations of the summer. A perfectly safe skating-pond is in the neighbourhood of the school.[60]

By 1887 the school had prefects and was divided into several houses, each with its own colours, societies and sports teams; and whereas for boys the house system meant restraint from too much liberty, for girls it meant escape from excessive gentility by providing unprecedented scope for activity.[61] In 1888, to encourage regular practice in games, the mistresses presented a handsome challenge shield for the thrice yearly house competitions in cricket, goals and gymnastics; and immediately the desire to gain the glory attached to the name of the shield winners 'added zest to play and great excitement among spectators'.[62] When gymnastics proved unsuitable for inter-house competition, the school magazine invited suggestions for an outdoor game to replace it. Athletic sports and golf were proposed, but it was finally decided 'to award the shield on a competition in lacrosse'.[63] Considering that lacrosse did not appear at university colleges until 1912, St Leonards' adoption of it in 1890 was very early indeed. In her autobiography Miss Lumsden recalled that she had watched a lacrosse match between teams of Montrealers and local Indians while visiting New Hampshire in 1884, and thinking the game graceful and beautiful, introduced it at the school.[64] But, since she was no longer principal, a more likely explanation is that she recommended lacrosse to a willing Miss Dove. During the next quarter of a century, lacrosse developed into a major sport at St Leonards and was introduced into schools and colleges all over the country by former mistresses and students.[65]

Meanwhile, the growth of opportunities for physical recreation proceeded apace. Three hours a day were set aside for exercise; the playground was enlarged to 16 acres; trained gymnastics and games mistresses were appointed; a fully equipped Swedish gymnasium and a nine-hole golf course were acquired. In 1896 hockey finally replaced goals in shield competition, and the house mistresses presented a challenge cup to be competed for three times a year in fives, golf and tennis. In the late 1890s outside matches, which had been infrequent because of the school's geographical isolation and head start in games rather than any philosophical inhibitions, began to be played against ladies' clubs and schools such as Wycombe Abbey and Roedean.[66] And in addition, students fenced, swam, skated, rode and took part in special bowling, batting and throwing competitions, gymnastic displays, and an annual athletic sports day.

Sports were a virtual passion at St Leonards by the turn of the century, as one of the school songs implies.[67] Every girl without a medical excuse was expected to play at least once a week, and match days were times of breathless anxiety. The *St Leonards School Gazette* devoted much more space to games than to any other subject. Players were urged to give their all for the sake of house and school, and spectators to turn out *en masse*, as if each match were a public contest that exposed moral fibre.[68] Games meant an unaccustomed degree of physical freedom, but:

> No mere physical enjoyment can explain the intensity of excitement in matches. The truth is that each . . . team is conscious of being put to a public test. Not only quickness and skill but staying power, combination, resource, the courage to play a losing game and the generosity to be a good winner, all those qualities once supposed to be untypical of girls, are there. . . .[69]

The school magazine's denunciations of the cheering of opponents' mistakes and of confusing rough with spirited play indicate that at times enthusiasm went to extremes.[70] Distinguished players were lionized; the names of captains of games were inscribed for posterity on a board in the gymnasium; special brooches were awarded to the considerable number who played in the first teams in the three major sports;[71] and as in boys' schools, the initiative in games being left to students, house captains wielded considerable power.

Misses Lumsden and Dove lost no opportunity to extol the virtues of games. On her frequent visits back to the school Miss Lumsden asserted that St Leonards' experience proved that girls could play so-called rough games without becoming at all unwomanly. Indeed, she claimed, they produced beauty, grace, mental lucidity, good health and steady nerves. More importantly, they were better than any other medium for imparting moral qualities, such as self-control, generosity, and courage, that were as essential to girls as to boys.[72] For her part Miss Dove went even further and insisted that ' . . . most of the qualities, if not all, that conduce to the supremacy of our country in so many quarters of the globe, are fostered if not solely developed by means of games'.[73]

Fortunately, headmistresses were sensitive to charges that St Leonards was a 'games' school, and they made certain the academic side of life was neither neglected nor interfered with. To assure that sport was not overdone, no student was allowed to play in more than four matches a week, and somewhat belatedly, in 1904, it was decided that 'No Shield Match shall be played on a day upon which a Certificate Examination is being held'.[74] The honours lists and results of the Oxford and Cambridge Higher Certificate examinations were regularly pointed to as proof of the vigour of St Leonards' academic work in general and among athletes in particular.

Games were even more important at Roedean School, which opened to middle-class girls in Brighton in 1885 under the joint principalship of the Misses Penelope, Dorothy and Millicent Lawrence.[75] The Lawrences believed there was a strong connection between a vigorous, healthy body and a mind similarly endowed, and they regretted that physical training was the branch of girls' education most generally neglected. Thus, they determined to make exercise a top priority.

The original prospectus stated:

> The aim of the school will be to give a thorough education, physical, intellectual, and moral. Special pains will be taken to guard against overwork, from two to three hours daily will be allotted to outdoor exercise and games. Opportunities will be given for Swimming, Riding, Dancing and Gymnastics.[76]

That aim was still revolutionary in the mid 1880s, but the Lawrences felt they were carrying on a crusade.[77] Despite the hostility of some Brightonians, who found the idea of school-girls playing 'boys' ' games offensive, they encouraged hockey and cricket from the first as part of a full programme of physical activity that eventually included riding, archery, tennis, fencing, swimming, water-polo, life-saving, running, walking, drill, Swedish gymnastics, golf, cycling, rounders, fives, hockey, cricket, lacrosse and netball.

Roedean, like a boys' public school, was organized on the house system. Games were arranged by a student committee which selected teams, scheduled matches and practices, assigned grounds, awarded colours and trophies, superintended the election of team captains from among those who had held colours the longest, and intimidated shirkers.[78] As at St Leonards, members of major teams were hero-worshipped, and great prestige was attached to playing for the school.

For several years lack of competition confined outside matches to the odd contest in tennis, drilling or gymnastics against a few other schools, or in hockey against Newnham, Penelope Lawrence's old college.[79] However, opportunities in hockey improved greatly when, in 1895, Roedean became the only school among the eight original members of the All-England Women's Hockey Association;[80] and, as the cult of athletics spread, inter-school games gradually became more frequent, culminating in a great rivalry with Wycombe Abbey. Meanwhile, there was no shortage of intra- and inter-house matches.[81] By 1897, when the school moved to a large new building, there were eight cricket and ten hockey teams out of a student population of about 100. All contests were reported on at great length in the school magazine, which liked to call players 'men'.[82] Unlike St Leonards, Roedean students did not relinquish the 'healthy pleasure in games acquired in school . . . on departure',[83] and over the years the Lawrences proudly congratulated old Roedeanians who played hockey for county clubs or for England.

In a detailed report to the Education Department in 1898 Penelope Lawrence explained the nature and philosophy of physical education at Roedean. A graduated programme existed, she said, adapted to the needs and abilities of each girl and designed to make her 'owner of herself' by giving equal development and balance to every muscle and organ. This programme included walking, riding, fencing, swimming, and drill and gymnastics which the whole school got for one hour a week. Training was tough, for, whereas a few years earlier not a single girl could show her head above the horizontal bar in a hanging position, in 1898 half the upper school could do so, as well as many in the lower division, while nearly all could go hand over hand up a 16-foot rope.

However, Miss Lawrence said, it was games that provided the staple form of exercise. Like Jane Frances Dove she went to extremes in evaluating the influence of games on the national character, claiming they 'make us able to evolve and preserve free institutions, and make us law abiding and moderate'.[84] Games, she asserted, combined healthy, pleasant exercise with training in physical skills. They improved *esprit* by promoting friendliness and mutual appreciation between teachers and students and by teaching self-respect to the athletic but dull student. Moreover, they taught fortitude, persistence, self-control, and judgement – precisely those elements that had hitherto been lacking in female education and which it was thus the school's responsibility to cultivate. With so many benefits accruing, it was imperative that every girl without a medical excuse participate; and since the very girls who most needed them were the ones who tended to avoid games, evasion was made difficult and somewhat unpleasant.

By games Miss Lawrence meant not tennis or rounders but the great team games of hockey and cricket. Hockey she regarded as an admirable substitute for boys' football, about the unsuitability of which for girls there was no question, while cricket supposedly admitted girls to a world far wider than their own. To those who claimed that cricket was quite beyond girls' powers she retorted that practice could produce quite a respectable standard of performance;

while to the argument that cricket and hockey were rough and dangerous her response was that nothing in life was completely risk-free, that risks were minimal if rules were obeyed and reasonable precautions taken to guard against fatigue and overstrain, and that they were more than outweighed by the obvious benefits.

Finally, to those who objected that games were filling too large a place in school life, she conceded a point. However, she said, this was not true of Roedean. Girls were always warned not to think of games as merely a means of acquiring strength, but rather as a key to health, happiness, mental acuity and moral virtues. In addition, the games mistress had duties apart from sport so that she was not separated from the intellectual life of the school. Roedean's experience demonstrated that earnestness in games and in study tended to go hand in hand. Girls who showed energy and vigour in sports usually applied the same qualities to their academic work, while those who played games but neglected books would probably have done so regardless. The annual examination results at Roedean revealed no incompatibility whatsoever between athletic and academic excellence, Miss Lawrence concluded.[85]

V

By 1914 certainly not all schools for middle-class girls had adopted the games-playing ethic. There remained considerable differences of opinion about the types and amount of exercise appropriate for pubescent girls and considerable variety in the degree of compulsion and time devoted to it. Nevertheless, a striking indication of the change in the attitudes of educators and the public to girls' sport is the fact that the prospectuses of most schools with pretensions to excellence boasted of playing fields and opportunities provided for games and physical education.[86] One to two hours of exercise a day had become common, as had a tradition of games-playing mistresses, many of whom, as in boys' schools, were 'old' students. Games leagues and associations had even been formed in many parts of the country by schools in the same district for competition in tennis, swimming, hockey, lacrosse, netball and rounders. On the whole students were games-mad. Entire student bodies turned out for major house and school matches, during which they participated in many of the same socializing rituals that had come to be associated with male athleticism. Militant school songs, inspired by the untrammelled freedom of the playing field, were sung with religious fervour. A plethora of trophies were objects of grail-like devotion, as were the colours awarded to outstanding athletes who themselves were virtually worshipped. Photographing teams for posterity was an annual rite, and sporting language conjuring up masculine images was considered smart.[87]

A few late Victorian educators, such as Dorothea Beale of Cheltenham and Sara Burstall of the Manchester High School for Girls, complained about the excessive zeal with which some girls pursued games.[88] However, athleticism never acquired anything like the same hold on girls' schools that it did on boys'. In both games provided a ritualistic agent of socialization that created cohesion and social control,[89] but in the last analysis the Victorian girls' and boys' public schools had different aims and ends. The function of the latter was to produce leaders of the country and empire who conformed to the middle- and upper-class image of the 'decent chap', and who would transmit the loyalty and patriotism they developed at school to the trading company, the regiment or the Foreign Office. What Mangan calls the crude Darwinism and pretentiousness of the boys' school came out most clearly on the playing field where the physical and moral qualities of manliness were supposedly best developed in struggles which emphasized that success in the endless battles of life went to the strong and the powerful, the brave and the true.[90]

The aims of the girls' public school were to provide girls with unprecedented opportunities for intellectual and physical development, to establish their intellectual equality with males, and to fit them more adequately for domestic or professional careers. Within them games were never worshipped in isolated splendour, but were always viewed as a part – albeit the most important part – of a systematic programme of physical training and medical inspection intended to make students fitter for academic toil.[91] The strengthening of character was certainly stressed, but the Darwinistic emphasis on conflict and power was not, nor were the unathletic and intellectual despised.

Manliness and womanliness remained very different concepts. The latter, unlike the former, did not conjure up images involving physical strength and authority, but rather those of mutual sharing, and intimacy and obedience in a domestic rather than public environment.[92] While reforming educators at girls' public schools were largely responsible for making sports a respectable activity for adolescent girls and for encouraging girls to be physically fit and to develop new ambitions and temperamental qualities, they remained committed to the preservation of many conventional Victorian values relating to family life and womanliness. Whether their students were writing the Cambridge Higher Local Examinations or playing an energetic game of hockey, they always insisted on femininity in mental outlook and physical manner.[93]

The Victorian path to social change was very uneven, and a genuine alteration in the attitudes of both sexes towards appropriate gender roles occurred very slowly indeed. Because momentous social, economic and political developments encouraged people of both sexes and various classes to aspire to greater independence and self-fulfilment, disoriented and anxious members of dominant groups thought they saw the symbolic and actual mechanisms that maintained the structure of society threatened at every turn.[94] In the face of social disruption and feminist challenges to male domination and to traditional definitions of woman's proper sphere, deviations from the norm were censured; and efforts were made to preserve sexual and familial relations unchanged by attacking not only the concept of women's emancipation but also the activities through which women expressed their quest for freedom, like studying men's subjects and playing their games.[95]

As women struggled to gain control over their own bodies through games and physical exercise, attempts were made to re-establish social control by raising high the spectre of women's inferior biology on the back of strident scientific and pseudo-scientific arguments.[96] Women, it had to be admitted, could compete with men in the classroom, but there was no way even the remote possibility of their competition on the sports ground could be countenanced.[97] So a new line of defence was drawn up. Whereas initially the scientific and medical professions had supported moderate exercise for women because of its potential to improve maternal health and combat the dangers of intellectual overwork, when females began to play games vigorously some of their arguments became distinctly negative. The old limited energy theory was revived and revised. Just as it had been maintained that women who attempted to compete with men academically and professionally would put their femininity and reproductivity at risk, so it began to be argued that muscular fatigue was no remedy for mental exhaustion and would have similar dreadful effects. Eugenic and social Darwinist claims were particularly potent, for they posited, apparently beyond any shadow of a doubt, that strenuous games, especially during puberty and menstrual periods, drained energy from vital organs, thus damaging women's bodies irreparably and threatening the survival of the race.[98]

Although games-playing inside and outside schools became increasingly widespread and in some cases actually valued for its physiological and social benefits, there remained a strong feeling of unease about serious sports competition for women, particularly in so-called rough games like hockey and cricket which in certain circumstances were viewed as 'unsexing'. Sport continued to be perceived as a basically masculine phenomenon in which female participation, apart from providing applause and respectability as spectators, was an anomaly. This continued as long as sport was regarded as the idealized socialization of masculine traits that were essential to national and military leadership; as long as the ideals of femininity regarded such traits as inessential to women's success in the Victorian social world; and as long as that world kept the doors to real political and economic power firmly closed to them.[99]

The academic and physical educations which girls received at public schools may have made their sex's potential better understood, but that potential remained only incompletely attainable.[100] On the one hand, they appeared to be a breakthrough into the staunchest of male domains and seemed to imply that women with educations similar to men's should be able to lead similar lives; and indeed, by the end of the nineteenth century there were an unprecedented number of independent and innovative young women in English society. On the other hand, however, such women were frequently in an ambiguous position. They might have been freed of many traditional trammels in their efforts to acquire knowledge, health and careers. Yet they were still restricted by social conventions relating to their sex and class, and by the striking contradictions that were implicit in reformed ideas about the socialization of women. Girls were encouraged to develop opposite sides of their personalities at the same time. They were allowed to pursue study that was serious and goal-directed; they were allowed to be ambitious and self-disciplined, and to aspire to careers before marriage; they were taught that excellence and achievement were appropriate for ladies; they were permitted good health and physical stamina, and to bicycle and play tennis and hockey. But simultaneously they were taught to be self-sacrificing, that their highest duty was to perform well as wives and mothers, and that they must accept the limits that society continued to impose on their sex. In other words, the characteristics prominent in the socialization of middle-class males that were developed in women by sound intellectual and physical training were to be used ideally in the private not the public sector.[101]

VI

The gradual acceptance of sport as compatible with socialization for femininity was the result of protracted negotiations and compromises that reconciled the apparent conflict between games and womanhood and between change and continuity.[102] Sport as an institutionalized form of activity required accommodation to predetermined roles and to expectations concerning appropriate behaviour.[103] Even many feminists who advocated a diminution of the inequalities between the sexes and a widening sphere for women accepted the idea of certain innate differences and of social norms that conditioned roles and conduct. The majority of the games pioneers at public schools were not active feminists and were willing to go even further in the direction of adaptation to the dominant value system. While they encouraged increased physical activity for girls, they perceived games-playing girls as acting in a boyish manner. Hence they themselves contributed to the continued identification of vigorous activity with masculinity. As an antidote to this they went out of their way to ensure that players projected an image of moderation and respectable femininity. They accepted the notion of limited sport, that is, that certain sports and ways of playing were off limits, such as those requiring physical contact, awkward positions, endurance and great strength. The introduction of new sports like hockey, netball and lacrosse, that did not carry the stigma of overt masculinity, helped as well as long as they took place under conditions that minimized threats to femininity. If these conditions – special rules, time limits, cumbersome dress – hindered skilful play, that was the price that had to be paid to preserve modesty and gain acceptance.[104] Propagandists for women's sport denounced the few sports-crazy girls, who eschewed conformity and went to extremes by exhibiting the roughness and off-hand manners of young men, as 'hoydens' who were untypical of the majority of sportswomen and who did the cause of women's sport irreparable damage.[105] 'The image of the new sportswoman thus accommodated to traditional, Victorian bourgeois mores without radically challenging them at the same time as it revitalized them in a way which allowed some adaptation to the broader social changes occurring at the time'.[106]

The story of women's sport and physical recreation during the later part of the nineteenth century comprises themes of continuity as well as change; contradictions and ambivalences, advances and compromises characterised the complicated processes of its history. The biologically determined stereotype co-existed along with the more vigorous model of the sporting woman. There continued to be common opposition to sport for women because of its believed negative effects on sexuality and childbirth, at the same time as it became an increasingly popular and acceptable pursuit. By their actions in sport women were affecting a change in public opinion about their physical image at the same time as they were having to accommodate to social pressures.[107]

This accommodation worked in the short run in that it gained for women's sports a degree of approval, and it was probably the only viable alternative at the time. However, it created problems in the long run. The acceptance of the basic masculinity of sport meant that for generations its female devotees adopted an apologetic tone when they justified even a modest invasion by women of 'man's' domain. Girls came to understand that they could play games but only if they took great care to demonstrate their basic femininity, and they learned that there would be no autonomous assessment of their real athletic worth as long as the standards of men were tl universal criteria of excellence. Thus, women in sport remained the 'other', the 'second sex', well into the twentieth century.[108]

Nevertheless, the evolution of women's sport was most important to general advancement of women. The majority of middle-class girls neither attended a public school nor participated in sports, and to them self-realization through proper mental and physical development was virtually meaningless. Furthermore, for years women's sport was confined to a small, elite group and largely to an educational setting which insulated it from public view. Yet the late Victorian public schools for girls were an ideal locale for promoting women's rights, and battles almost as important as those fought in examination and lecture halls were played out on sports grounds and in gymnasia. As has been demonstrated, 'the concession that physical exertion was suitable for Victorian young ladies coincided with the acknowledgement of their right to an education designed to make them more than superficially accomplished';[109] and a most important concession that was, for it made possible the inclusion of games and physical training in the curricula of the best girls' high schools and ensured an all-round education.

By 1914 female sport had effectively come out of the closet, and it could be said with some justice that 'few changes in Queen Victoria's reign are more complete than the position of the fair sex in modern sport'.[110] The range of women's sporting activities was in marked contrast to the severe constraints of the past. Whereas a little walking, croquet and gentle callisthenics were thought sufficient exercise for the young lady of the 1860s, her grand-daughter could run, bicycle, climb mountains, play tennis at Wimbledon, golf at St Andrews, hockey for England, and any number of team and individual games at college and school, and then she could read about so doing in features on 'The Sportswoman' or 'The Outdoor Girl' in respectable periodicals and newspapers. Despite prejudice, discrimination and restrictions, the lure of sport was obviously irresistible to some Victorian girls, who apparently found the rewards of participation sufficient to counteract whatever social costs were involved, and sufficient to offset the stress and role conflict they must have experienced as a result of the clash between their own desire to play and social norms to the contrary.[111]

The images and activities of women in sport remained circumscribed by outworn social values and sanctions that reinforced a negative attitude to women by perpetuating myths about male superiority and female weakness and inferiority.[112] But while sport could act as the ultimate idiom of conformity, it could also be a deviant activity, a channel for expressing hostility to social norms.[113] Whether they realized it or not, the Victorian educators who argued that exercise was a necessary prerequisite to successful schooling and the first generations of games players at public schools were involved in affirmative action on behalf of the sovereignty of the individual woman and the general worth of the female sex.

Sports participation, hedged in as it was by compromises with the social system, was symbolic both of progress in the direction of women's emancipation and of battles yet to be won. It mirrored the degree of middle-class women's acceptance outside the home and their release from the restraints of Victorian prudery, for there was a direct relationship between women's acceptance in sport and in other social situations. Sport gave women the opportunity to be physically active, to be mobile, to be vigorous and hardy, and to compete – in other words to try almost anything with a reasonable hope of succeeding. As the memoirs of public school girls repeatedly demonstrate, it provided a unique taste of freedom and whetted appetites for more.[114] Sport also heightened women's consciousness of their own bodies and provided a means of greater control over them through dress reform and increased physical activity. Modern studies show that sportswomen generally have positive feelings about their bodies and that such feelings are directly related to self-confidence and self-esteem.[115] Obviously there were no studies measuring the psychological effects of sport on Victorian women, but it is logical to surmise that if there had been they would have revealed similar positive results.

Finally, while women's sport had to compromise with the traditional concept of femininity in order to gain acceptance, it contributed to a revised definition of woman's nature, rights and abilities. The public schools in general succeeded in refuting the accusation that sound intellectual and physical education would produce creatures uninterested in and incapable of motherhood and domesticity. Their student-athletes in particular presented women in non-traditional roles and contributed important modifications to the feminine ideal by replacing an image of lassitude and inaction with one of energy and action.[116]

As Victorian women became more active in the public sphere and as the women's movement gained credibility and recruits, women's sport became increasingly strenuous and competitive and at the same time more plausible. The emergence of the female athlete, inside the girls' public schools and outside, was part of the same broad movement of social reform that saw middle-class women become university students, medical doctors and municipal voters; and in its own way it was just as significant to the ultimate goals of feminism.

The late nineteenth-century drive for greater equality initiated an on-going process of social change that slowly led to more freedom for women, and greater status and self-respect. Although sport was not a major site of feminist intervention, the women's movement gave a powerful stimulus to female participation in sporting activities at least partially free of traditional restraints, and conversely the physical rebellion that sport represented was part of the process that enabled Victorian women to contradict received definitions of their sex's true character. The nature of the debate on women's sport was of universal significance, since it involved many of the crucial factors influencing the course women might take in adapting to changing economic and social conditions. Neither the extent of women's sport nor that of their sporting accomplishments should be exaggerated, however.

Sport by 1914 remained overwhelmingly a symbol of masculinity and male power, and its female participants were only a small, elite sector of the total female population. Well into the twentieth century the inequality of women in society continued to be reinforced by sporting theories and practices that implied restriction and control. The tyranny of medical ignorance and social sentiment caused the belief to persist that competitive sports developed behaviour patterns contrary to the female nature and to the health of women and their unborn children. It took years for sportswomen to prove by their actions that no harm would befall either. Similarly, the ultimate test of women's sport long remained womanliness; the more attention female athletes paid to the requisites of ideal womanhood the more social acceptance they found.

Fundamental increases in the opportunities for women in sport had to wait for the second wave of feminism that began in the 1960s. With it finally came serious physiological research that dispelled the myths that for so long restricted women's physical attitudes and prejudiced their own and society's perceptions of their physical potential. With it too came recognition that women's limitations in sport have had less to do with genetics than with social and cultural codes that kept women alienated from their own bodies and protected the privileges and superiority of men.

NOTES

The author is pleased to acknowledge research grants from the Social Sciences and Humanities Research Council of Canada which greatly facilitated work on this project.

1. Among the works that link sport and women's history are Paul Atkinson, 'Fitness, Feminism and Schooling', in Sara Delamont and Lorna Duffin (eds.), *The Nineteenth Century Woman: Her Cultural and Physical World* (London, 1978), pp. 92–133; Sheila Fletcher, *Women First: The Female Tradition in English Physical Education 1880–1980* (London, 1984); Jennifer A. Hargreaves, 'Playing Like Gentlemen While Behaving Like Ladies: The Social Significance of Physical Activity for Females in Late Nineteenth and Early Twentieth Century Britain' (unpublished MA thesis, University of London Institute of Education, 1979; also see below, pp. 130–44); June A. Kennard, 'Women, Sport and Society in Victorian England' (unpublished Ed.D dissertation, University of North Carolina at Greensboro, 1974). See also Shirley H.M. Reekie, 'The History of Sport and Recreation for Women in Britain, 1700–1850' (unpublished PhD dissertation, Ohio State University, 1982).
2. Deborah Gorham, whose *The Victorian Girl and the Feminine Ideal* (Bloomington, IN, 1982) gives some attention to the subject of physical activity, is an encouraging exception.
3. W.J. Baker, 'The State of British Sport History', *Journal of Sport History*, X (1983), 64.
4. For example Nancy Joy, *Maiden Over: A Short History of Women's Cricket* (London, 1950); Ida M. Webb, 'Women's Hockey in England', in R. Renson *et al* (eds.), *History, the Evolution and Diffusion of Sports and Games in Different Cultures* (Brussels, 1976), pp. 490–6. The same criticism can be levelled at the treatment of women's sports in general histories of sports such as golf and lawn tennis and in standard histories of girls' schools.
5. Melvin L. Adelman, 'Academicians and American Athletics: A Decade of Progress', *J. Sports History*, X (1983), 96–7; Baker, op. cit., p. 64; Don Morrow, 'Canadian Sports History: A Critical Essay', *J. Sport History*, X (1983), 71–3.
6. Kennard, op. cit., p. 167; Carroll Smith-Rosenberg and Charles Rosenberg, 'The Female Animal: Medical and Biological Views of Woman and her Role in Nineteenth-Century America', *Journal of American History*, IX (1973), 354; see above, pp. 13–37.
7. Harry Edwards, *Sociology of Sport* (Homewood, IL, 1973), pp. 55–6, 81–2; Jan Felshin, 'The Triple Option . . . For Women in Sport', in M. Marie Hart (ed.), *Sport in the Socio-Cultural Process* (Dubuque, IA, 1972), p. 431; R.S. Gruneau and J.G. Albinson (eds.), *Canadian Sport: Sociological Perspectives* (Don Mills, ON, 1976), pp. 33–5; J.W.T. Hughes, 'Socialization of the Body within British Educational Institutions – An Historical View' (unpublished M.Sc thesis, University of London Institute of Education, 1975), pp. 10–12, 64–78; J.A. Mangan, *Athleticism in the Victorian and Edwardian Public School* (Cambridge, 1981), pp. 142, 206; Gladys I. Stone, 'On Women and Sport', in March L. Krotee (ed.), *The Dimensions of Sport Sociology* (West Point, NY, 1979), p. 41; Eldon Snyder, Joseph E. Kivlin and Elmer E. Spreitzer,

'The Female Athlete: An Analysis of Objective and Subjective Role Conflict', in Andrew Yiannakis *et al.* (eds.), *Sport Sociology: Contemporary Themes* (Dubuque, IA, 1979), pp. 204–10.

8. Ellen W. Gerber *et al.*, *The American Woman in Sport* (Reading, MA, 1974), p. 12.

9. Smith-Rosenberg and Rosenberg, op. cit., 333. This chapter concentrates on middle-class women. Sport reflected social class, and as was the case with so many aspects of the advancement of women during the nineteenth century, it was the physical needs and aspirations of middle-class women that were asserted first. Games and sports for working-class women were virtually non-existent, since the requisite leisure, schooling, and money were lacking. Their gradual development would make an interesting subject for further study.

10. J.A. Banks and Olive Banks, *Feminism and Family Planning* (Liverpool, 1964), pp. ix–x.

11. Felshin, op. cit., pp. 434–5.

12. Ibid., p. 433; Stone, 'On Women and Sport', pp. 45–6.

13. P. Blaine, *Encyclopaedia of Rural Sports* (London, 1840), p. 103; Joseph Strutt, *The Sports and Pastimes of the People of England* (London, 1833), pp. lxv–lxvi, 11–14; Norman Wymer, *Sport in England: A History of Two Thousand Years of Games and Pastimes* (London, 1949), pp. 70–9.

14. Roberta J. Park, 'Concern for the Physical Education of the Female Sex from 1675 to 1800 in France, England and Spain', *Research Quarterly*, XLII (1974), 104–19.

15. Robert Browning, *A History of Golf: The Royal and Ancient Game* (London, 1955), p. 120; Henry Cotton, *The Picture Story of the Golf Game* (London, 1965), p. 103; Pierce E. Egan, *Anecdotes: Original and Selected of the Turf, the Chase, the Ring, and the Stage* (London, 1827), p. 216; Pierce E. Egan, *Book of Sports, and Mirror of Life* (London, 1832), pp. 129–31, 346–9; Joy, op. cit., pp. 9–21; Roger Longrigg, *The English Squire and his Sport* (London, 1977), pp. 113–14; Lily C. Stone, *English Sports and Recreations* (Washington, 1960), p. 7; Enid Wilson, *A Gallery of Women Golfers* (London, 1961), p.11.

16. John Armitage, *Man at Play: Nine Centuries of Pleasure Making* (London, 1977), p. 108; Erasmus Darwin, *A Plan for the Conduct of Female Education in Boarding Schools* (London, 1797), pp. 9–12, 68–70; Dorothy Gardiner, *English Girlhood at School: A Study of Women's Education through Twelve Centuries* (Oxford, 1929), p. 353; Catherine Macaulay Graham, *Letters on Education with Observations on Religious and Metaphysical Subjects* (London, 1790), pp. 203–09; Phyllis Stock, *Better Than Rubies: A History of Women's Education* (New York, 1978), p. 115; Mary Wollstonecraft, *Vindication of the Rights of Women* (ed. Miriam Kramnick, Harmondsworth, 1975). pp. 81–3, 112–13, 123–30, 182–3, 286–7, 291–9.

17. Blaine, op. cit., pp. 152–3; Franz Bernard, *The Physical Education of Young Ladies* (London, 1860); Lant Carpenter, *Principles of Education, Intellectual, Moral and Physical* (London, 1820); Sarah Stickney Ellis, *The Daughters of England* (London, 1845); Sarah Stickney Ellis, *The Mothers of England* (London, 1843); Sarah Stickney Ellis, *The Women of England* (London, 1839); Frances E. Slaughter (ed.), *The Sportswoman's Library* (Westminster, 1898), I, pp. 4–6; Priscilla Wakefield, *Reflections on the Present Condition of the Female Sex; With Suggestions for its Improvement* (2nd edn., London, 1817); Donald Walker, *Exercises for Ladies; Calculated to Preserve and Improve Beauty, and to Prevent and Correct Personal Defects, Inseparable from Constrained or Careless Habits* (2nd edn., London, 1837).

18. Herbert Spencer, *Essays on Education* (London, 1910), pp. 136–7, 150–1; Herbert Spencer, *The Principles of Biology* (Oxford, 1898), II, pp. 512–13.

19. Elizabeth Blackwell, 'Extracts from the Laws of Life, with Special Reference to the Physical Education of Girls', *English Woman's Journal*, I (1858), 189–90.

20. Hargreaves, op. cit., p. 111; Christabel Osborn, 'Newnham – and After', *Windsor Magazine*, IV (1896), 303.

21. Ellen W. Gerber, 'The Changing Female Image: A Brief Commentary on Sport Competition for Women', *Journal of Health, Physical Education and Recreation*, XLII (1971), 59.

22. Peter Bailey, 'A Mingled Mass of Perfectly Legitimate Pleasures: The Victorian Middle Class and the Problem of Leisure', *Victorian Studies*, XXI (1977), 25; Mangan, *Athleticism*, pp. 99–100; Charles Tennyson, 'They Taught the World to Play', *Vic. Stud.* II (1959), 211–22.
23. Great Britain, Royal Commission on the Public Schools, *Report 1864*, I, 40.
24. Mangan, *Athleticism*, p. 22.
25. J.G. Dixon *et al.*, *Landmarks in the History of Physical Education* (Newton Abbott, 1974), p. 45. Clement Dukes, 'Games and Athletics in Public and Private Boarding Schools', *Physique* (1891), 41–2; Jonathan Gathorne-Hardy, *The Public School Phenomenon, 1597–1977* (London, 1977), pp. 168–70; Bruce Haley, *The Healthy Body and Victorian Culture* (Cambridge, 1978); Bruce Haley, 'Sports in the Victorian World', *Western Humanities Review*, XXII (1968), 115–25; Edward Mack, *Public Schools and British Opinion Since 1860* (London, 1941), pp. 41–2, 123–30; Mangan, *Athleticism*, p. 132; M. Marples, *A History of Football* (London, 1954), pp. 123–31; David Newsome, *Godliness and Good Learning* (London, 1961), pp. 195–235; Vivian Ogilvie, *The English Public School* (London, 1957), pp. 188–9; W. David Smith, *Stretching Their Bodies: The History of Physical Education* (Newton Abbott, 1974), p. 45.
26. P.H. Ditchfield, *Old English Sports, Pastimes and Customs* (London, 1891), p. 24; George A. Hutchinson, *Outdoor Games and Recreations* (London, 1892), pp. v–vi.
27. Barry Turner, *Equality for Some: The Story of Girls' Education* (London, 1974), p. 134.
28. Great Britain, Royal Commission on School Education, *Report 1868*, I, 522; VI, 388–90.
29. Royal Commission on Education, *Report 1868*, VII, 556–7.
30. Association of Headmistresses, *Minutes* (9–10 March 1877); Sara A. Burstall, *Frances Mary Buss* (London, 1938), p. 51; Gathorne-Hardy, op. cit., p. 267; Girls' Public Day School Trust, *Norwich High School, 1875–1950* (Norwich, c. 1950), p. 39; Gorham, op. cit., p. 96.
31. Emily Davies, *Thoughts on Some Questions Relating to Women, 1860–1908* (Cambridge, 1910), pp. 68–9; Eleanor M. Sidgwick, *University Education of Women* (Cambridge, 1897), p. 8.
32. Pauline Marks, 'Femininity in the Classroom: An Account of Changing Attitudes', in Juliet Mitchell and Ann Oakley (eds.), *The Rights and Wrongs of Women* (Harmondsworth, 1976), p. 177; Smith-Rosenberg and Rosenberg, op. cit., pp. 332–3.
33. Edward H. Clarke, *Sex in Education: or a Fair Chance for Girls* (Boston, MA, 1873); Henry Maudsley, 'Sex in Mind and in Education', *Fortnightly Review*, XV n.s. (1874), 466–83. See also Atkinson, op. cit., pp. 100–04; Joan Burstyn, *Victorian Education and the Ideal of Womanhood* (London, 1980), pp. 84–98; Gorham, op. cit., pp. 86–90; Elaine and English Showalter, 'Victorian Women and Menstruation', in Martha Vicinus (ed.), *Suffer and Be Still: Women in the Victorian Age* (Bloomington, IN, 1973), pp. 41–3; Smith-Rosenberg and Rosenberg, op. cit., pp. 334–40.
34. Gerber *et al.*, *American Woman*, p. 16; Hargreaves, op. cit., pp. 40, 90; Arabella Kenealy, *Feminism and Sex Extinction* (London, 1920); Arabella Kenealy, 'Woman as Athlete', *Nineteenth Century*, XLV (1896), 636–45; Smith-Rosenberg and Rosenberg, op. cit., p. 342.
35. Elizabeth Garrett Anderson, 'Sex in Mind and Education: A Reply', *Fortnightly Rev.*, XV (1874), 582–94; Atkinson, op. cit., pp. 104–07; Eliza B. Duffey, *No Sex in Education* (Philadelphia, PA, 1874), p. 117; Edward W. Ellsworth, *Liberators of the Female Mind: The Shirreff Sisters, Educational Reform, and the Women's Movement* (Westport, CN, 1979), p. 55; Elizabeth Garrett, 'Physical Training of Girls', *Victoria Magazine*, XI (1868), 151–2.
36. Edwards, op. cit., p. 231; Hugh L. Ross, *Perspectives on the Social Order* (New York, 1963), p. 267; Stone, 'On Women and Sport', p. 44.
37. Gathorne-Hardy, op. cit., pp. 271–2.
38. The women's colleges at Cambridge University were Girton (1869) and Newnham (1871). Those at Oxford were Lady Margaret Hall (1879), Somerville (1879), St Hugh's (1886), St Hilda's (1893), and the Society of Oxford Home Students (1891).

39. Atkinson, op. cit., p. 92. Mrs Henry Sidgwick, just before assuming the Newnham College principalship, was responsible for a particularly interesting effort by college educators to demonstrate that higher education had no discernible physical disadvantages. In 1890, incensed by an article in the *Pall Mall Gazette* which repeated the familiar argument that women were being educated at the expense of the reserve strength needed for motherhood, she assembled a committee, representing Girton, Newnham and Somerville Colleges and Lady Margaret Hall, to collect health statistics on women students. A survey was conducted, and in the resulting publication the health of students was compared with that of relatives of similar age who had not been to college. Taken into consideration were hours of sleep, work, and exercise, and the health of parents and children. The conclusion reached was that, although there was some evidence students enjoyed a higher standard of health throughout their lives and that they produced healthier children, on the whole college education did not significantly affect health one way or the other. Mrs Sidgwick personally took the survey a step further by photographing former students' babies to prove that higher education was not damaging to the future of the race. (See Catherine Baldwin, 'Note on the Health of Women Students', *Century Magazine*, XLII (1890), 294–5; Eleanor M. Sidgwick, *Health Statistics of Women Students of Cambridge and Oxford and of their Sisters* (Cambridge, 1890); Ethel Sidgwick, *Mrs Henry Sidgwick* (London, 1938), p. 144.)

40. Ruth F. Butler and M.H. Prichard (eds.), *The Society of Oxford Home Students: Retrospects and Recollections 1879–1921* (Oxford, c. 1930), pp. 105, 114; Muriel S. Byrne and Catherine H. Mansfield, *Somerville College 1879–1921* (Oxford, 1922), p. 58; B.A. Clough, *A Memoir of Anne Jemima Clough* (London, 1897), p. 195; Vera Farnell, *A Somervillian Looks Back* (Oxford, 1948), p. 44; Gorham, op. cit., p. 165; *Newnham Roll* (October 1875); 'House Rules', *Newnham College Reports* (February 1887), 6; Ann Phillips (ed.), *A Newnham Anthology* (Cambridge, 1979), pp. 37–8; Somerville Students' Association, *Report* (October 1914), 57.

41. Gemma Bailey (ed.), *Lady Margaret Hall: A Short History* (Oxford, 1923), p. 48; Sara A. Burstall, *English High Schools for Girls: Their Aims, Organisation, and Management* (London, 1907), p. 99; Lady Margaret Hall, *Report of the Lady Principal* (May Term 1885); *Thersites* (6 December 1912); Elizabeth Wordsworth, *First Principles in Women's Education* (Oxford, 1894), p. 12.

42. Bailey, *Lady Margaret Hall*, p. 47; Sara A. Burstall, *Retrospect and Prospect: Sixty Years of Women's Education* (London, 1933), p. 131; Byrne and Mansfield, op. cit., p. 94; Lilian M. Faithfull, *In the House of My Pilgrimage* (London, 1924), p. 62; *Girton Review* (July 1887), 9; LMH, *Log Book* (22 October 1885), 22; LMH, *Council Minutes* (October 22, 1885); Newnham College Club, *Cambridge Letter* (1894), 11–12; Newnham College, *North Hall Diary* (May Term 1896); Sidgwick, op. cit., p. 168; Somerville Students' Association, *Report* (November 1897), 10; Barbara Stephen, *Girton College 1869–1932* (Cambridge, 1933), p. 155; *Thersites* (11 February 1910).

43. The main ones among them were the North London Collegiate School (1850), Cheltenham Ladies' College (1853), the schools of the Girls' Public Day School Company (1872), St Leonards School (1877), Roedean School (1885), and Wycombe Abbey School (1896). All of these will be examined in detail in a longer study, while in this article Cheltenham, St Leonards, and Roedean are used as case studies.

44. Gorham, op. cit., p. 26; Marks, op. cit., p. 186.

45. Burstall, *English High Schools*, p. 91; Sara Burstall and M.A. Douglas (eds.), *Public Schools for Girls* (London, 1911), pp. 211–13; Hargreaves, op. cit., pp. 135–7; *St Leonards School Gazette* (October 1898), 327. Games and gymnastics were also introduced by games mistresses trained at one of the new specialist colleges designed to produce female physical educators. The first was established in Hampstead in 1885 by Martina Bergman-Österberg, a Swedish woman who founded the physical education profession in England. As experts trained in the Swedish system of gymnastics filtered into schools a transformation occurred. Drill and callisthenics gave way to scientific physical training. (See *Chelsea College of Physical Education, 1898–1958*; Colin Crunden, *A History of Anstey College of Physical Education, 1897–1972* (Sutton

Coldfield, 1974); Fletcher, op. cit.; P.C. McIntosh, *Physical Education in England Since 1800* (London, 1952); Jonathan May, *Madame Bergman-Österberg* (London, 1969); *Nine Pioneers in Physical Education* (London, 1964); Ida M. Webb, 'Women's Physical Education in Great Britain, 1800–1966, with reference to teacher training' (unpublished M.Ed thesis, University of Leicester, 1967).)

46. J.T. Talamini and C.H. Page, *Sport and Society – An Anthology* (Boston, MA, 1973), p. 272.

47. Jane Frances Dove, 'Reminiscences Dictated to Lady Stephen' (March 20, 1925); Gathorne-Hardy, op. cit., pp. 270–2; *Girls' Schools Year Book* (1906), p. 389; Haley, 'Sports', p. 124; Hargreaves, op. cit., pp. 135–7; Alfred Schofield, *The Physical Education of Girls* (London, 1889).

48. Elizabeth Raikes, *Dorothea Beale of Cheltenham* (London, 1908), Appendix D.

49. Royal Commission on Education, *Report 1868*, V, 740.

50. *Cheltenham Ladies' College Magazine* (Spring 1893), 123, (Spring 1895), 182; F. Cecily Steadman, *In the Days of Miss Beale: A Study of Her Work and Influence* (London, 1931), p. 11.

51. Louisa Lumsden, 'A Great Headmistress', *Cheltenham Ladies' Coll. Mag.* (Centenary number 1931), 71; Steadman, op. cit., p. 84.

52. Cheltenham Ladies' College, *Report of the Lady Principal* (July 1890); Josephine Kamm, *How Different From Us: A Biography of Miss Buss and Miss Beale* (London, 1958), p. 222; Steadman, op. cit., p. 84.

53. 'Report of the Lady Principal for 1893–94', *Cheltenham Ladies' Coll. Mag.* (Spring 1895), 182. The story is told that when Miss Beale first watched a hockey match she was distinctly unimpressed, and exclaimed, 'The children will hurt themselves if they all run after one ball. Get some more balls at once!' (Kamm, op. cit., pp. 21–2.) Paradoxically, Miss Beale, at the age of 67, learned to ride a tricycle, and despite failing hearing and sight she replaced her regular morning walk with a ride.

54. Dorothea Beale, 'Does Modern Education Ennoble?' (1905), quoted in A.K. Clarke, *A History of the Cheltenham Ladies' College 1853–1979* (3rd edn. Great Glenham, Suffolk, 1979), p. 82.

55. Cheltenham Ladies' College, *Report of the Lady Principal* (1903–04); *Cheltenham Ladies' Coll. Mag.* (Spring 1906), 94.

56. Cheltenham Ladies' College, *Prospectus* (1905); L.T. Meade, 'Girls' Schools of Today: Cheltenham College', *Strand Magazine* IX (1895), 287.

57. Cheltenham Ladies' College, *Report of the Principal* (1907–08); *Cheltenham Ladies' Coll. Mag.* (Autumn 1908), 272–3. Deborah Gorham notes that Lilian Faithfull, although one of the first students at Somerville College, a distinguished athlete and athletic administrator, and a notable educator, believed that women were inferior to men and so never really challenged prevailing ideas about the secondary role of women in middle-class social, economic, and family life. Girls, she felt, had less creative capacity than boys, less desire for independence, and less real intellectual ability. (Gorham, op. cit., pp. 164–5, 179, 183).

58. Barbara Stephen, *Emily Davies and Girton College* (London, 1927), pp. 291–2.

59. J.S.A. Macaulay (ed.), *St Leonards School 1877–1977* (Glasgow, 1977), pp. 3, 8; *St Leonards School Gazette* (June 1891), 26, (November 1902), 569.

60. St Leonards School, *School List* (August 1883), 3–4.

61. Atkinson, op. cit., p. 115; Julia M. Grant, Katharine McCutcheon and Ethel F. Sanders (eds.), *St Leonards School, 1877–1927* (Oxford, 1927), p. 60.

62. *St Leonards School Gaz.* (June 1888), 47.

63. St Leonards School, 'Rules and Records of the Challenge Shield Competition', (January 1888–July 1900). See also Jane Claydon, 'Lacrosse at St Leonards School', *Lacrosse*, XXXIV (1980), 9; *St Leonards School Gaz.* (June 1889), 81.

64. Lumsden, op. cit., p. 81.

65. In 1896 Miss Dove left St Leonards to establish a new school, Wycombe Abbey, in Buckinghamshire, which was patterned upon St Leonards. There she introduced lacrosse and put a strong emphasis on games in general. Lacrosse was introduced to

Roedean by a former St Leonards student who was invited to teach it in 1902.
66. *St Leonards School Gaz.* (March 1896), 200, (June 1896), 208, (October 1896), 225, (February 1897), 246.
67. Celia Haddon, *Great Days and Jolly Days: The Story of Girls' School Songs* (London, 1977), p. 54; *St Leonards School Gaz.* (Reprints 1901), 16–17.
68. *St Leonards School Gaz.* (November 1899), 385–90, (June 1900), 436.
69. Grant, McCutcheon, and Sanders, op. cit., p. 63.
70. *St Leonards School Gaz.* (November 1899), 385–90, (March 1903), 599; Webb, 'Women's Hockey in England', p. 493.
71. *St Leonards School Gaz.* (February 1899), 350.
72. *St Leonards School Gaz.* (June 1891), 27, (October 1891), 45, (November 1907), 854–55.
73. Dorothea Beale, Lucy H.M. Soulsby and Jane Frances Dove (eds.), *Work and Play in Girls' Schools* (London, 1901), p. 397. Miss Dove believed so completely in the value of exercise that she had each girl weighed on her return to school, and if she were found to be below what was considered the average weight, she was required to study less and play games more.
74. *St Leonards School Gaz.* (November 1904), 673.
75. The school was originally called Wimbledon House School. The name Roedean was adopted in 1897 with the move to a new site.
76. Dorothy E. de Zouche, *Roedean School, 1885–1955* (Brighton, 1955), p. 27.
77. Penelope Lawrence, 'Games and Athletics in Secondary Schools for Girls'. Great Britain, Parliamentary Papers, Reports from Commissioners, Inspectors and Others. *Education Department, Special Reports on Educational Subjects* (1898), II, 145.
78. Ibid., pp. 151–2.
79. *Wimbledon House School News* (Summer Term 1891), 3–4, (Christmas Term 1891), 3–4, (Easter Term 1892), 2–3, (Lent Term 1894), 2–4.
80. *Wimb. House School News* (Lent Term 1896), 3–4; *Roedean School Magazine* (Lent Term 1898), 4–5.
81. *Wimb. House School News* (Easter Term 1893), 2.
82. Ibid. (Michaelmas Term 1891), 3–11.
83. Grant, McCutcheon, and Sanders, op. cit., p. 97; 'St Leonards School', *Ladies Field* (9 September 1911), 57; *Wimb. House School News* (Lent Term 1896), 3–4.
84. Lawrence, op. cit., p. 149.
85. Ibid., pp. 145–58. See also de Zouche, op. cit., p. 36; McIntosh, op. cit., pp. 132–3; *Wimb. House School News* (Christmas Term 1893), 6–8.
86. *Girls' School Year Books* (1906–1914); Turner, *Equality*, p. 149.
87. Gathorne-Hardy, op. cit., p. 272; Norrita Glenday and Mary Price, *Reluctant Revolutionaries: A Century of Head Mistresses 1874–1974* (London, 1974), p. 74; Haddon, op. cit., p. 51.
88. Dorothea Beale, 'Letter to the Editor', *Fortnightly Rev.*, LXVIII (1900), 1071; Burstall, *English High Schools*, pp. 98–101; *Girls' Schools Years Book* (1906), p. 389.
89. Mangan, *Athleticism*, p. 206.
90. Ibid., pp. 136–206; J.A. Mangan, 'Imitating their Betters and Disassociating from their Inferiors: Grammar Schools and the Games Ethic in the Late Nineteenth and Early Twentieth Centuries', paper presented at annual conference of History of Education Society, Loughborough University, December 1982, p. 36; J.A. Mangan, 'Physical Education as a Ritual Process', in J.A. Mangan (ed.), *Physical Education and Sport: Sociological and Cultural Perspectives* (Oxford, 1973), p. 94; J.A. Mangan, 'Social Darwinism, Sport and English Upper Class Education', paper presented at Conference on the Social History of Nineteenth Century Sport, Liverpool University, March 1982, pp. 10–15.
91. Atkinson, op. cit., p. 93; Cheltenham Ladies' College, *Report of the Principal* (1909–10); Hargreaves, op. cit., pp. 136–7; Lawrence, op. cit., p. 156; McIntosh, op. cit., pp. 132–3; Smith, op. cit., p. 27.
92. Gorham, op. cit., p. 115; Judith Okely, 'Privileged, Schooled and Finished: Boarding

Education for Girls', in Shirley Ardener (ed.), *Defining Females: The Nature of Women in Society* (London, 1978), p. 124.

93. Edwards, op. cit., pp. 102–03; Gorham, op. cit., pp. 26, 56–7, 95.

94. A.P. Donajgrodski (ed.), *Social Control in Nineteenth Century Britain* (London, 1977), p. 13; Marks, op. cit., pp. 187–8.

95. A.E. Hendry, 'Social Influences upon the Early Development of Physical Education in England', *Journal of Physical Education*, LXI (1969), 19. See also Allen Guttmann, *From Ritual to Record: The Nature of Modern Sports* (New York, 1978), p. 34; Hargreaves, op. cit., p. 95; Kennard, op. cit., p. 168; Turner, op. cit., p. 145.

96. Atkinson, op. cit., p. 128; Hughes, op. cit., pp. 120–2; Smith-Rosenberg and Rosenberg, op. cit., pp. 355–6. It goes almost without saying that the movements for dress reform and birth control were part of the same fight for body control.

97. Talamini and Page, op. cit., p. 29.

98. Atkinson, op. cit., pp. 126–9; James Crichton-Browne, 'Sex in Education', *Lancet* (7 May 1892), 1011–18; 'A Candid Friend on Feminism', *British Medical Journal* (15 October 1910), 1172–3; Carol Dyhouse, 'Towards a "Feminine" Curriculum for English Schoolgirls: The Demands of Ideology 1870–1963', *Women's Studies International Quarterly*, I (1978), 291–311; Carol Dyhouse, 'Social Darwinist Ideas and the Development of Women's Education in England, 1880–1920', *History of Education*, V (1976), 41–58; Lorna Duffin, 'Prisoners of Progress: Women and Evolution', in Delamont and Duffin (eds.), *Nineteenth Century Women*, pp. 57–91; Gerber *et al.*, *American Woman*, pp. 12–17; Kenealy, 'Woman', pp. 636–45; R. Murray Leslie, 'Women's Progress in Relation to Eugenics', *Eugenics Review*, II (April 1910–January 1911), 282–98; Marks, op. cit., pp. 193–4; Mary Scharlieb, 'Adolescent Girlhood Under Modern Conditions, with Special Reference to Motherhood', *Eugenics Rev.*, I (April 1909–January 1910), 174–83; Mary Scharlieb, 'The Health of Adolescent Girls in Relation to School Life', *Journal of Education* (November 1909), 736–7; John Thorburn, *Female Education from a Physiological Point of View* (Manchester, 1884); Pleasaunce Unite, 'Disillusioned Daughters', *Fortnightly Rev.*, LXVIII (1900), 850–7; Paul Weiss, *Sport: A Philosophic Enquiry* (Carbondale, IL, 1969), pp. 214–15, 228; Dr Withers-Moore, 'The Higher Education of Women', *Br. Med. J.* (14 August 1886), 295–9; Earle F. Zeigler, *Physical Education and Sports Philosophy* (Englewood Cliffs, NJ, 1977), pp. 175–7.

99. Edwards, op. cit., pp. 102–20, 227–30; Felshin, op. cit., p. 431; M. Marie Hart, 'Stigma or Prestige: The All American Choice', in Hart (ed.), *Sport in the Socio-Cultural Process*, p. 177; Talamini and Page, op. cit., pp. 271–2.

100. Gathorne-Hardy, op. cit., p. 273.

101. Burstall, *English High Schools* pp. 90–1; Jane Frances Dove, 'The Modern Girl: How far are we fitting her for her varied duties in life?' *Wycombe Abbey Gazette*, III (November 1907), 161–2; Edwards, op. cit., pp. 102–03, 227–30; Ellsworth, op. cit., pp. 200, 287; Gathorne-Hardy, op. cit., pp. 273–4; Gorham, op. cit., pp. 105–18; Hargreaves, op. cit., pp. 138–82; Kennard, op. cit., p. 181; Okely, op. cit., p. 109.

102. Gorham, op. cit., pp. 96–7; Edwards, op. cit., p. 355.

103. Edwards, op. cit., p. 348; Alan G. Ingham and John W. Loy, 'The Social System of Sport: A Humanistic Perspective', in Hart (ed.) *Sport in the Socio-cultural Process* p. 245; Martha M. Sevan, 'A Theoretical Consideration of the Internal Dynamics of Sport', in Hart (ed.), *Sport in the Socio-cultural Process*, p. 222.

104. Atkinson, op. cit., pp. 113, 127–9; Gerber *et al.*, *American Women*, pp. 12–13, 191–2, 203; Gerber, 'Changing Female Image', p. 59; Hargreaves, op. cit., pp. 57, 86; Kennard, op. cit., p. 182.

It is difficult to appreciate how much the clothes of the Victorian period affected women's physical activities. Cumbersome and tight, they made rapid and vigorous movement virtually impossible, dictated the habits of body in which girls were trained, and generally reflected social attitudes towards women's restricted sphere. The question of what to wear for athletic activity was long a vexing one, for it involved the necessity to allow freedom of movement without offending propriety. The development of the box-pleated gym tunic at Madame Bergman-Österberg's physical training college about 1893 eventually created a revolution in sporting dress. Meanwhile schools like St Leonards and Roedean developed their own sports costumes, which preluded the school uniform and were worn only within the private confines of school playgrounds – blue serge, long-sleeved, knee-length dresses, over bloomers and stockings. At women's colleges games-playing also produced a rationalizing of dress, as did the advent of the bicycle. However, because participants were adults, modesty was particularly essential, and innovation was limited to shortening skirts so that they were six to eight inches off the ground.

Despite limitations, the participation of women in physical activities was responsible for bringing some comfort and ease into women's fashions. Thus, the evolution of the sports costume is a significant aspect of the larger stories of women and sport and women's emancipation, and deserves detailed study elsewhere. (See Atkinson, op. cit., pp. 117–20; Burstall, *English High Schools*, p. 96; C.W. Cunnington, *English Women's Clothing in the Nineteenth Century* (London, 1937); P. Cunnington and A. Mansfield, *English Costume for Sports and Outdoor Recreation* (London, 1969); Elizabeth Ewing, *Women in Uniform Through the Centuries* (London, 1975), pp. 68–74; David Kunzle, *Fashion and Fetishism* (London, 1982), pp. 46–7; C.E. Thomas (ed.), *Athletic Training for Girls* (London, 1912), pp. 60–7.)

105. Burstall, *English High Schools*, p. 101; Edwards, op. cit., p. 231; Felshin, op. cit., p. 432–3; Gorham, op. cit., pp. 56–94; Evelyn M. Perry, 'School Games', *Teachers' Guild Quarterly* (March 1910), 16–17; Thomas, op. cit., pp. 10–17.
106. Hargreaves, op. cit., pp. 200–01.
107. Ibid., p. 87.
108. Felshin, op. cit., pp. 432–3; Stone, op. cit., pp. 43–4; Anne Summers, *Damned Whores and God's Place: The Colonization of Women in Australia* (London, 1975), p. 86; Talamini and Page, op. cit., p. 32; Thomas, op. cit., pp. 3–4.
109. GPDST, op. cit., p. 39.
110. Ignota, 'Fair Sportswomen', *Harmsworth Magazine,* III (August 1899–January 1900), 173.
111. Edwards, op. cit., p. 355; Talamini and Page, op. cit., pp. 271–2; Yiannakis *et al.*, op. cit., pp. 207–09.
112. Felshin, op. cit., pp. 431–5.
113. Hilmi Ibrahim, *Sport and Society: An Introduction to the Sociology of Sport* (Long Beach, CA, 1976), pp. 173, 183.
114. Thomas, op. cit., pp. 3–4.
115. Yiannakis *et al.*, op. cit., pp. 207–09.
116. Atkinson, op. cit., p. 92; Felshin, op. cit., pp. 434–5; Gorham, op. cit., p. 106; Hargreaves, op. cit., pp. 74, 83, 92.

5

Victorian Familism and the Formative Years of Female Sport

Jennifer A. Hargreaves

In this chapter it is argued that during the formative years of female sport – that is, from the mid-nineteenth century to the early twentieth century – the legitimate use of the female body was redefined to symbolize a more active yet nevertheless still subordinate role, when compared with men. This development is extremely complex and difficult to analyse because it touches upon many different domains, for example, the biological, psychological, medical, moral and military domains, and, importantly, incorporates elements of Social Darwinism.[1] However, because of the limited space available here, I have chosen to focus on the Victorian cult of the family because it makes connections between these apparently separate spheres, and is thus a unifying feature of nineteenth-century bourgeois ideology and acted as a dominant constraining force on the early development of women's sport. Furthermore, Victorian familism highlights the specific nature of some of the contradictions facing the nineteenth-century sportswoman which have had repercussions for the development of women's sport until the present day.

It has been argued that the association of the woman with the domestic sphere and her role in the nuclear family was a modern invention dating approximately from the eighteenth century.[2] However, it became a popular idea which defined what a woman was and which directly related to her being female. The solidification, most notably of the bourgeois family, developed concomitantly with the consolidation of industrial capitalism, and by the turn of the century it was a key institution in the 'social mythology that helped to keep women relatively powerless'.[3] The underlying assumption about the family as the 'natural unit' existing in separation from the total social formation was an intrinsic part of a system of patriarchy with which many women colluded, bound up as it was with ideas about family arrangements, gender identities, sexual mores and women's biological, psychological and moral characteristics.

The idealized model of the respectable family centred on the man as the 'head of the house', operating mainly in the economic sphere, the provider of the material requirements of his household and its dominant authority figure. The relationship between the man and the woman was viewed as a reciprocal one in that the woman's dependent role as wife, housekeeper and childbearer, which confined her to 'the inferior world of the family . . . left the bourgeois man "free" to accumulate capital' in order to maintain her adequately.[4] Additionally, the woman was viewed as the family member whose moral influence should be impeccable. It was from the 'saintly mother' in the home that children first learned about the sexual division of labour and associated attitudes of obedience, hard work, honesty and loyalty. Thus the family was effectively cemented and its continuity ensured.

The model of the Victorian family may have been a reality for the affluent middle classes, but it was an impossibility for the majority of working-class families, who depended not only on the wife's wage labour to finance the home, but also, in many cases, on the labour of children as well.[5] Nevertheless, in the public image, the woman's work role was always secondary to her role within the family which constituted the Victorian ideal of the sexual division of labour.

The taken-for-granted assumption that this was the 'natural order of things' was underpinned by the implicit belief that the differences between men and women were biologically determined and hence immutable. Women, it was argued, were eminently suited, because of their innate physical and emotional characteristics, to stay at home and be good wives and mothers, and, by the same argument, were poorly equipped for the productive sphere. This was an integral element of the rhetoric of Social Darwinism incorporating the medical case for women's physical inferiority which was employed to justify 'maternity as the "highest function" of womanhood – essential to the healthy progress of the nation'.[6]

To what extent this vision of family life was a reality is less important than the way it was elevated as a concept which permeated social consciousness. Its development to a form of institutionalized sexism dominated social relations, thus giving them a material base in the work and family domains and also in the educational and leisure contexts. I suggest that the early years of women's sport gave ideological legitimation to the confinement of women to their separate, private sphere of the home, and to the existing patterns of biological and social reproduction in the home. 'Behaving like a lady' meant adopting the bourgeois values associated with being female, and it appears to have been a prerequisite for the nineteenth-century sportswoman.

I have characterized early forms of female sport and physical activity to show how they incorporated the ideology of the family and I shall deal firstly with *conspicuous recreation*. Such activities as croquet, early tennis and spectating at the races were all part of a process of consumption linked to the technological developments which revolutionized industrial methods of production. The increasing specialization of labour created a multitude of new jobs for working-class women it narrowed the lives of middle-class women and robbed them of their economic usefulness.[7] The idleness of the bourgeois lady became symbolic of her husband's or her father's material success; her finery reflected his affluence and the way she organized her leisure defined his social standing.

The life-styles of the middle classes, in particular, reflected the increased opportunity for acquisitiveness associated with the garden suburb idea which flourished from the mid-century onwards as swelling numbers moved into detached, semi-detached and terraced houses in the newly developed areas.[8] The insular, self-contained nature of these modern homes made the family a spatially segregated recreation unit, with the woman as its focal object who publicized the spending power of her husband and her father. Homes became more palatial and gardens became part of the improved amenities of domestic life for the middle classes. By the mid-Victorian period the bourgeois family had reached a plateau of prosperity sufficient for domestic duties to be taken care of by a growing army of servants. Even when growth and prosperity seemed to suffer a more general contraction from the mid-1870s, the Victorian bourgeoisie were able to resist any serious curtailment of expenditure and consumption and this was reflected in all forms of women's leisure. A whole 'consumer-amusement-market' for the family developed[9] and the resultant conspicuous display of affluence was symbolic of the increasing economic dependence of middle-class women on men. It was, also, a reflection of the middle classes increasingly divorcing themselves from their inheritance of thrift and frugality and indulging more openly in social pleasure.[10]

Lavish, extravagant clothes and accoutrements were worn to afford evidence of a life of leisure but they restrained women from performing any but the smallest and meanest of movements. The bourgeois lady remained, even on the tennis court, the wifely ornament of beauty, a physically incapacitated player, inhibited and subdued by convention and, as Veblen put it, 'bound by the code of behaviour as tight as the stays she was compelled to wear'.[11]

Similarly, at competitive events such as horse-racing, regattas or cricket matches, women reinforced the superiority of men by adopting a spectator role as members of an admiring female audience watching the physical antics of men. Alternatively, women were absorbed into the leisure sphere by the provision for them of 'gentle, respectable games', eminently suited to the 'weaker sex', and exemplified by croquet and its indoor derivatives like 'Parlour Croquet', 'Carpet Croquet' or 'Table Croquet'.[12]

Prints and photographs provide some of the scant evidence available that this model of the conspicuous sporting lady prevailed throughout the nineteenth century, and even beyond 1900. For example, Brian Dobbs' book, entitled 'Edwardians at Play', includes fifty engravings, prints and photographs, many of which feature women as spectators: sitting in the stands in flamboyant, wasp-waisted dresses, or walking in a leisurely and self-conscious fashion through the grounds. The one, isolated illustration of a woman participant shows her to be a most decorative lady partnering the sporting Prince of Wales at lawn tennis. She is undoubtedly wearing corsets, has a most fashionable pair of shoes, a pretty hat perched on her head, and even with a racquet in her hand, looks for all the world unable to move an inch or two in any direction.[13]

'Tight croquet', as it was originally called, featured all the most pronounced manifestations of bourgeois 'conspicuous recreation',

> Nobody could have called it a good game played, as it was, with only one hand in order that the womenfolk might be able to guard their complexions from the sun . . . a game of frills and fancies, of petticoats, giggles and maidenly blushes.[14]

Croquet was a highly social and fashionable pastime and became something of a craze so that 'hardly a house with a lawn was without its croquet set'.[15] Tennis also became a mania for the affluent which 'swept like a wind of change through the quiet countryside and brought the sexes together on the courts in a wave of exciting activity'.[16] For example, tennis parties 'were the highlight of Cambridge society in the 80s and 90s', although by this time the game had become a good deal more active for women and tennis attire was less restricted – the ladies sometimes tying their long dresses back with an apron.

Generally speaking, women's participatory role in conspicuous recreation embodied the characteristics of passivity rather than activity, subordination rather than ascendancy. The female croquet and tennis player represented the embellishment of man with no natural, organic connection to physical action of the sort that epitomizes the essence of sport as we know it today. Women were obliged to show restraint, be refined and respectable, and confirm at all times the 'ladylike' modes of behaviour prescribed for them. In the home context, the 'playing of games' became an important, fashionable accomplishment for the middle-class woman, in the same category as those much admired genteel activities like playing the piano, singing, drawing and painting, reciting poetry and doing needlework. It was a new, comparatively enjoyable way for the middle-class wife to display her talents as a 'cultured' lady of whom her husband could be truly proud, and since the daughter's chief objective was to find a husband,[17] it gave her scope to disport herself in appealing fashion to the opposite sex, in a seemingly innocent and acceptable form. Furthermore, playing games in the family context was viewed as positively desirable, as well as respectable, because it reflected the close-knit nature of family relationships and promoted the image of family life. The range of family sports increased to include various forms of hockey, badminton, cricket, bowls and skittles.

The schooling of middle-class girls provided an ideal preparation for all the features of 'conspicuous living' in the ambit of the family. The 'accomplishments' were given primacy in the majority of private girls' schools until 1850, and remained a feature of the curriculum, in a decreasing number of schools, for around 50 more years. In so far as it is possible to describe the crocodile walks and callisthenics and social dance as forms of physical education, done as they were in a self-conscious manner and in the restricting and fashionable clothes of the time,[18] then it is possible to observe that they invoked an attitude – a way of thinking and feeling – about what it was to be feminine, which became internalized and hence 'real'. This image of femininity can be recognized as the same one that applied to 'conspicuous recreation' in the sphere of the home and the family and so they mutually reinforced one another.

Another feature of bourgeois conspicuous living for middle-class women was the development of *therapeutic forms of exercise*. Middle-class women fulfilled their own stereotype of the 'delicate' females who took to their beds with consistent regularity and thus provided confirmation of the dominant medical account that this should be so. Women 'were' manifestly physically and biologically inferior because they actually 'did' swoon, 'were' unable to eat, suffered continual maladies, and consistently expressed passivity and submissiveness in various forms. The acceptance by women of their own incapacitation gave both a humane and moral weighting to the established scientific so called 'facts'. One way to avoid constitutional degeneration – a benefit to women as well as to the nation as a whole – was by way of medically prescribed exercise, and middle-class women with affluent husbands made ideal patients who, in addition, supported the economic status of doctors. Gentle exercises, remedial gymnastics and massage were the prescribed treatments for a whole range of female complaints and became integrated into a new 'medical-business-complex'. There was a boom in the number of clinics, health spas and seaside holidays and a proliferation in the number and type of personnel employed. A new range of semi-specialists such as dieticians, masseuses and remedial gymnasts emerged[19] and students trained at the new specialist colleges of physical education were incorporated into this movement to service the bodies of middle class ladies. The prescribed treatments promoted the identification of these women as a group who had similar delicate natures and in-built frailties. Rude health in this context was considered quite vulgar – gentle exercise on the other hand was intended to enable women to return to the ambit of their families in order to service their husbands and children and to be able to procreate successfully. Throughout the 1880s the stereotype of the middle-class lady with her associated limitations remained intact, in one form or another, in the family setting, and she supplied the predominantly institutionalized female image of the late nineteenth century which provided a backward-looking scenario for the 'new woman' to enter.

Gradually, a qualitatively different image connected with the notion of 'positive health' evolved but it co-existed with medical opinion opposing exercise for women because it was claimed to be damaging to health – a position which was in evidence for a long time. For example, in 1837, riding was condemned because it was believed to produce an 'unnatural consolidation of the bones of the lower part of the body, ensuring a frightful impediment to future functions . . .[20] and not so differently, in 1910–11, it was claimed that emphasis on games and athletics was likely to do irreparable damage to the adolescent girl and that hockey, specifically, could disable women from breastfeeding.[21]

These positions for and against exercise for women were not really in opposition in that they were both related to women's procreative functions, and were underpinned by a belief in Social Darwinism and its concern for the future of the human race and the national good by transposing the 'laws' of nature to social phenomena. Only exercise of a suitable kind, in moderation, without over-indulgence or risk of strain, was considered to enhance the health of women and their potential to conceive healthy children. In other words, there was a unity of the medical and moral opinions concerning female sport and exercise.

This trend can also be viewed as part of the discourse of sexual constraints embodied in Victorian familism. As Foucault says:

> There was scarcely a malady or physical disturbance to which the 19th century did not impute at least some degree of sexual etiology and which were susceptible to pathological processes and requiring therapeutic interventions.[22]

The prudishness associated with sport was also a way of censoring sex. In all forms of exercise for women, a 'proper' demeanour, decency and modesty were required: the avoidance of over-exertion, bodily display and sensual pleasure was essential. The dominance of this position as the century progressed explains how the eroticism of the false contours of the flamboyant dresses worn for 'conspicuous recreation' were replaced by the blouses and skirts of the hockey era which, though more natural and flowing, covered all possible parts of the body from sight. As activities took on a more vigorous form the sporting attire for ladies became distinctly shapeless and 'sexless'. The blue serge box-pleated gymslip, with tights sewn into knickers, and black and brown woollen stockings and laced shoes was the attire worn increasingly by numbers of lady gymnasts and games players right into the 1920s.[23] A *Daily News* report of 1890 describes how 'Their costume consists of a dark blue tunic and knickerbockers with a red sash with falling ends tied at the side. A knot of blue ribbon ties the bodice in front, and the stockings are dark blue with red ribbons'.[24] The splashes of colour added a 'feminine' touch to the proceedings but in no way affected the strict uniformity and depersonalizing nature of their clothing.

The implication that sport could detract attention from sexuality was made quite explicit in the 1912 *Handbook for Girl Guides*:

> All secret habits are evil and dangerous, lead to hysteria and lunatic asylums, and serious illness is the result. . . Evil practices dare not face an honest person; they lead you on to blindness, paralysis and loss of memory.[25]

The precise nature of the practices was not specified but we may guess what they were because cold baths and healthy exercise were the preferred antidote to sexual desire.

An important feature of late Victorian mores was the de-emphasis of the sensuous nature of its woman and the predominance given to their actions, missions, qualities of character and home life.[26] Their conscience or soul, duty or reason, were expressions of the highest part of their nature, whereas the body or appetite, or animalism – in reality the sexual instinct or desire – represented the lowest part of female nature.[27]

Moral purity continued to be embraced by better-off middle-class families whose reputation rested upon the chastity of their daughters, opposition to sports which were viewed as a threat to this convention was commonplace. Cycling for women was described as an indolent and indecent practice which would even transport girls to prostitution; it was said to be an activity far beyond a girl's strength and one which made women incapable of bearing children. Cycling, it was said, ' . . . tends to destroy the sweet simplicity of her girlish nature; besides, how dreadful it would be if, by some accident, she were to fall into the arms of a strange man'.[28]

In the context of swimming, the closeness of near-naked bodies smacked of depravity. Separate swimming was rigidly adhered to until the 1920s, and even then, in some areas, mixed participation was only possible in the guise of family bathing. There were separate entrances for men and women, and strict rules of procedure disallowed men from getting out of the water on the 'women's side' of the pool, and vice versa.[29] Even as a feature of the seaside family holiday, bathing was organized with great propriety to avoid embarrassment and to ensure absolute modesty and morality.[30]

It becomes clear from this account so far that changes in women's sport were not abrupt or dramatic but rather a process of adjustment and accommodation, new forms of activity being formulated concomitantly with established conservative attitudes. Patriarchal ideology was the most consistent and sustaining set of values which women learnt to accommodate to, although there was no reason to suspect that the new sportswomen did not believe its basic premises anyway. In order to achieve social approval for their involvement in sport, women had to demonstrate that femininity and more active participation in physical activity were not incompatible. If the activity could be shown to have a utilitarian function, if there was no associated immodesty or impropriety, and if women remained cautious in the level of exertion, then they could extend their physical horizons without threatening their existing set of social relationships with men – in fact, they could actually show that they positively supported their men in their ventures into sport. In all the different forms of sport this process of accommodation can be seen and those from the most wealthy sections of society were no exception.

The following examples from pre-1900 publications concerned exclusively with women in sport had distinctly aristocratic overtones, but interestingly rested upon similar justifications to those of the sports of other social groups. I have characterized these as *elite sports*

and they exemplify the moral imperatives of women's sport. An
unusually diverse assortment of activities – riding, hunting, team and
tandem riding, tiger shooting, rifle shooting, deer stalking and
driving, covert shooting, kangaroo hunting, cycling and punting –
were all deemed highly suitable and desirable pastimes for rich
women with a potential to enrich their lives in respect, most
particularly, to their essential femininity, to the state of their moral
welfare and to their general health. For example:

> Women . . . who are afraid neither of a little fatigue nor of a little
> exertion are the better, the truer, and the healthier, and can yet
> remain essentially feminine in their thoughts and manners.[31]

This account of Lady Grenville rests upon the implicit assumption
that there is an innate psychological difference between the sexes and
that 'characteristically' women possess an improving nature, an ethical
disposition which can 'refine the coarser ways of men' . . . 'contribute
to the disuse of bad language', and lead the way to 'habits of courtesy
and kindness' in the world of sport. We read that riding tends greatly
to moral and physical well-being and improves the temper, the spirits
and the appetite.[32] It is stated that hunting in the Shires provides a
healthy way of making a man active and training his character, while
the woman's most significant contribution as she rides by his side
through the countryside is 'Tact, kindness . . . courtesy and politeness
. . . part of our ideal lady's nature . . . which go a long way towards
what is called "Keeping the country together".'[33] It was recognized
that the woman's innate potential to employ her moral influence to
improve the condition of the nation was as possible in the realm of
sport as in her family role. The influence of the patrician elements,
especially, set the cutural tone of women's sport and complemented
the restrictions imposed by Social Darwinist beliefs.

The equating of moral rectitude with physical well-being was a
fundamental feature of sport in the *physical education* colleges for
women and in the more advanced schools for middle-class girls. Like
the mother to her children, the college principals and the physical
education mistresses were the moral exemplars for their students and
pupils. The first principal of Bedford College (founded in 1903) was
described by an old student as 'a sort of moral yardstick', and one who
firmly believed that 'the discipline of the school emanates from the
gymnasium'.[34] This idea was an element of the ethos of the physical
education profession which made an indelible mark on its future
development in the twentieth century. Madame Bergman-Österberg,
the first principal of Dartford College, was herself an uncompromis-
ing disciplinarian exacting from her students the highest standards of

behaviour. She was an autocrat who restricted the students' activities in every practical detail, forbidding them to visit each other's rooms, enforcing an early lights out, imposing cold baths, and refusing weekend leave except in special circumstances.[35] In this way, Madame Österberg intended to raise the level of health, intellect and morality of her students. Her support of female emancipation was effectively a nationalist sentiment, confirming the contemporary Social Darwinist position about the vital importance of motherhood in evolution, and encompassing a belief that the educational arrangements should be geared to the role of women as mothers.[36] Familism was, therefore, incorporated into the rhetoric, ideology, and into the practical arrangements of college life at Dartford, and later in the other specialist colleges. It was argued that the complete course of training was, in itself, an education for a future life as a wife and mother. 'The outdoor exercise and the training here [at Dartford],' Madame Österberg said, would fit girls . . . 'to become the organiser of the perfect home, or the trainer of a vigorous and beautiful new generation'.[37]

Previous medical accounts of the female constitution had directed attention to the physiological vulnerability of the woman's procreative capacity. In a way they were now turned about face by the notion that Swedish gymnastics, with its systematized attention to every part of the human anatomy, could promote healthy procreative functions. The woman's body and her ability to bear healthy children were idealized by Madame Bergman-Österberg:

> [Gymnastics] is the best training for motherhood. Remember, it is not "hips firm" or "arms upward stretch", it is *not* "drill", but it is moulding and reshaping and reforming the most beautiful and plastic material in the world, the human body itself.[38]

The physical education women gained considerable ground by widening the definition of how they could legitimately use their bodies, but although the freedom gained had some reality in relation to what went on before, it was a very limited version of being free and natural. Women's freedom to move rested upon the taken-for-granted assumption about the different, innate characteristics and needs of men and women. 'Gymnastics,' Madame Österberg claimed, 'develop body, mind and morals simultaneously' and are a 'vital factor in making manly men and womanly women'.[39]

Encapsulating the physical notion of motherhood was the belief that national efficiency inevitably depended upon a strong tradition of home life. The college, *in loco parentis*, reproduced the structure and ideologies of the 'perfect' Victorian home with the college principal as both father and mother figure rolled into one – the 'head of the house' and ultimate authority and the inculcator of high moral standards. 'If you want to see something of the home life of my girls, you have come at the right moment' was Madame Österberg's greeting to a visitor.[40] 'A small college admits also of home life,' she said, 'always essential to women's happiness, and never more so than during the period of youth.'[41] The students represented the children in their relationship to the principal and the teaching staff were also, symbolically, part of the same family and their authority over the students was analagous to the authority of an older over a younger sibling. At Dartford the staff, as well as the students, were all referred to as 'Madame's girls'.

The family authority relations were also reproduced in the student body – 'seniors' had a responsibility to 'juniors', and the 'college mother' to her 'college daughter', to see that she was integrated into the family community. In a very practical, and taken-for-granted way, the general living arrangements of the college household consolidated the ideas about what a middle-class family should be like – meal times especially were formal occasions, with everyone in evening dress, and the principal sitting at the 'head of the table'. A student from Anstey College said, 'At meal times, in keeping with Rhoda Anstey's idea that we were one family, the whole company sat at one vast Victorian dining table.'[42] An old student at Bedford College observed, 'The first refresher course was like a family gathering.'[43] The idealization of the family was both a central feature of patriarchal ideology and of the version of feminism in the physical education colleges; it was an integral part of everyone's living and thinking. The theory and practice of familism in the colleges reproduced the structure and morality of the patriarchal Victorian bourgeois home and reinforced conventional sexual divisions in society.

Many of the students trained in the colleges became involved in *voluntary philanthropic activities*, as well as teaching, which seems to reflect a shift from their stereotypical and static wifely roles, to a less insular social position of an increasing participation in public life. However, their widening sphere of action posed no threat to the traditional family structure – their benevolence was confirmation of a deeply moralistic attitude extending from the home into the community.

The absence of any pecuniary profit established the impeccable nature of the enterprise. Feminists themselves often adopted a contradictory position: on the one hand subscribing to a lessening of inequalities between men and women, on the other implicitly accepting the notion of innate differences which predisposed women to certain occupations – 'best suited to work in the fields of Education and Pauperism'.[44] The National Association of Girls' Clubs was instituted in the 1880s, and its associate members included clubs organized by the Church of England, the Girls' Friendly Society, and Mothers' Unions. These clubs offered hockey, swimming and gymnastics for their 'improving' qualities.[45] Youth work of this sort provided an opportunity for enlightened women to escape from the confines of domesticity without contradicting prior duty to home and family. Middle-class women were the main carriers of ideology within their family context, and their work teaching sport in clubs and elementary schools was an extension of this role where they became carriers of bourgeois ideology into working-class spheres of life.

Early *rationalized forms of sport* were shared between sports clubs, girls schools, universities and the colleges of physical education, and began to unfold during the last third of the nineteenth century. They represented organized forms of sport including competitive team games with codified rules and bureaucratic procedures. In all forms of rationalized sport women had to accommodate to public hostility – the freer the activity in terms of bodily and spatial mobility, the more powerful was the opposition, always based on moral and biological criteria. In 1884, when women were first allowed at Wimbledon it was declared that 'tournament play was all too tiring for the weaker sex',[46] but athletics was viewed more seriously as synonymous with indecency – a corrupting influence for a 'properly brought up girl'. In addition, it was considered to be a form of exercise unsuited to women's physiques which would produce an unnatural race of Amazons, thus destroying the prospect of motherhood and hence affecting the deterioration of the human race.[47]

The proliferation of twentieth-century women's sports such as golf, tennis, badminton, skating, hockey, netball, lacrosse, rounders, cricket, gymnastics, swimming and athletics only became possible because they occurred in separate spheres from the sports of men. By being insular, sportswomen did not constitute a challenge in their relationship to men. If men and women never opposed one another in open competition the newly learned female 'aggressiveness' and 'competitiveness' could be defined as qualitatively different from men's. Although sportswomen opened a new 'social space' in which they exerted power it can be seen that the power they wielded was not always progressive. The division of social space between men and women was characteristic of the nineteenth century – part of the 'world view'. Separate male and female sport did nothing to minimize the polarization between masculine and feminine which was manifest in the separate spheres of private (or family) life and public life.

Sport was still overwhelmingly a symbol of masculinity – the core manly virtues of courage, aggression and the competitive instinct were intimately associated with it. The cult of athleticism was in essence a cult of manliness, and so if women joined in on an equal footing they could hardly be simultaneously projected as sexual objects by men, whose position was clear:

> . . . beauty of face and form is one of the chief essentials (for women), but unlimited indulgence in violent, outdoor sports, cricket, bicycling, beagling, otter-hunting, paper-chasing, and – most odious of all games for woman – hockey, cannot but have an unwomanly effect on a young girl's mind, no less on her appearance. . . . Let young girls ride, skate, dance and play lawn tennis and other games in moderation, but let them leave field sports to those for whom they were intended – men.[48]

Nevertheless, woman's participation in the traditionally all-male competitive sports was symbolic of her competition with men, and she faced harsh ridicule about their de-sexing characteristics. It was imperative, therefore, for women games players to be in every way 'ladylike' in their behaviour both on and off the pitch. It is difficult to conceive of hockey being played by Victorian women in contemporary ladylike fashion since it was potentially a more vigorous, aggressive and dirty game – but that was precisely what was achieved. The ball was frequently lost under the long skirts of the players, who wore hats, and usually gloves as well, and who tackled each other at all times 'gently and fairly'. In 1897 there was a complaint in a game at Frances Holland School that hockey players 'keep the ball too much under their petticoats'.[49] I suggest that even after the turn of the century, as women's games playing skills increased with the increased freedom of movement afforded by tunics and divided skirts, they none the less created and reproduced traditional gender divisions. The ambivalence of, and irony in, the way women accommodated to their role in sport is unwittingly, but perfectly, encapsulated in the compliment paid to a headmistress about the behaviour of her cricket team: 'Your girls play like gentlemen, and behave like ladies'.[50]

NOTES

1. For a full discussion of the formative years of female sport see J. A. Hargreaves, 'Playing Like Gentlemen While Behaving Like Ladies': The Social Significance of Physical Activity for Females in Late Nineteenth and Early Twentieth Century Britain' (unpublished M.A. dissertation, University of London Institute of Education, 1979).
2. E. Janeway, in H. Eisenstein, *Contemporary Feminist Thought* (London, 1984), p. 9.
3. Eisenstein, ibid.
4. S. Rowbotham, *Hidden from History* (London, 1973), p. 3.
5. R. Baxandall, E. Ewen and L. Gordon, 'The Working Class Has Two Sexes', *Monthly Review*, 28, (July–August 1976).
6. C. Dyhouse, 'Social Darwinist Ideas and the Development of Women's Education in England, 1880–1920; *History of Education*, 5, (1976), 41–2.
7. V. Klein, *The Feminine Character: History of an Ideology*, (London: 2nd edn., 1971), p. 14.
8. G. Best, *Mid-Victorian Britain* (London, 1971), p. 18.
9. P. Bailey, *Leisure and Class in Victorian England* (London, 1978), p. 18.
10. S. Margetson, *Leisure and Pleasure in the Nineteenth Century*, (New York, 1969). The principles of duty, self-sacrifice and discipline were no longer so emphatic, with a resultant tendency for the opulent leisure patterns of the upper classes to be imitated.
11. T. Veblen, *The Theory of the Leisure Class* (London, 1934), p. 181.
12. B. Jewell, *Sports and Games: Heritage of the Past* (Tunbridge Wells, 1977), pp. 96–98. A whole range of commercialized indoor versions of games was produced including billiards, snooker, German billiards, bagatelle, versions of shove halfpenny, quoits, skittles, table skittles and Aunt Sally.
13. B. Dobbs, *Edwardians at Play* (London, 1973), p. 80.
14. N. Wymer, *Sport in England* (London, 1949), p. 226.
15. Jewell, op. cit., p. 96.
16. Margetson, op. cit., p. 211.
17. Ibid., p. 100.
18. M.C. Borer, *Willingly to School: A History of Women's Education*, (Guildford, 1976), pp. 240–3.
19. L. Duffin, 'Conspicuous Consumptive' in S. Delamont and L. Duffin (eds.), *The Nineteenth Century Woman: Her Cultural World* (London, 1978), pp. 31–2, 41.
20. D. Walker, *Exercises for Women* (London, 2nd edn., 1937), quoted by R.A. Smith, *American Women's Sports in the Victorian Era* (Pennsylvania State University, 1972), p. 8.
21. L. Murray, 'Women's Progress in Relation to Eugenics', *Eugenics Review* II (1910–1911), quoted in C. Dyhouse, 'Social Darwinist Ideas about the Development of Women's Education in England, 1880–1920; *History of Education*, 5, (1976).
22. M. Foucault, *The History of Sexuality* (Harmondsworth, reprinted 1981), p. 65.
23. L. Desmond, 'Gymnastics in the Roaring Twenties', *B.A.G.A. Journal* (Autumn 1973), 6.
24. Cited by A. Winter, *'They Made Today' A History of the Hundred Years of the Polytechnic Sports Clubs and Societies* (London, 1979).
25. K. Middlemass, *High Society in the 1900s* (London, 1977), p. 146. From the *Handbook for Girl Guides* (London, 1912).
26. H.E. Roberts, 'Marriage, Redundancy or Sin', in M. Vicinus (ed.), *Suffer and Be Still: Women in the Victorian Age*, (Indiana, 1973).
27. P. Cominus, 'Innocent Femina Sensualis in Unconscious Conflict', ibid. p. 156.
28. C. Willett Cunnington, *Feminine Attitudes in the Nineteenth Century* (London, 1935), quoted in M.A. Hall, 'The Role of the Safety Bicycle in the Emancipation of Women', *Proceedings of the Second World Symposium on the History of Sport and Physical Education* (London, 1971), p. 245.
29. A. Rawlinson, personal interview (2 July 1979). When training for the 100 yards and 200 yards backstroke events he had to take his mother with him in order to gain entry during family bathing sessions.

30. B. Levitt Whitelaw, *E. Adair Impey, Letters of Rememberance* (1965), p. 8. Dartford College Archives.
31. Lady Grenville (ed.), *Ladies in the Field: Sketches of Sport* (Ward and Downey, 1894), p. iv.
32. Ibid., p. 3.
33. Ibid., pp. 31, 76–7.
34. M. Squire, 'Margaret Stansfield 1860–1951. Teaching, A Way of Life', in E. & W. Clarke, *Nine Pioneers of Physical Education* (London, 1964).
35. Kingsfield Book of Remembrance, Dartford College Archives.
36. Madame Österberg, 'Madame Bergman-Österberg's Physical Training College', *Educational Review*, XIII (1896), 7.
37. Ibid.
38. L.D. Swinerdon, *Madame Bergman-Österberg's Physical Training College Report 1895*, Dartford College Archives.
39. Ibid.
40. S. Mitford, 'A Physical Culture College in Kent,' *The Girls' Realm*, (April 1899) 555.
41. Madame Österberg, 'The Principal's Report, *Madame Bergman-Österberg's Physical Training College Report 1898*, Dartford College Archives.
42. C. Crunden, *A History of Anstey College of Physical Education 1897–1972* (Anstey College of Physical Education, 1974).
43. Quoted by I.M. Webb, 'Women's Place in Physical Education in Great Britain, 1800–1966, with special reference to teacher training' (unpublished thesis, University of Leicester, 1967).
44. J. Wedgewood, 'Female Suffrage, Considered Chiefly with Regard to its Indirect Results', in J. Butler (ed.), *Women's Work and Women's Culture* (London, 1869).
45. H. Meller, *Leisure and the Changing City 1870–1914* (London, 1976), p. 177.
46. Wymer, op. cit., p. 250.
47. Winter, op. cit. p. 12.
48. Dobbs, op. cit. Quote from the Badminton magazine (1900).
49. Borer, op.cit. p. 292.
50. J.F. Dove, 'Cultivation of the Body', in D. Beale *et al., Work and Play in Girls' Schools* (London, 1891), p. 407.

6

The Making and Breaking of a Female Tradition: Women's Physical Education in England 1880–1980

Sheila Fletcher

Probably one of the most vivid images of female emancipation at the turn of the century – one that recurred then in the illustrated journals and lodged itself in the popular mind – was that of the New Woman engaging in sport. The lady cyclists, the lady swimmers, the lady cricketers, the lady golfers, the ladies with hockey sticks, rackets, even footballs, seemed to embody the spirit then abroad that was driving women (some women, at least) to gain admittance to the world of men. 'Let our women remain women instead of entering into this insane rivalry with men,' wrote one critic in the 1870s.[1] Such voices grew shriller as time went on, under the influence of eugenist ideas and the concern with race perfection which marked the new century. Women, in the view of the eugenist doctor, Arabella Kenealy, in 1899, stood in danger of neutering themselves by over-indulgence in athletics. The sinews of games-playing schoolgirls repelled her. 'Stigmata of abnormal Sex-transformation' she called them later, likening their development to that of male antlers in female deer;[2] and she arraigned the 'muscular reformer' who 'sees as woman's highest goal her capacity for doing things that men do'.[3]

To those who advocated female sport this 'doing things that men do' appeared quite differently. The two headmistresses who took the lead in promoting team games for schoolgirls – Miss Lawrence of Roedean and Miss Dove of St Leonards – regarded the cricket field not as a place where girls should develop the sinews of men but certainly as one where they would gain advantages hitherto confined to the male sex: notably, a raising of moral consciousness through the experience of games-playing. Girls should be public-spirited, like boys; and it was in the playground, according to Miss Dove, that boys learnt 'the principles of corporate life'.[4] Cricket, wrote Miss Lawrence, taught 'the civic virtues' through 'the constant necessity for the subordination of self to the good of the side, for perfect fair dealing with other players, for patience and cheerfulness under reverse, for exertion in despite of inertia, for resource in emergency'.[5] This is a far cry from 'the cult of Mannishness' so much deplored by Dr Kenealy. But it is the other side of the same coin: another view of women entering a world where standards of comparison are masculine. In muscular achievement, says Dr Kenealy, women will always be inferior to men. Girls, says Miss Lawrence, do not play cricket as well as their brothers at Eton and Harrow, 'but after all, in what athletic accomplishments do they equal their brothers?'[6]

This is just the kind of comparison which, in a wider field, the Victorian women's movement was constantly provoking. Could women sit examinations like men? Could they be doctors in the same way as men? Could they vote and act politically as men did? Such comparisons were bound to accompany a movement imbued with what Eleanor Rathbone later described as 'me too' feminism:[7] the claims of women to do what men did. And as this spirit was nowhere more evident or more successful than in education, it comes as a surprise to find a major initiative taken by women in that field which had absolutely nothing of 'me too' about it: I mean, the promotion of physical education which had its roots in Swedish gymnastics.

I

What became known as the Swedish system originated in the early nineteenth century with the work of Per Henrik Ling, who looked beyond the military context in which gymnastics were located in his day to their remedial, educational and aesthetic possibilities. The strength of Ling's system – and this was emphasized time and again by its devotees – lay in his close attention to the principles of human anatomy and physiology. Where it was alleged that the German system then fashionable was obsessed with apparatus, to which it forced the body to conform, Ling's exercises were arranged in tables carefully graded to progress in their demands upon strength and skill. 'Everything useless, or injurious has been discarded', it was said.[8] The aim was to promote the most harmonious bodily development overall. Consistent with this, remedial gymnastics were an important part of his work; indeed, the only part to be taken up in England before the 1870s. By then in Sweden, Ling was practically a patron saint and the Royal Gymnastics Institute in Stockholm which he had founded had trained generations of both men and women to carry on his work. In England, one or two doctors made use of his remedial exercises and one in particular, Mathias Roth, pressed on the government for over 20 years the system's educational merits; but little was achieved before 1878 when the London School Board appointed Miss Löfving, trained in Stockholm, to introduce gymnastics in their elementary schools. Three years later Miss Löfving was replaced by another Swede, Martina Bergman; and it is Miss Bergman, or Madame Bergman-Österberg, as she became, who must be seen as the author of a distinctively female tradition in English physical education.[9]

There is nothing to suggest that she came to England with the idea of doing anything more than teach gymnastics to teachers in the Board Schools. For this milieu, as a modern writer comments, Ling's system was ideal, since it required little space.[10] Apparatus work was not essential. The essence was contained in the free-standing exercises which, like some perfectly-balanced diet, were physiologically complete; and these, as Madame Österberg herself pointed out, could be performed 'in any schoolroom as long as there are not more than two children at each desk'.[11] She was a forceful woman, a great publicist, and dedicated to the gospel of Ling. Under her direction countless Board School teachers were given a glimpse of the truths she saw there, and dozens of little Board School girls out of the slums displayed Swedish drill; once, at least, before royalty. But however impressive the results she achieved, given the material, it soon became clear that her ideal of a healthy womanhood could not be attained in the working classes. Too much was stacked against it. In her own words, 'The physique of this class was so lowered and impaired by neglect and by bad conditions of housing, food and clothing, that unless the conditions could be changed, no radical improvement could be effected.'

Feeling this, she eventually decided 'that the secondary schools must be attacked and the foundations laid for an invigorated womanhood in classes which enjoyed happier conditions'.[12] She parted from the School Board in 1887. Two years earlier she had launched her own college for the purpose of training gymnastic teachers for the new high schools for middle-class girls.

It was very good timing. The so-called Renaissance of girls' education was at its height then: some 70 girls' grammar schools had come into being, funded under the Endowed Schools Act, where, 20 years earlier, the genre was unknown.[13] Thirty girls' high schools had been established by the Girls' Public Day School Company alone, since its inception in 1872; and there were other similar developments. Madame Bergman-Österberg, wholly committed to Ling's ideal of physical education, fell upon this expanding market and, in effect, sold to the new headmistresses the view that any reputable girls' school should have its trained gymnastics teacher. Up to this time, as she recalled later, 'the English public had not recognised that a gymnastic teacher needed special training'; it was she who took up what she called 'the double task': 'to train the teachers and to create a demand for them'.[14] Her goal was ambitious and highly innovatory. The girls' secondary schools, after all, had been created in the image of the boys', where gymnastics scarcely existed.[15] Indeed, though a drill sergeant might be employed, the overriding obsession with team games left little room for anything else, and games were usually run by the boys themselves, with help from any master who was interested. By the time Madame Österberg started her college, team games were catching on with girls as well, especially with those at the new girls' public schools, St Leonards and Roedean; and she built on this, assimilating games into her college course, and also into her philosophy. 'English out-of-doors games combined with Swedish gymnastics form a safe and rational basis for Physical Education'. But while games on their own developed vigour and endurance, skill and character, they could also foster one-sided development. The remedy lay in 'Rational Gymnastics'. 'Applied with knowledge and intelligence, Swedish Gymnastics exactly supplement the English games.'[16] Together, they combined to form 'a perfect training system'.[17]

But though she was ready to acknowledge games as an integral part of this perfect system, there can be no doubt that the heart and soul of her vision was the work of Ling. When she sent a trained gymnast into a school she sent a missionary for what she and all others trained at the famous Institute in Stockholm venerated as holy writ. They knew beyond question that, in essentials, the ideal system had been made by Ling. 'No one today,' wrote one of these experts in 1903, 'can *invent* a system of physical education; he can merely repeat long-proven truths and add more details to the knowledge already defined by science.'[18] This was so because Ling's system was the only one to have been derived from 'mechanics, physiology and psychology'.[19]

It is worth dwelling on this missionary fervour because it was a very important factor in launching what I have called the female tradition and in projecting values different from those linked with the masculine sports and games which were being taken up by the New Woman. Madame Österberg was ready to endorse the advantages to health and even to morals of girls playing cricket and lacrosse, but the civic virtues did not speak to her as they did to Miss Lawrence and Miss Dove. Madame Bergman-Österberg spoke most freely in the language of race regeneration:

I try to train my girls to help raise their own sex, and so to accelerate the progress of the race; for unless the women are strong, healthy, pure and true, how can the race progress?[20]

4. The redoubtable Madame Bergman-Österberg, founder of the first women's physical training college in Britain

Illus 1

Illus. 2

Illus. 3.

5. Madame Österberg's system was based on Swedish exercises, for which practical dress became essential.

AN INDUCEMENT.

Swedish Exercise Instructress. "NOW, LADIES, IF YOU WILL ONLY FOLLOW MY DIRECTIONS CAREFULLY, IT IS QUITE POSSIBLE THAT YOU MAY BECOME EVEN AS I AM!"

MORE SWEDISH INSTRUCTION.

Instructress (to exhausted class, who have been hopping round room for some time). "COME! COME! THAT WON'T DO AT ALL. YOU *MUST* LOOK CHEERFUL. KEEP SMILING— SMILING ALL THE TIME!"

6. The new popularity of Swedish gymnastics for girls naturally attracted ridicule from *Punch* (11 April 1906 and 25 April 1906)

The goals of physical education she defined as '*individual* and *race* perfection', to be attained by

> the maximum of *health*, through increased organic development and activity; by the maximum of *beauty*, by harmonious development of the human form, and by increased *moral consciousness* through a more perfect . . . balance between the physical, intellectual and moral qualities. These qualities, transmitted by inheritance, will perfect the race.[21]

Woman, she held to be 'the first factor' in that race regeneration which was now so urgent;[22] for, as she wrote in 1905, 'At the present moment the physical condition of our race causes a certain amount of national anxiety'.[23] Her 'gymnastics teacher and health mistress' was to do battle in this cause; and it was with pride in the importance of the work that this *new kind* of teacher went into the girls' schools to teach gymnastic tables and measure flat feet.

II

If we turn from the spirit to the organization of this female tradition, we enter a world in which all authority and standards of excellence pertain to women. Comparisons with men do not arise since men, in these early formative years, took virtually no interest in gymnastics. There were no colleges of physical training for men, in England, before the 1930s. But the women's colleges flourished from the start. In 1895, ten years after she had founded her college in London, Madame Österberg moved it out to a rural location at Dartford Heath. In 1897 a second college, Anstey, was launched in the Midlands by one of her students. In 1903 another former student started a similar college in Bedford. In 1905 a women's College of Hygiene and Physical Training was launched at Dunfermline by the Carnegie Trust, and one of Madame Österberg's students became its principal the following year. Two other colleges, Liverpool and Chelsea, made up the group of pioneers. Unlike the women pioneers in other fields of education, who had to seek the imprint of male authority, these were free to establish their own.

In 1899, impressed by the need to promote the interests of their new profession, a number of Madame Österberg's students founded the Ling Association. Much of its early work was concerned with defining standards and inspecting courses and in 1904 it assumed the role of an external examining body, awarding the Gymnastic Teacher's Diploma. In many other ways it was a key factor in fostering the growth of professional identity. Members from all the colleges took part in the Association's holiday courses, while its literature kept them abreast of every twist and turn in the engrossing business of interpreting the work of Ling. The Association was concerned as well with questions of salary and status, and these represent another important aspect of the female tradition. For Madame Bergman-Österberg, despite the fact that some of her utterances on Woman and The Race are reminiscent of Dr Kenealy, did not let concern for race regeneration lead her back into the mists of Victorian femininity. She was always very proud of having created a totally new profession for women. Looking back, towards the end of her life, she recalled that, through her efforts, 'a new profession, adequately remunerated, was . . . created for woman, *one of the few which she herself has initiated*'.[24] There is more than a touch of feminist pride in her declaration

> Let us once for all discard man as a physical trainer of woman. Let us send the drill sergeant right-about-face to his awkward squad. This work we women do better, as our very success in training depends upon our having felt like women, able to calculate the possibilities of our sex, knowing our weakness and our strength.[25]

The Gymnastic Teachers' Suffrage Society was established in 1909 and a gymnasts' contingent marched behind its banner in the great suffrage procession in London in the summer of 1911. Madame Österberg did not take part but her sympathy is not in question. Many years earlier she had gone on record as keen that women should have the vote. 'She is a warm supporter of her own sex,' wrote the *Woman's Herald* in 1891, 'and hopes to see all professions and trades open to women equally with men. She maintains that woman's *economical independence* will be of the very greatest importance in the question of her general emancipation.'[26] That the gymnast had a means to 'economical independence' gave her particular satisfaction.

By 1915, when Madame Österberg died, Ling had not only captured the girls' schools but the elementary schools as well. The therapeutic bias of the Swedish system strongly appealed to a Board of Education which, under its new Secretary, Robert Morant, saw the schools as crucial in the battle to check the nation's physical decline. It was Morant who introduced school medical inspection in 1907 and who brought in as the Board's first Medical Officer George Newman, a crusader for health. The Ling Association, which had always fought against military drill in the elementary schools, found itself pushing now against an open door. Newman appointed a woman inspector of physical instruction to his staff; physical training was made compulsory in the Elementary Teacher Training Colleges, and in 1909 the Board's new syllabus for physical training in the elementary schools was unequivocally Swedish in character. Well might the gymnasts, in the opening number of their *Journal of Scientific Physical Training*, affirm that the time was ripe 'to push forward those methods which have proved to be good in the educational service of the race'.[27]

The pioneers had become the establishment. During the war, and through the 1920s, they were in the van of Newman's efforts to raise physique in the elementary schools – as physical training organizers, inspectors, training college lecturers, remedial gymnasts in school clinics, and so on. The few men with comparable expertise acquired it abroad or in Scotland, at Dunfermline. No attempt in England to set up specialist courses for them achieved permanent success before 1930 when Carnegie College started a one-year course for men.[28] The women, meanwhile, had enlarged their course from two to three years in 1919, though the curriculum changed very little from what Madame Österberg had laid down: educational and remedial gymnastics; anatomy, physiology and hygiene; dancing; teaching practice; clinic work; games. The ethos, too, of the specialist colleges was very much what she had created. It was compounded of charismatic leadership (the other college principals were scarcely less powerful than Madame Bergman-Österberg herself), intensely hard work (some 44 hours a week, *excluding* private study and matches), formidable discipline, fierce criticism – plus the camaraderie of small institutions and a shared faith in the common goal. Did students really sign on for all this? Did they really come to these colleges committed to 'the educational service of the race'? The answer must be, probably not. There is certainly anecdotal evidence that some of them cared much more for games than for the niceties of Swedish gymnastics. They came to play cricket, hockey and lacrosse. The colleges were nurseries for internationals. None the less, the prevailing spirit was more the spirit of Ling than of Arnold. It was interventionist, even bossy. College students did not run their own games with the freedom allowed at the public schools,[29] and when they themselves went out as teachers it was part of their job to organize the games. In 1923 the official report on Differentiation of the Curriculum recommended that, in girls' schools, 'games should be left more to the girls themselves on the lines adopted in most boys' schools . . . games mistresses should not supervise girls' sports so much as at present' – a recommendation which the Board of Education singled out for emphatic approval.

The gym and games mistress continued, none the less, to occupy a role in girls' secondary schools which was *sui generis*; it had no parallel, and it was full of conflicting elements. On the one hand, she was a figure of authority. The gym mistress was the 'man' of the school, doing all the things which in a mixed society men would automatically have taken on. It was she who organized the children *en masse* – the movement of large numbers, in the daily routine, on special occasions and, of course, in emergency. If fire had broken out or a lunatic broken in, the odds are that it would have been the gym mistress, not the headmistress, who would have coped. The habit of authority came easily to her, for Ling's exercises were done to commands and 'commanding' was something she had learnt at college. The moral basis of her authority derived, though, from her own conviction of the value of what she was doing. 'The gymnastic mistress has so much influence that she should regard it as a sacred trust,' declared one doctor in the early 1920s;[30] and, broadly, she did so. That was the ideal set before her in the colleges. Harmonious bodily development and moral development went together; bodily discipline meant discipline in mind; and the gym mistress not only stood for the highest standards in physical attainment but for the highest standards generally. Many recollections of schooldays support this.[31]

This somewhat masculine authoritative role went along, though, with something much less imposing; more characteristic, one might say, of women than of men: the role of dogsbody. The gym mistress was frequently exploited, called on to perform a host of petty duties, from dealing with stationery and lost property to 'filling in' for any absent teacher. She might be the rock on which the whole school rested but she earned something like 20 per cent less than her graduate colleagues in the staffroom. The inter-war years saw the Ling Association fighting a long and unsuccessful battle to get gymnasts on to the graduate scale. But professional aggressiveness was sometimes at odds with attitudes which might well be called 'womanly'. 'A gymnast without a sense of vocation is a poor thing,' the *Journal* had written, when salaries were cut in the early 1920s, 'and while salaries wax and wane, those who have this precious gift can still put in their quota of work in raising the standard of national health, self-respect and conduct.'[32]

III

If the period between the wars was the heyday of the female tradition, there were signs none the less of some of those changes which eventually undermined it. One was implicit in the idea of 'secondary education for all', a yeast working slowly in the inter-war years but ultimately destined to transform a system dominated by the grammar schools. Another was the establishment at last of physical training colleges for men, and here an important difference must be noted. The men's colleges – Carnegie and Loughborough – offered not a three-year specialist course but a year of physical training to teachers who had already done their general training; and this broader approach was in line with the emerging official view that physical education should not be left entirely in the hands of narrow specialists.

By now, the kind of certainty that Madame Bergman-Österberg had felt about Ling was under challenge. 'Those engaged in physical training must . . . experiment with new methods to suit the altered conditions of life', a speaker at the Ling Association Conference had declared as early as 1921.[33] She went on to talk about the challenge presented by the work of Elli Björkstén, the Finnish gymnast who had drawn attention to the limitations of Ling's approach, with its impeccable knowledge of the body and almost total disregard of the mind. Gymnastic teachers should study psychology. They should use rhythm. They should even use music. 'The younger teachers,' it was admitted, 'certainly have not the same fixed idea of the incompatibilities of music and gymnastics which was held . . . some years ago.' The argument went on at conference after conference, those who called for change at pains to make clear that they were not *abandoning* the principles of Ling. Probably few could have foreseen, pre-war, how utterly these were to be rejected; still less, that deep disputes about the nature of their subject would arise between men and women, till the time came when it could be said that gymnastics meant different things in England 'according to the sex of the individual'.[34]

The change came indirectly; through dance. From the beginning dance had had its place in the curricula of the colleges, usually in the form of national dancing, folk dancing and ballroom dancing. The Modern Dance movement did not impinge upon this world until the 1930s when enthusiasts who had studied in Germany, where it developed through the influence of Laban, introduced their students to expressive movement. Rudolf Laban himself came to England as a refugee in 1938, to be welcomed by these pioneers; and in almost no time Modern Dance had become Modern Educational Dance. By 1948 when Laban's celebrated *Modern Educational Dance* was published, the Art of Movement Studio had been launched, with backing from the Ministry of Education, and teachers were queueing up to take its courses. In retrospect it is not surprising that a non-functional view of Movement, Movement as a means to 'body awareness', should have found response in the post-war world of child-centred education; nor that the metamorphosis of Dance should have put tremendous pressure on the line which separated Dance and Gymnastics.

The breaking of that line cannot easily be marked – it broke at different times in different places – but that moment around 1950 when a tutor at one college said to her Principal, 'I can't go on teaching "Arms Bend" any longer!' may be taken as representative.[35] She could not follow Laban's principles for Dance, helping every child to seek and develop her own movement potentiality, and then go and rap out commands in gymnastics. 'We no longer think of giving instruction,' that same tutor, Ruth Morrison, wrote later, 'we set out to provide the environment . . . and give the stimulus which will help the individual to grow and develop naturally.'[36] The idea of absolute standards of performance had become obsolete. 'We accept and welcome . . . individual differences, recognising in them a vast field of potential ability of every kind.' So the teacher would choose a movement theme and the children develop it themselves. As for apparatus, 'instead of teaching skills invented by Ling' the teacher would set problems, 'capable of many different solutions' and the children would solve them in their own way.[37]

It was probably this question of skills, more than anything, which caused the bitter split that developed now between those who favoured Movement and those who did not; between those who held that, with basic training geared to Laban's principles of Weight, Space and Time, specific skills could easily be learnt, and those who thought that such claims were nonsense. Broadly, the first group consisted of women and the second consisted of men.

In the 1940s when concepts of Movement began to be absorbed into physical education, many men were away in the army and subject to the very different experience of combat and commando training. After the war such experience was reflected in the development of physical activities which capitalized on an element of danger; physical education broke out of the gymnasium and took to the mountains and rivers, it was said. *In* the gymnasium, men became interested in extending the physiological approach. They became absorbed in measuring strength and stamina. They developed circuit training and other techniques for exploiting the principle of 'overload'. To many men, Movement was undermining 'the specifically physical and physiological aims of gymnastics';[38] while to many women it reflected values which they saw as integral to true education. 'There is a crying need . . . for people to co-operate, to work with respect for each other's qualities' wrote one Movement lecturer in 1970;[39] and certainly that kind of respect was fundamental to the concept of Movement.

The Movement/Anti-Movement battle raged, in a fashion, over 20 years. No other subject has been cleft ideologically as physical education was, along sex lines, and more could be said of this curious phenomenon. It concerns us here, though, as a manifestation of the rising influence of men, to which in the 1960s and 1970s various other factors contributed. One was the movement towards comprehensive schooling and co-education. The female tradition, firmly rooted in the girls' grammar schools, did not transplant well to a less sheltered environment. Other factors have been contingent on the development of higher education as a public service in the later twentieth century. It is strange to think now that a major influence in English physical education was exerted, till well beyond the Second World War, by a handful of autonomous, private colleges. By the early 1950s it had become clear that such colleges could not survive without support from local authorities, and one by one they were taken over. The implications of this change were far-reaching. For the public sector, as the colleges discovered, was a very variable creature over which they had no control. In the 1960s they were hugely inflated, like other colleges, to meet the teacher shortage; a decade later the balloon was let down. They, with others, were then merged and closed and engrossed into institutions with which they had no natural affinity till, like minor Soviet republics, they at length lost that sense of identity which had been a driving force.

Equally significant, one might say, was the fact that, over these years, they also lost control of their subject. We may recall that Madame Österberg had simply decided what that subject should be and then set out to sell the product. Later, seeking an acknowledged standard, the gymnasts had set up their Ling Diploma. Later still, in the 1930s, they succeeded in persuading London University to award an appropriate qualification, themselves effectively retaining control of it through the representation of college principals on the examiners' committee. When they came into the public sector, however, in the 1950s, they were brought in line with groups of other, general colleges for the award of the teacher's certificate, and had to share control of what that should constitute. In the 1960s, when survival depended on providing courses for a B.Ed. degree, they had to whistle whatever tune was acceptable to the awarding authority. And by the late 1970s, when survival depended on teacher training colleges showing their capacity to diversify beyond teacher training, they had to convince the CNAA – Council for National Academic Awards – that physical education was just as worthy *academically* as any other subject for a *BA* degree.[40] For better or worse, one effect of such pressure was to academicize beyond recognition what had started out as a practical thing; and another effect was to give the leadership to philosophers, and committees, and those who were pursuing higher degrees. Which brings us back to men, for more men than women were to be found in all such categories. And it was men who took the lead with physical education at the universities.

The demise of what I have called a female tradition is very much harder to define than its beginning. But some things are clear. If Madame Bergman-Österberg had returned in 1985 for the centenary celebrations of her own college (now in Thames Polytechnic) she would have found the physical education course had been terminated.[41] And if she had enquired about 'human movement studies' in what remains of the specialist colleges she would have found very few women in charge. For this there is no simple explanation. Their loss of influence has to be seen in the context of a range of educational and social developments over the past century. It raises some interesting questions, however, not least, how far their remarkable success should be regarded as a phenomenon of the old world of single women, single-sex education and 'separate spheres'. Professor Park has called the women's enclave which still exists in physical education in the USA a 'sheltered refuge' which its denizens would go to some lengths to defend.[42] Circumstances forced their English counterparts out of such an enclave – with results which seem to justify American fears. The implications of this, I suggest, extend far beyond the field of Physical Education to the whole question of the balance of influence between men and women in a mixed society.

NOTES

1. Quoted in D.D. Molyneux, 'Early Excursions by Birmingham Women into Games and Sports', *Physical Education*, LI (July 1959), 48.
2. Arabella Kenealy, *Feminism and Sex Extinction* (London, 1920), p. 139.
3. Arabella Kenealy, 'Woman as an Athlete: A Rejoinder', *Nineteenth Century*, XLV (June 1899), 927.
4. Jane Frances Dove, 'Cultivation of the Body', in Dorothea Beale *et al., Work and Play in Girls' Schools* (London, 1898), p. 402.
5. 'Games and Athletics in Secondary Schools for Girls' by Miss P. Lawrence, in *Special Reports on Educational Subjects* (London, 1898), II, p. 149.
6. Ibid., p. 156.
7. Eleanor Rathbone, 'Changes in Public Life', in Ray Strachey (ed.), *Our Freedom and its Results* (London, 1936), p. 57.
8. Dartford College Archives, (hereafter Dartford) M. Österberg, 'The Training of Teachers in Methods of Physical Education' (n.d.), p. 4. For a general account of Ling's work see Peter McIntosh, *Landmarks in the History of Physical Education* (London, 1957), and *Physical Education in England since 1800* (London, 1968); also Sheila Fletcher, *Women First: The Female Tradition in English Physical Education 1880–1980* (London, 1984).

9. For an account of Madame Österberg's career see Jonathan May, *Madame Bergman-Österberg* (London, 1969) and Sheila Fletcher, op. cit.
10. A.D. Munrow, 'Looking Back and Looking Forward in Gymnastics', *Physical Education*, XLVIII (March 1956), 18.
11. Royal Commission to Inquire into the working of the Elementary Education Acts in England and Wales (Parl. Papers 1887, XXX) Q 52,219.
12. Quoted in Ida M. Webb, 'Woman's Physical Education in Great Britain, 1800–1965' (unpublished M.Ed. thesis, University of Leicester, 1967), pp. 193–4.
13. See Sheila Fletcher, *Feminists and Bureaucrats: A Study in the Development of Girls' Education in the Nineteenth Century* (Cambridge, 1980).
14. Dartford, M. Österberg, 'The Physical Education of Girls in England' (c. 1913), pp. 4,5.
15. Uppingham and Loretto were exceptional among public schools in having gymnasia in the 1860s.
16. Dartford, M. Österberg, 'The Training of Teachers', p. 3.
17. Dartford, M. Österberg, 'The Physical Education of Girls in England' (1913), p. 7.
18. Baron Nils Posse, *The Special Kinesiology of Educational Gymnastics*, (Boston, 1903), p. vi.
19. Ibid. p.v.
20. Quoted, May, op. cit. p. 52.
21. Dartford, M. Österberg, 'The Training of Teachers', p. 1.
22. Ibid. p. 14.
23. Dartford, M. Österberg, 'Physical Education', p. 1.
24. Dartford, M. Österberg, 'The Physical Education of Girls in England', p. 5. (My italics.)
25. Dartford, M. Österberg, 'Physical Training as a Profession' (Women's International Congress, 1899), p. v.
26. *Woman's Herald*, 20 June 1891.
27. *Journal of Scientific Physical Training*, I (October 1908), 1.
28. The men's course at Dunfermline began in 1908. From 1908–12 a one-year men's course ran at the South Western Polytechnic. After the First World War a training course for men was launched at Sheffield, with an eye to the needs of the Day Continuation Schools, but it survived only till 1923.
29. While J.A. Mangan, *Athleticism in the Victorian and Edwardian Public School*, shows that this freedom, in origin at least, was sometimes more apparent than real, it did become deeply institutionalized.
30. H. Crichton-Miller, 'The Emotional Development of Boys and Girls', *Journal of Scientific Physical Training*, XIII (1920–21), 49–51.
31. See Fletcher, *Women First* pp. 79–81.
32. *Journal of School Hygiene and Physical Education*, XV (1922–3) 81.
33. *Journal of Scientific Physical Training* XIII (1920–21), 27.
34. Marjorie Randall, *Basic Movement* (London, 1961), p. 12.
35. Ruth Morison at I.M. Marsh College. The anecdote appears in Webb, op. cit., p. 374.
36. Ruth Morison, *Educational Gymnastics* (Liverpool, 1956).
37. Ibid.
38. Munrow, op. cit. p. 21.
39. Hilary Corlett, in *British Journal of Physical Education*, I (March 1970), 37.
40. For discussion of the effect of these changes see Fletcher, *Women First*, Chapters 7, 8.
41. The last students of the last intake finished in 1985–86.
42. Professor Roberta J. Park, 'Sport, Gender and Society: A Transatlantic Victorian Perspective' (lecture given at the annual conference of the British Society of Sports History, June/July 1984); see above, pp. 58–93.

PART THREE

COMMONWEALTH PERSPECTIVES

7

'One's Nerves and Courage are in Very Different Order out in New Zealand': Recreational and Sporting Opportunities for Women in a Remote Colonial Setting

Scott A.G.M. Crawford

Many observers of life in New Zealand have commented on the considerable place which sport fills in the public consciousness throughout all classes of society. In New Zealand's short history, New Zealanders have thought of themselves as belonging to a great sporting nation and a country devoted to sport, and these images have been important foundations for the development of national identity. Despite this, few scholars have attempted to study sport, and even in general histories of nineteenth-century New Zealand society little mention is made of either sport or recreation. Clearly then, to explore the notion of recreation and sport as potential avenues for achieving an emancipation of sorts for women in colonial New Zealand suffers from several weaknesses. There was no 'national history of sport' to use as a starting-point and archival primary source documents with an athletic flavour, such as records of Caledonian Societies, early rugby clubs and voluntary associations were, at least in their executive memberships, exclusively male.

Although New Zealand was exposed to the transplantation of British recreation and sport, the assimilation of this 'cultural baggage' was understandably shaped by the cultural values of the pioneer settlement. By the 1860s, the increasing levels of discretionary time and income created an expanding recreational consumer base which supported numerous projects in commercialized leisure. Recreational and sporting bureaucratic organizations, while modelled along British lines, reflected more of a frontier-style society. They were not dominated by the upper class, and drew support from all sectors of the community. Sporting success forged a national pride and placed athletics, not art, as the most valued form of cultural achievement.

The 'muscular Christianity' ethos influenced the leading schools, but the result was an emphasis on games-playing, rather than an embrace of a philosophy of moral education and character-training. The amateur ethos, while resistant to pressure, especially in the sphere of rugby, had an openness reflecting the egalitarian composition of much of society. New forms of technology affected society and shaped sport in terms of instrumentalization and rationalization. Increasingly, values were attached to achievement and high performance, and nowhere was this displayed with more assurance and excellence than on the rugby field. However, the less severe divisions of social class and the relatively spontaneous tenor of community life in New Zealand in contrast to Britain provided some opportunities for certain women to gain a degree of emancipation. Nevertheless, the paucity of reference sources on the 'invisible women' of the nineteenth century is a limiting factor. There were a lot of areas of activity where women were busy but which were not thought to be important, such as midwifery. In the 1940 *Dictionary of New Zealand Biography* only about two per cent of entries related to women.[1]

PIONEERING WOMEN

One fascinating collection of historical material is found, however, in the provincial museums of New Zealand. For the pioneering women settlers who migrated from Great Britain to New Zealand in the 1840s, 1850s and 1860s the three-month sea voyage provided an opportunity to compile diary accounts of sights, sounds, impressions, values and meanings. Jane Bannerman, a teenage cabin passenger on the *Philip Laing*, describes how she always had 'work': 'I sewed all the time and read instructive books. We had our piano in the cabin, and many were the songs we sang'.[2] She writes that her younger sister had rosy cheeks, loved to go running on the deck, was full of fun, and used to play for hours with her dolls and picture books.[3] Sarah Low found healthful recreation by sitting out on the open deck.

> I have been on deck (for the sake of air when I have been ill), that always proving my best medicine, no matter what weather, with no other female creature, and there, wrapped in some half a dozen coats and cloaks and lashed firmly to the side, seated on the ground, I have passed many hours. . . .[4]

Jane McGlashan, writing on the *Rajah* in 1853, noted:

> The day has been spent very pleasantly on deck. We, with our friends . . . form a sewing or knitting party while one reads aloud

. . . The elder Miss D. has been for several years on the Continent, and reads and speaks French fluently. We read French with her and have many conversations on manners and customs, persons and places abroad.[5]

In 1863 a Mrs Alexander described how there were 'games on deck'[6] by the light of the moon and confessed her enthusiasm for 'Scotch reels, country dances, quadrilles, polkas. . .'.[7] In 1868 Helen Ritchie, as the *William Davie* crossed the equator, observed that 'it is no easy work to dance reels in such warm weather'.[8] Two weeks later with the vessel moving towards southerly latitudes a diary entry spoke of the necessity for some form of exercise and concluded, 'The ladies have had a game of quoits today'.[9] The emigrant 'sailing' diaries are a most valuable primary source for the analysis of women and pioneering society. For example, they illustrate that there were approved parameters of behaviour which determined the socially accepted 'play opportunities' for both women and children, and the cathartic influence of recreation in a milieu that was essentially dominated by a male, utilitarian viewpoint.

A point to be emphasized, during the early years of settlement, is that in addition to episodic free time punctuating the working year, diversions of various sorts also seem to have penetrated or rather to have been a natural part of the work rhythm itself. Two sisters who settled in Otago as early as 1844 wrote in their diary of 'amusements', but in every case (gardening, fishing, boating and hunting) the activity was directly related to survival.[10] For the rural-agricultural-pastoral inhabitant, although recreation was dominated by work, it was possible to make games of some chores. Many women combined domestic duties with sewing, weaving, cooking and decorating that inserted a more creative element into their dawn-to-dusk work schedule. The frontier nature of colonial New Zealand life tended to avoid the rigid compartmentalization of women's roles that dominated English middle-class society in the nineteenth century. Catherine Squires described the fun and excitement of bareback horse riding (a most immodest activity for a genteel Englishwoman!) as she mustered cattle on a remote farm.[11]

As the process of industrialization in the 1860s began to make some impact on New Zealand society new doors were opened for colonial women. For example, the arrival of small steamships meant weekend recreation cruises took place from Dunedin and Wellington ports. This marks the first occasion that contemporary records indicate large numbers of women attending a formally organized recreational activity. 'The ladies sat in rows on the seats surrounding the quarter deck, very prim and nice and careful not to crease their dresses'.[12] Despite bouts of seasickness the women took a full part in enjoying the 'cake and wine' and dancing with 'energy which never flagged'.[13]

The Sunday church service, the market day and the sports meeting were the main avenues for facilitating social exchanges. In 1864 for example, the cricket team from Kaitangata embarked on the *Tuapeka*, called at Balclutha to collect the local team and then sailed up to Te Houka to play a game on a privately owned paddock in the company of sheep and cattle. Such occasions were much more than sporting encounters. Batting scores, bowling figures and the result paled into insignificance beside the vital functions of communal relaxation and convivial interaction: 'It was a real picnic, and the wives and children had a great time'.[14]

The lifestyle adopted by any settler in New Zealand depended upon the time and place of arrival, on income and occupation, and most unpredictably of all, upon the immigrant's readiness and capacity for adjustment. Adaptation of the imported heritage appears to have been most rapid and most thorough in every day matters. Dress and diet, housing styles and housekeeping methods, all soon reflected a distinctive colonial air. Attitudes and values were much slower to alter, the degree of adaptation depending upon the person's position in society. The higher up the social scale the less likely was significant change. Indeed, the most remarkable single document on recreation and sport in nineteenth-century New Zealand was a diary written by a Lady Barker on a South Canterbury sheep station. While the animated accounts of days full of physical activity are authentic, the attitude of Lady Barker and a handful of others like her was always that of being colonials. The colony was never regarded as home and their attitude 'perpetuated a sentimentalized version of the British way of life'.[15] In other words, their interests did not reflect a wider social trend of female involvement in outdoor activities. Nevertheless it is possible to argue that the scope of Lady Barker's physical pursuits and her enthusiastic embrace of recreational interests were the result of the attractive challenges of the New Zealand countryside. Although Lady Barker remained for only a few years in New Zealand (the late 1860s and early 1870s), her accounts of spending a freezing night by a creek catching eels, riding for 45 miles in a day over the roughest imaginable country, or tobogganing down a mountainside on an improvised sled, stand as a testament to a most unusual woman who was devoid of Victorian primness:

> . . . one's nerves and courage are in very different order out in

New Zealand to the low standard which rules for ladies in England, who 'live at home in ease!'[16]

In the 1860s and 1870s there are records of wives settled on isolated sheep stations who did not see another woman for months at a time. During the 'gold rush' period respectable women stayed away from the pubs known as 'sly-grog shanties'. In the Otago goldfields there were over 700 establishments, one to every 75 inhabitants.[17] The number of females on the Tuapeka goldfield in July 1862 was 150 while the male population numbered 11,500.[18] Many of the goldminers focused their attention on these pubs and hotels and sought the company of resident barmaids or dancing girls.[19] Hotel proprietors and entertainment entrepreneurs were constantly finding that female employees were eagerly sought, often as wives. One publican, determined to retain a barmaid, advertised to his friends in Dunedin to send him the ugliest woman they could find. 'Her single blessedness lasted two weeks.'[20] Fortunately, in 1871 an Act was passed prohibiting music and dancing in all public houses. The suppression of dance houses effectively reduced the number of bar girls being drawn into prostitution and virtually stopped the importation of a class of women designated dance-girls who were already convicted prostitutes.

Even by the late 1880s neither the bicycle nor the long swimsuit and hat had appreciably altered a restrictive social attitude towards female participation in sport and recreation. This did not merely apply to New Zealand – a similar situation existed in Britain and America. In fact, New Zealand women escaped the hostility that made Australian females ostracized by Victorian and Queensland swimming associations throughout the nineteenth century. However, the 1873 'Employment of Females Act' did give up the Saturday afternoon as a half-holiday to 'working girls' and allowed them at least an opportunity to ramble and picnic. Some of the earliest photographs of women in Otago (outside of the myriad staged head shots of family groups) show them in just such a milieu.

> A number of them [the working girls] turned their half holiday to good account by getting as much fresh air as they could, some of them taking walks, and others going down to the Port.[21]

For female students at the Otago Girls' High School (opened in 1871), however, there were a few opportunities for athletic endeavours. The original core curriculum set health and physical training as complementary activities to English, French, Linear Drawing, Needlework and so on.[22] The girls were able to have drill classes in the

Otago Boys' High School gymnasium, but Victorian morality decreed that a walled pathway be constructed so that the girls could reach the exercise area 'without the contamination of contact with, or sight of, the boys'.[23] A retired army sergeant spent much of the time parading the girls in army-style marching manoeuvres, and even the gym uniforms and knickerbockers had military braiding. While club exercises and apparatus work – climbing, swinging and vaulting – were also taught, Principal Burn found, in 1879, that less than 20 per cent of the girls were taking physical training as they found it dull and repetitive and the uniform an abomination.[24]

From the founding of the Dunedin Teachers' College in 1876 (originally housed in the Otago Normal School), military drill was taught to all student teachers. Moreover, Principal Frederick wanted the construction of a gymnasium and the services of a qualified gymnast, and in 1879 passed regulations preventing female trainee graduates from instructing drill in schools unless they themselves were of a satisfactory level of physical fitness.[25]

In pre-industrial England it has been claimed that single women held key positions in the work force – managing convents and large estates, and running inns, shops and small businesses.[26] But, by the middle of the nineteenth century, Victorian social ideology had defined unmarried women as 'superfluous' and 'redundant', and Victorian society had condemned spinsters to marginal positions in the home, church and workplace. The desperate shortage of raw labour, however, in pioneering New Zealand, combined with the meagre population base and a community rather than class consciousness led to the legitimization of women engaged in physical activity. Jobs had to be done, vegetable gardens had to be dug, sheep were to be mustered and a primitive landscape had to be farmed. Rural and agricultural settlements witnessed men and women, boys and girls buckling to as co-workers. In the literature that has been written about women during the 'pioneer' period words such as 'strength', 'courage' and 'determination' appear regularly. In Victorian England notions of femininity would not normally have included such characteristics.

AN EMANCIPATION OF SORTS

The 1880s in New Zealand witnessed the growing demand for the right of women and girls to unrestricted physical development and the beginnings of female participation in institutionalized forms of recreation. Certainly, sport and recreation were made incredibly difficult for women because of the long, bulky and restrictive nature of their clothes, and 'the attitude of a society where even an ankle could not be displayed in public'.[27] While women in the rural communities of Otago had always been able to enjoy horse-riding, dressed informally in work clothes, social custom demanded that attendance at hunt club meetings meant 'decent' attire.

> Ladies rode side-saddle and habits were shaped to allow for the protruding knee. Under the skirts they wore drawers of suede or other strong material. Jackets were usually tight-fitting and cravats, gloves, boots and hats completed the outfit.[28]

Daring young ladies did flout convention and risked the censure of society by wearing bloomers for bicycling following the example set by Amelia Bloomer in the USA in 1849. In fact a feminist group in Christchurch in the 1890s campaigned to reject the corset and urged women to wear a type of culotte.[29] The two leaders of this group, Miss K. Walker and Mr J.L. Wilkinson, advocated the divided skirt and baggy knickers and at their wedding saw to it that bride and bridesmaids wore the knickerbocker 'cycling' costume.[30]

Yet again the British influence was considerable. Once games were accepted as part of a girl's schooling in England during the 1870s, the social stigma was removed from participation in sport. Participation in cricket, athletics, curling, tennis and swimming was possible, although such involvement often went on in an atmosphere of 'amused tolerance'[31] created by patronizing males. Nevertheless, rigid Victorian thinking dictated that dress modes remained conservative.

> At first women were expected to cope with the physical activity in their usual heavy, concealing garments. In the seventies women played tennis in flannel quilted dresses, long of course, with an apron with a pocket to hold the balls, and a tweed cap of masculine appearance. In 1885 women still played in ankle-length skirts, teamed with high-necked blouses, belted waists and straw hats. At this time white stockings appeared for tennis.[32]

The Carisbrook Lawn Tennis Club of Dunedin in the 1880s became the first major sports club that recruited a significant number of female participants. Of 150 members, 60 were women. Indeed, the club went out of its way to attract lady members by means of a half a guinea annual subscription compared with a male's fee of one guinea. Nevertheless, in accordance with the prevailing societal attitude towards the role of women, it was made clear that 'the afternoons of Monday and Tuesday are the days when the ladies take their share in the game'.[33] The philosophy was affirmative to limited participation and negative to equal status.

Unquestionably the greatest opportunity for women, in seeking emancipation from their stereotyped roles, came with the advent of the safety bicycle in 1884. Hyslop, writing of Christchurch in the 1890s, recalls bands of 50 or more male and female cyclists off on a club run: 'Ladies rode in bloomers and men in knickers'.[34] The New Zealand Cyclist's Touring Club, founded in 1883, readily accepted female members and urged regional and urban clubs to actively recruit lady cyclists.[35] The bicycle gave females an inexpensive form of mobility and, in terms of revolutionary dress, allowed them to achieve their own identity as women.

> The effect of the bicycle on women's clothing was truly revolutionary – within a period of two or three years the bicycle gave . . . the liberty of dress which reformers have been seeking for generations.[36]

This rebellious attitude towards what was seen to be as appropriate dress for women was put to verse in an entry of *New Zealand Wheelman*:

> Come Dolly and Trix,
> Quick into your knicks.
> We'll off to the gorge and back . . .
> The neighbours may say
> 'How shocking!' but what care we?
> Our strong ripe joy, hath no alloy
> And the skirted may skirted be . . .
> Are we not God's children all?
> And what father ever meant
> That only his son should enjoy the fun
> While his daughter sat still content?[37]

Reeves claimed that the invention of the safety bicycle (1884) and the Dunlop pneumatic tyre (1888) did more to widen the daily lives of women 'than any change yet worked in them by the possessing of political rights'.[38] This is not to say that there was no entrenched opposition to this form of social innovation. The Woman's Rescue League of Washington, D.C., claimed that 'cycling prevented married women from having children, that the new dress was shocking and indecent, and that the new familiarity and companionship with men led to immorality'.[39] As late as 1903 in New Zealand, Helen Wilson commented upon the bicycling expedition that she made with her sister.

We made ourselves short, heavy serge skirts exactly alike and a navy and white blouse to be worn with a red tie and belt. We bought mushroom hats with red frills. The skirts were shockingly short; they came only just to the ankles, so of course it would be impossible to appear in civilised places, or even to stay with friends, without a change.[40]

The remarkable Mrs Wilson went off on her three-week long North Island tour leaving her husband to look after their three young children. On returning home she was faced by a mother who was 'shocked' by the 'barbarism' of her mode of travel, and a husband who 'didn't seem pleased with some of the details'.[41]

Helen Wilson was representative of a small group of women who found recreational participation helpful in breaking down the prejudices that categorized women as servers and home providers. Her activity interests made her both a friend and a companion to her husband. She speaks of tennis and river swimming with him, and gives a marvellous account of a duck shoot where she shot the birds, he stripped off and dived into the river to recover them while their young child wandered off to be rescued from 'twelve great Hereford bullocks'.[42] In 1896 she remarked that 'football became a fashion' and that she relished the joys of being 'a football fan' and the 'glories of a win'.[43] It has been noted that female interest in athletics was not considerable at Otago Girls' High School at the end of the 1870s. However, in 1885 Alexander Wilson became Headmaster and in a talk to the Otago Education Institute he described the values of 'body training' through the avenue of gymnastics.[44] Wilson played fives against female students with 'skill and cunning' and created a much more positive attitude towards physical activities. His encouragement of sporting activity can be best gauged by the account of his first prizegiving in 1885, when two prizes were awarded for tennis, six for fives, and seven for gymnastics.[45]

From 1880 onwards there was the emergence of 'a progressive spirit among some women'[46] in recreational matters, although there were rigid lines of demarcation preventing women from achieving athletic parity. For example, in 1891 when Miss Nita Webbe attempted to become the promoter and manageress of a women's rugby team to tour New Zealand the public roar of outrage was such that the project was scrapped.[47] For many women in colonial New Zealand recreational forms were more cerebral that athletic. The private scrapbook of Mrs Janet McLaren, compiled from 1884 to 1887, had 110 pages with 375 press clippings. Of these clippings 86 were poems cut out from Otago newspapers followed by English-based long newspaper essays on European history. Mrs McLaren idolized Queen Victoria and General Gordon and, for her, 'recreation' was reading the newspapers, learning poems and writing her own verse and putting together, with loving care, a beautifully bound scrapbook.[48] The puritan ethic and the Christian concept of the family had a strong impact on the expected role of women. Morality at home would stem from women who had found their true vocation as 'wives, mothers, homemakers, nation builders and moral arbiters'.[49]

While references to women as participants in New Zealand sport and recreation during the period 1848–1907 are limited, it seems clear that the subsequent years, 1907–20, would yield a rich body of information on the expansion, in New Zealand, of female involvement in physical activity.

> Sport, for so long an outpost of male chauvinism, a symbol of masculinity, was by the 1880s beginning to be infiltrated by the Englishwoman who was gradually freeing herself from the bounds of the Victorian drawing room. The sports and past-times which these women adopted were, in line with the colonial process, transported to New Zealand to take firm root.[50]

The 1870s in England marked the high point in Victorian ornamentation whether reflected in house embellishment or exuberant costume design. Elaborate flounces, aprons, looped-up skirts and tunics were at the height of fashion. Sport, it is argued, became increasingly popular among women and did much to rationalize dress. Nevertheless, the bathing dresses and tennis frocks of the last decade of the nineteenth century still allowed only a moderate degree of freedom in movement. Swimming dresses were made of seven yards of twilled flannel with long sleeves and a high neck. The aim was to cover not reveal.[51] The standard tennis outfit of a long quilted, blue flannel dress rounded off with a tweed cap emphasized good taste and style rather than granting freedom of movement over a grass playing-surface.

The woman of the time was heaped high with impedimenta. Costume designers and outfitters used a language and terminology that is now redundant; it was the day of the Dolman, the mantle, the ulster; of jet, ribbon, and passementerie trimming. Within New Zealand many women displayed a pronounced ambivalence towards the introduction and acceptance of imported fashion. On the one hand they did not want to display a colonial provincialism and unsophisticated parochialism. Indeed in some communities (the 'gentry' of Canterbury?) it may be that they sought to outdo the most fashionably dressed ladies of Regent's Park, London! However, a major hypothesis of this chapter is that in New Zealand many women were working alongside their husbands, brothers and neighbours to break in the country. For these women there was plenty to do in a practical way. Members of societies attribute certain characteristics to the individuals of the different sexes. Nevertheless the situation in Victorian New Zealand shaped a process of gender socialization where certain women worked with men. The primary sources of information reinforce a picture of an absence of that feeling of antagonism to the environment or to the opposite sex which characterized English society of the day.

The influence of the 'Cult of True Womanhood'[52] should not be underestimated. The colony's Church of Scotland ministers, Church of England clergy and Methodist preachers reflected an American and British concern to see women as 'revered and admired but locked into hoop skirts and home'.[53] While such an ethos permeated the respectable suburbs of Christchurch and the social network of the Governor General's activities in the capital of Wellington, it had neither credibility nor relevance for the demands of life in the isolated townships, hamlets and sheep stations.

CONCLUSION

The short, loosely fitting gymnastic tunic worn by girl students at Otago High School in the 1880s 'personified the spirit of emancipation of women who were beginning to break free of some of the more restrictive elements of the Victorian code of behaviour and morality'.[54] In a 1891 New Zealand magazine, a high school student confided to her father that the thing she wanted to do most was to go to an out-of-the-way place and paddle about without shoes or stockings.[55] Nevertheless, despite women voting for the first time in 1893, the formation of the National Council of Women in 1896 and Emily Siedeberg graduating, in the same year, as the country's first female physician, there were still barriers. For climber Freda de Faur, the physical challenges were compounded by the cherished conventions of the middle-aged who railed at her for being alone with a guide, as it would ruin her 'reputation'.[56] However, as her climbing reputation grew she was more free to do as she pleased without protest from the self-appointed guardians of private morals at the Hermitage Hotel. Miss de Faur would leave the Hermitage in a 'proper skirt' but discard it as soon as she was out of range of the tourists to climb in a serge jacket, a knee-length skirt, knickerbockers, puttees and clinker boots.

Women like Freda de Faur were controversial figures because by their personality and physical vitality they ran counter to the 'biomedical thought of the mid-nineteenth century [which] both reflected and encouraged women's passive role in society'.[57] The theory of the 'dictatorship of the ovaries' reasoned that through her inherent fragility and weakness a woman should be 'prevented from doing anything that might cause damage to her delicate reproductive system'.[58] Lady Barker and Freda de Faur, though by education and, social background representatives of the upper class, were *not* primarily involved in the 'croquet, bowling, tennis, golf, and archery . . . of coeducational recreation, which were designed more for social contact than for competition'.[59] They sought competitive challenges outdoors with, against *and* without men and, by example, became a part of an international move towards the acceptance of a new view, that exercise was indeed good for women.

Photographs of Miss de Faur show her as lithe and fit, looking more in the 1980s ideal of female attractiveness as an adjunct to an athletic shape. It should be remembered that with Victorian fashion the woman was ethereal and emaciated, with a heightened bust to set off the ankle and the features of the face. For some women in pursuit of the hourglass figure of a Lillie Langtry, fasting, whalebone corsets and even surgical removal of the lower ribs were acceptable. This societal notion of the perfect body, then, played its part in steering women away from vigorous activities such as running. However, it should be emphasized that social pressure clearly discriminated against women. A Canadian observer, in 1890, while patronizingly declaring that women could swim, dance and ride affirmed that as for running 'nature most surely did not construct her'.[60] Women did participate in bicycling, roller skating and tennis. On the tennis court or the open road there was a physical liberation of sorts. There is the impression that for the colonial girl a multiplicity of roles while not encouraged were accepted, albeit in an atmosphere of patronizing good humour. A fascinating photographic profile of a 'Maid of Maoriland', published in 1901, epitomizes this glimpse of the greater freedom that seems to have been afforded the young female in New Zealand. The eight snapshots show a woman in her early twenties in a series of different poses – milking a cow; riding a horse; cooking; washing clothes; arranging flowers; playing tennis; painting (or sketching) in the outdoors; getting into a canoe; standing with a bicycle. The captions were in verse:

> What is there that she cannot do,
> The sweet New Zealand girl?

> She's milkmaid, cook, and groom in one . . .
> And after dinner, on the lawn
> She'll beat you four to love.
> What charming metamorphoses,
> This girl goes daily through –
> From washing tub to bicycle,
> From easel to canoe.[61]

With such a regime of life-style interests and occupations it is no wonder that firms targeted their advertising towards women such as the 'Maid of Maoriland' or Helen Wilson. In 1907 a Fry's cocoa slogan stated that, 'The Outdoor Girl, the Athletic Girl, aye, every Girl who aspires to a healthy vigorous body should drink. . .'.[62]

From the beginnings of organized sports competitions early in the nineteenth century, sport has determined that men behave in one way and women another. Sports fields, and in New Zealand society even more so the sports club, were an influential adjunct to the workplace and home in the ascription and acceptance of male–female relations. In late nineteenth-century New Zealand, as elsewhere, women were kept from involvement in all leisure which did not serve their basic functions of motherhood and providing the basis for stable families. Marriage in New Zealand was the main occupation of women. However, the colonial environment opened new doors. The census of 1874 showed 245 women running medium to large farms.[63] There was:

> . . . a feeling of usefulness and a greater degree of independence than the women migrants had experienced before. To reach the same end in England they would have had to break out of the shell of home and family and emerge into the world a rebel against position and role.[64]

Although New Zealand did not witness the emergence of a Florence Nightingale, a George Eliot or a Harriet Beecher Stowe (all to a greater or lesser extent involved in the controversial interpretation of moral dilemmas) there were other landmarks to be set by colonial women. New Zealand female social reformers could not change the world but had the spiritual and physical resources to achieve voting parity. These women knew themselves to be 'useful'. They had nourished a pioneering settlement not by passivity, expressiveness and dependence, but with a generous sprinkling of instrumental qualities.

In 1893 New Zealand became the first national state in the world to allow women to vote,[65] the result of the outcome of a feminist movement comparable with movements elsewhere in the world and more effective in terms of legislative change. However, while women in the USA emerged as persuasive political levers via the abolitionist movement, in New Zealand women came to the fore because of learning how to organize themselves and adopting a new outlook on their basic rights in the sphere of temperance. Through the temperance movement there was 'an apprenticeship in the art of political agitation'.[66] This political concern for women's voting rights was not translated into a movement for equal representation in sport. Although the first national women's sports association was founded in 1908,[67] before the 1914–18 war there was only one national championship event for women.[68] Nevertheless, this particular championship, for tennis, was founded as early as 1886 and provided New Zealand with its first female sports star. Miss K.M. Nunneley won the ladies' national tennis title on 13 consecutive occasions from 1895 to 1907.

In colonial New Zealand almost exclusively within the umbrella of home, family and property, there were significant opportunities for a degree of recreational freedom unknown in the motherland. Sporting associations, on the other hand, following the conservative restrictions of male-dominated athletic clubs throughout the British Empire, allowed only limited access to women in activities such as tennis, golf, bicycling and swimming, as well as rambling, tramping and curling. Yet again, the potential opportunities for women in colonial New Zealand have to be stressed. The founding of the YWCA in 1878 represented the first branch of this now very large international body to be formed in the southern hemisphere.[69] By the end of the 1880s over 300 members enjoyed lectures, craft activities and 'every kind of sport'.[70] Recreation and sports provided some opportunities for certain women to gain, if not a degree of emancipation, then an expansion of freedom, choice and physical pleasure within colonial New Zealand.[71] The spirit of independence fostered by a favourable employment market encouraged equality rather than servility in master/servant relationships. Even the best-treated servants would leave for a better place or to get married and be mistress of their own homes.

In the 60 or so years under study the nature of recreation and sport in New Zealand changed dramatically. For the early settlers recreational pursuits were few and far between with the effort of establishing a new home being of fundamental importance. It should be emphasized, however, that this process allowed men and women to work together as partners and combine physical resources to overcome challenges and realize long term objectives.[72] On a surprising number of expeditions into mountainous areas by government survey workers wives, sisters and their female friends accompanied the 'work' party.[73] Leisure activities in pioneering society were spontaneous affairs in which everyone joined with great enthusiasm and informality. As communities became more established there was more time, energy and opportunity to formalize recreational exchanges. Sport became a regular part of community life and was organized into a complex network of institutions throughout the colony.

While rugby as a patriarchal institution dominated the social and cultural side of life and served as a singular *rite de passage*, in the early 1900s women's sport also experienced a major breakthrough with field hockey growing from one club in 1897 to ten regional associations becoming affiliated to the newly formed New Zealand Women's Hockey Association in 1908. The feminine ideal in the late nineteenth and early twentieth century carried with it the acceptance of a philosophy of legitimate and illegitimate activity. Gentleness, not aggression, co-operation, not competition and graceful movement, not the vigorous play of muscles, were the rubric. Legitimate activity within New Zealand included many of the genteel and leisured sports. Golf, tennis, swimming, recreational horseback riding, curling and skating were accepted in a single sex and mixed setting. What was unusual is that the contact-sport competition of women's field hockey was not considered inappropriate for women. It came to enjoy great popularity not only at the girls' schools but by the first World War was the major female club/team sport in the rural villages of New Zealand. In the 1980s field hockey and netball are the two leading women's sports, and New Zealand's world number one ranking in netball reflects female commitment to tough competition. There is much evidence that the 'cultural image of women rather than physical limitations . . . [have] made women's participation in sport limited and unequal'.[74] The New Zealand culture has always been wholly accepting of sport *per se* and the level of structural discrimination in the twentieth century has never been such that it has blocked off feminine involvement or resulted in their unequal treatment. What is noteworthy today is the extent of gender role changes whereby several rugby administrators are female and women in increasingly large numbers are coaching boys' and men's sports teams.

Women in colonial New Zealand did not have the variety of recreational options available in the 'motherland'.[75] Nevertheless, there was a social climate of acceptance if not for the female athlete then certainly for the woman eager to enjoy the fun and freedom of recreational activities.[76] Some oral history data of the early 1900s re-affirm a social ideology where many facets of sport and recreation were seen to be appropriate and legitimate for women. The following are three separate female interviews: 'I was brought up in the country, on a farm. At school . . . the girls used to play with the boys – they played football, and we played cricket with them'; 'I guess I was a bit of a fitness fanatic! I played 'A' grade tennis. . . . I also played a little bit of golf. I loved rollerskating. . . . Every winter I would go skating. . . .'; 'At primary school there was hockey for the girls and rugby for the boys – there was lots of pleasure in sport. My parents' attitude was that they believed in us playing sport and enjoying ourselves. We were kept happy.'[77] On the fringe of the British Empire sport and recreation may have opened fresh doors for women. A writer in a 1895 New Zealand bicycling magazine spoke of the 'new woman': 'A being of cool brain, warm heart, courage and strong muscle'.[78]

NOTES

This chapter is an extended version of a paper, 'An Emancipation of Sorts: Recreational and Sporting Opportunities for Women in Nineteenth Century Colonial New Zealand', that appeared in the *Canadian Journal of History of Sport*, Vol. XVI, No. 1, May 1985, pp. 38–56.

   To gain an unusual and fascinating treatment of women's opportunities for 'liberation' in the middle of the twentieth century see E. Ebbett, *When the Boys were Away: New Zealand Women in World War II* (Wellington, 1985). Since actual hostilities occurred well away from New Zealand, the impact of the war on most women was second-hand and probably greatest on young women of an age to have husbands serving in the forces, or to join up themselves; to be man-powered or to tackle jobs hitherto reserved for men; to fall in love with American servicemen. Ebbett's book builds up a vivid picture of the bleakness, the irritations and inconveniences of the war period and the new employment opportunities it opened for women leading to a new spirit of independence. Future social historians must examine the extent to which these new opportunities occurred in the sporting and recreational domain.

   Indications show that many experiences of sportswomen in contemporary New Zealand are common to other countries, suggesting that universal experiences of women are more strongly reflected in the institutions of sport and leisure than are cultural differences. See S.M. Thompson, 'Women in Sport: Some Participation Patterns in New Zealand', a paper presented at the Leisure Studies Association International Conference, Sussex University, England, 1984.

1. G.H. Scholefield (ed.), *A Dictionary of New Zealand Biography* (Wellington, 1940), 2 vols. At the time of writing the new *Dictionary of New Zealand Biography* was being compiled with the firm intention by the editorial staff of redressing the imbalance of male over female. There were special problems in finding nineteenth-century women the working parties drawing up prospective biography entries considered suitable. The women did not seem significant in the way men were in their contribution to the making of New Zealand. They were not whalers or sealers or explorers, they were not usually runholders or farmers in their own right, or big businessmen or members of the professions or the colonial intelligentsia. Moreover, women somehow seemed to leave fewer records than men on which to base their biographies – fewer mentions in newspapers, for example. And many, perhaps most, nineteenth-century women believed that their sphere of influence was personal, domestic rather than public. D.P. Page, 'Finding Our Lost Foremothers', Otago University Radio Cassette – first broadcast 10 April 1985.

In the Making of New Zealand series (also published in 1940) of 30 volumes not one is devoted to women. In the volume devoted to 'Dress', of 15 sub-sections 11 predominantly are devoted to male dress attire, manners, fashions and so on. The most recent New Zealand reference source supports the view on the dearth of useful material and has no sections on either sport or recreation. P.A. Sargison, *Victoria's Furthest Daughters – A Bibliography of Published Sources for the Study of Women in New Zealand 1830–1914* (Wellington, 1984).

2. J. Bannerman, unpublished diary, 1849, p. 71, Otago Early Settlers' Museum (hereafter OESM), Dunedin.
3. Ibid.
4. Letters of Sarah Low, unpublished material, 1849, OESM, p. XV.
5. J. McGlashan, unpublished diary, 1853, OESM, entry of 11 July.
6. Mrs Alexander, unpublished diary, 1863, OESM, entry of 19 September.
7. Ibid., entry of 21 September.
8. H. Ritchie, unpublished diary, 1868, OESM, entry of 28 August.
9. Ibid., entry of 11 September. For a detailed classification of ship recreations see, S.A.G.M. Crawford, 'Recreation at Sea: Leisure Pursuits on the Otago (New Zealand) Bound Emigrant Ships 1847–1869', *International Journal of the Society for Nautical Research (Mariner's Mirror)*, (1986).
10. I. Anderson and J. McKay, *Tales of Pioneer Women* (Christchurch, 1940), p. 268. The Short sisters of Bannockburn describe 'school-days' in the 1880s beginning with a 5.00 a.m. start cutting lucerne fields. *Cromwellian* (Magazine of Cromwell District High School, 1977), 8.
11. C. Squires, unpublished diary, 1859, OESM p. 17. For young children the tendency was to enjoy 'adventures offered by the natural environment, rather than playing traditional games'. B. Sutton-Smith, *The Folk Games of Children* (Los Angeles, 1959), p. 1.
12. *Otago Witness*, November 1860.
13. Ibid.
14. F. White, *Pioneering in South Otago* (Christchurch, 1958), p. 150.
15. Graham, 'Settler Society'. In, W.H. Oliver and R. Williams (eds.), *The Oxford History of New Zealand* (Wellington, 1981), p. 133.
16. Lady Barker, *Station Amusements in New Zealand* (London, 1873), p. 74. There is scarcely a recreation or sport that Lady Barker does not attempt to master. 'I do not believe that even in Canada the skating can be better than that which was within our reach in the Malvern Hills [Of New Zealand]', p. 58.
17. F.W. Craddock, *Golden Canyon* (Christchurch 1973), p. 52.
18. Ibid., p. 54.
19. Ibid.
20. Ibid., pp. 55–6.
21. *Otago Daily Times*, 13 October 1873.
22. E. Wallis, *A Most Rare Vision* (Dunedin, 1972), p. 19.
23. Ibid., p. 32.
24. Ibid.
25. C.M. Johnstone and H. Morton, *Dunedin Teachers' College* (Dunedin, 1976), p. 32.
26. M. Vicinus, *Independent Women: Work and the Community for Single Women, 1850–1920* (Chicago, 1985).
27. E. Ebbett, *In True Colonial Fashion* (Wellington, 1977), p. 65.
28. Ibid., p. 67.
29. Ibid., p. 65.
30. P. Grimshaw, *Woman's Suffrage in New Zealand* (Auckland, 1972), p. 10.
31. Ibid., p. 9. One feminist sees the pattern of modern sport in Britain stemming from its dual origins – the Public School cult of 'muscular Christianity' and the Industrial Revolution. So, it is argued, in common with other institutions sport 'was developed for men, and by men'. J. Graydon, 'But it's more than a game. It's an institution! Feminist Perspectives on Sport'. *Feminist Review*, 13 (1983), 7–8. Again, for New Zealand, the 'muscular Christianity' impact popularized games playing but played down the

masculine and moral nature of sport. Secondly, industrialization in New Zealand never assumed the magnitude of the English model. In colonial New Zealand recreation and sport never became a 'self-indulgent festival of masculinity'. One anecdote of the 1890s recalls a young girl's primary school sport. Organized coeducational sports took part daily, with boys and girls combining in rounders and in a non-tackle 'tag' type of rugby football. See, E. Hosken, *Turn Back the Clock* (Wellington, 1968), p. 44.

32. Ebbett, op. cit., p. 69.

33. J. Bathgate, *An Illustrated Guide to Dunedin* (Dunedin, 1883), p. 35.

34. W.E. Hyslop, *Bill Hyslop Remembers: The Autobiography of a Motorist from Horse and Buggy and Bicycle Days* (Hastings, 1968), p. 8.

35. See various issues of *New Zealand Wheelman*, 1894–1896. One writer claims that the Atlanta Ladies Cycling Club, established in Christchurch in 1892, was the first women's cycling club in the world. J.A. Wood, *Victorian New Zealand* (Christchurch, 1974), p. 70.

36. S.H.Aronson, 'The Sociology of the Bicycle', in T.E. Lasswell *et al.* (eds.), *Life in Society* (Chicago, 1965), p. 62.

37. *New Zealand Wheelman*, 3: 49 (28 November 1894).

38. W.P. Reeves, *State Experiments in Australia and New Zealand* (London, 1902), Vol. 1, p. 137.

39. Aronson, op cit., p. 62.

40. H. Wilson, *My First Eighty Years* (Hamilton, 1951), p. 154.

41. Ibid., p. 158.

42. Ibid., p. 137.

43. Ibid., p. 150.

44. Wallis, *Rare Vision*, p. 42. Twenty years later the Morris sisters in Australia, despite a conservative education scene, established physical education as an essential component in all-around education. R. Crawford, 'The Morris Sisters of Melbourne Girls' Grammar School: 1898–1913' (paper presented at the VII Commonwealth and International Conference, Brisbane, September 1982). In rural New Zealand, diet, climate and the physical nature of the life-style meant that girls in the primary schools were encouraged to throw themselves into games – 'romping in all the bounding vigour of perfect health'. *Cromwell Argus*, 2 November 1870.

45. Ibid., p. 43. Wilson popularized active outdoor exercise and ordered the school grounds to remain open one hour after school so that the girls might play longer. *Principal's Annual Report and Prospectus*, 1885, p. 6. From 1885–1891, in his annual school reports, Wilson always made some encouraging remark about the importance of physical education. *Principal's Annual Report Prospectus*, 1886–1891.

46. R. Bushby and I. Jobling, 'Decades of Sport and the Shape of Australian Womanhood' (paper presented at the First National Conference on Women, Sport and Physical Recreation, University of NSW, Sydney, January 1980), p. 7. Golf, by the turn of the century, rivalled the impact of the bicycle on women. Golf reaffirmed, not rejected, the expected role of women to be fashionably present. So the golfing cape, flowing skirt, and designer hat made golf an 'accepted' activity for women. Thus the official bulletin of the United States Golf Association (December 1899) had a frontispiece depicting a chic female dressed in the height of fashion – for golf! Pears, the English soap company, in their first 'recreational' advertisement using women, showed a beautifully attired lady golfer saying 'After a royal game use soap of equal fame'. See C. Price, *The World of Golf* (London, 1963), pp. 86 and 122.

47. Grimshaw, *op. cit.*, p. 10.

48. Survey of the Janet McLaren scrapbooks and an interview with her great-granddaughter, Elizabeth Lumb, in Dunedin, November 1977. Contemporary research on romance writing and reading points to possible reasons why women like McLaren projected themselves into fiction and identified with historical characters. A substitute for the 'nurturance' women were denied in a patriarchal and Calvinistic New Zealand? See the critique of Ms Radway's recent book *Reading the Romance*. B. Yagoda's feature on 'Scholarship', *Chronicle of Higher Education*, 22 May 1985, 5 and 8.

49. A.R. Grigg, 'Shaping a Social Ideology – Puritanism' (three parts) Radio New Zealand, 14 October 1982. The physical and emotional demands of carrying out these differing roles must have been considerable. 'The energy, endurance and adventurousness of most women was satisfied by the conditions of their daily lives.' H.M. Simpson, *The Women of New Zealand* (London, 1962), p. 143. 'Manliness and womanliness remained very different concepts'. K.E. McCrone, 'Play Up! Play Up! And Play the Game! Sport at the Late Victorian Girls' Public School', *Journal of British Studies*, XXIII, 2 (1984), 127. This excellent 28 page paper represents a most useful, concise inter-disciplinary analysis of women, sport and Victorian society (see above, pp. 97–129).

50. J. Barclay, 'An Analysis of Trends in New Zealand Sport, from 1840 to 1900' (unpublished B.A. thesis, Massey University, 1977), p. 57. The influence of scouting was to see the publications in 1908 of *Peace Scouting for Girls* with sections on hiking, tent-pitching, tracking, knotting, signalling and self-defence. However, society at large was reluctant to accept equal sports provision for boys and girls at school. In 1912 the School Board (responsible for fiscal policy at the Otago Girls' High School and the Otago Boys' High School) turned down a request for £5 to rent a hockey ground, but approved a much larger amount to be used for the boys' sport fund. *Otago Girls' High School Magazine*, 1912, 30. However, in the early 1900s a female hockey coach was added to the faculty and various girls' teams took part in local competitions. Wallis, *op. cit.*, p. 64. The six-part 1983 New Zealand Television Series, *Pioneering Women*, while not devoted to women and sport, explored the theme that it may well have been the pioneer women, rather than the men who determined who we are. Certainly women at the turn of the century were the educators and keepers of morals. In terms of a moral and attitudinal climate they had an enormously strong influence on the New Zealand character. For example, Ettie Rout (1877–1936), a feminist and socialist, had views on health and exercise far advanced for her time and spoke out against the pollution of the rivers. Nurse Sibylla Maude (1862–1935) advocated outdoors camps for tuber-culosis patients and founded the District Nursing Association in 1896. She and her younger nursing recruits were able to reach the far-flung suburbs in Christchurch by bicycle.

51. Societal values and cultural mores were to change in New Zealand. A caption from a post First World War beach comic strip read: He: 'Phil is only here to show her new costume'. She: 'Looks as if the costume is only here to show Phil'. *New Zealand Sporting and Dramatic Review*, 11 February 1926. By the 1930s a survey of the articles in the *New Zealand Woman's Weekly* found that several advocated 'all over' tanning and that 'sun oils' were advertised with swimsuits being 'so brief' and the sun so 'tempting'. G.R. Rowlands, 'Advertising and Commercial Promotion of Sport in New Zealand: 1880–1939' (research essay, Faculty of Physical Education, Otago University, 1985).

52. P.J. Murphy, 'Sport and Gender' in W.M. Leonard, *A Sociological Perspective of Sport* (Minneapolis, 1984), p. 189.

53. Ibid.

54. C. Crunden, 'The Care of the Body in the late 19th and 20th Centuries in England', *Bulletin of Physical Education*, XI: 1, (1975). In March 1884 the publisher of a new magazine on recreation and sport announced that there would be regular contributions by a female athlete. *The Athlete and New Zealand Exchange and Mart*, 28 March 1884, 2.

55. Ebbett, op. cit., p. 65. The reduced levels of social restriction in colonial New Zealand allowed women to row competitively – such an event at England's Henley Regatta would have been unthinkable. See, for example, an inter-provincial race between Auckland and Taranaki women's crews. *New Zealand Herald*, 19 April 1897.

56. F. de Faur, *The Conquest of Mount Cook* (Christchurch, 1977), p. 36. A recent study makes the points that a) de Faur was one of a number of female mountaineers in New Zealand; b) mountaineering was a catalyst in the emancipation of women; c) mountaineering costumes and new climbing techniques were an avenue of self-expression for women; d) sex role stereotypes were eroded by the rigours of climbing and the necessities for 'team co-operation'. P. Lynch, 'A History of Women

Mountaineers in Victorian New Zealand' (special study, Faculty of Physical Education, Otago University, 1985).
57. Murphy, op. cit., p. 189.
58. Ibid.
59. Ibid., p. 194.
60. J. Cochrane, A. Hoffman and P. Kincaid, *Women in Canadian Life-Sports* (Toronto, 1977), p. 17. In Wellington at Te Aro baths there was still segregated swimming in the 1890s. 'The hours for ladies were from 9 am to 2 pm and for gentlemen, a red flag was hoisted, and a blue flag for the ladies.' L. Ward, *Early Wellington* (Wellington, 1928), p. 282. The sporting ethos of the period was built upon appropriate role behaviour. 'Sport for boys was to teach them spirit, leadership, loyalty and how to take the initiative in life. Since women were destined only for home life, sport for them could only be seen as of secondary importance, at the most a means by which they could keep physically healthy, with the right proportions.' H. King, 'The Sexual Politics of Sport: An Australian Perspective', in R. Cashman and M. McKernan (eds.), *Sport in History* (St Lucia, 1979), p. 72. In other words it was appropriate role behaviour to *support* the male. For example, in tennis mixed doubles a female writer observed, 'Ladies should try to improve their play and not spoil the sport for men, as they too frequently do'. K. Dodd, 'Ladies' Lawn Tennis' in Duke of Beauford (ed.), *The Badminton Library Tennis, Lawn Tennis, Rackets, Fives*, (London, 4th Edn. 1897), p. 314. Nevertheless, within rural New Zealand, there were very real opportunities for outdoor recreation with the nature of pastoral life. One lady recalled in 1900: 'I used to go riding with my uncle every day, well before I was five years old. I'd stand on the back of his saddle with my arms around his neck; I'd even canter with him like that'. C. Hunt, *Something in the Hills – Yesterday in Central Otago*, (Wellington, 1979), p. 132. By the 1920s there was encouragement for women to exercise. ' . . . too often in their zeal and love of their work, they (women) forgot the recreation, the physical recreation that alone can keep old age at bay and retain a natural vitality and beauty and that only comes from wholesome exercise in the open air.' *Otago Witness*, 20 July 1920. This was but part of the gradual movement within society for women's rights. By l914, women had become an essential and sometimes respected part of the workforce.
61. *New Zealand Graphic* (Christmas Issue), 1901.
62. Ibid., (Christmas Issue), 1907. How women have been athletically portrayed in the sphere of commercial advertising warrants sociological investigation. By the mid-1930s: ' . . . Ascot, Goodwood, Cowes and Wimbledon, wherever the sport-loving British girl is to be found, Yardley Lavender greets you'. *New Zealand Woman's Weekly*, 19 November 1936. The advertising promotional campaign that tied into the exploits of New Zealand aviatrix Jean Batten is intriguing: a woman flying in an age of male folk heroes from Charles Lindbergh to Antoine de Saint Exupéry.
63. R. Dalziel, 'The Colonial Helpmeet: Women's Role and the Vote in the Nineteenth Century New Zealand' *New Zealand Journal of History*, 11: 2, (1977), 116. The notion of the colonial environment opening new doors *vis à vis* the inter-relationship of sport, class and community has been looked at. See S.A.G.M.Crawford, 'Muscles and character are there the first object of necessity': An Overview of Sport and Recreation in a Colonial Setting – Otago, Province, New Zealand', *British Journal of Sports History*, 2: 2 (1985), 109–126.
64. Ibid., p. 115.
65. It should be noted that women had the right to vote in Wyoming since 1869 and in Utah since 1870. Grimshaw, op. cit., p. 23.
66. Ibid., p. 24.
67. 'Winter Sports', *Making New Zealand* 2: 27 (Wellington, 1940), 30.
68. 'Summer Sports', *Making New Zealand*, 2: 26, 20.
69. Ibid., 16–17.
70. Simpson, op. cit., p. 167.
71. Ibid., p. 169. It is of significance that the New Zealand Alpine Club in 1891, unlike its British counterpart, allowed women members from the outset.

72. If one adopts the essential feminist concept of men's power over women and the form of women's resistance then clearly that 'resistance' found an outlet in areas of recreation and sport. 'Women found ways to resist the suffocating confines of the traditional female role'. *The Sexual Dynamics of History* (London, 1983), p. 5. The London Feminist History Group examining emigrant women in a patriarchal past describe them as 'brave and intrepid' and 'heroines in their venturesomeness' (p. 86). Such terms could have been applied, in the context of this essay, to the persona of Freda de Faur. Other researchers see the notions of male brutality and female submission as too categorical. Affection and companionship were critical necessities to survival. E. Shorter, *A History of Women's Bodies* (New York, 1982). In the rural and outback settings of colonial New Zealand the isolation of the pioneering communities may well have consolidated husband-wife relationships as friends and partners. This was certainly the case for the New Zealand housewife Helen Wilson, discussed earlier in this chapter. The 'ideal of companionate marriage' and the reality of life in nineteenth-century America is discussed in C. Strickland's, *Victorian Domesticity – Families in the Life and Art of Louisa May Alcott* (Alabama, 1985), pp. 111–17. The sheer number of adult women in New Zealand (140,000) should be emphasized. They comprised almost half of the total adult population in 1893. Reeves, *State Experiments*, p. 114. Mature, older and independent women were able to settle and establish themselves in New Zealand and avoid the social stigma of being labelled 'spinster'. Mary Taylor, a friend of Charlotte Bronte, came out in 1846 to join her brother. 'Freed from the social and class restrictions of England, she set up a small shop in Wellington and had a flourishing business'. J. Millen, *Colonial Tears and Sweat : The Working Class in Nineteenth Century New Zealand* (Wellington, 1984), p. 64.

73. One of the earliest forays into the Southern Alps (1871) saw women using ice-axes on a glacier at an altitude of 5,100 feet. M.B. Scott, 'Women Climbers of New Zealand', *New Zealand Alpine Journal*, 10 (1943).

74. Murphy, op. cit., p. 197.

75. See for example *Illustrated London News*, 19 January 1906, for a description of a new sport for women, football on rollerskates; 26 May 1906, a lithograph of a basketball match ('The finest athletic sport for girls'); 21 July 1906, a full-page drawing of 'boat polo for ladies'.

76. See for example the section on 'Sports, Games and Pastimes' in *The Cyclopedia of New Zealand*, (Otago and Southland), 4, (Christchurch, 1905), pp. 203–9. The actual numbers of women registered with formal sporting associations was not large. 'The association [gymnastic] has two ladies' clubs affiliated to it, and good work is being done by the lady gymnasts, some of whom are exceedingly clever'. In one township, of the 460 members of the amateur swimming club, only 60 were women. Volume 3 (on Canterbury province) indicates that there were not significant regional variations within New Zealand although it was noted that the Avon rowing Club had a 'ladies' ' dressing room (p. 215); in Volume 2 (Auckland province) there was the landmark of a woman appearing in the elected officials listed for a recreational association. Miss Statham, as assistant secretary of the Auckland Cycle Roads League (p. 246); in Volume 1 (Wellington district) there was a description of the Wellington Golf Club and an announcement that 'the Mirimar ladies succeeded in defeating the Hutt ladies in their first match in 1895', p. 429.

77. M. Moran, 'A Century Beginning: An Oral History of Leisure and Sporting Activities in Otago from 1895 to 1925' (research essay, Faculty of Physical Education, Otago University, 1985), p. 25.

78. *New Zealand Wheelman*, 3: 62 (July 1895).

8

Moral and Manly: Girls and Games in the Prestigious Church Secondary Schools of Melbourne 1901–1914

Ray Crawford

In a special edition of the *Melbourne Morning Herald* on Monday 1 January 1901 the large and broad headlines that spread across the front page of the newspaper proclaimed the fact of Federation, the birth of a new nation, and the 'glorious news' that the people of Australia were at last free of English rule. The more conservative *Age* carried the declaration of the Commonwealth in a less vivid display and chose to give prominent attention to a message from the Prime Minister, Edmund Barton, which pointed out that it was the duty of his 'fellow Australians' to assist the first Federal government to meet its highest aspirations.[1] The leader article had little option but to point out that people were now living in the twentieth century, and though they 'had done with the Nineteenth' it was necessary to consider the argument that time alone was not something which made sharp divisions in human affairs. Indeed, the heritage of the past had not been seriously interrupted or greatly disturbed by the momentous events of the day. It almost appears that the editor chose to offer the evidence of this belief by retaining, as much as possible, the everyday appearance of the newspaper's carefully laid out columns and reporting on a normal range of domestic news concerned with the details of beer adulteration, cemetery problems, the quicker delivery of letters and the introduction of concentrated milk. The news from overseas was dominated by reports of the Boer War. In an article on the conduct of the war, and recent developments in the South African campaign, it had been observed by the correspondent that 'some of the sublimest heroism of the war came from weak women who devoted themselves to the assignment of the battlefield's heroes'.[2] There is nothing in the report to indicate that the reference to the physical constitution and character of women is anything other than a solemn comment. Two or three days after those eventful hours of a brand-new century both Melbourne newspapers returned to their regular reporting activities. The sober reflections of the *Age* that changes in the chain of human events are slow-moving seemed all too apparent. Nevertheless, the start of 1901 would be forever judged as a significant landmark in the nation's history.

If the public sealing of political emancipation from England now gave an additional patriotic dimension to the concept of nationhood for all Australians, it is worth emphasizing that sport had been an important identifying element in the latter part of the nineteenth century in leading the various colonies into an emotional acceptance of a united Australian commonwealth. The colonists of English descent were the foremost and most forceful voice in colonial society, and from the earliest days of settlement they had held true to the sports and pastimes practised in the mother country. Distance was a tyranny to be endured and tolerated, but the 'sports of Old England gave the colonists a sense of continuity with the culture from which they had sprung, the comforting assurance that they were legitimate heirs to the Anglo-Saxon inheritance'.[3]

The more favourable and well-disposed climate of the Antipodes, readily available open spaces close to towns and cities, and generally improved economic circumstances for a majority of the population, combined to bring a variety of sports within the practical reach of many colonists. Some confirmation of the growth and broad development of the sporting scene in Australia can be taken from the observations of the English novelist Anthony Trollope. On his visit in 1871 he was drawn to the conclusion that sport was almost 'a national necessity' and 'cricket, athletics, rowing matches, shooting, hunting, flat-racing and steeplechasing' held as strong a passion for Australians as they did for those 'at home'.[4] An equally detailed account of Australian society was first published in London in 1883. *Town Life in Australia*, a blunt yet engaging description of Victorian Australia, was written by English-born Richard Twopeny, a former Marlborough College schoolboy who eventually settled in Adelaide in 1876. Twopeny considered that outdoor sports were the 'principal amusements of the Australians' and using the criteria of general interest taken in sport and matching this against the size of population, Australia could lay claim to being 'the most sporting country in the world'.[5] Cricket was singled out by Twopeny as the paramount Australian sport because all ages and all classes were interested in the game and 'there is no class too poor to play, as at home (England)'.[6] Indeed, Twopeny's admiration for Australian deeds on the cricket field against the mother country was to bring from him the enthusiastic assessment that 'cricket is the colonial *carrière ouverte aux talents*'.[7]

The reasons why sport became so rapidly an important element in the lives of most Australians have yet to be fully explored or explained. What Trollope and Twopeny failed to appreciate in their discussions of colonial sport was the seriousness with which Australians pursued their playing and spectating. Both authors observed the sporting scene through essentially English eyes and drew their pictures of the colonies as Southland outcrops of the British way of life, inspired by English ideas and wedded to the beliefs and virtues of the English middle class. While much of this picture was true there were already aspects of the Australian sporting make-up which took their cue from attitudes and values generated from making the best of a 'new home'. Winning, perseverance, success, mateship, and refusing to concede that one man was better than another were taken on board as features of the Australian character, and as a natural corollary Australian sportsmen were prepared to portray the image and enhance the myth. However, the extent to which Australians had embraced the sporting world late in the nineteenth century was not to everyone's liking or approval. The dissident voice of the Rev. Dr Bevan protested to his church congregation in 1892 about the amount of space Melbourne newspapers gave to sports coverage; he was equally scathing about a community that considered a pugilist to be 'a much more important member of society than any monarch'.[8]

Dr Bevan's remarks contained more than a grain of truth. The 1880s and 1890s were a remarkable period in the growth of sport in all of the colonies. Moreover, there was wide interest throughout the community in the success of Australian sportsmen. Middle-class support for organized team games, and in particular the sports transported from the English public schools, had grown quickly, but this movement was now augmented by an upsurge of working-class interest in rowing, athletics, the codes of football, boxing, cycling and horse racing. And gambling, an already well entrenched tradition with the Australian community,[9] served to increase the excitement and boost the size of crowds at many sporting events. However, as the nineteenth century drew to its close, it was the ability of most men in the colonies to engage and participate in a wide range of sports that made the clearest picture in the Australian sporting scene. In sharp contrast it was equally evident that women of all classes, and especially those from the lower orders, were severely restricted to the narrow confines of a limited sporting world.[10] In all the Australian colonies 'sport for all' meant sport for all men.

I

Until the early 1880s croquet had been the principal athletic exercise available to a small percentage of women, but this game was quickly superseded when the more active, energetic and enjoyable lawn tennis boomed among the middle classes. Since it was the preferred and fashionable game played on the courts that were rapidly being attachèd to many suburban and country homes, girls transported the sport into their prestigious private schools.[11] It was tennis that effectively opened the way for women to enter a much wider sporting world and participate in a physical and social environment where there was less prohibition and inhibition. Marriage for the 'colonial woman' remained an important and culminating mark of social success, much as it did in Victorian England, but the idea that playing sport would 'unsex' women and erode their femininity and physical health had been successfully challenged. As a result the medical and physiological arguments mounted in the case against women playing sport lost much of their potency. Archery and boating clubs extended the recreational opportunities of women in the 1880s but it was cycling which captured the sporting imagination of women from all social classes in the final decade of the century. To complete the sporting liberation of women hockey made its debut on the playing fields of Adelaide in 1899, brought to that city by the Waterhouse sisters on their return from Cheltenham Ladies' College.[12] It was towards the end of the nineteenth century, at the time when legislation and legal sanctions in Australia were creating a more democratic society and the women's suffrage movement was making important headway,[13] that sport began to offer women the opportunity to break away from a purely domestic role and reveal their increasing self-reliance and desire for self-improvement.

Against this broad and general social background the education of middle-class girls in Melbourne's prestigious church secondary schools at the turn of the century entered into a period of quite radical change. Curriculum innovations were about to be set in train in a small and select number of prestigious girls' private schools that would alter the essential nature of education for their clientele. Moreover, these initiatives would spread and have a vital impact upon the education systems throughout Victoria, and eventually induce new social attitudes in many Australian women. In her Speech Day report of 1901 the youthful and deeply religious Mary Morris, co-principal at Melbourne Church of England Girls' Grammar School, announced a distinct change of educational policy towards schoolgirl sport. She declared:

> The great importance of sport in schoolgirl life should at once be recognised. Our girls need open-air exercise just as boys do,

especially if they are doing good mental work. More especially they need the discipline of the playground which boys get, and which enables them to understand the value of co-operative effort in later life.[14]

Unfortunately there is no recorded account of the reaction of the audience to this statement, but a declaration suggesting a more persuasive and dominant role for organized sport in girls' schools was something of a bold action, particularly in the case of Mary Morris. Only three years previously William Morris had bought Merton Hall, then a small private school located at Domain Road in the Melbourne suburb of South Yarra, and installed his two daughters, Mary and Edith, as co-principals of an insignificant educational establishment. Fewer than twenty pupils enrolled at the school in 1898, yet the talents of the two sisters made Merton Hall an immediate success which forced their move to larger buildings in 1900. In the same year the Church of England announced its own highly favourable impressions of the school and concluded that Merton Hall was capable of bearing the Church's aspirations in girls' education. By allowing the use of the name Church of England Girls' Grammar School, and advertising the obvious religious affiliation to the Melbourne community, it assured the future prospects of the Morris school.[15]

Despite this propitious link and advantageous development, the courage of Mary Morris in calling for a more profound review of the place of sport in girls' secondary education should be recognized. She was fully aware of the long and acrimonious debate that had preceded the establishment of a girls' school supported by the Melbourne Church of England Diocese. As recently as 1895 Judge Molesworth had bitterly opposed the involvement of the Church 'with ordinary branches of a ladies' [sic] education, including dancing and gymnastics'.[16] Bishop Moorhouse, an equally fierce and enthusiastic supporter of a girls' school, provided the perfect counter-balance in the battle of words and perceptions of serious education. In an astute reference to the public school education received by boys in the city, the Bishop concluded that 'dancing and callisthenics are no more incongruous with religious principles than football and cricket'.[17] By signalling her intent that a new physical education would be introduced into her school and that sport would be included as an integral part of this educational development, Mary Morris was departing quite radically from the accepted practices and organiza-tions that existed for physical exercise in the major girls' schools in Melbourne. Equally significant, the proposition was being put forward that the school authorities should accept their responsibilities and control these new developments for the ultimate benefit of all girls. It would become increasingly clear that the laissez-faire approach of a gentle physical culture that had operated in the schools during the final quarter of the nineteenth century was about to be replaced by more highly structured physical training. A twentieth-century *mens sana in corpore sano* was being called into existence by a woman, which was unusual in a city where men had played the dominant role in supporting new educational ventures and widening the curriculum opportunities for girls. Further, the whole question of organized sport for girls was a challenge to the conventions rigorously held, and applied, about acceptable 'feminine' behaviour. Reforms to girls' education that were not suggested by men would have to be well-argued and gain the support of parents and powerful pressure groups in the community.

The plea by Mary Morris for a thorough review of the physical activity practices operating in the Melbourne girls' schools was not entirely original, although previous canvassing for greater attention to be paid to the physical needs of girls tended to exclude games and sport. The focus of this reform debate centred on the better provision of systematic gymnastic exercises that would aid the health and physical development of girls. Miss Bromby, headmistress at Ruyton Girls' School, had returned from England in 1894 impressed by the work she had seen in the schools and considered it time that a more serious approach was taken to the provision of physical training in girls' schools in the colony. At the Ruyton Speech Day in late 1894 the headmistress commented:

> We have a large dancing class, but I do not consider this sufficient for physical training. I should like to see drill established throughout the school, and the gymnastic and fencing classes revived, for I think it much to be desired that the systematic development of the bodily powers should not be neglected.[18]

Such a message in the mid-1890s was a small part of a slow-moving and wider concern being gradually expressed at the inadequacies of education throughout Victoria. It was being realized that education in the colony, especially in the government schools, had made little progress in over two decades and the school systems had failed to come to grips with many of the fundamental deficiencies that had grown with their own evolution.

In the establishment of the Presbyterian Ladies' College in 1875, the first Australian school to offer secondary education to girls equivalent to that being provided in the foremost boys' schools in the colony,[19] two quite separate and distinct strands of an extra-curricular physical culture emerged and developed in a piecemeal manner.[20] The 'extra' of gymnastics was taught from the outset and it became the common practice of the private girls' schools to employ 'specialist' staff from the commercial gymnasiums operating in Melbourne to visit them and teach those girls who had signed up for the subject. The second strand of the system had its origins in the recreative games encouraged by the schools as 'healthful exercise' for girls now engaged in strong intellectual pursuits. Yet these games, played mainly in recess times and after school, relied very much on the enthusiasm of the girls themselves for their existence and development. School clubs were formed by the girls and acted as the basis for the organization of competition, but this often meant a fluctuating rise and fall in enthusiasm and the opportunity to play in games. It was clear that the schools considered the loosely composed and weakly operated physical culture to be at the periphery of their mainstream educational developments, however mindful they were forced to be in their advertising in newspapers and brochures that health was a high priority in their educational thinking. In all of the notable girls' schools in Melbourne in the latter part of the nineteenth century the common feature of physical culture was its undulating fortunes that had much to do with the social and economic changes occurring at that time.

The system of physical culture that did exist in girls' schools, whatever its vacillating course, owed as much to fear as to anything else. Pioneers of female education were extremely wary of the medical arguments in circulation that girls engaged in serious mental study were being exposed to a 'brain pressure' that their 'delicate' physical constitutions might not cope with.[21] Charles Pearson, the first headmaster at the Presbyterian Ladies' College, was very much aware of these physiological arguments and the concerns of middle-class parents needing reassurance that their daughters would not be handicapped in any way, and especially in the marriage market, by the path which led towards academic achievement. At the opening of the College in 1875 Pearson went out of his way in his inaugural address, which generally championed the cause of 'higher culture' for women, to point out that careful consideration would be given in his new school to the health and physical development of the pupils.[22] There would be no neglect of 'wholesome forms of recreation' and the weighty authority of Herbert Spencer was used to construct the case for girls being allowed to take part in 'physical culture'.[23] Yet Pearson's insistence on physical exercise for schoolgirls owed a great deal to his own background and first-hand knowledge of how hard girls would work in the classroom to achieve success in their academic studies. The former Rugby schoolboy and Oxford don had had experience in lecturing to women and older girls in England and had been an examiner at Queen's College, tasks that had given him an insight into the zealous approach and dedicated application of many female students and their meticulous production of written assignments. Above all, however, Pearson probably had to allay the fears of parents that higher education for girls would not destroy their bodily health which might reduce their chances of marriage and a capacity to manage a home or function as a mother.[24] Unfortunately, and like many educators before him, Pearson's rhetoric outstripped his practical ability, and he was unable, in the two short years that he acted as headmaster, to organize a curriculum that gave any serious attention to the development of a worthwhile system of physical culture.

The reasons why Presbyterian Ladies' College, and the other new girls' schools that were founded in the colony before the end of the nineteenth century, moved extremely slowly in developing a comprehensive system of physical education are not hard to find. Overall, the schools were confronted by a double problem. On the one hand they had to demonstrate that girls had the intellectual capacity to cope with academic syllabuses that had been rigorously constructed to test the best in the boys' schools, aware that any marked inferiority shown by the girls could hinder the advance of women's higher education. On the other hand, this open competition in mental excellence was not to detract in any way from the 'greatest ornament of the sex', a reference to the female feelings of 'sweetness, refinement and womanliness' which supposedly gave women their major influence in a male-oriented world.[25] Games and sport were therefore difficult to justify in an already crowded timetable geared to mental education; moreover, their boisterous nature had to be considered in case they adversely affected womanly feelings.

Nevertheless, as new girls' schools were established, notably Tintern Ladies' College (1877), Ruyton Girls' School (1878), and the Methodist Ladies' College (1882), games and a limited sport competition slowly evolved and gained popularity. The initiative in these areas was largely taken by the girls, though the school authorities sanctioned the playing of all games and kept a benevolent supervision over these activities. Serious rivalry was to be reserved for the examination hall and the paths that would take girls down the 'matriculation road'. By 1880 the right of women to enter Melbourne University had been won and the first group of women matriculants had been allowed to sign the matriculation roll.[26] From this point onwards, and clearly up to the end of the nineteenth century, the academic competition between the principal girls' schools was a matter of some considerable prestige, despite the occasional statements that denied a race for university honours. When the Presbyterian Ladies' College sent out a challenge to the Methodist Ladies' College in October 1885 for a tennis match between the best four players in each school, the event was given prominent mention in the Methodist girls' school magazine. The challenge was seen as an audacious gesture – 'I fancy I still hear the exclamation of the girls as they repeat the words, and try to realise their meaning'. But it is also noticeable that two of the best players in the Methodist Ladies' College team found it impossible to practise for the match because they 'were working hard for University examinations'.[27] Visible proof that the educational experiment in the colony should be seen as a success took precedence over any sporting contest.

II

In fairness to the schools, the progress of games and competitive sport in them during the final decades of the nineteenth century was determined very largely by social rules and etiquette laid down by the Melbourne middle-class community. Whatever the sporting passions of schoolgirls, fledgeling schools were not likely to contravene the strict conventions and moral codes established by an unforgiving stratum of society. In the second year of the Presbyterian Ladies' College operations one girl was bold enough to suggest that 'a football club be established' at the school because she had observed how much 'fun, enjoyment and excitement' boys seem to have in that game.[28] Her request was probably considered by the school authorities with mild amusement, but here was one girl obviously dissatisfied with the gentility of croquet, the game that had supposedly established itself as the 'favourite pastime' of the girls at the Presbyterian Ladies' College in 1875.[29] The first of the school clubs was formed in the following year for the purpose of 'friendly contests', but such tame exercise did not appeal to every girl at the school, particularly the country boarders who were probably used to more spirited forms of physical play at home. They petitioned the Principal, the Rev. George Tait, for the use of the gymnasium at certain free times for roller skating practice, a request that gained qualified support from an unknown author writing in the school magazine:

    Skating is a much more healthful amusement than croquet, and we wish them (the boarders) great enjoyment in it, only warning them to be aware of fractured limbs or skulls, and such facial disfigurements as broken noses and scarred cheeks.[30]

The message was clear. Skating was a risky activity and the school was not going to accept any liability for any resultant injuries.

The rapid adoption of tennis in the girls' schools early in the 1880s was due to two major reasons. Here was a game that offered far greater opportunities for movement, physical exercise, enjoyment and challenge to the majority of girls who found croquet an activity unable to meet their demands and needs for harder physical play. In addition, the Wimbledon championships in 1877 and the Victorian titles meeting two years later quickly established tennis as the most popular game among the colony's middle class, many of whom had the space to set up grass courts adjacent to their homes. Cement and grass courts were hastily laid in the schools, and challenge matches between teams of the 'best four' in each school became a regular feature of tennis by the end of the 1880s. Reporting of these early inter-school matches is marked by the delicacy of the language used to describe the competition. There is no hint of athletic glory and sporting honour for the victorious team, or for any individual performance. Indeed, the actual result in some of the first competitions is hard to find, gestures of modesty and propriety in keeping with the expectations of women in the best of society in the Australian colonies.[31] The breakthrough and acceptance of tennis as a game suitable for schoolgirls patently aided a more liberal interpretation of 'healthful exercise' among the school authorities. Before the end of the 1880s a select band of team games – rounders, lacrosse and cricket – were being played by the girls in the major secondary schools, although each game suffered in its development from varying numbers of participants and fluctuating enthusiasm.[32] The total number of girls in schools was not large (the Presbyterian Ladies' College enrolled 277 pupils in 1882 and advertised this proud fact around Melbourne) and there was no established pattern of girls attending secondary school on a consistent year-to-year basis. Enthusiasm for games therefore depended highly on the efforts of the girls who held the responsible offices in the school clubs, or form organisations, to drum up support for a particular game at any time.

Throughout the nineteenth century the schools continued to view the playground and the games field as a necessary, but quite separate, development to the mainstream of their educational and cultural activities. A loosely organized physical culture was condoned for health reasons, but the nature of this work and involvement remained subsidiary to the goals set by those in charge of the schools. The largest and most prestigious schools were the brain-children of various religious groups in the colony but they held the common aspiration of producing 'Christian ladies'. Such a concept was bound up in education theory which placed the greatest value in 'a spirit of industry' and gave the highest priority to the moral behaviour and development of girls. Thus the schools strove to create within their walls an atmosphere and a tone built around a 'corporate conscience' and the exaltation of behaviour mirrored in modesty, truth, honour and obedience. Sin was exhibited in falsehood, laziness, meanness and disobedience.[33] A rigid application to mental achievement was considered to be the true pathway to the desired virtues that marked out a dutiful wife and mother, while there remained in the minds of many church and education leaders the idea that play had the propensity to encourage the sinful characteristics in the young. In setting themselves the primary task of providing girls with a standard of education equivalent to that in the best of the boys' schools, the Melbourne girls' schools argued that they were equipping the daughters of middle-class parents 'for a successful life'. Unmistakably, success could only be measured in the terms set down by the church, a life devoted to the service of Christian beliefs, a message strongly emphasized by the Rev. W.H. Fitchett, president at Methodist Ladies' College:

> Education, if it is not to be a curse, if it is to fulfil its highest office, must be not divorced from Christianity, but wedded indissolubly with it. . . . God's Word must be taught as well as human science; Christian virtues as well as social accomplishments.[34]

The prestigious church secondary schools educating Melbourne girls were to discover very early in the twentieth century that the games field was an ideal and practical environment to be trusted with the Christian message and inculcation of Christian virtues. From this time the mercurial growth and development of games and organized sport in these schools was never in doubt.

The reasons for the rapid deployment of games and sport in the Melbourne girls' schools at the turn of the century, and their equally quick promotion to the centre of the education stage, have been simply explained as the straightforward imitation of similar events that were already occurring in girls' schools in England. Australian public school and private education did take many of its cues, directly and indirectly, from England, and boys' schools plainly drew much of their inspiration from the Arnoldian traditions. Yet the motive of imitation should be considered against a broader tapestry of events and explanations, many of them more subtle and complex than a singular reason or simple repetitive action. Whether by accident or design, the plea by Mary Morris in 1901 for the re-evaluation of the place that games should occupy in the education of girls was presented at an opportune time. Her desire for change coincided with a more general call for education reform in the state, a movement launched on a crescendo of criticism of the government schools.

III

The case for changes in the state school system could no longer be ignored, and if the strongest accusations were levelled against the narrow and inflexible elementary education offered in these schools, a broader mood for educational reform had developed in the community. Alfred Deakin's specific charges against state education in 1898, and Theodore Fink's Royal Commission on Technical Education between 1899 and 1901, condemned an antiquated school curriculum and the extreme formalism of 'old' education which over-valued 'book learning' and memory training teaching methods.[35] The need for education in schools to become more practical received a great deal of attention by the reformists, and at the Federal Education Congress held in the Melbourne Town Hall in January 1901 some speakers called on schools to consider the 'total child' and give more sympathetic treatment to his 'individuality'. Although the three-day conference was suddenly curtailed by the news of the death of Queen Victoria, the sustained and strong message seeking educational reform had reached a wide audience. Frank Tate, about to take up his appointment as the first Director of Education in Victoria, exemplified the determination of the reform movement in his paper which, though not read, was published in the congress proceedings. He concluded:

> There is a great tide coming in. The great tidal wave of the new education has swept round the globe, and it is not to be kept back from Victoria by a few Dame Partingtons who are busy, mop in hand, trying to sweep back the Southern Ocean.[36]

Perhaps the true greatness of Mary Morris might be judged in the fact that here was a reform voice caught up with the 'New Education' rhetoric, but she was to prove that she was more than a fashionable echo that stopped short of practical action.

The idea of nurturing a new physical education in girls' schools to replace a redundant eclectic physical culture should be seen as a fresh pioneering development in female education. By the turn of the twentieth century it was being gradually accepted that the battle for the right of women to a higher education had been won even if some major skirmishes still lay ahead. The first woman had graduated from the University of Melbourne in arts in 1883, in medicine in 1891 and in science in 1893, which meant that questions of the wider social aspects of emancipation, including women's suffrage, could be taken up in public debate.[37] But as the numbers of women graduating from universities increased and significant breakthroughs occurred in their acceptance into professional and public life, the physiological arguments of the nineteenth century about the dangers of 'brain pressure' in women quietly disappeared. Mrs Garrett Anderson, a leader of the Women's Movement in England, had always rejected the theories about the weakness and smaller size of the female brain and argued that it was a lack of physical development, not mental capacity, which hampered women in their competition with men.[38] Yet with little help from an insipid physical culture the prizes of higher education had fallen to girls. The deduction may well have been drawn. A new and more demanding physical training, controlled by the schools and incorporating organized games and competitive sport, could produce a physical development in girls that might yield even greater intellectual and academic rewards.

A much more straightforward argument has been put forward to explain the development of the games cult in girls' schools. As soon as the opportunity arose, the leaders in the field of girls' education were keen to make their schools as much like boys' schools as possible.[39] The rationale was simple. Similar education would aid the emancipation of women and allow them the chance 'to lead the same lives as men'.[40] Attractive as this argument might be, it needed to be treated with some caution as far as the Australian scene was concerned. Undoubtedly, there was a clear sociological purpose behind the pioneering efforts of the women involved with secondary education for girls. In a society troubled and concerned with 'women's rights', and debating the entry of women into the professions and public affairs, an education with the characteristics of equality might improve the work opportunities of females. Many of the Melbourne middle class had been affected by the economic crash of the early 1890s and the continuing struggle between capital and labour in the state where commerce and industry were the most advanced.[41] Women had been induced to become wage-earners, and by the turn of the century the parents of the middle classes were sending their daughters to private schools for the same reasons that they packed off their sons to public schools – to improve their prospects of finding gainful employment. Further, in a stratum of society that had long regarded women as 'physically delicate' and in need of male protection 'from the harsh realities of life', it was a highly visible demonstration of equality to let girls take part in team games and enter into sporting competition. Clearly, team games and playing field rivalry for girls was a venture that could help to dispel the generally held view that there was an acceptable but narrow role for women in society. Importantly, the view was partly based on the belief that the female personality had natural weaknesses, marked by pronounced feelings of emotionalism in a crisis or in the face of every minor hurt. The bumps and bruises of sport would help to eradicate the myth of 'weak women' and reveal characters capable of physical courage. Christian ladies could now demonstrate that Christian gentlemen were not the only inheritors of those prized manly virtues: loyalty, honour, purity and strenuousness.

Local developments in sport obviously influenced the renewed and strengthened interest the Melbourne girls' schools were to take in games. Sport had become a national interest by the end of the nineteenth century and since the 1870s Australian sporting success against overseas competitors had played a considerable part in the achievement of a national, rather than a colonial identity.[42] Stimulated by this, women in the Melbourne community began to take part in a wider range of sporting events and activities. Golf, archery, boating, roller skating, cycling and lawn bowls increased in popularity with women,[43] and undoubtedly the new-found enthusiasms rubbed off on younger girls. At the University High School in 1900, a private co-educational school run by Lawrence Adamson and Otto Krome, two men who were to make high reputations as headmasters at Wesley College and the Methodist Ladies' College in the early decades of the twentieth century, girls had begun to take the initiative in an expansion of their sporting interest. 'Ludo', writing in the school magazine, noted the promising development of the formation of a Girls' Games Committee:

This year of 1900 has been a remarkable one in the annals of U.H.S. Not that the girls have unduly asserted themselves, for that would be inconsistent with their dignity, nor have the boys fallen into the background, for that their inborn nature would shudder at and revolt from. But from the Sports Club, which hitherto has been too exclusively a gymnastic, cricket and football association, there has sprung a little offshoot which bids fair to becoming a working institution. . . . This is the Girls' Games Committee, as yet no bigger than a grain of mustard seed in influence and power, but which shows very fair promise of a career.[44]

Perhaps in a mixed secondary school in 1900 the noticeable uncertainty of the author could be expected but her powers of foresight were well founded. Within five years the larger girls' schools would be operating games committees and sporting organizations would be set up to promote and control a burgeoning games movement in them.

The games movement that was chafing at the bit in girls' schools now appeared to be released from the confines of a narrow and restricted operation by the Morris proclamation. Margaret Irving, who with her sister Lilian founded Lauriston Girls' High School in 1901, had been much impressed during her visit to English schools in the same year by the enthusiasm of girls for the game of hockey. On her return to Melbourne she immediately introduced hockey as a winter sport at Lauriston and called on the other girls' schools in the city to follow her lead.[45] The first inter-school match was held between Lauriston and Ruyton in 1903 on a pitch which was little more than 'a level piece of ground', but the news of the fixture reached girls from the Melbourne Girls' Grammar School and a group attended the match as interested spectators. It was also in 1903 that Mary and Edith Morris, with a thriving school of 200 girls on their books, felt confident enough to leave their responsibilities and travel overseas to study and examine programmes and teaching methods in other schools. What they saw in English schools had the greatest impact upon them and plainly influenced the direction of educational events at their own school when they returned to Melbourne.[46] The breadth and intensity of the games sentiment in English girls' schools confirmed Mary's beliefs about the importance of systematic physical exercise and games for girls, and she may well have observed the progress of the new physical education at schools such as Roedean, Godolphin, Wycombe Abbey and Cheltenham Ladies' College. At these schools the games programme had grown to include tennis, hockey, cricket, golf, rounders, lacrosse, basketball and fives, but crucially, several of the prestigious schools were now employing specialist teachers in 'physical training' as they graduated from Madame Bergman-Österberg's College at Dartford.

This modern trend was keenly noted by the Morris sisters. As soon as Mary Morris returned to her post at the Girls' Grammar School she encouraged 'friendly' hockey matches with Lauriston and Ruyton. The immediate popularity of these fixtures among the girls encouraged her to take the additional step of harnessing the obvious enthusiasm for more regular and formalized competition. At a meeting held in Merton Hall in 1905 representatives from the 1904 contesting girls' schools were joined by those from Tintern Ladies' College and the Girls' Schools Hockey Association was formed. Basic regulations governing the inter-school matches were set by the committee and certain playing rules were agreed upon to assist the movement skills of the players and reduce the element of dangerous play. It was decided that the skirts used in playing had to be eight inches from the ground, white petticoats were not to be worn underneath, and hard-rimmed hats and hatpins would be banned from the playing area,[47] all precautions that seem as wise as they were patently necessary.

These first developments in organized competitive sport were not without some teething problems. Emma Cook, headmistress at Tintern, felt it wise to inform parents in her 1906 school prospectus that she was fully aware of 'the dangers of girls becoming boisterous at games' but she would ensure that 'the behaviour at play is such as is becoming of ladies'.[48] Although Oberwyl School and Toorak College joined the Hockey Association in 1906 it was noticeable that the two largest schools, the Presbyterian Ladies' College and the Methodist Ladies' College, remained on the sidelines, somewhat unsure of a radical development which broke with the casual arrangements built in the past and that appeared, at least in their eyes, to work well. There may, however, have been an element of jealousy in the situation. Neither of the two premier schools had been first to think of, and produce, the popular initiative. Further, the men in control at both schools may not have been keen to follow an educational lead given by a relatively young headmistress in charge of the newest denominational girls' school. And clearly, the exalted importance of the games field was not to the liking of every school administration. The Rev. S.G. McLaren, principal at the Presbyterian Ladies' College in 1904, was quite obviously disturbed by the increased attention being given to games in girls' schools and the risk of their interfering with the academic side of school life. In his annual report of that year McLaren issued a warning 'against elevating what ought to be a pastime into the serious business of the school'.[49]

Yet, within two years of this pronouncement his own school was to take a leading part in raising sport to a new eminence by appointing a headmaster, James Bee, who regarded games as a greatest help in producing school spirit and fostering *esprit de corps*. Despite these early uncertainties the team spirit and team loyalty that was precipitated by the introduction of hockey was quickly seized upon by the girls' schools for their own purposes, and explains, in part, the rapid advance of organized inter-school competitions in tennis, rounders and cricket and the introduction of basketball and baseball as new team games. The Registration of Schools Act in 1905 laid down minimum standards of facilities and teaching operations for all non-government schools, which threw them into even greater competition with each other and the small number of government secondary schools dealing with a carefully selected group of intelligent students. Since the open publishing of examination results was a public aspect of this competition and was taken as a mark of a school's status and image, it had the effect of sparking off even keener rivalry between schools.[50] School authorities wanted girls to develop a close identity with the achievements of their own school, demonstrate a loyalty to it, and a patriotism for its ideals.[51] The activities of the games field were now considered a valuable instrument in the promotion of this much desired identity, loyalty and patriotism.

IV

There can be no doubt, however, that the most significant event in the development of the games movement in Melbourne girls' schools occurred with the decision of Mary and Edith Morris to send their younger sister Gwynneth to England in 1904 to train at Madame Bergman-Österberg's Physical Training College. Gwynneth had been a pupil at Merton Hall since 1898 and her all-round ability at sport and overall interest in physical training led to her appointment as games captain at the school. The bold and imaginative action of the elder sisters was repaid by Gwynneth who graduated in her two-year diploma course at the college with first-class honours. Few girls who trained under the redoubtable principal at Dartford were likely to emerge from the college without some of Bergman-Österberg's philosophy being absorbed into their own beliefs and carried with them wherever they went to teach in the world. She was prepared to let it be widely known that her main objective in life and education was to 'train my girls to help raise their own sex, and so accelerate the progress of the race; for unless the women are healthy, strong, pure and true, how can the race progress?'.[52] On Gwynneth's return in 1906 Mary Morris installed her at the Girls' Grammar School to run a newly created Department of Physical Training and Recreation, an innovation that the other leading girls' schools could not ignore for long. Moreover, the advent of the specialist-trained gym and sport mistress was a staffing appointment trend that was, again, eventually adopted in the other schools.

7. Gwynneth Morris, first head
of Melbourne Girls' Grammar
school's innovatory Department
of Physical Training and
Recreation

8. Working girls in Dunedin, New Zealand, 1899, on
a picnic organized by their employer,
Cadbury Fry Hudson (Hocken Library)

9. 'Free exercise' for girls in an Otago school, c. 1906 (Hocken Library)

10. In the early nineteenth century Alexandra, Otago, had clubs for croquet (top),
hockey (centre) and tennis (bottom): the last two were actually mixed at this time
(Hocken Library)

In the meantime, the pacesetters at Merton Hall were not to be seen altogether as the leaders of educational experiment by the older and more established church secondary schools. Cautiously, the Methodist Ladies' College appointed Miss Tannock, a full-time class teacher, into the additional role of 'Sports Mistress' in 1906, the same year that Otto Krome arrived at the school as headmaster. A close friend of the sport-loving Adamson at Wesley College, Krome immediately gave his personal sponsorship to the activities of the playground and games field. He began the habit of attending every inter-school tennis match, talked about 'the honour of the school', and indicated that he was keenly interested in the results of the matches which involved the school. Suddenly, four out of 15 pages in *Bluebell*, the school magazine, were taken up with reports of sporting contests and events, and Krome added his own touch of encouragement by presenting a trophy to the winners of an inter-form tennis competition.[53]

From around 1906 *'esprit de corps'* was to become as much an overworked phrase in girls' schools as *'mens sana in corpore sano'* had become in the boys' public schools, but it effectively carried the message that school authorities urgently wanted to transmit to their girls and the fee-paying parents. The corporate life of a school was its most important feature and the highest aim should be for a school to be 'one living organism, and not a mere assemblage of individuals',[54] sentiments long expressed and deliberately manufactured in boys' secondary education. In the 'battle of life' the boys' public schools had sought to make their clients makers and rulers of an empire or captains of business and commerce. Changing patterns in society now made it imperative that girls should be trained to take up the new challenges confronting them in motherhood and the rigours of professional and public life. Games had already demonstrated their practical efficiency in turning individualism to collectivism in boys' schools and it was clear that the girls' schools, to some degree, merely copied from this tradition. But the girls' schools also recognized that as their clients were about to become involved in their own 'battle of life', which would expose them to a range of experiences previously unknown to the feminine role, then a stronger conditioning programme in moral development and character training was essential. With these ideals now in forefront of the minds of those who controlled the affairs of the Melbourne girls' schools, the future of organized games within a broad scheme of physical training was never brighter.

The revised attitudes towards sports and games in the girls' schools were revealed in the role and influence of James Bee during his term as headmaster at Presbyterian Ladies' College between 1906 and

1913. He invoked the authority of Anne Jemina Clough, the first principal of Newnham College, Cambridge, who considered that active games for girls produced in them a 'healthy outlook on things. . . . because of the concentration, the complete forgetfulness of self'.[55] Bee's coaching of the sports teams at the school, an unusual occurrence in the first place, was made more distinct by his teaching philosophy of 'hit hard and play to win', an attitude that appears to have won him undying loyalty from the girls under his influence.[56] Such an approach and outlook towards the playing field may have been responsible for the article that appeared in *School Notes*, the magazine produced by Melbourne Girls' Grammar School. Excessive sporting rivalry at inter-school matches, the promotion of athletic glory and an exaggerated emphasis on winning brought a terse rebuke from the young Gwynneth Morris. She was concerned that the prime virtue in games should be seen in their moral value and the true nature of 'manliness' expressed in physical skill, pride in effort, winning and losing decently, courage, honour and loyalty. Written under the name of 'Kingsfield', Gwynneth's pointed message carried the title 'The Spirit of the Game':

> The greatest element of evil which may creep into our view of athletics is the idea that one must win at all costs . . . we need to cultivate the spirit for which fair play comes first – defeat or victory afterwards . . . teamwork. . . . This develops traits of character which we all wish to encourage – fair play, impersonal interest, earnestness of purpose, the ability to give one's best not for one's own glorification, but for the good of the team – the cause.[57]

Clearly the girls' schools were now finding out, as Gwynneth's words show, that the course of competitive sport is never smooth for very long, however much the organizers might play down the aspect of winning. Whatever Gwynneth's beliefs that team games were primarily organized to develop the moral well-being of the individual and draw girls together in a sense of 'communal solidarity', a sentiment that might then transfer from the playing field into the corridors of the school, she would be forced to recognize, as others would, that any level of devotion to the games field bred a complex set of behaviour in both players and teachers. During the first decade of the twentieth century most of the Melbourne girls' schools believed that competitive games were a valuable instrument in the attainment of high-minded educational goals. It was equally true, however, that they were having to realize, as a result of this remarkable growth of interest in games, that the playing field was just as capable of a more perverse indoctrination into a less desirable system of virtues.

V

The minor problems and conflicts that appeared with the rise of the organized games movement in the principal girls' schools perhaps need a deeper analysis, but it is fairly clear that a majority of girls welcomed the new games curriculum and enjoyed the competitive side of sporting contests. In short, games were highly popular in all schools, and these feelings were expressed in a welter of songs and poems that burst from the pages of the school magazines, most of which extolled the 'love of the game'. At the Methodist Ladies' College the Old Girls' song now gave two of its four verses to sport and young reporters were telling of the 'fervent hopes' for the new season and promoting the hardy image of those who had 'learned to ignore the ruffled skin and bruises'.[58] It is a debatable point whether or not James Bee's tough approach to games at the Presbyterian Ladies' College contained the belief that the rough and tumble of the playing field should act as a remedy for purported feminine physical and psychological weaknesses. But many girls now saw themselves in a stronger image as the result of playing games, and chose to express this and their recently acquired spirit for games in verse:

> Here when our hearts were strong and keen
> Gaily we fought our fight
> Guarding our tempers, scorning knocks
> Learning to love the right.[59]

The enthusiasm for sport was further strengthened in the years leading up to the Great War by the introduction of new games that spread the chances of playing for the school or form teams. Basketball was being played in some schools by 1907, lacrosse on a regular basis by 1908, baseball by 1909, and swimming sports were added around 1910 in several schools.[60] Indeed, Melbourne Girls' Grammar School felt so confident about the sports boom that Edith Morris, the sole headmistress now that Mary had married and retired in 1908, announced that all girls in the senior school would take part in at least one compulsory game.[61] Membership of the 'Sports Committee' and the election to the captaincy of first school teams became important positions within a school, while school magazines became heavily involved in reporting inter-school sport, yet offering modest reference to any star performer in a winning or losing team. This particular emphasis on team performance and faint praise of the elite individual athlete characterize the reporting during this era and stand out in sharp contrast to the exaltation of the athletic hero in the Melbourne boys' public schools.

It should not be forgotten, however, that the popularity of games in girls' schools during the period under review could be simply explained by the immense pleasure they gave to most pupils. In particular, team games offered an excitement through their challenge and a joy in their freedom of movement that was denied in the classrooms and in Swedish drill, the second arm of the physical training syllabus. Ling's gymnastic exercise system had been fully explored by Gwynneth Morris in England, and when her team of school gymnasts performed at the end of year Speech Day in 1907, the large audience of parents, local doctors and leading educators were sufficiently impressed by the demonstration to give their total approval of the work.[62] The health and physical development objectives of the 'free standing and living-support movements' were potent arguments in favour of Ling's system, and the idea of regulated and systematic exercises to increase the strength and stamina of girls, especially if they wanted to play games, added to the positive report.

Yet, the rigidly controlled and intricate evolutions of Swedish drill may not have been enjoyed by many of the girls. A boarder at Melbourne Girls' Grammar School in 1908 possibly captured in verse the true feelings of girls towards the daily drill lesson that had become standard practice in most girls' secondary schools by the end of the decade. She wrote:

> Out in the quad the bell in tolling
> Out of the door come boarders rolling
> In blouses white and tunics short
> To learn ideas that Gwynneth brought
> Then at last, 'tis time to stop.
> And finish with a march called "Hop".
> A brighter glance comes o'er their faces,
> As out of the door each poor girl races.[63]

Games were a release from closely supervised physical and mental effort and if the class notes within school magazines can be seen as something of a fair reflection of the attitudes of the 'ordinary girl' towards games, the comments of a Form VB girl at Tintern in 1912 are an interesting example of these attitudes. She remarked: 'Last drill day Miss Thompson gave us a lesson in basketball, instead of our usual work; we enjoyed it very much . . . and we had a good game'.[64]

Motives and reasons preached from a denominational platform held strong sway with a cautious middle class. Quite clearly, the games movement in the girls' schools did a great deal to assist in women's wider participation in community activities at a time when their involvement continued to be restricted. Further, the public image of the athletic schoolgirl helped to dispel the idea that female athletes were something of a curiosity or a freak, open to ridicule, as this song from the late nineteenth century portrayed:

> She rises with the lark and scorches in the park
> She's a lady there's a lot of wear and tear about;
> Her shoes are number nine, and her foot's as big as mine;
> So I don't think she's the kind of girl I'd care about.[65]

By 1910 sport had shown its powers of widening social contact. Mixed hockey games were being played in Melbourne parks, the Methodist Ladies' College played tennis against its sister college in Adelaide and in 1913 the first of the women's inter-state hockey championships were held by the Victorian Association. However, the spread of girls' games was not to everyone's liking and an 'anxious parent' expressed concern in a letter to the Melbourne *Argus* in 1910. On the subject of 'Girls and Rough Games' the correspondent complained that while walking through a public park deep shock had been given by the vigorous characteristics of a hockey game in which girls 'rushed about, flourishing their sticks and dealing terrific blows, not only to themselves, but to each other'.[66] Replies to the newspaper on the next day disagreed wholeheartedly with the first interpretation of the activity. It was 'to be hoped that the day was long past when girls were kept in the seclusion of their homes engaged in sewing and knitting', and it was foolish to 'deny that the Australian girl today is one of the finest types of young womanhood in this world and this is largely due to sport in which she engages'.[67]

VI

Nineteenth-century sport in Australia has been considered as a part of the colonists' desire to recreate 'a new Britannia in another world' and their need to feel an attachment to 'the culture from which they had sprung'.[68] The development of the games movement in girls' schools at the very beginning of the twentieth century may well be examined within the context of this particular theory. Sport did play a vital role in the dissemination of British cultural values in the first place, yet in the period between 1901 and 1914 the cultural and national values peculiar to Australia emerge, and some of these – mateship, fierce patriotism, extreme competitiveness – can be detected in the games of girls' secondary schools. Nevertheless, reliance upon English example and inspiration was strong throughout the period leading up to the First World War. In her Speech Day report of 1908 Edith Morris referred to the 'spirit of true patriotism' which was the 'great tradition handed down from English Public Schools', and this was a major reason in her complete acceptance of games for girls.[69] Again, speaking to the National Council of Women in 1912 on modern trends in the education of women, Edith spent a long time talking about the necessity of games in girls' schools and largely supported her case with ample references to English authorities. She was firm in the belief that games were of material aid in moral training and the formation of 'good character' and they fostered 'a spirit of comradeship rather than sentimental affection'.[70] This last comment has particular interest and relevance. Games, at least in the minds of the girls' school leaders, were principally about solidarity, not individuality. At the same time, they were helping to remove traditionally held attitudes to women and replace them with those previously associated exclusively with men, in particular the highly regarded characteristics of 'mateship'. What is clear, some much greater analysis is required before a picture is likely to develop on the extent to which girls' games did act as a medium for the transfer of a male-oriented value system marked by independence, individuality and competitiveness.

Finally, there should be strong challenge to the assumption that until comparatively recent times the exclusion of women from sport denied them the opportunity to develop certain traits such as healthy body–healthy mind, manliness, and its characteristic displays of courage, physical prowess, honour, loyalty and the gentlemanly tradition epitomized by fair play and a show of decency. 'Women, by definition, could not become either gentlemanly or manly, and because women's contribution to the society was undervalued, the development for them of a healthy mind in a healthy body was also less important'.[71] The games and competitive sports that evolved and established themselves in the lives of some schoolgirls early in the twentieth century require a review of this statement. The major girls' schools in Melbourne were enthusiastic in their cultivation of humanism and the spirit of fair play, and the girls, through their use of sporting metaphors and vivid language in match descriptions, had been quick to show their mettle.

Regrettably, there is no major work in existence which considers the sporting traditions in Australian girls' schools, and it is impossible in a short article to present anything more than a brief explanation and analysis of some focal points in the nature and structure of this important but complex movement. Indeed, the investigation of the phenomenon in one state covering a limited time span has its own problems. Certainly, it is not always easy to find the truth about major happenings. Human records and personal testimony throw up many perplexing contradictions while the investigator inadvertently drifts into his own prejudices which influence his interpretations. Yet interpretations must be offered even if they are the catalyst of immediate disputation. The era under review, 1901 to 1914, has special significance in the history of private secondary education for girls in Australia. These 13 or so years were marked by the rapid transition of a *laissez-faire* physical culture to a powerful and highly controlled comprehensive system of physical training in a small number of selective independent schools.

Although this system of physical exercise affected relatively few girls in its first years of operation, it was to have an immense influence in all schools in the state thereafter. The nature of the system, an unlikely combination of Swedish gymnastic exercises and English games, preached a primary responsibility to health, physical development and moral training, objectives that seemed, at least in part, to steer it away from the accusations often levelled at over-athleticism in boys' public schools.[72] As the Great War began, organized games and competitive sport had established a permanent and thriving position in girls' schools. Beyond 1918 the games movement continued on a course of wide acclaim to a point where one historian, recording the history of a Melbourne girls' school, considered the school magazines of the 1920s 'depressingly full of sport' and 'tedious' in their details and descriptions of countless form and inter-school matches.[73]

Several Melbourne girls' schools might lay claim to a crucial role in the growth and development of games and sport among their ranks but it should be recognized that the prestigious church schools carried the day and played the crucial part in the general acceptance and progress of the movement. It was their voices, and reputations, which gave legitimacy to a controversial educational development and gained from the community approval of their actions.

NOTES

1. *Age*, 1 January, 1901, p. 2.
2. Ibid., p. 1.
3. L. Sandercock and I. Turner, *Up Where, Cazaly, The Great Australian Game* (London, 1981), p. 13.
4. T.D. Jaques and G.R. Pavia, *Sport in Australia* (Sydney, 1976), pp. 24–5.
5. R. Twopeny, *Town Life in Australia* (Harmandsworth, 1973) p. 204.
6. Ibid.
7. Ibid.

8. K. Dunstan, 'Our Sporting Obsession' in Jaques and Pavia, *Sport in Australia*, pp. 2–3.
9. See J. O'Hara, 'The Australian Gambling Tradition' in R. Cashman and M. McKernan, *Sport: Money, Morality and the Media* (NSW University Press, n.d.a.), pp. 68–85.
10. John Daly emphasises these points in his study of sport, class and community in Colonial South Australia 1836–1890. See J.A. Daly, *Elysian Fields*, (Adelaide, 1982), pp. 173 and 183.
11. R. Crawford, 'Sport for Young Ladies: The Victorian Independent Schools 1875–1925' in *Sporting Traditions*, 1: 1, (November 1984), 66–67.
12. Daly, *Elysian Fields*, p. 183.
13. See N. MacKenzie, 'Vida Goldstein: the Australian Suffragette', in *Australian Journal of Politics and History* 6: 2 (November 1960), 129–204. MacKenzie makes the point that Australia was the first large country to introduce universal adult suffrage and he quotes Alice Zimmern, who in her 1909 survey of the women's suffrage movement commented, 'In Europe and America we may watch the struggles and aspirations after freedom, but we must turn to the Antipodes to see the achievement' (p. 190).
14. *Jubilee History* (The Melbourne Church of England Girls' Grammar School, 1953), pp. 68–9.
15. Ibid., p. 24.
16. Ibid., p. 16.
17. loc. cit.
18. *Church of England Messenger*, 11 January 1895, 10.
19. See J. Tregenza, *Professor of Democracy* (Melbourne, 1968), p. 75.
20. A fuller explanation of physical culture in the girls' schools is given in Crawford, 'Sport for Young Ladies'.
21. Ibid., 2.
22. C.H. Pearson, *The Higher Culture of Women* (Melbourne, 1875), p. 10.
23. Ibid.
24. Dr Maudesley, a leading mental specialist in England, was an opponent of advanced education for women. In 1875 he had raised the argument that the health and functions of a woman would be adversely affected by mental studies. See R. Strachey, *The Cause*, (London, 1978), p. 251.
25. Ailsa Zainu'ddin, *They Dreamt of a School*, (Melbourne, 1982), pp. 34–5.
26. Ailsa Zainu'ddin, 'The Admission of Women to the University of Melbourne, 1869–1903', in S. Murray-Smith (ed.), *Melbourne Studies in Education* (Melbourne, 1973), p. 82.
27. *Bluebell* 4 (December 1885) 61.
28. *Patchwork* (October 1876), 78.
29. *Patchwork* (August 1876), 45.
30. *Patchwork* (September 1876), 50.
31. See the conventions, rules and codes of behaviour set out in *Australian Etiquette, on the Rules and Usages of the Best Society in the Australian Colonies*, People's Publishing Company, Melbourne, 1885.
32. This statement is based on an examination of the school magazines of the Presbyterian Ladies' College and the Methodist Ladies' College by the author.
33. As an example of the concepts and views expressed here see the *Prospectus* of the Methodist Ladies' College (1885–86), 6. The 'Prize Day' speech of Reverend W.H. Fitchett gives a good indication of the educational aims of the schools in the 1880s.
34. Zainu'ddin, *They Dreamt of a School*, pp. 48–9.
35. See A.G. Austin, *Australian Education 1788–1900* (Victoria, 1972), pp. 266–70.
36. Quoted in R.J.W. Selleck, *Frank Tate* (Melbourne 1982), p. 127.
37. N. MacKenzie, *Women in Australia* (Melbourne, 1962), p. 25.
38. Strachey, loc. cit.
39. J. Gathorne-Hardy, *The Public School Phenomenon* (London, 1977), p. 273.
40. Ibid.
41. MacKenzie, op. cit., p. 49.
42. S. Bennett, *The Clarence Comet* (Sydney, 1973), pp. 10–11.

43. See Bruce Howard, *The Proud Australians* (Melbourne, 1978), pp. 12–45.
44. *The School* (June 1900), p. 31.
45. M.E.L. Irving, 'Hockey – Its Development in Our Girls' Schools', *Ruytonian* (April 1928), 19–20.
46. Though Mary went on to America, and Edith to Europe, to study other schools, the English girls' schools left the deepest impression on the co-principals and influenced their educational thinking. This information is given in a letter to the school magazine in 1974 by Gwynneth Morris, the youngest of the three sisters. See *Melbourne Girls' Grammar School Magazine*, 157 (December 1974), 16.
47. Irving, loc. cit.
48. Quoted in Lyndsay Gardiner, *Tintern School and Anglican Girls' Education 1877–1977*, (East Ringwood, 1977), p. 26.
49. M.O. Reid, *The Ladies Came to Stay* (Melbourne, 1961), p. 63.
50. Patriotism to a school, a developing identity through prestige, was also important in the competition for student enrolments. At the start of the twentieth century there were 81 boys' schools, 54 girls' schools, and 747 mixed schools in the private education system in Victoria, holding nearly 32,000 students. *Age*, (23 October 1901), 9.
51. Zainu'ddin, *They Dreamt of a School*, p. 125.
52. J. May, 'The Relevance of Historical Studies in Physical Education', *Physical Education*, 60: 179 (March 1968), 28.
53. Zainu'ddin, *They Dreamt of a School*, p. 130.
54. F.P. Bevill Shipham, 'Corporate Life and Games in Secondary Schools', *Education Times* (January 1899), 4.
55. Quoted in Reid, op. cit., p. 18.
56. Ibid.
57. *School Notes* (April 1907), 21.
58. Zainu'ddin, *They Dreamt of a School*, p. 130.
59. Ibid.
60. The author does not claim that the date set against each sport is accurate. His survey of several school magazines show when the games first appear in discussion.
61. *Jubilee History*, p. 72.
62. *Melbourne Girls' Grammar School Magazine*, 157 (December 1974), 48. This information is contained in a letter to the magazine from Gwynneth Morris (Mrs Coles) who died on 14 January 1974.
63. Ibid.
64. *Brook* (April 1912), n.p.n.
65. *Sport in Schools: The Participation of Girls*, Social Development Unit, NSW Ministry of Education, 1980, p. 13.
66. *Argus*, 27 May 1910, 5.
67. *Argus*, 28 May 1910, 17.
68. Sandercock and Turner, *Up Where Cazaly?*, p. 7.
69. *Speech Day Report* 1908, p. 5, M.C.E.G.G.S. archives.
70. *School Notes* 23 (April 1912), 266–7.
71. *Sport in Schools: The Participation of Girls*, p. 12.
72. For information on the accusations of athleticism made against the Melbourne boys' public schools see R. Crawford, 'Athleticism, Gentlemen and Empire: L.A. Adamson and Wesley College', History of Sporting Traditions IV Conference, Melbourne Cricket Ground, August 1983, organized by La Trobe University.
73. Gardiner, op. cit., p. 78.

9
Physical Activity for Canadian Women, 1890–1930: Media Views

Helen Lenskyj

The 1890s represented a starting point in the movement towards Canadian women's educational, political and economic equality, all of which had implications for their sporting participation and leisure activities. These developments were correctly perceived as a threat to patriarchal hegemony by members of the dominant class/gender – middle-class males.

The medical profession served as a cornerstone for the hegemonic apparatus which defined woman's physical, intellectual and moral ranking in relation to man, and, by extension, her proper place in the world of sport and leisure. Medical pronouncements on safe and acceptable types and levels of physical activity for women reinforced, and in turn were shaped by, the assumption that women's primary function was child-bearing. Like other influential members of the community, doctors were able to express their views on male supremacy and female frailty in the pages of newspapers and periodicals and in the prescriptive literature of the time. Controlled, for the most part, by middle-class males, the print media served class as well as gender interests.

Similar themes characterized many women's magazines, as well as the women's pages of newspapers and periodicals, further evidence of the pervasiveness of an ideology which assigned women a special, albeit inferior, status in society. Journalists frequently solicited the views of leaders of the women's movement or women active in reform organizations like the National Council of Women of Canada (NCWC); with few exceptions, these articles stressed special women's role, not as equals but rather as helpmates to men and moral guardians of society. More explicit examples of the 'separate spheres' ideology were found in the prescriptive literature directed at girls and women, produced by teachers, clergymen and moralists; these publications typically portrayed women's primary interests and duties as domestic.

I

The separate spheres ideology formed the basis for most early pronouncements regarding appropriate sport and leisure pursuits for women. At one pole were the traditionalists like Toronto newspaper man C.S. Clark, writing in 1898, who saw the beginnings of social evil and moral decay in every change in women's lifestyles, ranging from bicycle-riding to choir practice.[1] These critics usually advocated a return to a golden age when young women were modest and selfless, restrained and domesticated.

At the other pole, middle-class women in the social reform movement, whom Canadian historians have subsequently labelled 'maternal feminists', were developing a rationale for their new role in society based on women's innate propensities for nurturing and mothering; it was assumed that these qualities were distributed among all (middle-class) women by virtue of their gender, whether or not they had actually borne children.[2] Thus, they argued that it was the duty of these women to devote their free time to the 'mothering' of the poor and needy, especially at a time when mass immigration, urbanization and industrialization were changing the face of Canada. Maternal feminists stressed, however, that their 'new duties in social services and reform' did not detract from their domestic life: as the author of a *Canadian Pictorial* article expressed it, 'Now, . . . while the home is the centre, it is not also the "circumference" of "women's sphere".'[3] This perspective, reformist rather than revolutionary, served to entrench women's service role, reinforcing the double standard which discouraged women's frivolous or unproductive use of leisure time.

At a time when women's maternal and domestic leanings were considered inherent, and their childhood socialization was geared to a future as wife and mother, public reaction to the changes in dress and lifestyle which resulted from the 'bicycle craze' of the 1890s was predictably mixed. Clark, for example, maintained that girls on bicycles had only one purpose in mind, to associate with boys. 'A girl would be considered decidedly immodest,' he wrote, 'did she go on long tramps with boys, but on her bicycle she can at the same time satisfy her taste for boys' society and satisfy the demands of propriety.'[4] Of course, it was probably this feature of cycling – the opportunity to conduct social and leisure activities beyond the scrutiny of the customary guardians of female virtue – that contributed to its popularity among young women.

The close association between the bicycle and the bloomer was responsible for much of the criticism directed at female cyclists.

Commenting on a current controversy over a picture of ballet dancers, Clark asserted 'that one girl in a bloomer costume will create far greater and more widespread corruption among boys than a city full of show bills [of dancers], so will a well developed girl in short dresses'.[5] Apparently some Toronto trustees agreed with him: in 1895, six out of 19 trustees voted in favour of a motion 'that the inspectors be instructed to report at the next meeting the names of all female teachers who have been riding bicycles in male attire, commonly called "bloomers".'[6] To adopt an article of clothing reserved for man's exclusive use and symbolic of his superior status was, it seems, an offence equally as serious as riding a bicycle.

Not all observers were shocked by the sight of women on bicycles. The editor, as well as several contributors to the Toronto magazine *Athletic Life*, first published in 1895, wholeheartedly endorsed cycling for women, but one journalist did not extend this enthusiasm to the bloomer: '[in Montreal] the fair devotees of the wheel have shown no tendency towards any radical novelty in the way of special bicycle costume, ordinary street clothes being worn. Thank goodness! Save, oh save us from the bloomer girl'.[7]

Articles in *Athletic Life* made some reference to the recreational side of cycling for women, but most of its advocates relied on the guaranteed health and beauty argument which doctors had pioneered when they were promoting activities like physical culture and housework. As the editor of the Women's Pages asserted, even opponents of exercise for women admired 'the increased vitality, the suppleness of body and roundness of limb, to say nothing of the presence of mind' resulting from activities like cycling, rowing and gymnastics.[8] The health gains for men were recognized, too, but references to the psychological benefits seem to have been confined to women, presumably because it was, by that time, axiomatic that sport served to build character and promote mental alacrity in boys and men.

Writing in *Massey's Magazine* of her experiences as a 'lady cyclist', Grace Denison noted the gains to the heart, lungs and head, but she devoted most of the article to her cycling adventures in Canada and the USA. Throughout these amusing accounts, however, there were scattered reminders to the reader that the author was, after all, still a 'lady', sweet and helpless, neither man-hating nor man-aping. She admitted, for example, that 'men are handy to have around when tires blow up, or nuts loosen, or hills are steep, and then there might be cows!' – cows invariably caused Denison and her friends to seek male assistance. Her account of a women's cycling race, too, served to reinforce the prevailing stereotype of women's physical and mental incapacity for the rigours of sporting competition, while, at the same time, her uncharitable depiction of the winner's appearance pandered to the myth of the 'masculine' sportswoman:

> . . . the winner, a fat lady, with a moustache and snapping black eyes . . . promptly fell off in a faint and was immediately sat upon, by a scraggy lady whose hair had gotten loose . . . Being revived [she] snapped her eyes at the dishevelled one and said acidly, "I beat you, anyway, smartie!" It was the most ludicrously feminine way of expressing sport, taking, as woman contests nearly always do, such a pointedly personal turn.[9]

Grace Denison skilfully dissociated herself from this breed of 'lady cyclist' and these 'undesirable exhibitions', her own participation being limited, for the most part, to competition for attendance, not for speed. The 'scorcher', she claimed, was always a man; women were 'too cowardly' to speed. In contrast to this apologetic treatment of the subject, a short item in *Athletic Life* portrayed the female cyclist, at least her Australian version, as an aggressive woman intent on dominating men:

> The 'new woman', according to an Australian exchange, permits 'man, poor man' to be associate members [*sic*] only of their cycling clubs, and proposes to *make* them repair punctures, inflate tires, clean wheels, etc. (emphasis in original)[10]

The apparent inversion of power relations evident in articles like this served to draw public attention away from the more important implications of women's physical activity, presenting this isolated incident as if it were the tip of the iceberg. It is significant, however, that the women in this story were still portrayed as dependent on men. Similarly, columnists like 'Lady Gay', writing for the Toronto newspaper *Saturday Night*, described her cycling tours in a thoroughly feminine manner, thus reassuring readers that lady cyclists were not really a threat to the patriarchal order.[11]

II

A more striking example of media distortion of women's athleticism appeared in *Blackwood's Magazine* (London) in an 1890 article on 'Modern Mannish Maidens'. The unnamed author, using arguments which Dr Arabella Kenealy revived nine years later, depicted women everywhere as abandoning 'the 'old sweet ways' of womanhood' in their quest to conquer men in the work-place, the playing field and the drawing room. This 'hybrid tomboyism', the woman was warned, threatened 'to disturb the seemliness, the dignity, the attractiveness, the lustre' of her sex; it was in 'her sweetness, her weakness, her lovingness' that her alleged 'divinity' lay. In addition to her clever redefinition of weakness as strength, the author set out a new criterion for women's sports: they must not require that a woman 'exhibit herself in an ungainly manner, least of all before men'.[12]

In a section from 'Modern Mannish Maidens' which the editor of the Toronto *Globe's* Women's World saw fit to reprint a month later, the author identified running as one activity for which 'nature most surely did not construct [women]'. They ran, he claimed, with 'a kind of precipitate waddle with neither grace, fitness nor dignity'.[13] Nearly half a century later, Montreal journalist Elmer Ferguson exhumed these arguments in a *MacLean's* article entitled 'I Don't Like Amazon Athletes': 'No sweet feminine girl (and, I repeat, what male doesn't want girls to be sweetly feminine, and nice and sweet and frilly?) can be much good at the more robust forms of athletics'.[14]

Few critics at the turn of the century were so explicit in asserting 'what males want', but, nevertheless, more subtle appeals to feminine modesty and sweetness served to constrain physically active women just as effectively as Ferguson's more direct warnings. Women who cycled, for example, were handicapped by the bulky and restrictive clothing considered modest and feminine. For reasons of safety and comfort, they began to modify the long skirt, struggling with versions 'hobbled by bands of elastic' or weighted down with leaden sinkers, or lightweight skirts which blew in the wind.[15]

As well as these physical handicaps, the belief that women lacked strength and mechanical leanings made them good candidates for the cycling schools which opened up in some Ontario cities in the 1890s, operated by bicycle manufacturers intent on increasing sales. Men, it seems, needed no such instruction, although complaints about the danger posed to pedestrians by cyclists (of both sexes) suggest that men's cycling skill was by no means faultless.[16]

Magazines like *Athletic Life* promoted only a narrow range of physical activities for women. In addition to cycling, its contributors were strong advocates of physical training for women. A four-part series on the subject, written by Captain Seaholm, appeared in 1895, its first year of publication, and subsequent issues regularly included news items related to 'the beneficial results of gymnastic exercises upon the figure and health of a growing girl', in the words of the editor of the Women's Pages.[17] A report on Helen Barnjum's classes for McGill women cited a Montreal reporter's response to their gymnastic ability: 'It encourages faith in the future of a country that will be able to draw from so bright-eyed, healthy-bodied, clean-limbed a host, for the mothers of a coming generation'.[18] The McGill students would have been startled, no doubt, to discover that, during the performance, their bodies had been scrutinized for their breeding potential.

A Montreal newspaper report of the same event a year earlier was somewhat more discreet, commending the women for their 'well-trained flexible muscles which showed that when the time should come for them in the trials of future years to be put to the actual test they would not be found wanting'. These trials were obviously related to the child-bearing and child-rearing which were seen as women's inevitable destiny. This journalist was impressed with the students' marching, too, claiming that it 'would have done credit to a veteran infantry corps'.[19]

In a similar vein, the Women's Pages editor of *Athletic Life* described the achievements of a girl who had trained in the gymnasium for two years: '[she] could take the end of a Martini-Henry rifle of which the butt end was resting on the ground, and raise it easily to the level of her shoulder'.[20] Early issues of *Athletic Life* featured a Military Department, published, according to an editorial, at the request of men connected with the militia. At a time when military men frequently served as physical training instructors for both sexes, the military emphasis was probably not surprising; it demonstrated, too, the tendency to measure athletic competence by male-defined standards.

The Women's Pages of *Athletic Life*, which first appeared in 1896, devoted considerable space to descriptions and illustrations of the gowns worn by women attending the Royal Canadian Yacht Club ball. Social notes like these appeared regularly, as did full-page photographs of female 'beauties', often unidentified, with captions like 'Tall and Divinely Fair'. The only other women whose photographs appeared with any regularity were the actresses featured in the theatre section. There were clear inconsistencies in the editorial policy of a magazine which, in 1895, published Seaholm's critique of North American women – 'pale, weakly, indolent . . . whose interest nothing will arouse outside of the fashion plate, a dress ball or – a flirtation' – and, the following year, proceeded to introduce a section for female readers catering to this (alleged) narrowness of interest and aversion to healthful activity.[21]

Two American magazines first published in the late 1800s also influenced views and practices related to women's physical activity. *Outing*, a New York publication, appeared first as *The Wheelman* in 1883, and *Physical Culture* was published in Boston in 1899. Other popular magazines, American and Canadian, published relevant articles from time to time. Physical activity for women received more comprehensive coverage in *Outing* and *Physical Culture* than in their Canadian counterpart, *Athletic Life*, but the emphasis on health and beauty remained. The titles of some of the early articles in *Outing* indicated this kind of perspective: 'Physical Training for Women: The Attainment of Normal Weight'; 'Women in Athletics: The Athletic Girl not Unfeminine'; and 'How Athletics May Develop Style in Women'.[22]

While articles addressing specific women's issues appeared on a fairly regular basis, the content of *Outing* was intended primarily for men. It was clear that the authors were addressing a middle-class audience: the article on physical training, for example, began by stating that 'there has never before been a time when so many women of culture and refinement were working to improve their general physical development', while 'Women in Athletics' addressed the problems associated with private education for girls who were destined for college or for 'the career of a young lady in society'. References to 'the peculiar demands of twentieth century womanhood' and methods of strengthening 'the organs which are peculiarly feminine' did nothing to dispel the myth of woman's inherent weakness and susceptibility to the strain of modern living. The familiar view of the female as a defective male surfaced, too, in Christine Herrick's article on athletics, where she discussed the way in which physical training served to destroy 'many womanish – not womanly – traits' like lack of self-control, vanity and impatience, while it promoted accuracy, logical thought and a sense of humour, all of which women commonly lacked. A girl's athletic ability, however, 'need not convert her into a mannish woman. It would only ingraft into her nature the gifts she lacks'. Nor would it render her 'unattractive to men', Herrick reassured her readers: the ability to 'endure material hardships' improved her chances in this regard.[23]

Articles like 'Womanhood – Muscles' and 'Strong, Beautiful Bodies for Girls and Women' are indicative of the radically different approach taken by the editor of *Physical Culture*, Benarr MacFadden – an approach which generated considerable criticism and controversy:

> The writer has maintained in this magazine since its inception that there should be but very slight difference between the strength of man and woman – that the proverbial feminine weakness is simply the result of growing into womanhood hampered by the conventional skirt, the bigoted prejudice of parents against play of a romping nature and with the internal organs distorted, bruised and diseased by the terrible corset.[24]

MacFadden's position was exceptional in 1900, as was his rationale for promoting girls' physical development: nowhere did he refer to their role as wife and mother, a remarkable omission for a physical educator of his time. Instead, he stressed the ideals of strength and beauty: girls 'need not be acrobats, but develop within their bodies the same strength, grace and superb beauty'.[25]

Some writers used the growing interest in physical culture to remind female readers of the health benefits to be derived from housework. In a *Popular Science Monthly* article, for example, Alice Tweedy told the story of a doctor whose prescription for a woman's 'fashionable ills' read: 'one broom: use in two hours of housework daily'. For the numerous women who needed more exercise, Tweedy advised additional housework, even to the point of doing without a servant. These housewives, she claimed, 'need not rashly bestride the bicycle, nor rush through the *non-productive* drill of the gymnasium'.[26] (emphasis added) By 1900, more detailed advice was being offered: one article explained how to perform housework in a manner beneficial to the body, paying attention to good posture and bending from the waist rather than the back. The author recommended, too, that housewives rest for five or ten minutes in the middle of the day, but, anticipating that some might view this as the mark of a 'shiftless' woman, she provided a substitute – stretching exercises to promote flexibility and relaxation.[27]

A Hamilton social reformer, Adelaide Hoodless, was more generous to the busy housewife: in her 1898 text for Ontario schoolgirls, *Public School Domestic Science*, she proposed a 'scientifically' organized daily schedule which allowed, after the morning's cooking and cleaning, 'by a systematic and energetic effort . . . at least one hour to rest before preparing dinner or lunch'.[28]

It was probably advice like this which the editor of 'Woman's Sphere' in *The Canadian Magazine* had in mind when she wrote a some-what satirical piece about exercising on a ladder. Commenting on a health and beauty hint in a Sunday newspaper, which had advocated this method for developing grace and agility, the editor suggested that climbing the ladder 'with a pail of water in one hand and a washcloth in the other' would bring even better results; after all, she observed wryly, cleaning and sweeping had 'long been advocated – by those who never do it – as a healthful and stimulating pastime'. She concluded that her personal choice would be 'the regular gymnasium and "its scientific instructor"', but *chacun à son goût*.[29]

Not everyone agreed on the benefits of gymnasium classes; outdoor activities were considered by many to be more beneficial than those conducted under poorly ventilated conditions indoors. Some traditionalists, too, clung to a pastoral image of the ideal 'Canadian Girl' which was incompatible with 'scientific' indoor exercise: she was depicted as 'the flower of this strong, beautiful, northern land', 'a child of nature', 'an authority of outdoor sports' and a lover of 'sun and air and freshness'.[30]

III

Clearly, the two men who described this ideal in *Canadian Magazine* articles were referring to the young women whose social status permitted such a lifestyle. For the large numbers of young working women who laboured up to 60 hours a week for minimal pay, the freedom to enjoy outdoor sports, summer and winter, was limited by both time and money. Organizations like the YWCA, which organized lunch-hour and evening physical training classes, recognized these limitations on employed women, providing facilities, equipment and instructors. At a time when maternal feminists firmly believed that 'working girls' required protection, in the form of sex-segregated lunchrooms and supervised leisure activities, the YWCA's provision of these classes fulfilled a social control function, as well, by discouraging indiscriminate, unchaperoned association with men.[31]

By the war years, in line with the usual premium placed on manpower and womanpower in times of national crisis, there was increased emphasis on women's responsibility to develop to their full physical potential. The views and practices of maternal feminists were compatible with this goal: although they emphasized moral rather than physical strength, they were vocal critics of women of their own class who indulged their alleged weakness by living frivolous, unproductive lives. This advice, for example, appeared in a 1915 edition of *Woman's Century*, the official publication of the NCWC: 'When you cling to the idea of weakness, you are not using the strength which God has given you. You are refusing to accept it and your ability to use it seems to become very small'.[32] Similarly, the principal of Havergal College in Toronto used the 'playing fields of Eton' analogy as a rationale for girls' sporting participation, pointing out that the physical and mental endurance acquired through sport prepared young (middle-class) women for 'professional' and married life.[33]

The advice offered by Marjorie MacMurchy, in *The Canadian Girl at Work*, was directed more towards young working-class women. Alluding to their religious and patriotic duties, she wrote: 'The girl must learn to be her own captain, her own commanding officer. She should give herself orders to take daily exercise . . . we should think of our bodies as fine instruments which are given into our keeping'.[34] Finally, in a 1917 article, Adelaide Plumptre, a leader in the Canadian Red Cross Society and a prominent social reformer, summarized the changes of the preceding few years:

> Co-education and open-air holidays began to lessen the difference between boy and girl, the necessary emergence of women from the stuffy femininity of the drawing-room into the human life of industry and business has been accelerated – though not initiated – by the demands of war, and has disposed for ever of the theory that there is no place for a woman outside her home.[35]

'Stuffy femininity' may have disappeared, but many traditional views and practices were resistant to sudden change. The notion that women were purer than men, and hence, more suited for the role of moral guardians of the home and society, was a popular platform for maternal feminists. At the same time, women were often depicted as temptresses, responsible for the downfall of innocent 'boys'. Blanche Johnson, a 'pioneer leader in temperance, rescue, prison reform' and an editor for the Women's Christian Temperance Union, portrayed women in this light, in a 1918 *Woman's Century* article entitled 'Our Girls and the Post Bellum'. After praising young women for the selflessness and strength they had displayed during the war years, she proceeded to condemn their improper dress – blouses, for example, 'open many inches below the bounds of modesty' – which put temptation 'before that fine type of Canadian manhood', the man in military uniform.[36] The soldier who succumbed was, it seemed, quite blameless; in fact, Johnson expressed greater sympathy for 'the boys exposed to the temptation' than for the young women involved. As well as the sexual double standard implied by such thinking – a typical manifestation of the 'moral guardian' role assigned to women – there were serious implications for the girls and women who wished to adopt less restrictive dress in order to participate more fully in physical activities.

In the early decades of the century, journalists seldom reported women's sporting activities without including details of the participants' clothing and personal appearance, apparently for the purpose of reassuring readers that these women were feminine, that is, charming and attractive, as well as athletic. It was sometimes difficult to carry out this intent, since many athletic women defied prevailing standards of femininity. Mary Trotter, reporting on 'prominent women' for *Everywoman's World*, a Toronto publication, in 1914, included a section on 'A Title Holder in Golf, Miss Florence Harvey'. This golfer, it seemed, could not be fitted into the conventional feminine mould, but Trotter managed to portray an attractive woman, using criteria that differed from those usually employed in the popular press: 'Sportswoman she is from her generous feet to her clear, direct and glowing brown eyes . . . in figure the champion is strongly-knit, in carriage confident, in conversation brilliant. . .'.[37]

Another article in *Everywoman's World*, published one month earlier, expressed a different kind of admiration for sportswomen, reducing their participation in outdoor activities to a kind of fashion show: 'It is something of an axiom', according to journalist Geraldine Dare, 'that the feminine world is ruled by the mandate of fashion'. Women took up rowing, for example, because of 'the decorative possibilities', including the 'natty blouses' which were part of the rowing costume. Moreover, exercise promoted female beauty: 'A full chest and graceful shoulders' were by-products of rowing, while archery was 'conducive to grace of movement' and discus-throwing demonstrated the 'poetry of motion'. One positive note in the article was the author's dismissal of the claim, by some 'prosaic individual', that sweeping constituted better exercise than rowing – apparently, there remained some diehard advocates of the 'housework as exercise' message.[38]

Another distortion in the reporting of women's sporting activity was the tendency to present the achievements of exceptional sportswomen as if they were typical of all women, regardless of such factors as social class, age, opportunity and talent. This kind of journalism, at a time when most Canadian women did not even have the right to vote, evoked a false picture of an egalitarian society where women's access to sport was totally unrestricted. Dare's report, for example, began with the claim that women were now participating in all men's sports, and 'yet more disconcerting to masculine vanity and sense of superiority', the sportswoman, while not receiving any special concessions, still 'more often than not . . . proves herself the "better man" in a competitive contest on equal terms'.[39] It was somewhat premature, too, for Dare to suggest that women's performance in activities like cycling, riding, tennis and golf matched men's. When men and women competed informally against each other, there might well have been women who outperformed men, but, at this very early stage in women's sporting history, there were considerable gaps between the best female and best male performance in virtually every sport.

IV

On the questions of fashion, lifestyle and leisure, middle-class women in the 1920s continued to be influenced by the numerous periodicals which delivered advice on these topics. Advertisers, as well as editors and journalists, played an important part in shaping the public view of female health and beauty, at a time when the manufacturers of feminine hygiene products like deodorants and sanitary napkins, as well as sports clothing, were trying to establish a market. Varying in accordance with the interests of these groups, women were depicted alternatively as active sporting types concerned with functional clothing and healthy lifestyles, and lethargic beauties whose most profound thoughts were related to fashion and men.

Corset advertisements continued to dictate how the female form should be moulded: 'The alteration of styles necessitates a study of the best corsets for the new figure', according to an advertisement in a 1924 issue of the *Canadian Magazine*, which proceeded to recommend a style 'imparting correct lines both front and back'. By 1928, a *Chatelaine* advertisement for Lovers-Form Corset, 'The Corset of Youth', was promising 'a glorious sense of physical freedom'. At the same time, less restrictive undergarments appeared on the market, including the 'knickernick', described as 'the comfortable, charming, lasting underdress . . . no strains, no binding, no blousing'.[40] The writer of a *Chatelaine* fashion column observed, too, that 'today, fashion decrees that sports' clothes and especially bathing suits must be practical as well as decorative'. The clothes illustrated were, as well, 'quite boyish in design', a feature which the writer apparently viewed as adding, rather than detracting from their appeal.[41] The flapper image, of course, required a 'boyish' figure, but the writer's claim that fashion (and not function) decreed practicality was misleading, since it implied that women's involvement in sport and the popularity of comfortable, functional clothing were merely passing fads.

The 1920s brought a marked increase in the number of articles in women's magazines stressing the relationship between exercise, health and beauty, with titles like 'Your Figure and Your Health', 'Exercising for the New Silhouette' and 'Stretch and Stretch Again'.[42] Advice of this kind was directed to the woman employed in an office or shop, who would benefit from vigorous outdoor activities, and to the housewife, whose busy schedule would be relieved by doing some stretching or relaxing exercises. Some of these writers revealed the same traditionalist yearnings for the simpler life of a past era as their nineteenth-century counterparts. A 1927 column on 'Running the

Home', in the *Canadian Magazine's* women's section, warned readers: 'The stress and strain of modern life is increasingly hard on the nerves which become weak and irritable, and sometimes results in temporary or permanent insanity.' While relaxation used to take the form of 'quiet conversation', according to columnist Jane Addison, it had now been replaced by loud jazz music, movies and dancing, which left the brain 'excited but not stimulated'. Concluding on a familiar note, Addison urged women to view their bodies 'as very important machines which need proper care and repair', including adequate rest and moderate exercise.[43]

It was implied, in articles like these, that marriage and motherhood put an end to women's participation in most outdoor sports. A personal story appearing in a 1929 issue of *Chatelaine*, 'Sport Bound: The Plaint of a Mother of a Thundering Herd', listed the problems of a woman whose sons and husband were sports enthusiasts. Her biggest challenge, it appeared, was to perform her domestic duties in 'a hodge-podge of hockey pads, guns, fishing rods, boxing gloves and tennis racquets'.[44] It was clear, however, that she approved of her family's activities and was perhaps envious of the fun and camaraderie which ensued. Doris Butwell Craig recalled that her competence in activities like fishing, skating and badminton enabled her, in adult life, to enjoy the friendship of her brothers and her husband. Moreover, she claimed, the same daring and resilience that contributed to her success in sports before her marriage helped her to cope with the problems of life on a farm with two small children.[45] Most of her contemporaries, however, continued to treat physical activity as a more pressing need for boys than for girls. A mother who gave her views on homework in a 1931 *Chatelaine* article claimed: 'Children need exercise . . . unless one's boys have time to go out in the backyard and play games properly, they will be handicapped through all their school years'.[46]

In addition to the personal stories and advice columns in magazines like *Chatelaine*, advertisements served to reinforce sex-differentiated practices related to physical activity: physiological processes like sweating and menstruating took on new dimensions when deodorants and sanitary napkins appeared on the market. Consistent with patriarchal ideology which expected women to correct their physical imperfections in order to increase their heterosexual appeal, these advertisements made frequent references to the various odours which rendered the female body unattractive. Advertisements for Mum deodorant used the feminine charm argument: 'The whole charming effect of feminine daintiness can so easily be destroyed by the faintest suggestion of perspiration odour'.[47] Clearly, the athletic woman could not hope to maintain the required aura of 'feminine daintiness' which, this advertisement implied, was a prerequisite for male attention.

An effective marketing device used in Mum and Lysol advertisements was to extend the applications of the product. Mum was presented as a multi-purpose deodorant: 'All body odors are instantly and harmlessly neutralized, whether from perspiration or other causes . . . Mum is entirely harmless to the most delicate tissue'. Lysol's pioneering efforts in lifestyle advertising, however, were more direct and pernicious in their allusions to vaginal odour. In a series of husband/wife exchanges, the woman was blamed for her 'misunderstanding' and 'neglect' of feminine hygiene. The consequence of this oversight ranged from chronic tiredness and inertia to 'premature old age' and marital problems. One episode, entitled 'Detained at the Office – Again', hinted that the husband's frequent overtime work, and possibly his extra-marital activities, were to be excused on the grounds that the wife should have paid more attention to feminine hygiene: she 'only has herself to blame' if her vitality and heterosexual appeal are lacking.[48]

To mystify the 'feminine hygiene problem' further, a booklet entitled 'The Scientific Side of Health and Youth' was available from the manufacturers of Lysol. By providing no clues as to the exact cause and nature of these varied health problems, and no indication of the product's application, these advertisements preyed on women's fears, conveying the clear message that the female genitals harboured dirt and disease.[49]

Advertising for sanitary napkins and other 'personal necessities' followed a similar pattern, making reference to doctors' recommendations and to the superiority of 'scientific' products. 'Homemade pads', women were advised, were 'unsanitary and so often dangerous to health'. There were appeals to social class, as well: '8 in 10 better-class women employ Kotex'. Perhaps the only valid claims in these 1928 Kotex advertisements were the promises of greater freedom and comfort, although the euphemism for menstruation – 'times of hygienic distress' – tended to detract from the image of an active woman enjoying these benefits.[50] Advertisements for other products of this kind, like sanitary belts and underwear, portrayed menstruation as a disability. The 'Hickory Personal Necessities' advertisement, for example, offered this explanation: 'Feminine nerves are so sensitive at a time of physical strain, and apprehension about protection just adds to the burden'.[51]

An exception to this trend was a 1929 Modess advertisement which described 'the modern girl – graceful as a greyhound, a lover of the outdoor life – how she has shattered hidebound tradition'.[52] The emphasis on youth here was significant, indicating that the advertisers associated young women with outdoor activities and predicted higher sales among this group. As well, female athletes had attracted considerable media attention in the preceding years and advertisers were probably correct in anticipating that the 'active woman' image would help to sell their product. For the most part, however, the health emphasis prevailed in this kind of advertising. *Chatelaine*, a publication intended almost exclusively for female readers, rarely acknowledged women's growing participation in sport; the outstanding success of the Canadian women's track and field team at the 1928 Olympics, for example, went unnoticed in this, Canada's major women's periodical.

V

By the late 1920s, with many successful women's athletic clubs operating in Ontario, the sportswoman was beginning to share some of the legitimacy as well as some of the censure to which autonomous women in other fields were subjected. A 1927 article in the *Canadian Magazine*, for example, described such women in this way: 'It is difficult to think that a woman who can be a leader in social life and in sports . . . should have anything but a man's broad outlook on life in general'. The writer, Mona Clark, was addressing the question, 'Are Brains a Handicap to a Woman?' She considered the trend towards a 'melting pot' of distinctly masculine and feminine traits to be a healthy one, but concluded that the tendency for talented women to hide their ability was inevitable: 'As long as men are men, they will want to worship rather than admire, and as long as women are women, they will want to be worshipped rather than admired.'[53] A contributor to *Chatelaine*, in 1931, took a similar stand in an article entitled 'I'd Rather Have Beauty Than Brains'.[54]

In contrast to the complacent acceptance of a double standard which made brains in women permissible only if they were accompanied by beauty, Laura Salverson, a prominent Canadian novelist of Icelandic origin, assessed the problem in her typically satirical style:

> Brilliance in a woman is always a grave mistake – a slip on the Creator – and could not be borne except for the happy coincidence that most intellectual women are plain if not ugly. Which proves, of course, that they should have been men, and that only an ox-eyed stare, red sensuous lips, a round voluptuous body and simpering speech constitute feminine loveliness.[55]

There were important parallels between intellectual women and athletic women, as the media preoccupation with the physical appearances of each demonstrated. Then, as now, athletes who met prevailing standards of heterosexual attractiveness received more favourable press coverage: Ethel Catherwood, for example, dubbed the 'Saskatoon Lily' by Canadian journalists, attracted the attention of photographers and reporters in Amsterdam *before* she won the high jump event at the 1928 Olympics. After the track and field team's spectacular success – four medals and the women's team title – media attention, of course, escalated. Canadian papers reacted with an outpouring of national pride, typified by this verse which appeared on the front page of the *Toronto Star* in August 1928:

> The equal of her brother she has proved
> Her worth and holds her solid place unmoved
> In letters, art and every kind of lore
> And calmly waits new kingdoms to explore;
> In mental fitness she has well excelled,
> And now, a record makes in track and field,
> Proving her mettle for the stronger role,
> Where man had thought he held complete control.[56]

Subsequent decisions concerning the elimination of some track and field events for women clearly demonstrated that man's 'complete control' in this realm remained, for the most part, intact. Women's sport had, however, achieved a higher profile in the Canadian press by the late 1920s. Toronto's major newspapers introduced women's sports columns, written by former athletes: 'The No Man's Land of Sport: News and Views of Feminine Sport' by Alexandrine Gibb, appeared in the *Toronto Star* and 'The Girl and the Game', by Phyllis Griffiths in the *Toronto Telegram*. While the *Globe and Mail's* policy, as stated in the 1920s, was 'to encourage frank, open, manly sport', it followed the lead of the other Toronto papers in 1933, when Bobbie Rosenfeld, 1928 Olympic track athlete and one of the leading Canadian sportswomen of the 1920s and 30s, began writing a column entitled 'Sports Reel'.

Women's sports columns in Toronto papers usually included opinion as well as fact: Alexandrine Gibb, for example, added her own interpretation of the proceedings of the Recreation Congress, held in Toronto in 1931. Amazed at some of the retrogressive steps proposed by a small group of American women in physical education – dropping admission charges, eliminating male coaches and restricting women's competition – Gibb demonstrated to readers that these changes were neither necessary nor practical. One of the most energetic exponents of this position at the Congress, Ann Hodgkins, was a former director of the Eaton Girls' Club in Toronto; in 1931, she was working in New York as field secretary for the Women's Division of the National Amateur Athletic Federation (NAAF), a group which, as Gibb pointed out, had been responsible for sending letters to each participating country urging the elimination of women's track and field events from the Olympics.[57] Gibb failed to mention that John Degruchy, a Toronto sportsman who co-chaired the session with her, had taken a position similar to that of the American women. According to another *Star* report, Degruchy had posed several leading questions to the group: 'Has woman sacrificed her great charm of femininity by entering the field of sport?' 'Has the desire to excel in sport relegated the home to the field?' 'Is there any danger of commercializing women's sport?' Gibb, it seemed, preferred to explain the difference of opinion along national rather than gender lines. 'The people of Canada are proud of their girl athletes,' she was quoted as saying. 'The interest is not only because of their success, but also on account of the general good conduct of the girls.'[58]

As manager/chaperone of the women's team during their overseas travels in 1925 and 1928, Gibb had played an important part in ensuring that their morals were above reproach, and she obviously believed that this was an important aspect of female athletes' public image. 'Athletics are good for girls' morals,' she said in an interview with another *Star* journalist, Frederick Griffin, whose article, 'Sport Enhances Womanhood', appeared the Saturday following the Recreation Congress. Gibb explained the moral benefits in this way: 'An athlete can't go out messing around, smoking, drinking, dancing to all hours. She has to stay fit'. Asked the inevitable questions about athletics and reproduction, Gibb was happy to report that the women were not 'neglecting motherhood': Myrtle Cook, an Olympic sprinter, had recently given birth to a healthy baby. A Toronto gynaecologist cited by Griffin claimed, too, that exercise was good preparation for motherhood.[59]

The argument in the press did not die, however; in 1934, another *Star* sports columnist, Andy Lyttle, revived the health arguments. Griffin again took the position that sport was physically and socially beneficial to women, citing the views of Alexandrine Gibb and Lou Marsh, as well as medical opinion. In response to questions about loss of femininity, Gibb stated that poise and charm were enhanced by sport: female athletes were 'just as concerned about their clothes and appearance as their sisters who sit at home, more so'. Griffin added his own interpretation – 'They believe in manicuring and marcel waves' – as well as citing a Los Angeles reporter who had been impressed with the appearance of the Canadian women's team at the 1932 Olympics: 'A close-up of the Canadian gals and one wants to send out a hurry call for the casting directors'. Marsh agreed with Gibb and Griffin: Canadian female athletes were 'feminine' both on and off the field, they were not 'shy or diffident', nor were they 'rough or repellent'. During overseas tours, they had been complimented on their 'sweet and ladylike' behaviour, according to Marsh.[60]

These articles were typical of the press debate in the early 1930s. It was significant that women like Gibb, a former athlete and a leader in women's sport, participated on terms dictated, for the most part, by male journalists and sportsmen, as she defended female athletes against the charges of 'lost femininity'. Gibb, of course, shared their concern for the morals and deportment of athletes representing Canada, and, under her supervision, their conduct appears to have been exemplary. Commenting on Gibb's statements, however, Hilda Thomas Smith maintained that, as a journalist, Gibb used public interest in the femininity issue for her own ends.[61] Whatever the reasons, this kind of reporting gave the issue unnecessary prominence, with the coverage of women's athletic performance often suffering as a consequence.

Another distortion evident in the femininity debate was the tendency to dissociate contemporary developments from their early roots. One article after another began with criticism, verging on ridicule, of the women who, in fact, paved the way for their daughters' and granddaughters' sporting participation. These included the early cyclists, golfers, tennis players, physical culturists and dress reform advocates. Gibb was among the journalists who adopted this approach, as she emphasized how much progress women had made since those early days: 'The masculine girl was an oddity of the Victorian age. Nowadays, a girl, essentially feminine, does not become masculine because she sprints or plays softball'.[62] Griffin, too, characterized the early female athlete as 'a mannish creature . . . she wore tweeds, took long, manly strides and spoke in a deep voice'.[63]

It was understandable, of course, that the unprecedented level of women's participation evoked rhetoric and hyperbole in the press. One sportswriter, however, noted that it was the sceptical journalists and critics at the turn of the century who had been responsible for labelling the female athlete a 'strident, belligerent Amazon whom the militant suffragette atrociously exemplifies'. Henry Roxborough's article, 'The Illusion of Masculine Supremacy', published in a 1935 issue of the *Canadian Magazine*, was not only unusual for this insight, but also because it was one of the first to compare male and female

performance in terms of rates of improvement. In a variety of sports –
track and field, golf, tennis, rowing, swimming – women were making
more dramatic improvements than men, so that the gap between the
sexes was narrowing.[64] Clearly, these were more valid comparisons
and more convincing evidence of women's physical potential than
many of the earlier commentaries produced. Roxborough's reporting, however, was not totally free of the biases of his times: a 1930
article, 'Are We Sport Crazy?', made only passing reference to
women's participation, and even in his 1966 history of nineteenth-
century Canadian sport, *One Hundred – Not Out*, his treatment of
women's sport occupied only one of the 27 chapters, and it bore the
title, 'The Invasion of Women'.[65]

VI

It was probably recognition that women's performance was steadily
improving and that their participation was not a passing fad that
prompted *MacLean's* journalist Elmer Ferguson to launch his attack
on the 'Amazons' of women's sport. Anxious to defend himself from
the 'girl sports columnists' who had taken issue with him in the past,
Ferguson agreed that 'girls have a place in sport' – a place
characterized by 'grace, sweetness, rhythm, freedom from sweat and
freedom from grime'. In contrast, sports producing sweat and strain
were unfeminine, clearly an indictment from a man who assumed that
his female readers were more concerned with attracting male
attention than with developing their athletic ability. Giving the views
of doctors, journalists and even a female athlete to support what he
called a 'sensible' position on the issue, Ferguson pointed out that few
men enjoyed seeing their 'girlfriends' sweating and straining, nor
were women particularly 'alluring' with bare legs and dirty faces. His
arguments were indistinguishable from those of his nineteenth-
century counterparts, as was his particularly scathing attack on the
athletes whom he considered unattractive. One was a successful
sprinter, identified only as the 'Galloping Ace', whom he described as
'a big, lanky, flat-chested, muscular girl, with as much sex appeal as
grandmother's old sewing machine'. The 'pretty girl runners', he
claimed, were less successful than the 'leather-limbed, horselike-
looking stars', a pattern which 'proved' that masculinity was a
prerequisite for success in 'violent sports'.[66]

Critics like Ferguson made it clear to their readers that strain, sweat
and dirt were incompatible with their view of femininity. According to
advertising for feminine hygiene products, however, the source of
odours, dirt and disease was the female body itself, with even mild

forms of physical activity exacerbating the problem. Clearly, it was unlikely that physically active women would satisfy these criteria of femininity, unless they met or surpassed other measures of feminine beauty. Most vulnerable to Ferguson's brand of criticism, both in the 1930s and today, were women who lacked aesthetic qualities like grace and beauty, both in personal appearance and in performing their chosen sport. Definitions of these qualities were, of course, sex-specific: Ferguson's adjectives 'big' and 'muscular', applied to male athletes, would have conveyed the writer's admiration, not, as applied to female athletes, his contempt.

With criticism of women's sports mediated by these kinds of criteria, one activity, swimming, appeared to escape much of the censure directed at track and field. Included in the 1912 Olympic Games and in the first British Empire Games in 1930, swimming and diving were generally accepted as appropriate activities for women, even at a competitive level. Gracefulness of movement was facilitated by the water and the problem of body odour was eliminated; with the kind of 'sanitary' protection available early in the century, it appears unlikely that many women swam while menstruating, and thus the problem of over-exertion at this time was alleviated. Moreover, the masculine body type was not a prerequisite for success; in fact, additional body fat proved valuable for the maintenance of body temperature, especially in long-distance swimming.

Despite these advantages, the problem of dress, ever present in women's sport, had served to limit girls' and women's access to swimming for decades. In Toronto at the turn of the century, for example, it was common for boys to swim in the rivers or at the lake and island beaches without clothes. The city provided free street car and ferry service and, according to one account, 'free bathing beaches swarmed with boys' during the summer months.[67] It was not until 1925, however, that public money was used to provide free swimming instruction for both girls and boys, in Board of Education facilities, a step which corrected some of the earlier inequalities of access experienced by girls who could not enjoy the 'gloriously free, untrammelled' play of their brothers.[68] Even in the privacy of a segregated pool, girls, as late as 1913, swam almost fully clothed, in a full-skirted dress and cotton stockings. The modern style of one-piece swimsuit was available by the 1920s, made of '100% pure wool', according to one advertisement. A necessary feature of the early suits was a 'skirt' to protect female modesty; even as late as 1937, there was opposition to a proposed skirtless tank suit which University of Toronto women wished to adopt, with 'The Great Swim Suit Controversy' debated in the pages of Toronto newspapers.[69]

Long-distance swimming for women, following Gertrude Ederle's success, gained recognition in Ontario in 1926 when the Canadian National Exhibition introduced an annual World Championship Lake Swim. Several shorter lake and river races, up to three miles in length, were held in the Toronto and Hamilton areas in the late 1920s, as well as indoor championships conducted in YMCA pools. Girls and women participated in almost all of these events, with the Toronto women's club, the Dolphinets, producing most of the record-holders. The level of public interest at this time was reflected in a new sport magazine, *The Canadian Athlete*, published in Toronto in 1928; its first issue was devoted to swimming and, unlike many contemporary publications, the reporting of women's performances was notable for the absence of irrelevant comments on their physical attractiveness.[70]

Despite the apparent progress made in the post-war period – the relaxation of earlier restrictions on women's lifestyle and clothing, greater access to a variety of team and individual sports, the higher visibility of female athletes in the media – many traditional views and practices remained. Although women were participating in increasing numbers and proving their competence in many areas of sport, patriarchal definitions of femininity, stressing sweetness, passivity and dependence, were slow to change. For the female athlete, this ideology was manifested in the widespread acceptability of activities believed to promote grace, agility and charm, and the subsequent media attention which the graceful and charming female athlete received confirmed the efficacy of these definitions. On the other hand, sweat and strain on women's faces, like clothing which revealed the limbs, destroyed the mystery of femininity as well as eroding a major rationale for women's subordinate position in society: women were not innately frail and weak, nor would they always need or want male protection. In other words, women's sporting activities were counter-hegemonic.

NOTES

This chapter is an edited version of Chapter 5 of my dissertation, 'The Role of Physical Education in the Socialization of Girls in Ontario, 1890–1930' (unpublished Ph.D. thesis, University of Toronto, 1983).

1. C.S. Clark, *Of Toronto the Good* (Montreal 1898).
2. See, for example, the essays in Linda Kealey (ed.), *A Not Unreasonable Claim* (Toronto: Women's Educational Press, 1979), especially Wayne Roberts, ' "Rocking the Cradle for the World": The New Woman and Maternal Feminism, Toronto 1877–1914', pp. 15–45.
3. 'Women's Movement and Progress', *Canadian Pictorial* (January 1911), 19.
4. Ibid., 112.
5. Ibid.

6. Toronto Board of Education minutes, cited in 'Women in Education' series, Toronto Board of Education, 1975.
7. 'Notes from Montreal', *Athletic Life* 1 (June 1895), 275.
8. 'Women's Pages', *Athletic Life* 3 (March 1896), 124.
9. Grace Denison, 'The Evolution of the Lady Cyclist', *Massey's Magazine* (April 1897), 283.
10. Ibid., 1 (April 1895), 195.
11. See, for example, *Saturday Night* Women's Pages (March 1896).
12. 'Modern Mannish Maidens', *Blackwood's Magazine* 147 (February 1890), 252–64; Arabella Kenealy, 'Woman as an Athlete', *Living Age* 3 (May 1899), 363–70; 'Woman as an Athlete: A Rejoinder', *Living Age* 4 (July 1899), 201–13.
13. 'Woman's World', *Globe* (15 March, 1890), 12. See also Helen Lenskyj, ' "A Kind of Precipitate Waddle"': Early Opposition to Women Running', in Nancy Theberge and Peter Donnelly (eds.), *Sport and the Sociological Imagination* (Fort Worth, 1983), pp. 153–61.
14. Elmer Ferguson, 'I Don't Like Amazon Athletes', *MacLean's Magazine* 51 (1 August, 1938), 9, 32.
15. Denison, op. cit., 281–2.
16. See, for example, the advertisement for women's bicycles and cycling instruction in *Saturday Night* (21 March 1896), 8.
17. Captain A.W. Seaholm, 'Physical Training', *Athletic Life* 1 (May 1895), 207–9; (June) 266–9; 2 (July) 22–5; (August) 73–6; 'Women's Pages', 3 (March 1896), 125.
18. 'Montreal Sport', *Athletic Life* 3 (April 1896), 231.
19. Jesse Harriott, 'The Department of Physical Education for Women', *McGill News* (Autumn 1935), 36.
20. *Athletic Life* 3 (April 1896), 171–2.
21. Seaholm, op. cit., 208.
22. J.V. Gillman, 'Physical Training for Women', *Outing* 39 (December 1901), 319–26; Christine Herrick, 'Women in Athletics', *Outing* 40 (September 1902), 713–21; Elizabeth Dryden, 'How Athletics May Develop Style in Women', *Outing* 42 (July 1903), 413–18.
23. Gillman, 319–20, 324; Herrick, 714, 716, 721.
24. Editorial, 'Womanhood – Muscle', *Physical Culture* 1 (August 1899). 181–4. This was a rebuttal to Kenealy's article, cited above. Benarr MacFadden, 'Strong, Beautiful Bodies for Girls and Young Women', *Physical Culture* 3 (May 1900), 113.
25. Ibid., 115.
26. Alice Tweedy, 'Homely Gymnastics', *Popular Science Monthly* 40 (February 1892), 526–7.
27. Martha van Rensselaer, 'Physical Education Applied to Housework', *The Chatauquan* 34 (February 1902), 532.
28. Adelaide Hoodless, *Public School Domestic Science* (Toronto, 1898), p. 122.
29. 'Woman's Sphere', *Canadian Magazine* 21 (September 1903), 469–70.
30. Reginald Gourlay, 'The Canadian Girl', *Canadian Magazine* 7 (October 1896), 508; Hector Charlesworth, 'The Canadian Girl', *Canadian Magazine* 1 (May 1893), 187–8.
31. For YWCA programs and policy, see, for example, Josephine Harshaw, *When Women Work Together: A History of the Young Women's Christian Association in Canada* (Toronto, 1966).
32. *Woman's Century* 3 (October 1915), 19.
33. Ellen Knox, *Girl of the New Day* (Toronto, 1919), pp. 19, 28.
34. Marjorie MacMurchy, *The Canadian Girl at Work* (Toronto 1919), pp. 118–9.
35. Adelaide Plumptre, 'Some Thoughts on the Suffrage', in John Miller (ed.), *The New Era in Canada* (Toronto, 1917), p. 311.
36. Blanche Read Johnson, 'Our Girls and the Post Bellum', *Woman's Century* (Special Number, 1918), 77, 79.
37. Mary Trotter, 'Prominent Women', *Everywoman's World* (July 1914), 33.
38. Geraldine Dare, 'Fun in the Open Air', *Everywoman's World* (June 1914), 11.
39. Ibid.

40. Advertisements, *Canadian Magazine* 62 (March 1924), 11; *Chatelaine* 1 (March and November, 1928), *passim.*
41. 'Knitted Things for Out-of-Doors', *Chatelaine* 1 (May 1928) 28.
      Chatelaine was first published in 1928, subsuming the *Canadian Home Journal*. It was well received and widely read: when an advertisement asking readers to submit names for a new women's magazine appeared in *MacLean's* that year, 75,000 people responded. The magazine focused on fashion, beauty, consumer news, investigative reporting and fiction. See Marjorie Harris, 'Fifty Golden Years of Chatelaine, 1928–1978', *Chatelaine* 51 (March 1978), 43–55.
42. 'Your Figure and Your Health', *Everywoman's World* (November 1919), 14; M. Agniel, 'Exercising for the New Silhouette', *Ladies' Home Journal* 47 (March 1930), 62; Helen Hathaway and Barbara Beattie, M.D., 'Stretch and Stretch Again', *Good Housekeeping* 90 (June 1930), 38–9, 230–3; Margaret Fox, 'Every Woman Should Lead a Double Life', *Chatelaine* 1 (April 1928), 1, 42.
      American magazines like *Ladies' Home Journal* and *Good Housekeeping* were widely read in Canada; the influx of untaxed 'foreign' periodicals, estimated at 60 million copies in 1928, prompted the Canadian National Newspaper and Periodicals Association to publish an advertisement in the *Canadian Magazine* 69 (February 1928), 37, which warned readers of the dangers of permitting incorrect ideas regarding Canada and the Empire to be spread in this way.
43. Jane Addison, 'Running the Home', *Canadian Magazine* 68 (September 1927), 27, 41.
44. Mrs H.D. McCorquodale, 'Sport Bound: The Plaint of a Mother of a Thundering Herd', *Chatelaine* 2 (May 1929), 9, 73.
45. Doris Butwell Craig interview, 23 January 1983, Toronto.
46. 'Is Homework a Necessity?' *Chatelaine* 4 (April 1931), 13.
47. Deodorant advertisement, *Chatelaine* 1 (April 1928), back cover.
48. Ibid.
49. See Lysol advertisements, *Chatelaine* 1 (1928), *passim*. These parallels between personal and domestic hygiene were discussed by Veronica Strong-Boag in 'Canadian Domestic Technology in the 1920s and 1930s', a paper presented at the University of Toronto Conference on Women, Power and Consciousness, 30 October – 1 November 1981.
50. See, for example, Kotex advertisement, *Chatelaine* 1 (March 1928), 65.
51. Hickory Personal Necessities advertisement, *Chatelaine* 1 (April 1928), 76.
52. Modess advertisement, *Chatelaine* 2 (May 1929), 44.
53. Mona Clark, 'Are Brains a Handicap to Women?' *Canadian Magazine* 67 (February 1928), 27.
54. Nan Robins, 'I'd Rather Have Beauty Than Brains', *Chatelaine* 4 (February 1931), 3–6, 57.
55. Laura Salverson, *The Viking Heart* (Toronto, 1947), p. 139. Salverson was writing about attitudes in the early 1900s.
56. Joseph Cook, 'Canadian Women and the Olympic Games', *Toronto Star* (8 August 1928), 1.
57. See Alexandrine Gibb's column, 'The No Man's Land of Sport', *Toronto Star*, for the week of 5 October 1931.
58. 'Would Train Women to Run Girls' Sport', *Toronto Star* (6 October 1931).
59. Frederick Griffin, 'Sport Enhances Womanhood', *Toronto Star Weekly* (10 October 1931), 16.
60. Griffin, 'Girls, Is Sport Good For You?' *Toronto Star Weekly* (31 March 1934), 3.
61. Hilda Thomas Smith interview, 1 February 1983.
62. Gibb, cited in Griffin, 'Girls'.
63. Griffin, 'Sport'.
64. H.H. Roxborough, 'The Illusion of Male Supremacy', *Canadian Magazine* 84 (May 1935), 45, 55.
65. Roxborough, 'Are We Sport Crazy?' *Canadian Magazine* 73 (March 1930), 7, 54–5; *One Hundred – Not Out* (Toronto, 1966), 239–44.
66. Ferguson, op. cit.

67. 'Toronto's Free Swimming Schools', *The Canadian Athlete* 1 (March 1928), 13. See also Clark, op. cit., 4–5.
68. This was the phrase used by Margaret Galloway in *I Lived in Paradise* (Winnipeg, 1925), p. 151, in reference to her memories of childhood swimming, where boys and girls each had their own swimming holes.
69. Swimming costume advertisement, back cover of *The Canadian Athlete* 1 (March 1928); see also A.E. Marie Parkes, *The Development of Women's Athletics at the University of Toronto* (Toronto, 1961), p. 33.
70. 'A Review of Swimming History During 1927', *The Canadian Athlete* 1 (March 1928), 5–9; 'Here are the Six Best Lady Natators in Canada', ibid., 16.

PART FOUR

AMERICAN PERSPECTIVES

10

'Good Wives' and 'Gardeners', Spinners and 'Fearless Riders': Middle- and Upper-rank Women in the Early American Sporting Culture

Nancy L. Struna

In the social history of early American sport, women have been ambiguous creatures. Out of this work, some will emerge slightly less ambiguous, but ideally no longer as creatures. Except for the initial years of settling Virginia, women were both agents and clients in the definition of colonial and early nineteenth-century society and its sport. This piece suggestively sketches the involvement of white, middling and upper rank Anglo-American and, eventually, American women in this era's sporting life.[1]

The evidence about women's sporting experience suggests three primary historical sub-periods. The first spanned much of the seventeenth and the initial decades of the eighteenth centuries, a relatively long time when women were secondary and complementary to male colonials. The first half of this era receives little treatment here, and it remains poorly understood in large part because women themselves were few and the records are fragmentary at best. From the 1680s until about 1720, however, one can suggest more numerous and firmer inferences about the emergence of distinct patterns predicated on gender. As 'good wives' and 'gardeners' women entered what was a male domain as 'outlivers', complements in several ways to the main sporting action. The years between the 1720s and the 1760s comprise the second sub-period, a comparatively short, transitional one. Subtle changes began to affect the earlier patterns as women became more involved and involved in different ways in the sporting culture. The 1760s marked the beginning of the third and final sub-period. Pre- and post-Revolutionary women began to privatize sport, a movement which, when combined with late eighteenth- and early nineteenth-century reality and the ideal of the republican mother, precipitated a separate sphere of women's sport. Women's privatization of sport achieved its fullest expression and its ideological sanction in the cult of domesticity during and after the 1820s.

I

At first glance, the extant records would seem to transmit very little information about women in the colonial Anglo-American sporting experience before the second quarter of the eighteenth century. In fact, during much of the seventeenth century women's presence was occasionally implicated but rarely defined. In 1635, for example, the emigré minister Richard Mather presumably spoke for the female as well as the male travellers to Massachusetts Bay when he acclaimed the shipboard slaughter and carving of a porpoise as 'wonderful to us all and marvelous merry sport'.[2] Estate inventories from the 1640s, 1670s and 1680s in the two earliest British colonized regions, Massachusetts and the Chesapeake, also suggest that a few women had access to instruments for sport, especially horses, carbines, and cards. Such records do not, of course, verify the use of these in sport by women at a time when traditional British notions of sport as diversion (a 'carrying away from') and recreation (a 'carrying toward') still prevailed.[3] Nor does the presence of women at communal gatherings uniting work and sport in raisings, huskings, and trainings clarify the female role.[4]

From all of this, the historian might conclude that the records are simply too few and too fragmentary to permit any discussion of the earliest colonial women's sporting experience. And given the small number of women within the seventeenth century population, this might be the safest decision.[5] However, the very nature of the evidence – indirect and implication-oriented – may itself be revealing. Such records do at least suggest that the Anglo-American women's experience was both secondary and complementary to that of colonial men.

This seems to be precisely the point of a court case near Springfield, Massachusetts in 1662. Accused of breaking a law against playing cards in private dwellings, John Henryson admitted his guilt. Three or four other times, in fact, he had been 'willing to have recreation for my wife to drive away melancholy'. The act occurred from John's decision 'to [do] anything when his wife was ill to make her merry', but the cards belonged to the sickly Martha. In the end, the court fined both of the Henrysons in line with their perceived responsibility in the matter. Martha paid five shillings for playing, while John's penalty was four times as costly. He submitted twenty shillings because in the court's view, he had 'suffered that unlawful Game . . . to be played in his howse'.[6]

The Henrysons' case may have been an anomaly in the middle third of the seventeenth century. Other women do not appear to have been as visible in any sporting venture as Martha was, and they would not be for two more decades. From the 1680s until the 1720s, however, some middling and upper-rank women did become more evident in the colonial sporting life as sport itself assumed definition and consistency and as the colonial sex ratio became more nearly equal.[7] Two patterns in particular emerged. First, men and women engaged together in card and billiard games, in boating, and in horseback riding. Occasionally these were private activities, in one's home, fields, or on a nearby river or bay. Sporting activities by men and women also appeared at public rituals which were events of commemoration, celebration, and cohesion. At farms, plantations, and towns in the northern and the southern colonies, these public events ranged from harvest festivals and trainings, to ministers' ordinations, to entertainments for weddings and anniversaries, elections and appointments, and deaths.[8]

The second pattern placed women in a position which was ancillary to the main action, the public sporting contests of colonial men. This pattern appears to have been more common in the south than in New England, partly at least because of differences in the stability of regional institutions. In the Chesapeake in particular as the largest landowners and merchant planters established horse races as public domonstrations of prowess and social order, both of which were essential to the organization of an ordered society, women began to appear. They did so for certain not as contestants but as observers, albeit not necessarily inert ones. As did common planters, servants and slaves, the women watched as their husbands, fathers and brothers competed over quarter-mile distances. The fact that many Chesapeake women, perhaps most, could and indeed did ride and even sat upon their horses as the match took place apparently did not alter the evident gender and rank definition of these events.[9]

Both patterns, though different in structure, share common features. First, in neither case did women appear as competitors. In fact when men and women engaged together, the event was primarily a ride rather than a race, or a manifestation of skill and agility rather than a test. The physicality of women was not an item for public consumption; indeed, no evidence indicates that women displayed the physical aggressiveness inherent in public sporting contests. Second, women did not make the rules which separated sport from ordinary tasks; nor did they define the social performance, although they may well have been instrumental in ordering the behaviour of the male participants and spectators. In sum, women came as complements, as 'good wives' and friends, as tenders of order and propriety.[10] To borrow Annette Kolody's metaphors, women came as 'gardeners' to the sporting scene; men, as 'conquerors'.[11]

Both the Henryson anecdote and the broader late seventeenth- and early eighteenth-century patterns support historians' descriptions of other male-female relationships of the time. The seventeenth and the early eighteenth centuries beget a hierarchical world in which the 'pervasive realities of ordinary existence', as well as ideology, sustained both patriarchy and male–female complementariness.[12] Martha Henryson was the 'good wife' who supplied her husband with what he needed, the cards and her participation, to improve her condition. So, too, was Maria Byrd, the wife of the early eighteenth-century Virginia planter, William Byrd II. On numerous occasions, and usually when no one else was present, the two played cards. At least once he made her 'out of humor by cheating' at piquet, but Maria apparently never turned the tables or sought redress.[13]

Whether as owner and dispenser of equipment as in the case of Martha Henryson and other women who owned taverns, or as the second player who made sporting participation possible, or even as race observer, seventeenth- and early eighteenth-century women were essentially 'outlivers' in what was a predominantly male enterprise. This does not mean, of course, that colonial women were passive onlookers. It does mean, however, that women did not ordinarily and regularly perform as did men, although on small plantations and rural farms the lines between men's and women's physical actions certainly could and did blur. Mrs Francis Jones, the wife of a small planter in southern Virginia, is a case in point. She could 'perform the most manfull Exercises as well as most men in those parts'.[14] Such exceptions notwithstanding, sport – useful, competitive recreation among Anglo-Americans after 1680 – was first and foremost a part of the male domain. It was a 'manfull Exercise' characterized by physical prowess, competition and conquest, and prestige in both the public and private arenas. These were also the qualities embedded in the male role and acted out by men who, for the most part, were bound to the land or sea and to the husbandry of either. No comparable feminine-defined experiences appear to have occurred within women's lives at this stage, experiences which derived from daily tasks and were ordered and replicable cultural performances.[15]

II

As early as the 1720s and particularly during the middle third of the century, the actions of women began to change. New England townswomen availed themselves of the increase in horses to ride either in the saddle or in a chaise 'to take air'.[16] Horseback riding also enabled women like Mrs Walcott of Salem to travel to join her husband and to go fishing in 1724.[17] Enterprising southern women, some of whom were widows, used two of the era's developments, the newspaper and the printing trade, to announce their arrangements for balls, assemblies and dancing lessons, as well as to obtain cards and other equipment for their taverns and, in some cases, their homes.[18] Further, by the 1740s the *Virginia Gazette* had begun to advertise the goods and services offered by upholsterers and other craftsmen to both sexes, to 'all Gentlemen, Ladies, and others'.[19] Then, too, in that decade and the next 'well-legged' girls had opportunities to run foot and horse races at local fairs.[20]

These examples represent subtle rather than radical changes in the approach of women to life and to sport in public, at least, as well as in the perceptions of some women by some men. Clearly, Mrs Walcott remained a 'good wife', but one whose role as such now encompassed the previously male activity of fishing. Nor had the women who arranged and advertised balls and who purchased sporting equipment subverted their positions as mistresses. As colonial women traditionally had, they acted in ways which enabled them to manage their economies. Only the races for girls actually suggest a significant departure in practice. However, given that the term specified was that of 'girl', at a time when gender was less of a factor in children's activities than it was for adults, even this defies revolutionary change.[21]

Another set of actions reinforces the impression of subtle change in the activities of middle- and upper-rank women in the middle third of the eighteenth century. Both as private endeavours and in public, gatherings of men and women for sport became almost commonplace, and they certainly involved patterned action. In the south the key event was the horse race, and after mid-century cockfights also became fairly common. In the case of horse races, women attended as before, but two differences emerged. First, women occasionally observed from the centre of what had become bona fide tracks, and by the 1760s they had begun to sponsor purses and even occasionally to wager on the contestants. Second, the match itself was followed by a dance, a ball in colonial parlance. Together, the race or cockfight and the ball constituted a virtual social formula.[22]

In New England, especially in eastern Massachusetts, the 'frolic' became standard social fare. For adults in their thirties and forties, and even older, a set of patterned actions appeared. Walks on commons or malls, minuets and country dances, sailing in the harbours, or sleigh rides formed the first act. A dinner or picnic followed, and the evening ended at cards or a lecture. For younger colonials, the action was likely to be more demanding and to last longer into the night, occasionally at a tavern for fiddling and dancing.[23]

Both sets of activities suggest two differences in women's involvement in sporting engagements, compared with what it had been in the decades before the 1720s. First, the position of women, the location within the sporting scene, had altered. They had moved closer to the action, be that to the centre of the track, on the rail, or in the boat or sleigh. Second, the action formula clearly incorporated them. Indeed, within the dances and balls men and women participated equally.

Again, these were subtle changes in the sporting culture. Although women appeared to share in the event in ways not evident earlier, they did not yet fully mediate or define or provoke it. Other alterations which would have revolutionized women's involvement in sport had not, of course, occurred. The primary factor absent from the sporting scene among women was that of competition, or even some alternative perception of the heart of the action in sport. Neither races nor cockfights involved women competing, nor did harbour sails or sleigh journeys. In fact, the older sense of 'ride' persisted in the walks, the boat trips, and the sleighing ventures. In sum, the precise rendering of women's complementariness had changed, but they remained complementary none the less.

Why then did these changes, however subtle, occur, and what did they mean for the broader Anglo-American colonial sporting culture? A part of the answer to the first question lies in the expanding eighteenth-century economy and demographic changes which altered women's activities even as they left gender role essentially unaffected. Women in households with income above the level needed for subsistence had more access to imports and colonial-made goods, to horses and equipment for sport. Also, particularly in the cases of taverners and sponsors of assemblies and balls, governments and customers expected and encouraged economic enterprise among women, especially those without husbands, as an alternative to relying on ill-developed public relief. Then, too, the mortality rate declined, more than half of the colonial population consisted of people under 16 years of age, and families stabilized and became significant agents in colonial culture. Combined with the individualization of religious experience, these factors emphasized the maternal and wifely responsibilities and functions of women, especially those of moral arbiter, teacher, and friend. Thus, it is not surprising that Mrs Walcott rode to join her husband and went fishing, or that southern planter women in particular moved to centre-stage at horse races and dances, where both husbands and children were also found.[24]

A second part of the answer lies in the fact that colonials during the middle third of the eighteenth century turned towards the body and physical expression, rather than away from these as had their predecessors in the previous century. By the 1740s Boston had a 'Physical Club', and learned men like Benjamin Franklin and John Adams extolled the importance of bodily development and exercise.[25] 'Exercise invigorates, and enlivens all the Faculties of Body and of Mind', wrote Adams in 1756. 'It spreads a gladness and Satisfaction over our minds and qualifies us for every Sort of Buisiness [sic], and every Sort of Pleasure.'[26] Such sentiments did not, for certain, apply specifically to women, although Adams for one would later entreat his wife, Abigail, to interest herself in the physical development of both their children and herself. But the absence of conscious attention to women's bodies and physicality did not deny changes in practice and, perhaps, awareness. Besides Mrs Walcott's fishing and other women's rides 'to take air', public rituals also belied a physical expressiveness not evident earlier in the century or in the previous century. Whether it was a ritual of abasement, as in the case of religious revivals, or a ritual of fulfilment, such as the frolics, women participated actively.[27] One astute observer also perceived women using their bodies to their advantage while dancing. At a ball in Annapolis in 1744, William Black, a travelling Virginian, concluded that the 'Ladies' who were dancing appeared to be flirting. In his view, they seemed to be trying to test the 'strength and vigor' of their partners and to convince the men of their own 'Activity and Sprightliness'.[28]

It is important to emphasize that Black found these women testing, rather than contesting, their male counterparts. His conclusion confirms that mostly subtle changes had occurred in women's actions, particularly in relation to men and primarily in the public scene. Yet even that he should have recorded such a process, which occurred away from the home at a ball, suggests that another more fundamental change was occurring in the middle third of the eighteenth century. John Adams's separation of 'Buisiness' and 'Pleasure' and his virtual order to Abigail – 'you will,' he wrote to her before they married, 'make a better Figure in the elegant and necessary Accomplishment' of card play – also indicate that such a significant change was occurring in the conception of the place of sport in the lives of middling and upper rank colonials.[29] Neither the testing of men by women nor card play were germane to the working lives of these middle- and upper-rank colonials. None the less, they occurred because work and sport, or the broader leisure, had begun to emerge as separable entities in the middle third of the eighteenth century. Such a separation, even in the initial stage as it was at mid-century, was itself a part of the broader reconceptualization of colonial life which would eventually, certainly by the end of the century, result in other dichotomies: in the divorce of church and state, in debates and discussions involving the ideal types of freedom and slavery and yeomen and townsmen, and in the gradual idealization of domesticity, a clearly distinct women's sphere.[30]

The initial divorce of work and sport, as well as the organization of opportunities for sport which did not depend solely or even primarily on traditional utilitarian endeavours and cycles, occurred in the easternmost regions of the Anglo-American colonies after the 1720s. Compared with the traditional forms of sport which might be characterized as 'natural' ones – those tied to historical ways of life and rituals, to the utility of land and sea – newer, even 'artificial' forms emerged. Cockfighting, fox-hunting, and, of course, sailing and sleighing for pleasure, for example, appeared. None of these, for certain, was distinguished by movement forms or outcomes which translated directly into work practices. The times for such events and even the codes of conduct which governed, or failed to govern, the actions of the participants also negated traditional work-discipline. Indeed, days-long shooting and gambling contests and forays, New Englanders' frolics, and races between Chesapeake galley-style crafts manned by slaves were time- and energy-consuming affairs which actually required recovery time.[31]

Whether women were agents in the separation of work and sport, or work and leisure, and whether such a reconceptualization of human affairs affected them as significantly at the same point in time as it did the activities of their male counterparts remains unknown. Other historians have confirmed that women did affect the changes in religious thought and practice which eventually precipitated its privatization. In the case of sport and leisure, however, the evidence is still too meagre to enable one to establish, or deny, women's agency. The emergence of the horse race – ball formula and the pattern of action within the frolics suggests that women may have had a defining role, particularly in the social ordering process, in such public events. But one must also consider the possibility that men simply added such activities to accommodate their wives or to enhance their control over their spouses at a time when the spectre of the wife-mother was on the ascendant.[32]

Regardless of which conception, or even another, is ultimately established, the middle third of the eighteenth century will probably remain as period of subtle change, a period of transition for middle- and upper-rank Anglo-American women in the public sporting culture. Compared with what had occurred before the 1720s, women's activity did become more central to the events of sport, and they did move, in a physical sense, as they had not in the past. Still, they had not made sport a private activity and their place and their action in public complemented those of their husbands, brothers and friends. A new relationship and indeed new forms of sport emerged only in the 1760s and afterwards.

III

Historians of Revolutionary and post-Revolutionary women have suggested contrasting views of women's role and responsibilities in American society in the late eighteenth and early nineteenth centuries. In *Women of the Republic* Linda Kerber argued that the Revolutionary War encouraged women to undertake more predomi- nantly male responsibilities and activities. As men moved to the fronts, to the legislatures, or even out of the colonies, the actions women took essentially expanded their traditional roles as 'deputy husbands'. After the war, however, Kerber maintained, American society reverted to earlier patterns and in some cases even more severely restricted women's lives and roles. The other position, presented succinctly in the works of Mary Beth Norton and Suzanne Lebsock, claimed meaningful, even positive and beneficial, altera- tions in women's responsibilities and opportunities, facilitated in part by women themselves. Norton contended that women had substantial responsibilities and autonomy, the bases for new roles, in religion and education in *Liberty's Daughters*. In *The Free Women of Petersburg* Lebsock echoed Norton's conclusion. She emphasized that the Virginia women in this town developed female networks and benevolent societies which served as the primary mechanisms for gaining autonomy.[33]

Depending on which facets of women's lives one examines, either view, or neither, may be wholly accurate. Evidence from the sporting culture, for certain, both supports and rejects these positions. In part at least, this ambivalence appears because the war was not a pivotal event in the history of the sporting culture and because of regional variations in post-Revolutionary involvement. Among middle- and upper-rank women, the pre-war decade of the 1760s actually precipitated some change, which was to be completed some 60 years later. This was the decade in which women began to define a sporting sphere for themselves and to form new relationships which augmented older connections with public contests for men.

In the 1760s some Anglo-American women appear to have been in the same stage of culture formation in sport as men had been in the latter decades of the seventeenth century. Beginning in eastern Massachusetts, townswomen rearranged what had been traditional individual and communal work into contests – spinning matches. At least partly encouraged by the Non-Importation Acts, these competitions were clearly purposeful, and they emerged in other regions as well. Divided, or dividing, into groups on the basis of age, marital status or location, the women and girls spun skeins and knots of yarn from raw linen and cotton. Pride rather than prizes motivated the spinners, who intended either to use the products to offset the loss of British manufacturers or to turn them over to the local militias.[34]

These spinning matches apparently were the first of colonial women's useful, competitive recreations – their initial feminine-defined sport form. As colonial men had with horse-racing a century earlier, women transformed a significant domestic activity into a contest, the goal of which was to alter the normal outcome of the endeavour. This is precisely what happened. Compared with an individual spinner's output of two or three skeins a day, the group produced in excess of 100 and nearer to 200 skeins when the competitors numbered more than 70.[35]

As was the case with horse-racing, too, part of the significance of the spinning matches was symbolic. In fact, more than any other activity, spinning itself represented the women's domestic role, and two terms – 'spinster', the unmarried female, and the 'distaff' side, referring to the sex in general – derived from the activity.[36] The matches may have had more meaningful symbolic consequences than practical ones, for the actual products did not fulfil the colonies' demands for home manufactures. What they provided for certain, however, was 'the most pleasing Satisfaction' among the women about their efforts on behalf of the 'Welfare of our Country'.[37] They also united women in what the Philadelphian Elizabeth Graeme Fergusson later termed 'a train of Female Hands/Chearful uniting in Industry Bands'.[38] Mrs Fergusson had recognized the networks of women that spinning engaged.

What she did not clarify, however, was that the spinning contests had emerged among townswomen. This appears to be of some significance both for the sport of women and for the beginnings of 'modern' sport in the immediate pre-Revolutionary years. In contrast to their rural contemporaries of both sexes, the female participants in these contests had not spun regularly; instead, they had purchased or traded for yarns and fabrics. Even though the interruption of imports encouraged townswomen to return to the task, that they should do so within a framework of competition suggests a different conception of what it was that they were doing. More than either a task of labour or even a simple utilitarian pastime or diversion, albeit a joyful and entertaining one, the spinning contest was an act of autonomy carved out of domestic endeavour and facilitated by corporate life in the towns. Its very nature, however, reinforced women's traditional sphere.[39]

This experiment in 'modern' sport – an activity simultaneously separated from and embedded in the culture – was short-lived. Spinning contests did not survive long past the end of the Revolution. Both urban and rural women returned to what had been: little or no spinning for townswomen and those on large plantations, and the daily individual labor and occasional communal 'bees' for rural ones.[40] This is not to say, however, that the post-war years heralded no sport and the possibility for social relationships in it. The networks, for certain, remained.

Neither the emergence nor the demise of spinning contests pre-empted other more traditional relationships within the broader pre- and post-Revolutionary sporting culture. Boat and foot races, marksmanship matches, and even games of ball on village greens for men and skating and sleighing forays for both sexes continued, at least until the fighting began locally. Even after the war began, the Continental Congress and local committees of safety which inveighed against some sport forms and the gambling which accompanied them did not change the sporting culture significantly. Not until late in the war, when the stock of horses in the southern colonies had been depleted, was the most popular of southern forms, racing, interrupted. To all of these events, women continued to come.[41]

In addition to the innovation of spinning contests, middle- and upper-class women augmented their traditional complementariness in another way during the 1760s and early 1770s. The arrangement, rather than the form of sport, is the key here, as three examples suggest. First, having learned to gamble at cards with her Virginia neighbours, the young Sally Fairfax began to do so with her mother at home. Second, along with a neighbour, the three daughters of Councillor Robert Carter rode in a boat down the Rappahannock River until they reached the spot where they could begin the main event, their fishing.[42] Finally, a Virginia tutor travelling to Philadelphia recorded what may have been the most common event among middle- and upper-class women throughout the eastern regions of the colonies. In the spring of 1774 Philip Fithian arrived in that city to find his 'old Aunt' and three partners at a table playing 'that vulgar game fit only for the meanest gamblers "All Fours" '.[43]

Fithian clearly did not approve of his aunt's enterprise. But his moral indignation did not hide the fact that what she and other women, young and old alike, had begun to form before the Revolution were networks, sometimes joined in sport. In pairs, fours, and even in larger groups, women engaged with and competed against other women. Precisely what caused these networks remains unknown. The motivation may simply have been a desire for enjoyable camaraderie.[44] Particularly in the Chesapeake, however, where such networks seem to have been most common, they may have formed in reaction to two phenomena. The first involved the absences of men. Husbands, fathers, and brothers travelled away on business or sporting ventures for several weeks or longer. These trips interrupted male–female relationships and may have either encouraged or enabled women to spend more time among themselves. The second development involved conversions to one of the numerous evangelical sects active in the Chesapeake during the 1760s and afterwards. Genteel fathers and mothers who became 'new lights' occasionally did withdraw themselves and their families from the common and traditional social gatherings and relationships, leaving themselves and their offspring to form new ones.[45]

Regardless of the precise, or imprecise, cause of these sporting-bound networks which formed before the war, it is clear that they continued afterwards. In 1791, for example, Ferdinand Bayard, a Frenchman travelling near the warm springs in western Virginia, observed groups of women on horseback who 'would challenge each other to a race'. They were, he concluded, 'skilful and fearless riders'.[46] A year later Mary Palmer Tyler described a similar gathering swimming in Massachusetts. Although she preferred to simply descend 'the steps for my bath', her companions 'would dive off the platform'. Afterwards, they told her that she 'was foolish not to share so great a luxury'.[47]

Although striking, Tyler's comment about the 'luxury' of swimming is not particularly meaningful to one's understanding of what happened to women who sported in the final decades of the eighteenth century. Swimming was neither common nor valued among many Anglo-American colonials or, after independence, American citizens. It would not become so until later in the nineteenth century when habits of personal and public health and cleanliness changed.[48] Tyler's and Bayard's descriptions do, however, suggest that the networks and the essentially private settings combined to enable women to do what they had not done before the 1760s, except on occasion and usually in public: they involved themselves directly in sporting activities. They raced horses, they swam, and as the Fairfax, Carter and Fithian examples indicate, they played cards, gambled and fished. Among members of their own sex and in private, in sum, women had begun to engage in some of the common and even some of the not-so-common sport forms known to eighteenth-century Anglo-Americans.

The decade of the 1760s, then, marked the beginning of a new and distinct phase in the social history of the colonial and early national sporting culture. Women emerged within it via their networks and in private settings as active participants. As seen first in the spinning contests, middle- and upper-rank women had begun to personalize sport, both literally and figuratively, even as some maintained their complementariness in contests among men. Coupled with the post-Revolutionary ideal of republican motherhood, this privatization of women's sport by women would ultimately result in a domestic sphere of sport by the 1820s, an adjunct to the cult of domesticity.

As it was initially discussed, by both men and women, the ideal of the 'republican mother' implied a positive, even enhanced, social role and place for American women. In fact, as the learned New Englander, Judith Sargent Murray, wrote in 1798, 'I expect to see our young women forming a new era in female history'.[49] Murray's projection of this new era depended in large part on the emphasis which much of early national rhetoric placed on the family. The argument was quite straightforward. The family was the bedrock of the new nation, the source of good and intelligent citizens. As women fulfilled their maternal responsibilities and exerted their moral influence on the family, they also affected, and positively so went the assumption, the process of nation-building. But, to fully realize their contributions, women required education and religious involvement. These, in turn, provided some avenues for extra-familial activities, especially those reinforcing desired maternal functions. Hence, Murray's new era in female history offered respect, opportunity and meaningful action for post-Revolutionary women. In short, the 'republican mother' could expect a more complete and appreciated existence than her predecessors.[50]

After 1790, however, the everyday sporting life of 'republican mothers' changed little. Instead, middle- and upper-rank women essentially sustained and in some cases very slightly redirected action in sport. Among northern women, especially townswomen, active participation in sport when it occurred remained tied to networks of neighbours and kinswomen and to individual rides and walks, occasionally recommended by doctors to improve one's health. Such was the case, as well, in the plantation south where the formation of women's networks apparently depended more on the cycle of agricultural tasks and on both their husbands' and their willingness to arrange gatherings and annual excursions.[51] Here, too, planters arranged events 'for the amusement of the Ladies', events which would eventually, certainly within the third and fourth decades of the century, celebrate the ornamental presence of women with separate observation posts.[52]

None of these experiences suggests, of course, any truly novel arrangements and forms of sport. Nor did practices appear more regularly as the nineteenth century progressed. In the case of the 'new' American women's sporting life, sustenance and redirection were merely opposite sides of the same coin – reinforcement of what had been. Murray's 'new era of female history' did not emerge, nor would it when the children of the first generation of 'republican mothers' became adults.

What those children provided when they became adults were the ideology and regularized programming for women's privatized sporting sphere and their complementary responsibilities in the public world of men's sport. Known as domesticity, and to historians as the 'cult of domesticity', this system of beliefs and its practical renderings in sport clarified and even reified women's role and women's sphere. Domesticity maintained that women's duties – those of wife, mother, nurturer, teacher and moral arbiter – were gender-specific and culturally significant. Indeed, women's sphere, with both public and private connotations, was a virtual *sine qua non* of human and national goodness and growth.

The lines of continuity between the republican mother ideal and domesticity are striking. It is certain that the latter concept emerged among women who as children had been reared in households where work and rhetoric introduced them to the republican mother's culture, including its sport. An increasing number of schools also reinforced that culture among the young daughters of the Republic who became *ante bellum* adults. As did the earlier ideal, domesticity stressed and elevated women's private endeavours which could be turned to the public, the male, benefit. So the dichotomy between public and private persisted. So, too, did the propelling mechanisms. Domesticity facilitated and was preached and practised within networks; in fact, there was a bindingness emanating from the emphasis on women's common tasks and role which transcended distance and regions.[53]

The only major distinction between the two phrasings of women's sphere, and one which affected the sporting culture, was the younger generation's emphasis on health. Proponents of the republican mother ideal had, of course, at least recognized the importance of health as the state in which women must exist to fulfil that ideal. They had not, however, moved as concertedly to link physical performance and sport to health and, hence, both to the post-Revolutionary ideal as did their predecessors. That connection remained to be made by the daughters of the first republican mothers. These women included Catharine Beecher, Mary Lyon, and Lydia Sigourney, as well as other definers and proponents of domesticity, both male and female. Such writers and activists perceived of health as a condition of harmony which existed when both the systems of the body and the body-environment relationship achieved equilibrium. Failure to achieve this two-fold bodily state resulted in foiled life and reproductive function. As Beecher stated the worst case scenario, without health women suffered such 'a delicacy of constitution' that they became 'early victims to disease and decay' and 'a cloud of gloom settles over the whole family circle'.[54]

Health, then, emerged as the major publicly espoused justification, even the ideological goal of domesticity, during and after the 1820s. Such a goal did not, however, either necessitate or inject new forms and conceptions of sport among middle and upper-rank women. What the proponents of domesticity stressed for women were precisely the forms of and arrangements for sport that they had seen in their republican mothers' homes and in their own schools: walks in the open air, horseback riding, 'wholesome' games, and regimented bodily exercise (callisthenics).[55] Beecher even harked back to the spinning contests of the 1760s, albeit without competition but certainly for the common good, as she recommended 'domestic employments'.[56] Through these 'old' forms of sport and exercise, in the house as well as outside it, the 'new' goal of health – and future generations of virile, moral Americans – was to be achieved.

IV

In the American 'cult of domesticity', in sum, the period of middle- and upper-rank Anglo-American women's experience which emerged in the 1760s would appear to have achieved completion. The pre-Revolutionary decade saw the initial defining of a women's sporting sphere, a process which was and would continue to be simultaneously radical and conservative. The women's sporting sphere was radical in so far as it was innovative: 'new' networks and activities engaged in by women in a 'new' domain, private leisure. But the sport of women by women also retained traditional elements. What remained were the persisting Anglo-American conception of sport as useful recreation; the action of the female participant as gardener, albeit now of her body, rather than as conqueror; and the seemingly imperceptibly distinct roles of agent and client. Further, however much women's sporting sphere complemented the lives of the participants, it did not destroy the centuries-old position of women as spectators in the public domain of male competition.

Whether the emergence of a distinguishable women's sporting sphere between the 1760s and the 1820s actually empowered women or enhanced their value to men remains a significant question to be answered in future research. Age, rank, and regional variations also remain to be examined.[57] About the general lines of this sphere, however, one thing is certain: it was a logical result of the pre-1760s Anglo-American colonial experience. In the two sub-periods before the 1760s, Anglo-American middle- and upper-rank women gradually altered their action and influence. They moved from providing their husbands with sporting equipment to using it themselves, from appearing in public rituals to privatizing new ones, from being 'outlivers' to becoming 'skilful and fearless riders'. All the while, to be sure, domestic endeavours and complementariness to their husbands remained critical to the Anglo-American and the American women's identities. These were not to be abandoned in the women's separate and private sporting sphere of the late eighteenth and early nineteenth centuries.

NOTES

1. The few, descriptive treatments of colonial and post-Revolutionary women's sport include: Reet Howell, 'Recreational Activities of Women in the Colonial Period', *Arena Review*, IV (May 1980), 3–10; Jennie Holliman, *American Sports (1785–1835)* (Durham, NC, 1931), Ch. 11; Julia C. Spruill, *Women's Life and Work in the Southern Colonies* (Chapel Hill, NC, 1938), Ch. 5; Mary Sumner Benson, *Women in Eighteenth-Century America* (New York, 1935); Jane Carson, *Colonial Virginians at Play* (Williamsburg, 1965). For the most recent complete synthesis of historical works on white colonial women, see Mary Beth Norton, 'The Evolution of White Women's Experience in Early America', *American Historical Review*, LXXXIX (June 1984), 593–619.
2. Richard Mather, 'Journal, 1635', in Alexander Young (ed.), *Chronicles of the First Planters of the Colony of Massachusetts Bay, From 1623 to 1636* (Boston, 1846), p. 460.
3. Nancy L. Struna, 'Colonial Sport: More Questions Than Answers' (paper presented at the North American Society for Sport History annual conference, May 1984).
4. *Records and Files of the Quarterly Courts of Essex County Massachusetts* (Salem, 1911–14), Vols. I–IV; Inventories and Accounts, Vol. I, pt. 1, 1674–1704, Maryland Hall of Records.
5. White Anglo-American sex ratios in the 1630s were 6:1 in Virginia and 3:2 in Massachusetts, 5:2 across the colonies in 1700, and 3:2 at mid-century. Total population

of the eastern seaboard colonies: 4600 in 1630; 50,000 in 1650; and 250,000 in 1700. Robert V. Wells, *Revolutions in Americans' Lives. A Demographic Perspective on the History of Americans, Their Families, and Their Society* (Westport, CN, 1982), esp. Chs. 2–4; Walter Nugent, *Structures of American Social History* (Bloomington, IN, 1981), pp. 26–53; Lorena S. Walsh, ' "Till Death Us Do Part": Marriage and Family in Seventeenth-Century Maryland', in Thad W. Tate and David Ammerman (eds.), *The Chesapeake in the Seventeenth Century. Essays on Anglo-American Society* (Chapel Hill, 1979), pp. 126–52; Russell R. Menard, 'Immigrants and Their Increase: The Process of Population Growth in Early Colonial Maryland', in Aubrey C. Land, Lois Green Carr and Edward C. Papenfuse (eds.), *Law, Society, and Politics in Early Maryland* (Baltimore, 1977), pp. 88–110; Roger Thompson, *Women in Stuart England and America: A Comparative Study* (London, 1974), Ch. 2.

6. Joseph H. Smith (ed.), *Colonial Justice in Western Massachusetts, 1639–1702: The Pynchon Court Record* (Cambridge, 1961), p. 257.

7. Nancy L. Struna, 'Defining Sport in the American Colonial Experience' (paper presented at the Olympic Scientific Congress, July 1984); Wells, *Revolutions in Americans' Lives*, p. 81.

8. Philip A. Bruce, *Social Life of Virginia in the Seventeenth Century* (New York, 1907), pp. 182–3; Francis Louis Michel, 'Report of the Journey of Francis Louis Michel from Berne, Switzerland, to Virginia, October 2, 1701–December 1, 1702', *Virginia Magazine of History and Biography*, XXIV (April 1916), 125–9; Spruill, *Women's Life and Work*, pp. 86–8; Durand of Dauphine', *A Huguenot Exile in Virginia; or, Voyages of a Frenchman Exiled for His Religion, with a Description of Virginia and Maryland*, (ed. and trans.) Gilbert Chinard (New York, reprint edn., 1934), p. 117; Sara Kemble Knight, *The Journal of Madam Knight* (Boston, 1971), pp. 20, 56, 57; Carl Bridenbaugh, *Cities of the Wilderness. The First Century of Urban Life in America* (London, 1938), pp. 265–80; Worthington C. Ford (ed.), *The Diary of Cotton Mather* (New York, 1911), pp. 11, 367.

9. Nancy L. Struna, 'The Formalizing of Sport and the Formation of an Elite: The Chespeake Gentry, 1650–1720s', *Journal of Sport History*, XIII (Winter 1986).

10. The term 'good wives' comes from Laurel Thatcher Ulrich, *Good Wives. Image and Reality in the Lives of Women in Northern New England 1650–1750* (New York, 1983). For a fine discussion of the symbolic significance of women's bodies, see Peggy Reeves Sanday, *Female Power and Male Dominance. On the Origins of Sexual Inequality* (Cambridge, 1981), esp. Chs. 4–5.

11. Annette Kolodny, *The Land Before Her. Fantasy and Experience of the American Frontiers, 1630–1860* (Chapel Hill, 1984), pp. 7–8, 17–54.

12. Ulrich, *Good Wives*, p. 8.

13. Louis B. Wright and Marion Tinling (eds.), *The Secret Diary of William Byrd of Westover, 1709–1712* (Richmond, 1941), p. 75. See, also, Michael Zuckerman, 'William Byrd's Family', *Perspectives in American History*, XII (1979), 253–312.

14. Philip Ludwell, 'Boundary Line Proceedings, 1710', *Virginia Magazine of History and Biography*, V (July 1897), 10.

15. Struna, 'Defining Sport in the American Colonial Experience'.

16. Joseph Bennett, 'History of New England' (1740), *Proceedings* Massachusetts Historical Society, first ser., V (January 1861), 124–5.

17. James Jeffrey, 'James Jeffrey's Journal for the Year 1724', *Essex Institute Historical Collections*, XXXVI (October 1900), 14 July 1724.

18. *Virginia Gazette*, 22 April 1737, 7 April 1738; *Virginia Gazette* Day Book, 1764–1766, pp. 98, 124, 168, Colonial Williamsburg Foundation photostat; York County Wills and Inventories, 1732–1740, XVIII, 58, Colonial Williamsburg Foundation film.

19. *Virginia Gazette*, 28 November 1745.

20. *Maryland Gazette*, 14 June 1753.

21. During much of the eighteenth century, more than half of the population was youthful (a majority under 20, and a third under ten years of age), and as Philip Greven has shown, colonial parents followed numerous modes of child-rearing. In all of these forms, the significance of gender was related to the age of the child. Before the age of

seven, gender mattered little in daily tending; after seven, boys and girls began to receive differential training and treatment; and after 12, children were clearly either males or females. See Greven, *The Protestant Temperament, Patterns of Child-Rearing, Religious Experience, and the Self in Early America* (New York, 1977); also, Wells, *Revolutions in Americans' Lives*, 80–83.

22. See, for example, *Maryland Gazette*, 4 October 1749, 25 April 1754, 2 November 1769; William Eddis, *Letters from America* (ed.) Aubrey Land (Cambridge, 1969), pp. 54–5.

23. Diary of Mrs Mary Vial Holyoke, 1760–1800, in George F. Dow (ed.), *The Holyoke Diaries* (Salem, 1911), pp. 47–79; Benjamin Lynde, *The Diaries of Benjamin Lynde and of Benjamin Lynde, Jr.* (Boston, 1880), pp. 132–3; Jonathan Green, Diary 1738–1756, 27 February 1740, 1 March 1741, Linscott Papers 1653–1922, Massachusetts Historical Society; Francis Goelet, 'Extracts From Captain Francis Goelet's Journal Relative to Boston, Salem, and Marblehead, etc. 1746–1759', *New England Historical and Genealogical Register*, XXIV (January 1870), 53, 55, 57; John Boyle, 'Boyle's Journal of Occurrences in Boston, 1759–1778', *New England Historical and Genealogical Register*, LXXXIV (October 1930), 364; Bennett, 'History of New England', 125–6; James Phillips, *Salem in the Eighteenth Century* (Boston 1937), pp. 179–80.

24. Carole Shammas, 'The Domestic Environment in Early Modern England and America', *Journal of Social History*, XIV (1980–81), 3–24; Ulrich, *Good Wives*, pp. 51–67; Wells, *Revolutions in Americans' Lives*, 83; Mary Beth Norton, *Liberty's Daughters: The Revolutionary Experiences of American Women, 1750–1800* (Boston, 1980), esp. Ch. 1; Daniel Blake Smith, *Inside the Great House: Planter Family Life in Eighteenth-Century Chesapeake Society* (Ithaca, NY, 1980); Laurel Thatcher Ulrich, 'Vertuous Women Found: New England Ministerial Literature, 1668–1735', *American Quarterly*, XXIII (1976), 20–40; Gerald Moran and Maris Vinovskis, 'The Puritan Family and Religion: A Critical Reappraisal', *William and Mary Quarterly*, XXXIX (April 1982), 29–63; Richard Shiels, 'The Feminization of American Congregationalism, 1730–1835', *American Quarterly*, XXXIII (1981), 46–62.

25. Carl Bridenbaugh (ed.), *Gentleman's Progress, the Itinerarium of Dr Alexander Hamilton 1744* (Chapel Hill, 1948), p. 115.

26. L.H. Butterfield (ed.), *Diary and Autobiography of John Adams* (Cambridge, 1961), I, p. 27.

27. For initial research on the changing nature of public rituals and the use of the body as a medium of expression within them, see Nancy L. Struna, 'A Physically Expressive Popular Culture: Eighteenth Century Massachusetts' (paper presented at the North American Society for Sport History annual conference, May 1985).

28. William Black, 'Journal', *Pennsylvania Magazine of History and Biography*, I (1877), 130–1.

29. L.H. Butterfield (ed.), *Adams Family Correspondence* (Cambridge, 1963), I, pp. 44–5.

30. Two fine works which have begun to treat the significance of dichotomies as possible products of modern personality formation are Michael Zuckerman, 'The Fabrication of Identity in Early America', *William and Mary Quarterly*, XXXIC (April 1977), 183–214; and Robert M. Weir, 'Rebelliousness: Personality Development and the American Revolution in the Southern Colonies', in Jeffrey J. Crow and Larry E. Tise (eds.), *The Southern Experience in the American Revolution* (Chapel Hill, 1978), pp. 25–54. See also Edmund Morgan, *American Slavery – American Freedom* (New York, 1975); and Michael Kammen, *People of Paradox* (New York, 1972). That the work – leisure dichotomy, at least among upper-rank colonials, pre-dated the industrial revolution is an intriguing probability suggested by numerous colonial records, but more work needs to be completed.

31. *Virginia Gazette*, 14 February 1751, 27 February 1752, 23 May 1755, 22 February 1773, 10 February 1774, 21 July 1774; John C. Fitzpatrick (ed.), *The Writings of George Washington, 1745–1799* (Washington, DC, 1931–44), XXIX, pp. 295–6, XXXII, p. 109, XXXVII, pp. 194–5; Anon., 'Journal of a French Traveler in the Colonies, 1765', *American Historical Review*, XXVI–XXVII (July, October 1921), 72, 742–3; Hunter Dickinson Farish (ed.), *Journal and Letters of Philip Vickers Fithian, 1773–1774: A Plantation Tutor of the Old Dominion* (Williamsburg, 1943), pp. 198, 201–203; Edward

M. Riley (ed.), *The Journal of John Harrower, An Indentured Servant in the Colony of Virginia, 1773–1776* (Williamsburg, 1963), p. 46; *Maryland Gazette*, 11 February 1768, 29 September 1774; Jack P. Greene (ed.), *The Diary of Colonel Landon Carter of Sabine Hall, 1752–1778* (Charlottesville, 1965), II, pp. 638, 640–641, 775, 870, 905, 996; Louis Morton, 'Robert Wormeley Carter of Sabine Hall', *Journal of Southern History*, XII (August 1946), 356–8; David Meade, 'Recollections of William Byrd III', *Virginia Magazine of History and Biography*, XXVII (October 1929), 310; E.P. Thompson, 'Time, Work-Discipline, and Industrial Capitalism', *Past and Present*, XXXVIII (1967), 56–97; Nancy L. Struna, 'Gentry "Right Actions" and the Ordering of Sport and Society in the Eighteenth Century Chesapeake' (paper presented at the International Association for the History of Sport and Physical Education ninth congress, July 1985).

32. Norton, 'The Evolution of White Women's Experience', 606–09. For women and religion in the post-Revolutionary period, see Nancy F. Cott, *The Bonds of Womanhood. 'Woman's Sphere' in New England 1780–1835* (New Haven, CN, 1977), esp. Ch. 4.

33. Linda K. Kerber, *Women of the Republic. Intellect and Ideology in Revolutionary America* (Chapel Hill, 1980); Norton, *Liberty's Daughters*; Suzanne Lebsock, *The Free Women of Petersburg; Status and Culture in a Southern Town, 1784–1860* (New York, 1984). See also Mary P. Ryan's well-developed description and analysis of women's associations in *Cradle of the Middle Class. The Family in Oneida County, New York, 1790–1865* (Cambridge, 1981); Jan Lewis, *The Pursuit of Happiness. Families and Values in Jefferson's Virginia* (Cambridge, 1983); and Catherine Clinton, *The Plantation Mistress. Women's World in the Old South* (New York, 1982). Clinton's assessment of post-Revolutionary southern women is both less convincing than and sometimes contradictory to Lebsock's conclusions. The term 'deputy husbands' is from Ulrich, *Good Wives*, Ch. 2.

34, *Essex Gazette*, 2 August 1768; *Boston Gazette and Country Journal*, 16 October 1769; Mary Cooper, Diary, 3 February, 17 March, 14 November 1769, New York Public Library; Joseph E.A. Smith, *The History of Pittsfield, Massachusetts, From the Year 1734 to the Year 1800* (Boston, 1869), pp. 205–6; James Parker, 'Extracts From the Diary of James Parker of Shirley, Massachusetts', *New England Historical and Genealogical Register*, LXIX (January 1915), 10, 14, 121.

35. *Essex Gazette*, 2 August 1768; Thomas Dublin, *Women at Work* (New York, 1979), esp. Ch. 2; Rolla M. Tryon, *Household Manufactures in the United States 1640–1860* (Chicago, 1917).

36. Norton, *Liberty's Daughters*, pp. 15–8.

37. *Boston Gazette and Country Journal*, 16 October 1769.

38. Cited in Norton, *Liberty's Daughters*, p. 20.

39. This notion of sport and its relationship to society derives largely from Richard S. Gruneau, 'Freedom and Constraint: The Paradoxes of Play, Games, and Sport', *Journal of Sport History*, VII (Winter 1980), 68–86.

40. Precisely why the spinning contests ended, perhaps even before the war itself, remains an important but at this point unanswerable question.

41. See, for example, Thomas Anburey, *Travels Through the Interior Parts of America* (Boston, 1923), II, p. 57; Robert G. Albion and Leonidas Dodson (eds.), *The Journal of Philip Vickers Fithian, 1775–1776* (Princeton, 1934), p. 126; Evelyn M. Acomb (ed.), 'The Journal of Baron von Closen', *William and Mary Quarterly*, X (April 1953), 213; Marquis François Jean de Chatellux, *Travels in North America in the Years 1780, 1781 and 1782*, (ed.) Howard C. Rice, Jr. (Chapel Hill, 1963), I, pp. 176–7, II, p. 507; Carson, *Colonial Virginians at Play*, p. 119; Bonnie Ledbetter, 'Sports and Games of the American Revolution', *Journal of Sport History*, VI (Winter 1979), 29–40.

42. Edmund Morgan, *Virginians at Home. Family Life in the Eighteenth Century* (Williamsburg, 1952), p. 77; Farish (ed.), *Journal and Letters of Philip Vickers Fithian, 1773–1774*, p. 248.

43. Ibid., 73–74.

44. The networks appear to have begun to form in the 1740s and 1750s, particularly in the

south, for as the young South Carolinian Eliza Pinckney wrote about two older women, they 'are partial enough to mee to wish to have mee with them'. Harriet H. Ravenel, *Eliza Pinckney* (New York, 1896), pp. 5–6. By the 1760s the appearance of sport as activities within these groupings was a part of the continuing gender specialization in social arrangements seen in women's eating first, leaving balls together, and visiting. See Rhys Isaac, *The Transformation of Virginia 1740–1790* (Chapel Hill, 1982), pp. 56–79; Norton, *Liberty's Daughters*, Ch. 1; Cott, *The Bonds of Womanhood*, pp. 160–96.

45. See, for example, Letter, Robert Carter to Francis Christian, 23 June 1775, Robert Carter (of Nominy) Letters and Day Book 29 June 1775 – 16 May 1780, Box 11, Duke University typescript. Also, Rhys Isaac, 'Evangelical Revolt: The Nature of the Baptists' Challenge to the Traditional Order in Virginia, 1765–1775', *William and Mary Quarterly*, XXXI (July 1974), 345–68.

46. Ferdinand Bayard, *Travels of a Frenchman in Maryland and Virginia with a Description of Philadelphia and Baltimore in 1791*, (ed.) Ben C. McCary (Williamsburg, 1950), p. 40.

47. Mary Palmer Tyler, *Recollections 1775–1866*, (ed.) Frederick Tupper and Helen Tyler Brown (New York, 1925), p. 164.

48. Benjamin Franklin ('The Art of Swimming Rendered Easy') and a few medical men and educators in the early nineteenth century recommended swimming, but there is little evidence to suggest that people outside of educational institutions followed this advice.

49. Judith Sargent Murray, *The Gleaner* (Boston, 1798), III, p. 189.

50. For discussions of the republican mother ideal, see Kerber, *Women of the Republic*, pp. 189–231; Cott, *The Bonds of Womanhood*, pp. 95–108; Norton, *Liberty's Daughters*, pp. 256–94; Nancy Woloch, *Women and the American Experience* (New York, 1984), p. 118; Barbara Miller Solomon, *In the Company of Educated Women* (New Haven, 1985), pp. 1–13.

51. Peter Smith (ed.), *The Diary of William Bentley* (Salem, 1905), IV, p. 610; Ryan, *Cradle of the Middle Class*, p. 26; Bertram Wyatt-Brown, *Southern Honor, Ethics and Behavior in the Old South* (Oxford, 1982), p. 234; Letter, Maria Campbell to Elizabeth Russell, 19 August 1809, Campbell Collection, Duke University; Letter, Benjamin Rush to David Campbell, 7 February 1807, Campbell Collection, Duke University; John Bernard, *Retrospectives of America, 1797–1811* (New York, 1887), p. 189; Letter, Sarah Rutherfoord to John Rutherfoord, 12 July 1811, Rutherfoord Collection, Duke University; Percival Reniers, *The Springs of Virginia: Life, Love and Death at the Waters, 1775–1900* (Chapel Hill, 1941), p. 37. This initial research has not quantified women's participation in order to discover whether it occurred more or less frequently after the turn of the century than before. This may, however, be an important task in order to discover why women's poor health became such a concern in the early and mid nineteenth century.

52. Letter, St George Coalter to Judith Coalter, 18, 21 July 1833, Brown-Tucker-Coalter Collection, William and Mary College.

53. Barbara J. Berg, *The Remembered Gate: Origins of American Feminism, The Woman and the City, 1800–1860* (New York, 1978); Cott, *The Bonds of Womanhood*, esp. Ch. 2; Deborah Gorham, *The Victorian Girl and the Feminine Ideal* (Bloomington, 1982), esp. Chs. 1 and 7; Kathryn Kish Sklar, *Catharine Beecher: A Study in American Domesticity* (New York, 1973); Barbara Welter, *Divinity Convictions: The American Woman in the Nineteenth Century* (Athens, OH, 1976), pp. 21–41; Mary Kelley, *Private Woman, Public Stage: Literary Domesticity in Nineteenth Century America* (New York, 1984); Roberta J. Park, ' "Embodied Selves": The Rise and Development of Concern for Physical Education, Active Games and Recreation for American Women, 1776–1865', *Journal of Sport History*, V (Summer 1978), 5–41; Roxanne Albertson, 'School Physical Activity Programs for the Antebellum Southern Females', in Reet Howell (ed.), *Her Story in Sport: A Historical Anthology of Women in Sports* (West Point, NY, 1982), pp. 369–79; idem., 'Sports and Games in Eastern Schools, 1780–1880', in Wayne M. Ladd and Angela Lumpkin (eds.), *Sport in American*

Education: History and Perspective (Washington, DC, 1979), pp. 19–32.
54. Catharine Beecher, *Treatise on Domestic Economy for the Use of Young Ladies at Home and at School* (Boston, 1841), p. 18; idem., *Physiology and Calisthenics for Schools and Families* (New York, 1856), p. 165.
55. Park, ' "Embodied Selves":' 9–19; Jack W. Berryman and Joann Brislin, 'The Ladies Department of the *American Farmer*, 1825–1830; A Locus for the Advocacy of Family Health and Exercise', *Associates National Agriculture Library Today*, II (September 1977), 8–15; Elizabeth A. Green, *Mary Lyon and Mount Holyoke* (Hanover, NH, 1979); Patricia Vertinsky, 'Sexual Equality and the Legacy of Catharine Beecher', *Journal of Sport History*, VI (September 1979), 38–49; Betty Spears and Richard Swanson, *History of Sport and Physical Activity in the United States* (Dubuque, IA, 1978, pp. 72–84.
56. Beecher, *Treatise on Domestic Economy*, p. 32.
57. Initial research on women's diaries in the post-Revolutionary decades suggests that significant differences in practice and expectation distinguished adolescent and adult females.

11

Body Shapes: The Role of the Medical Establishment in Informing Female Exercise and Physical Education in Nineteenth-Century North America

Patricia Vertinsky

Much of the rhetoric about the promotion of physical exercise and the subsequent development of physical education curricula for girls and women during the nineteenth century has portrayed the emerging popularity of female exercise and sport as a victory of feminist effort and scientific rationality over the tyrannies of fashion, sensuality, male dominance, and ignorant neglect about health matters. What is important, notes Howell in tracing the history of women's sport, 'is that the rise, one might exaggerate and say the emancipation, of womankind went hand in hand with the growth of physical education for girls and women'.[1]

Park more cautiously suggests that 'there are times when one might be almost inclined to believe that modern women's emancipation is intimately bound up with her athletic ability – and certainly with her physicality'.[2] In support, she has documented the many endeavours to draw attention to the physical needs and abilities of women, or attempts to improve their health and physical education, which developed between 1776 and 1865, suggesting that these cumulatively helped to establish a climate favourable to the development of physical education and sports programmes for females in the late nineteenth and twentieth centuries.

Certainly, the promotion of physical education and healthful exercise as a means for helping women attain their natural potential was an important platform of the emerging women's rights movement in *ante-bellum* North American society and continued as a general emphasis throughout the nineteenth century. Yet, the impetus for the enterprise, and the shifting (and sometimes contradictory) theoretical underpinnings of the calls for female exercise were enormously complex. They reflected the anxieties of middle-class Americans discovering their bodies and placing a new emphasis upon the human form. The notions that emerged about the ideal female form and function, however, were possibly more conservative than liberating.

This chapter explores this hypothesis by focusing upon the shifts in shared concepts of the ideal physical form of the woman throughout the nineteenth century. Our preoccupation with 'form' is in line with some new trusts in historical research which view styles and fashions as means of societal control rather than spurious human artifacts.

Indeed, Fellman and Fellman note that socio-political scholarship has broadened to encompass analyses of the ways people feed, clothe, nurture and educate each other, considering these as central means to the entrenchment and replication of political and economic forms.[3] Social historians of women's fashion and female beauty ideals, for example, have tried to show how complex, contradictory and controlling was much of the advice given to nineteenth-century women about how to conserve, or transform themselves into 'perfect women' – useful yet decorative, dainty but strong, slender and rounded, modest yet erotic.[4]

The pursuit of beauty (of face and physical form) has constituted a key element in women's separate experience of life yet it has been strongly influenced by both men and women. Appearance is a primary mark of identification, a signal of what women consider themselves to be and how others want them to look. Changes in popular standards of physical beauty thus reflect a complex interaction of women's changing expectations, evolving scientific and medical knowledge, social modernization and many other factors.[5]

Banner, in her analysis of *American Beauty*, has characterized successive types of ideal female forms which predominated among middle- and upper-class women of the nineteenth century:[6] 1. The 'steel engraving lady' of the *ante-bellum* years, frail, pale and willowy; 2. The voluptuous, large-breasted woman of the decades following the Civil War; and 3. The tall, athletic 'Gibson-girl' of the late 1890s.

Her explanations for the evolution of these fashions in physical form have been challenged as simplistic, especially the conclusion that dress and exercise reform were major influences in the genesis of the natural, athletic woman as a model of beauty.[7] More convincing is the argument which focuses upon the alignment of particular body physiques into socially defined and attributed gender roles. This argument can be derived by examining the paradigms underlying the formal legitimization of a particular form. The shift in control beliefs at the beginning of the nineteenth century entrusted the role of legitimization to the new earthly custodians of the body – the emerging medical profession. Thus, an examination of the evolution of the professional paradigm and its use to prescribe or legitimize certain forms and behaviours provides us with a vehicle for testing our hypothesis. The broad characterizations of desirable female body architecture serve as a useful backdrop for scrutinizing the orthodox medical arguments that were advanced to limit female functions and mobility by validating prevailing fashions of form among women of means.

THE ROLE OF MEDICINE IN 'FRAMING' IDEAL FEMALE FORMS AND FUNCTIONS

Medicine, notes Pellegrino, is an exquisitely sensitive indicator of the dominant cultural characteristics of any era,[8] and this was apparent throughout the nineteenth century as orthodox physicians largely ignored or distorted scientific evidence in their struggle to develop professional strength and social authority, while competing for business in a busy marketplace.[9] In particular, the emerging dominance of the medical profession was related to increasingly harsh efforts to control and regulate women's bodies. In a changing society, doctors came to see themselves as moral as well as physical guardians of women and they used their authority to interpret (and corrupt) new scientific findings in ways which might support their claims. Medical theory was used to reinforce social prescriptions of the appropriate female form and function.[10]

An examination of the therapeutic advice given by orthodox medical men to women, their pronouncements upon the ideal female form and their prescriptions for physical exercise provides support for the claim that physicians wholeheartedly sought to protect societal values with respect to women's roles and functions rather than alter them in line with scientific theories.[11]

Banner's three characterizations of ideal female forms – slender and fragile, plump and voluptuous, tall and athletic – cannot easily be strictly confined to particular time frames, for all models of beauty vied for attention throughout the century. Yet she provides considerable evidence to support her claim that the slim fragile and delicate model of beauty permeated *ante-bellum* middle- and upper-class society, at least until the 1850s; that this prototype was challenged by a plumper, more voluptuous model of female beauty after the 1870s which evolved into the taller, more vigorous and athletic ideal female shape of the late 1890s. By 1900, she says, social trends had 'signalled the downfall of the voluptuous woman as a standard of beauty for American women and the athletic frame became the ideal'.[12]

Retracing this time line with a view to medical support for female form and function, we shall see that medical explanations initially supported the idea that women were naturally small, frail and weak until physicians found it expedient, due to loss of popularity and licensure, and large-scale competition with quasi-medical reforms, to join forces with moral physiologists and support female physical education and other health reforms which fortified the female frame.[13] Through hygienic conditioning, some agreed, stronger, healthier women could become better mothers and more attractive wives. However, the effect of the health reforms, increased education, and especially the growing number of non-working middle-class women exacerbated male anxieties in an industrializing society increasingly fearful of a disintegrating social order. We hypothesize that the vogue among medical men for supporting the ideal of plump and voluptuous women after the Civil War was, in part, an effort to regain control of women by devaluing their minds and re-emphasizing their bodies. Large bosoms and swelling hips were extolled as a visual manifestation of woman's only purposeful role – maternity. 'Her bosom is the symbol of love and nutrition . . . Her maternal functions are indicated by greater breadth of hips . . . Her uterus and ovaries . . . mold her character, beautify and perfect her form.'[14]

Physicians and moralists united after the 1870s in the joint desire to rescue the American race (and generate good business) by restoring emphasis on the female body to counteract female independence and the weakness they believed was caused by too much brainwork. Systematic exercise seemed to offer an opportunity to regain control over the lazy body and to reintroduce substitute physical labour into the lives of workless middle-class women.[15] Sports and physical activity would provide the strength and muscle to improve women's maternal function, but would not, they were sure, destroy the beauty of feminine curves, or the harmony of the home. Exercise advocates were happy to report that physiological studies showed that women lost no body curves through exercise.[16] Morality and a moderate muscularity thus joined in a salvage plan supported by orthodox physicians to renovate the female body and fortify a lady's will to be a good mother. At its most extreme, bearing and rearing robust babies came to be seen as the sum of female existence in the physical culture world.[17]

Despite medical ambivalence about the amount and type of physical exercise appropriate for women, and volumes of wide-ranging advice about correct living and appropriate systems of exercise, popular standards of female beauty reflected a growing scientific consensus about female exercise needs as the twentieth century dawned. Neither female frailty nor voluptuous plumpness continued to be extolled as functional or as standards to emulate.

Though the change was hardly as dramatic as that noted by Mrozek where 'swooning damsel, pushed by physical educators, yielded to an emancipating sportswoman', in the last decade of the nineteenth century, a tall, strong, and athletic frame did become fashionably beautiful and the ideal promoted by physical educators.[18] 'No woman,' said Dr Dudley Sargent, 'could be beautiful without exercise.'[19] For the most part, the medical profession agreed. Many of them became leaders of the physical education profession. After all, the shape of the ideal woman represented (to a conservative profession) an adaptation, not a repudiation, of older values. It was also very attractive.

The relative importance placed upon improvements in body shape and body function fluctuated during the nineteenth century as different groups sought to imprint their ideas upon the purpose and practice of physical education for women and girls. We shall show, however, that in the *ante-bellum* years, and the decades following the Civil War, the orthodox medical profession played a critical and generally conservative role in defining female forms, modifying physiological knowledge, joining and withdrawing from health reform movements, supporting and attacking advances in female emancipation, and above all, in advancing their professional and masculine interest in controlling the female body.

ORTHODOX MEDICINE AND THE STEEL-ENGRAVING LADY OF THE ANTE-BELLUM YEARS

Banner has called the body shape that influenced females in the early years of the nineteenth century the steel-engraving lady. It is a familiar image to any reader of romantic Victorian novels.

> Her face is oval, or heart shaped. Her eyes . . . are downcast. Her chin is soft and retreating. Her mouth is tiny . . . her body is short and slight, rounded and curved. Her shoulders slope; her arms are round; a small waist lies between a rounded bosom and bell-shaped torso . . . Her hands are small, her fingers tapering. Her feet . . . are tiny and delicate.[20]

Small, soft and curved – these became popular descriptors of the ideal *ante-bellum* lady of industrializing North America. The portrait of feminine delicacy, echoing the crusader's chivalrous and spiritualized version of perfect womanhood, was a stereotype of physical uselessness. It denoted in part the loss of power among women caused by the economic shift from home to factory production as the nineteenth century progressed. Women's physical work, however ceaseless and hard it had been in earlier days, had at least been visible and recognized as a contribution to household and community.[21] Concomitant with the economic shift of the mode of production was a loss in female status. At the beginning of the nineteenth century women lost a number of their legal privileges, including the right of some to vote. Opportunities for exercising domestic medical skills declined, and 'despite their long record as expert midwives, they were barred from a newly defined and restricted medical profession', which pronounced upon their health and physical limitations.[22] Indeed, problems of women's health in the nineteenth century gained unprecedented attention from the medical profession.[23]

On every front, women's familiar roles, functions and ambitions seemed in the process of curtailment. Banned from production, women needed less muscular power. Their critical role in reproduction was increasingly emphasized by a developing base of scientific or quasi-scientific knowledge which reinforced and redefined the identification of female with nature and male with culture.[24] The scientific endeavour was conceived of and assigned as a masculine enterprise; nature was personified as woman and mother; and male medical men used this direction to channel women closely into the correct role of nature – reproduction and child nurture. Women's health was thus seen to be dependent on and defined as the ability to perform domestic functions. By limiting women to the family, and asserting their incapacity for rational scientific thought, men justified the economic inactivity of women and showed them to be physically feeble, unable to survive without the protection of the stronger male.

Medical and pseudo-scientific theories increasingly legitimized, and women subscribed to, the ideal model of physical shape and beauty for women that portrayed them as having a distinct physiology with small heads and thin, delicate, soft and curved characteristics. 'A woman has,' said Dr Meigs, 'a head almost too small for intellect but just big enough for love.'[25] The analogy here came from craniology which held that brain size indicated mental ability. Women and children had small brains, and thus limited mental capacity.[26] Scientific theories further suggested that the North American climate exacerbated the tendency for women to be physically frail and nervous. As *Harper's* put it, 'she is a very delicate plant, not generally strong in nerve and muscle'.[27] Feminist Elizabeth Cady Stanton believed this. She wrote that 'owing to the . . . climate . . . our women . . . are highly wrought, physically delicate and slender'.[28]

These views about women's physical and mental frailties and the development of therapeutic measures to cope with them reflected a system of beliefs about health and disease which strongly affected, in one way or another, ideas concerning female physical education as a means for obtaining health, beauty and physiological efficiency. Medical practice in the *ante-bellum* years was based upon a humoral doctrine that saw the emanation of disease as a result of an imbalance among the systems of the body or between the body and the environment. Popularized by Dr Benjamin Rush, one of the most prominent of early American physicians, this vitalist theory supported orthodox medical views that women were thin and weak because of the constant demands made upon their bodies by their reproductive system.[29]

Physicians prescribed rest or gentle exercise for women to preserve their delicate health, easily drained by menstruation and childbirth. The constitution of women could only bear a certain amount of moderate exercise. Walking was fine if pursued sedately.[30] Nature, it was felt, provided just enough energy for the body to function normally, but menstruation in particular made special and regular weakening forays upon the body. Furthermore, doctors generally believed that the onset of menstruation triggered the physical manifestations of femininity and convinced woman of her dependence. As a result, mothers were told to regard their adolescent daughters as physically fragile and vulnerable.[31]

Douglas, in her analysis of nineteenth-century American culture, notes that society forces members of a sub-culture, at any moment of intersection with the larger culture, into a constant, simplified and often demeaning process of self-identification. Convinced by the scientific and medical analyses of orthodox doctors about their innate weakness and the centrality of their reproductive function, and persuaded by popular literature which immortalized delicate slender women with flower-like natures, middle-class Victorian women identified themselves ever more closely and narcissistically with the 'steel-engraving' silhouette that epitomized perfect womanhood. The narcissist, says Kohut, 'lacking in adequate confirming responses – from the environment – turns to self-stimulation in order to retain (her) precarious cohesion'.[32] According to this explanation, women tried increasingly to assert themselves through narcissistically exploiting the female identity that medical man had defined for them and idealizing the very physical image that rendered them powerless. To stress their ill-health, says Douglas, 'was a way . . . punitively to dramatize their anxiety that their culture found them useless . . . but it supplied them with a means of getting attention'.[33] It was the mode and the zeal with which women pursued this image and the attendant health dangers rather than the representation itself which impelled irregular physicians, women reformers and a varied band of quasi-medical experts to seek a path of remedial action.

Concern arose from a number of directions that middle-class women's lifestyles were an important contribution to their ill-health: that women were unnaturally causing imbalances to occur within their bodies and in their interaction with the environment. The lament was constant that women were being corrupted by fashion and were courting illness in order to appear slender, more delicate and beautiful. Girls languishing of broken hearts or dying of flower-like natures were an immensely popular theme in Ladies' magazines. Impressionable females were accused by reformers of feigning chronic invalidism as a sign of their female delicacy.[34]

The over-zealous pursuit of slender beauty was also perceived in the popularity of too-tightly laced corsets. Corsets were usually recommended for adolescents and women as a necessary support for their internal organs, but many females were criticized for using corsets for modelling rather than support. Consumption and breast tumours, as well as the flattening of nipples, were all blamed upon too-tight lacing.[35] Similarly, women were accused of arranging their clothing for appearance rather than functionality, limiting movement and giving inadequate protection from the weather by wearing thin shoes and low-cut dresses. Despite these criticisms, however, the corset remained popular for most of the century. Its use, Sinclair has argued, represented the superiority of the upwardly mobile woman who could remain breathlessly idle while her working-class sisters could ill-afford the luxury of a corset.[36]

The cultivation of generalized hypochondria, and too frail an image, inevitably caused a perceived imbalance of form and function with a consequent loss of physiological efficiency. Women could not carry out their domestic functions effectively on a daily basis, and they appeared to be rendering themselves more susceptible to the ever-present dangers of disease. During the first half of the nineteenth century, disease contributed to the fact that women had an overwhelming physical disadvantage in relation to men. They bore numerous children, they were less well fed than men: 'They were dragged down by anemia and enervated by all kinds of diseases for which there is no male counterpart'.[37] After the age of five, the female death rate exceeded that of the males. Most particularly, many young middle-class females contracted tuberculosis which did indeed contribute to fragility and an early death.[38] Furthermore, the symptoms of the disease, erratic emotional behaviour, bright eyes and pale, translucent skin fitted popular expectations about how young women should look and behave.[39]

The poor state of American women's health influenced the

physician's determination to make an impression on his patients. Confronted with harsh diseases, orthodox physicians felt they must use harsh and active measures which produced immediate, symptomatic changes in the patient.[40] Blood-letting, purges or perspiration became common heroic measures which, despite the fact that they killed as often as they cured, were expected and demanded by patients. Copious bleeding was used for every kind of illness and was strongly recommended by eminent physicians of the day who felt that it was a genteel and elegant therapy.[41] Indeed, heroic therapeutic measures became normative among regular medical men despite their painful and often tragic consequences.[42]

As women felt the pain and anxiety of ill health, and saw the continued high rate of female mortality, it was hardly surprising that some would join the criticism of medical regulars and look for help from nostrums offered by a wide range of quasi-medical authorities. Women reformers especially denounced the ineffectiveness of orthodox physicians and attributed female frailty to ignorance about preventive health as much as to constitutional weakness.[43] Harriet Hunt was weary and tired with the regulars, Mary Gove dissatisfied with blue pills and bleeding.[44] Both of them felt it was their mission to educate women physiologically and lessen their reliance upon and prudish difficulties with orthodox physicians.[45]

During the *ante-bellum* years, numerous alternative systems of healing had appeared, each claiming to serve women better than regular medicine. Thomsonianism, homeopathy, hydropathy all stimulated the growing belief that hygienic measures could replace medical therapeutics and that physiological knowledge, rightly applied, could regenerate individual and social health. The growing health reform approach to prevention was spurred on by a tide of optimism and evangelical enthusiasm that fused pseudo-science and religion in the countenance of human perfection. If people would learn to regard physiological knowledge and hygienic living as Christian duties, the reformers promised, society could be purged of its corrupting influences and the millennium would be within grasp.[46]

As disease was increasingly perceived as a consequence of careless living, and health and its benefits to be earned by the individual rather than conferred by a physician, reaction crystallized against a fragmented and tradition-oriented medical profession and their excessive medications.[47] Doctors were criticized for using arcane medical terms in an attempt to gain a despotic sway over the public.[48] The licensing legislation adopted by most states at the beginning of the century was repealed in all but three states by 1845.[49] By the time of the Civil War, no effective medical licensing existed in any of the states.[50] Pressed into the health market-place, regular physicians often found it expedient to adopt and assimilate the methods of their competitors – the health reformers.

The health reformers showed varying degrees of hostility toward the medical profession but their feeling was that if physicians were to be accepted at all, they would have to be reformed physicians. William Alcott had already challenged the American Physiological Society to transform medical practice into a system that paid the doctor for preventing rather than curing illness. The way to do this, he suggested, was to teach the science of healthy living to the young, creating a new public demand for health. This would be a market for the new medicine and 'doctors would no longer find their healing mission in conflict with their economic interest'.[51] The message Alcott (himself a disaffected physician) brought to the orthodox medical profession, was that the teaching of physical education, rather than therapy, should be their appropriate mission.

'At the very least, health reformers forced physicians to wrestle with questions of hygiene and to assume a more aggressive interest in popular health (and physical) education'.[52] Preferring compromise to conflict, many doctors accommodated changes in their practice without relinquishing their own beliefs. Thus, lifestyle modifications in diet, dress and exercise for women were prescribed ever more frequently in the 1840s and 1850s as physicians sought to establish their professional dominance in a society which was rejecting their traditional, heroic remedial measures for disease and supporting quasi-medical personnel who were promoting a vision of perfect health and social harmony to be accomplished through the practice of exercise and good hygienic habits.

Physicians noted the popular clamour for active therapy to relieve sickness and, despite their continued ignorance about the etiology of disease, looked for various ways to renew their impression on their patients.[53] Dr Worthington-Hooker remarked that 'the science of patient-getting is often more assiduously studied than that of patient-curing. Real success is not so much desired as the appearance of it'.[54]

THE MEDICAL ESTABLISHMENT AND THE VOLUPTUOUS WOMEN OF THE POST-CIVIL WAR DECADES

The Civil War played a critical role in promoting a developing consensus about nationhood and formalizing new majoritarian expectations and ideas which could lead to order and stability in a rapidly changing world.[55] Mark Twain called the decades after the

Civil War the Gilded Age.[56] Ray Ginger termed the period the Age of Excess.[57] More instructively, Howard Mumford Jones called it the Age of Energy since the containment and control of the forces of industrialization and consumerism were critical questions of the age.[58] The amazing energy of the period in search of assurances for an orderly social life tended to sacrifice forms of voluntarism and to limit channels that had been carved for individual behaviour.[59]

The medical establishment responded to widespread anxieties for social control by strengthening professional control over entry and standards and developing new therapies and surgical practices for their female patients. In 1870, they admitted 'only such persons to membership in their various medical societies as a fully qualified practitioner, and who adhere to . . . legitimate practice'.[60] Given this professional strength, orthodox medicine was in a better position to force sectarian physicians to modify their views in line with regular medical practice.

Yet, no matter how hard they tried to avoid the pitfalls of the marketplace through regulatory measures, excessive numbers of physicians, the growth of specialist practices, and the continued ineffectiveness of medical therapies created a highly competitive environment. The practice of medicine remained a stern mistress and continued, 'neither a pure art nor a perfect science', to suffer both from the ignorance of those it served, and the desire of physicians to maintain their position of authority in a changing world.[61]

Male physicians were especially concerned with the growing strength of the women's rights movement, and the demands of middle-class women for higher education, easier access into the medical profession, and greater control over their bodies and their lives. The demands of emancipating women represented a deviation from the social order upon which doctors depended for their livelihood. Though only a few nineteenth-century American women were committed feminists, increasing numbers of middle-class, workless women had developed an interest in humanitarian reform, extended education and birth control. Increasingly, as the century advanced, male physicians attempted to develop arguments to explain to middle-class women that they could gain independence only at the expense of society. Such females, they said, were contributing to race suicide. Women, physicians warned, must from childhood see their role as that of robust and self-sacrificing mothers, or take responsibility for society's demise.[62] Rebellious women, said Dr Gardner, threatened the United States with disintegration on the scale of that of the Roman Empire.[63]

Freud has explained how fear of a revolt by suppressed elements in society can drive the dominant élite to stricter, precautionary measures.[64] Contemporary feminist scholars also have suggested that industrialism intensified the division between men's and women's spheres and increased the exploitation of women.[65] Certainly, the perceived need to control women and their bodies intensified with the stresses and strains of industrializing society,[66] and was reflected in the kinds of medical therapies and lifestyle advice that were advanced by the male medical establishment in the decades following the Civil War.

In particular, vigorous therapies replaced out-of-favour heroic measures in attempting to make an impression upon female patients. Stimulants of all kinds were offered. Quinine became a panacea for all ills in the 1870s and 1880s and was recommended by a committee of the American Medical Association who stated that 'with this in their hands (many physicians) do not need or desire any other articles of this class'.[67] By 1886, American doctors were using 40 per cent of the total world consumption of quinine.[68] Opium and morphine were widely used for any and all complaints, but most popular of all was alcohol since it 'furnishes our best means of counteracting the depressing action of disease in general'.[69] The use of alcohol became widespread, particularly as it was believed to have food value as well as being very agreeable to patients.[70] Physicians, noted Dr Carpenter in 1871, either had to prescribe alcohol or lose their patients.[71] The strengthening therapies accorded well with the advice of a number of physicians who were beginning to recommend that plumpness was a sure sign of female health and good nature, and that physiological evidence demanded women consume large quantities of food in order to counter-balance the rigours of climate and child-bearing.[72]

Plumpness became beautiful and fashionable in the years after the Civil War.[73] 'The women in all our great centres of population are yearly becoming more plump and more beautiful,' declared Dr George Beard with satisfaction in 1879. Plumpness, roundness and size, he continued, are rightly believed to indicate well-balanced health.[74] Foreign visitors, too, noted a change in women's shape after the 1850s, and attributed it to the influences of European fashion and new styles in art.[75] In sculpture and paintings after the Civil War female bodies became increasingly large with an emphasis on heavy bosoms and hips. John Gasts' enormously popular painting called the 'Spirit of the Frontier', but essentially heralding the triumph of order across the nation, had as its dominant motif a giant goddess, serene, majestic and ample-bosomed. Many of Thomas Nast's political cartoons of the 1870s featured a tall and plump Columbia.[76]

The emphasis placed by some on the need for women to fortify their bodies with food, alcohol and tonics as compensation for the physical efforts of pregnancy and childbirth is consistent with the argument that many physicians steadfastly maintained an indifference to the relationship between new scientific knowledge and medical practice. The medical promise of experimental physiology proclaimed by such eminent physiologists as Claude Bernard and Michael Foster in the 1860s and 70s was substantially ignored by practising physicians in North America.[77] As late as 1902, Dr Cathell's enormously popular *Book on the Physician Himself and Things That Concern His Reputation and Success* noted that the new scientific knowledge might actually be damaging to the general practitioner.[78]

The reasons for this indifference are complex, but Temkin suggests that when medicine comes to depend on basic scientific thought, it is 'usually of a sort that research physiologists might fail to recognize as scientific at all'.[79] More important, it seems, is the understanding that physicians continued to adapt their world view of health and disease to the expectations of their patients (upon whom they depended) and that changes in ways of looking at the body and its relationship to health and disease reflected economic and social shifts and the texture of personal experience more than changing intellectual paradigms. The eminent practitioner Dr Edward Clarke, in a famous essay of 1874, expounded at length upon the bedside achievements of his colleagues but gave 'barely a nod' to the findings of basic science.[80]

Instead, he and other orthodox physicians re-interpreted the vitalist theory that saw disease as an imbalance among the body systems by contributing to a general public uneasiness that shifting social and economic conditions were taking an unprecedented emotional and physical toll upon Americans, especially women. Nerve weakness, or neurasthenia, became a 'self-fulfilling medical prophecy', as doctors proclaimed it 'an epidemic of advanced civilization'.[81] (Also useful was the security that 'a nervous and irritable lady . . . may be worth from one to five hundred dollars a year' to medical men.)[82] Dr George Beard declared that increasing numbers of Americans were suffering from nervous bankruptcy, a physical state that demanded dramatic therapies to save the nation from sliding further into physical and moral decline. Women were in particular need of help, he noted, since they were 'more nervous immeasurably than men and suffer more from a general and special nervous disease'. Furthermore, he lamented, 'the weakness of women is all modern, and it is pre-eminently American'.[83] Others agreed, and showed how American women were liable to nervous breakdown because of the thinness of their blood, or because their brains were small and light.[84]

These problems were exacerbated, many physicians agreed, by

increasing female demands for higher education and their efforts to compete with men. Medical men were particularly worried about professional competition and made the strongest attack upon higher education for women. Women insisting upon joining the medical profession were considered to lack the necessary physical constitution, and to be too easily swayed by emotion.[85] Even at home, it was supposed that females had difficulty performing their legitimate domestic roles when their physiological abilities were disrupted by nervous exhaustion. Dr Edward Clarke blamed much of female ill-health upon mental exertion and education. Girls, he said, should be carefully protected from the excitements of study and helped to build up their bodies for their supreme – and only – function: reproduction. Over-educated women, he continued, could not help 'acquiring an Amazonian coarseness, becoming hysterical, anemic and incapable of maternal feeling'. They would become flat-chested and develop 'monstrous brains and puny bodies'.[86] Worse, education for women would result in their offspring being of an exhausted constitution.[87]

Arguments that women were created for beauty, not mental activity, and for motherhood, not professional activity, were extended by physicians to show that women needed physiological education not intellectual study. The most highly developed female physiologically would exhibit the most feminine characteristics. Ideally, the balance of the female body system would be maintained by rest during menstruation and compensatory exercise at other times to restore lost energy. Well-rounded physical education was thus seen as the chief reformist means to counterbalance brainwork, menstruation and reproduction.[88]

In this regard, regular physicians did not quarrel with their less orthodox counterparts and other moral reformers who were promoting gymnastics and physical activities as means to remedy the stress and poor health of American women and enforce the laws of health as a religious duty. Dio Lewis, physician turned temperance reformer, developed a popular system of light exercise that aimed at dampening sexual passions, developing self-control and providing robust mothers for the future.[89] He did not, however, offer women strength so that they could break their social bonds, agreeing with Dr Beard to the extent that if the new woman were to be a healthy woman she would have to be a woman in the old role.[90] Other physicians with a preventive inclination (many of whom were homeopaths) became heavily involved in promoting physical exercise for women in the female colleges and other institutions.[91] Dr Dudley Sargent especially promoted physical education for women through his Sargent system at Harvard, and was involved with William G. Anderson in spearheading an organized advocacy for physical educators through the founding of the American Association for the Advancement of Physical Education in 1885.[92] Yet reformers and educators were strongly influenced by the orthodox medical profession's pronouncements upon the health problems of female education and were most careful to adhere to medical recommendations that both bodily and mental fatigue should be avoided.

The importance of nurturing the female's reproductive ability was further underscored by fears that the birth rate among middle-class women was rapidly declining as a result of abortion and birth control.[93] Physicians came to regard women as the vessels and products of their reproductive system. Thus, the significance male physicians attached to the body part of woman increased in proportion to their devaluation of her mind. 'Woman was what she was,' said Dr Horatio Storer, 'because of her womb alone.'[94] Such beliefs identified women totally with their bodies and provided physicians with the authority to tell them how their bodies should look, and how they should behave in order to improve their physiological efficiency for child-bearing.[95]

Through strengthening therapies, food, tonics, compensatory exercise, and gynaecological surgery, orthodox medical men endorsed size, plumpness and rounded curves as female virtues, and as indications of female beauty which was equated with goodness and morality. Supporting Hogarth's view that the curved line is the line of beauty, Ralph Waldo Emerson had claimed that beauty reached its height in women.[96] In the decades after the Civil War, ample curves, especially of bosom and hips, epitomized the female form of beauty to strive for, and represented the ripeness of women for their maternal function.

Efficiency in childbirth, however, clearly required physical strength that seemed to demand more than gentle exercise, massage, tonics and surgery. Increasingly, physical renewal or regeneration for females became a catchword among physicians as new understandings of growth and development and interpretations of evolutionary theories slowly permeated medical thinking.[97] When growth studies were linked up with ideas on phrenology, the theory of compensation through exercise gained an expanded audience. Liberal interpretations of growth statistics allowed physicians to tie body morphology to intelligence and show that girls and women needed exercise to build body bulk and symmetry in order to be healthy mothers of potentially large and intelligent children. 'The size of an organ,' said Dr Ruschenberger, 'is a measure of its power. The growth impulse is impressed upon the germ at the moment of conception (and) is dependent upon the . . . vigor of the parents.'[98]

Thus strength, as well as size, came to be viewed as a desirable component in the ideal female form, though curves were not to be sacrificed. The difficulty lay in interpreting how much strength could be developed through healthful exercise without sacrificing societal demands for female modesty and the beauty of female curves. Again, the definition of the problem which faced the orthodox medical profession was not derived from their professional paradigm, but emerged rather as a shared concern of a broad coalition of societal conservative forces.[99]

The solution to the dilemma was personified in the 'Gibson Girl' who in appearance was tall, commanding and athletic.

> Her figure was thinner than that of the voluptuous woman but she remained large of bosom and hips . . . she was braver, stronger, more healthful and skillful . . .[100]

This body shape began to dominate standards of female beauty in the last decade of the nineteenth century.

SCIENTIFIC MEDICINE AND THE EMERGENCE OF THE TALL, ATHLETIC GIBSON GIRL

In the last years of the century, medicine began to change, as traditional dogmas and sectarianism became increasingly untenable in the face of massive scientific advances which inevitably informed orthodox diagnosis and practice. Slow but definite upward trends in female life expectancy at birth were evident by 1890.[101] By the 1890s, 35 states had either established or resurrected medical licensing laws and at the end of the century all states had licensing regulations except for the Alaskan territories.[102] In 1901, Dr Charles Reed, President of the American Medical Association, declared, 'Practice has changed. . . . I proclaim the existence of a new school of medicine'.[103]

Several developments were evident. Despite the continuing popularity of pills, the ordering of drugs or medicine for every disease was no longer regarded as the chief function of the doctor.[104] There was also a substantial shift of locus of medical practice from home to office beginning to take place which lessened the dominance of the physician within the family circle, but allowed him to advance his repertoire of techniques in a clinical setting.[105] Furthermore, regular physicians had managed to suppress the sectarian tendencies of the age, restricting the opportunities of homeopaths and other irregulars where convenient, and assimilating many of their techniques. After all, said Dr Hartford in 1898, 'I see no good reason why we should allow the army of irregulars to carry away the best part of our business'.[106]

Perhaps the major indication of change in medical beliefs and practice was the growing recognition of the importance of prevention among regular physicians. In 1882, Dr Nathan Allen noted that 'the time is fast approaching when prevention will be the watchword'.[107] The critical thrust to physicians' concern with preventive medicine, and consequently more serious interest in health and physical education, was an optimistic interpretation of evolutionary theory which became slowly evident in medical thinking and practice. Initially, many regular physicians accused the evolutionists of spreading materialist philosophy into all realms of society. During the 1880s, however, many of them had transformed evolution into a benevolent and progressive teleology overseen by God.[108]

Second generation evolutionists such as Lester Ward re-interpreted Herbert Spencer's initial pessimistic notions that mankind was helpless in the evolutionary march to show that men or women could use their telic ability, their will, to improve their evolutionary chances. Since only the fittest parents would pass on their acquired, superior health to their children in the march to a perfect race, mistreatment of one's body amounted to a calculated mistreatment of one's progeny.[109] Thus, in order to breed out unfitness, one had an obligation to be healthy. Men and women, said Dr Devendorf, 'have no right to bring into the world children . . . to drag out a miserable existence and transmit again to their children the fatal inheritance'.[110]

Women, as future mothers, played a potentially critical role in determining the fate of the race, and size in the form of ample bosom and broad hips was clearly an insufficient condition for vigorous motherhood. Doctors could see that without energy and strength a woman would be unable to fulfil her mission, yet physiological determinism had decreed that she was at the mercy of the influences of her reproductive organs. Little hope could be seen for women who 'by nature were defined by physical characteristics and driven helplessly by powerful emotions verging on the pathological'.[111]

The answer to the pessimism of hereditarianism and the seeming hopelessness of female biological determinism lay in acknowledging the primacy of the will – in developing character through strength of habit and strong will. Habits could be transmitted to the next generation and, as William James explained, habit was to be achieved through action, or more specifically, motor activity.[112]

One of the best ways of fostering good habits was through systematic, vigorous physical activity. 'Our habits do more to form our bodies as well as our minds than the conscious efforts at improvement.'[113] Thus, strengthening the body would develop the mind, the character and the will. Physical culture would help to 'unfold the natural and symmetrical beauty of the human body, making it fit and capable, in every phase of moral life, to adopt and carry out the will of its supreme master, the mind.'[114] Physical activity and sport, said an ardent promoter of female exercise, would strengthen the woman to serve as 'the mother of a race of stalwarts'.[115]

Evolutionary theory thus became 'a welcome kinsman to medicine's expanded definition as it moved to encompass prevention as well as cure'.[116] It was especially useful in providing the impetus for many physicians to support female exercise and sport as part of an essential salvage plan of bodily renovation, and to promote an ideal female body frame that was strong and muscular, but still feminine.[117] They generally agreed that 'women [should] not aim for an athlete's prodigious strength, but for the development of each muscle of the body to uniform strength and symmetry, giving those curves and lines of beauty which have made the feminine figure the model for all sculptors and painters'.[118]

As women began to participate more extensively in sports and exercise, however, especially in such activities as bicycle riding, many physicians became increasingly concerned and ambiguous in their support of healthful pursuits that threatened to promote greater female control over their bodies and their lives.[119] Muscle power was important for child-bearing and the medical literature of the 1890s noted that bicycle riding exercised all the muscles.[120] At the same time, many physicians began to feel a strong uneasiness about strenuous physical activity for women in sport or on bicycles. 'As women took to the roads, physicians took to their desks', says Whorton, and whether they applauded the benefits or worried about the hazards, the emphasis was inevitably the same: upon women's reproductive capacity.[121] 'Will the female rider throw aside her wheel long enough to have a baby,' asked Dr Love in 1895, 'let alone a respectable sized family?'[122]

The physician's concern for the physical betterment of the late nineteenth-century female, then, was not for her sake alone, but for the sake of her unborn children. Thus, even the gradual emergence of the scientific foundations of medicine did little to ameliorate the tendency of its establishment to serve as an instrument of social control rather than a vehicle for reform. This was at least true where the shape and function of women's bodies were concerned.

NOTES

1. Maxwell L. Howell and Reet A. Howell, 'Women in Sport and Physical Education in the United States, 1900–1914', in R. Howell (ed.), *Her Story in Sport: A Historical Anthology of Women in Sports* (New York, 1982), p. 162.
2. Roberta J. Park, 'Embodied Selves: The Rise and Development of Concern for Physical Education, Active Games and Recreation for American Women, 1776–1865', *Journal of Sport History*, 5:2 (Summer 1978), 5.
3. Anita Clair Fellman and Michael Fellman, *Making Sense of Self: Medical Advice Literature in Late Nineteenth Century America* (Philadelphia, 1981).
4. See Valerie Steele's review of Lois Banner's book, *American Beauty*, in *Journal of Social History* (Winter, 1984), 300–1.
   Herbert Blumer has illustrated the complexities involved in an historical analysis of fashion in 'Fashion: From Class Differentiation to Collective Selection', *Sociological Quarterly*, 10 (Spring 1969), 275–91.
5. Lois W, Banner, *American Beauty*. (New York, 1983). See also, E. Berscheid, 'Physical Attractiveness', *Advances in Experimental Social Psychology*, 7, (1974), 158–210; and S. Ewen, *Captains of Consciousness* (New York, 1976).
6. Though Thorstein Veblen in *Theory of the Leisure Class* (New York, 1915) located the source of fashion among the élite, recent analyses have shown a growing and pervasive middle-class influence upon models of beauty in the nineteenth century. See, for example, Mary Ellen Roach and Kathleen Musa, *New Perspectives on the History of Western Dress* (New York, 1980).
7. See Valerie Steele, *Review*; Robert Riegel, in his analysis of nineteenth-century dress reform has suggested that no real dress reform had taken place by the end of the nineteenth century; see 'Women's Clothes and Women's Rights', *American Quarterly*, XV:3 (Autumn, 1963), 390–401.
8. E.D. Pellegrino, 'Medicine, History and the Idea of Man', in J.A. Clausen and R. Straus (eds.), *Medicine and Society: Annals of the American Academy of Political Sciences*, 9 (1963), 346.
9. Paul Starr and others (Shryock, Rosenberg, Rothstein) have examined the rise to authority and power of a group of initially lowly, divided and poorly paid nineteenth-century medical practitioners. A number of explanations have been advanced to account for the degree of control that regular practitioners gradually managed to exert within industrializing America. Starr, for example, relates how early distrust of physicians was replaced by a fundamental faith in their value in evaluating and controlling large amounts of technical information. The reasons for this transformation of popular opinion are complex but are intricately connected to political and social forces of the time and especially to the growth of the medical market. Paul Starr, *The Social Transformation of American Medicine* (New York, 1982); see also George Rosen, *The Structure of American Medical Practice, 1875–1941* (Philadelphia, 1983), edited by Charles E. Rosenberg; William G. Rothstein, *American Physicians in the Nineteenth Century: From Sects to Science* (Baltimore, 1972); John S. Haller, Jr., *American Medicine in Transition, 1840–1910* (Urbana, 1981); Morris J. Vogel and Charles E. Rosenberg (eds.), *The Therapeutic Revolution: Essays in the Social History of American Medicine* (Philadelphia, 1979).
   Competition in a busy marketplace increasingly pressed orthodox doctors into the role of 'clear headed, shrewd and practical men . . . who had little love of science for its own sake and whose principal objective was to obtain money. John Shaw Billings, 'A Century of American Medicine, 1776–1876; Literature and Institutions', *American Journal of Medical Science*, 72 (1876), 438–80.
10. A number of feminist social historians have focused upon the role of the medical profession in medicalizing the bodies and sex of nineteenth-century American middle class women. Carroll Smith-Rosenberg and Charles Rosenberg, Ann Douglas Wood, and others have developed the idea of a medically-based male conspiracy, where physicians as protectors of the status quo asserted control over emancipating

middle-class women by developing prescriptions based upon a combination of scientific imprecision and emotionally charged conviction. Ann Douglas Wood, 'The Fashionable Diseases: Women's Complaints and Their Treatment in Nineteenth-Century America', *The Journal of Interdisciplinary History*, IV (1973), 25–52; Carroll Smith-Rosenberg and Charles Rosenberg, 'The Female Animal: Medical and Biological Views of Woman and Her Role in Nineteenth-Century America', *Journal of American History*, 60 (Sept. 1973), 332–56 (and see above, pp. 13–37). Sara Delamont and Lorna Duffin, *The Nineteenth Century Woman: Her Cultural and Physical World* (London, 1978) suggest that the analytic tools of social anthropology developed by Mary Douglas and Shirley and Edwin Ardener can be profitably used to analyse aspects of Victorian female experience, and to extend the Rosenberg model. Placed in an inferior category in the predominant system of society, women, as a muted group, 'transform their own unconscious perceptions into such conscious ideas as will accord with those generated by the dominant group'. See Shirley Ardener (ed.), *Perceiving Women* (London, 1975) p. xvii. Such theories help explain why many women so readily accepted male medical views as their own and why the most successful women reformers were those able to articulate their ideas in a form acceptable to the dominant male group of orthodox physicians.

Mary Douglas suggests that humans impose order upon complexity and disorder by strict classification – anything which weakens the boundaries of that classification is anomalous, a physical pollution, or a moral or social danger. Thus, a rigid separation of sex roles became essential to counteract the disruptive forces of rapid social change in nineteenth-century America. Eliminating dirt was not a negative movement but a positive effort to organize the environment. Mary Douglas, *Purity and Danger: An Analysis of the Concepts of Pollution and Taboo* (London, 1984).

Whether one accepts a conspiratorial theory borne out of masculine stress, one of dominant and muted groups, or accepts the medical marketplace explanation, medical theory and practice in the nineteenth century did mirror the emerging features of an industrializing society and helped to shape responses to the changing roles of men and women within it. Most important, perhaps, is to recognize that male medical therapies for nineteenth-century women cannot be viewed apart from the scientific ignorance and confusion of the age. See Regina Markell Morantz, 'The Perils of Feminist History', *The Journal of Interdisciplinary History*, IV (1973), 649–60; Susan Sleeth Mosedale, 'Science Corrupted, Victorian Biologists Consider "The Woman Question" ', *Journal of the History of Biology*, 11:1 (Spring 1978), 1–55.

11. Leading regular medical practitioners frequently provided the arguments (often inconsistent) and couched in scientific terms, to justify their role as physical guardians of women, and to legitimize the diagnoses and prescriptions for female disorders that they wished to market on a grand scale. This meant that medical knowledge was used to support attitudes about appropriate forms and functions of the human body. See, for example, Sara Delamont and Lorna Duffin, *The Nineteenth Century Woman: Her Cultural and Physical World* (London, 1978); John S. Haller and Robin M. Haller, *The Physician and Sexuality in Victorian America* (Illinois, 1974).

12. Banner, *American Beauty*, p. 146.

13. For example, when physicians did provide support for lifestyle modifications such as the physical and health education of girls and women, there were usually many motives, and they were not necessarily related to new physiological knowledge, or the desire for women to experience greater control over their bodies. Often, support for an exercise or diet regimen represented an intellectual compromise with physician's traditional understandings of health and disease, as well as a keen desire to compete in a crowded market of would-be healers. Rothstein, *American Physicians in the Nineteenth Century*.

14. R.V. Pierce, *The People's Common-Sense Medical Adviser* (21st edn., Buffalo, 1889), p. 208; S. Weir Mitchell, *Doctor and Patient* (Philadelphia, 1888), 707; George L. Austin, *Perils of American Women, or a Doctor's Talk with Maiden, Wife and Mother* (Boston, 1882), p. 185.

15. See James C. Whorton, *Crusaders for Fitness: The History of American Health Reformers* (New Jersey: Princeton University Press, 1982) for a detailed description of

the efforts of health reformers and moralists to promote physical education for women, in particular the writings of Martin Luther Holbrook; Fellman and Fellman, *Making Sense of Self*, p. 125; note, however, that it was significant that despite a burgeoning physical culture movement there was very little interest in encouraging working-class women to exercise or participate in sport.

16. Dudley Sargent, 'The Physical Development of Women', *Scribner's Magazine*, 5 (Feb. 1889), 181.

17. Bernarr Macfadden, *The Power and Beauty of Superb Womanhood* (New York, 1901).

18. Donald J. Mrozek, *Sport and American Mentality, 1880–1910* (Knoxville: The University of Tennessee Press, 1983), p. 137.

19. Sargent, 'Physical Development', 182.

20. Banner, *American Beauty*, p. 46, derives her use of the term steel-engraving lady from Caroline Ticknor, 'The New Woman and the Steel-Engraving Lady', *Atlantic Monthly*, 88 (July 1901), 105–110.

21. See Phillida Bunkle in 'Sentimental Womanhood and Domestic Education, 1830–1870', *History of Education Quarterly*, XIV:1 (Spring, 1974), 13–29, for an analysis of interpretations of the changing female role at this time.

22. Ann Douglas, *The Feminization of American Culture* (New York, 1977), p. 59, documents these shifts in female role. See, for example, Walter Channing, *Remarks on the Employment of Females as Practitioners in Midwifery* (Boston, 1820).

23. Patricia Branca, *Silent Sisterhood, Middle Class Women in the Victorian Home* (London, 1975), though mainly illustrating the British experience, also outlines North American concerns. See also Edward Shorter, *A History of Women's Bodies* (New York, 1982) in which he describes the changing health of women in the nineteenth century and physician's attitudes towards women's health; and Ann Douglas Wood, 'The Fashionable Diseases: Women's Complaints and Their Treatment in Nineteenth-Century America', *The Journal of Interdisciplinary History*, IV (1973) 25–52.

24. Penelope Brown and L. Jordanova, 'Oppressive Dichotomies: The Nature/Culture Debate', in Elizabeth Whitelegg *et al.* (eds.), *The Changing Experience of Women* (Oxford, 1982), pp. 389–401.

25. C.D. Meigs, *Females and Their Diseases* (Philadelphia, 1848), Introduction.

26. Elizabeth Lee, 'Nineteenth Century Craniology: The Study of the Female Skull', *Bulletin of the History of Medicine*, 53 (1979), 415–33; see also Stephen Jay Gould, *The Mismeasure of Man* (New York, 1981) for an excellent discussion on craniology.

27. Quoted in Thomas Woody, *A History of Women's Education in the United States*, Vol. 2 (New York, 1929), p. 105.

28. Elizabeth Cady Stanton, 'On the Social, Educational, Religious, and Political Position of Women in America. Delivered at Prince's Hall, 25 June, 1883', *Stanton Papers*, Library of Congress.

29. Benjamin Rush, *Medical Inquiries and Observations*, Vol. 4 (Philadelphia, 1794–98); Richard H. Shyrock, 'The Medical Reputation of Benjamin Rush', *Bulletin of the History of Medicine*, XLV: 6 (Nov.–Dec. 1969), 507–52; see also Richard H. Shyrock, *Medicine and Society in America, 1660–1860* (New York, 1960).

30. *Etiquette for Ladies: With Hints on the Preservation, Improvement and Display of Female Beauty* (Philadelphia, 1848).

31. For discussions of nineteenth-century views on girls and menstruation, see, for example, Vern Bullough and Martha Voght, 'Women, Menstruation and Nineteenth Century Medicine', *Bulletin of the History of Medicine*, 47:1 (Jan.–Feb., 1973), 66–82; Martha Vicinus (ed.), *Suffer and Be Still: Women in the Victorian Age* (Bloomington, IN, 1972).

32. Heinz Kohut, 'Thoughts on Narcissism and Narcissistic Rage', A.A. Brill Lecture of the New York Psychoanalytic Society (30 November 1971).

33. Douglas, *Feminization*, 109. Complaints from females about their general ill-health were frequent. See, for example, Catharine Beecher, *Letters to the People on Health and Happiness* (New York, 1855).

34. Arthur W. Calhoun, *The American Family from Colonial Times to the Present* (Cleveland, 1917), p. 213.

35. 'Action, not ornament, should be the goal for a woman', said Catharine Beecher, in *A Treatise on Domestic Economy* (Boston, 1841). This was typical of a constant anxiety among *ante-bellum* moral reformers over the deleterious effects of fashion and lack of attention to the laws of health; see also Catharine Beecher, *Letters to the People on Health and Happiness* (New York, 1855), pp. 93–4.

36. Andrew Sinclair, *The Better Half: The Emancipation of the American Woman* (London, 1966), p. 104; A number of historians have attempted to explain the reasons for the corset's popularity. See, for example, Helene E. Roberts, 'Submission, Masochism, and Narcissism: Three Aspects of Women's Role as Reflected in Dress', *Signs: Journal of Women in Culture and Society*, 3 (Spring, 1977), 7–29, and David Kunzle, *Fashion and Fetishism: A Social History of the Corset, Tight Lacing and Other Forms of Body Sculpture in the West* (Totowa, NJ, 1982).

37. Shorter, *Women's Bodies*, p. 285.

38. Deborah Gorham, *The Victorian Girl and the Feminine Ideal* (London, 1982).

39. Barbara Ehrenreich and Deidre English, *Complaints and Disorders: The Sexual Politics of Sickness* (Glass Mountain Pamphlet 2, The Feminist Press, 1973), p. 21.

40. Rothstein, *American Physicians*, p. 41.

41. John M. Scudder, 'Bloodletting', *Eclectic Medical Journal*, 36 (1878), 186.

42. Jacob Bigelow, *Modern Inquiries* (Boston, 1862). J.C. Furnas, *The Americans: A Social History, 1587–1914*, Vol. 1 (New York, 1969), p. 339.

43. Regina Morantz has documented how female health crusaders stood united in their criticism of heroic measures, and in their desire to disseminate health and physiological knowledge to the housewife. 'Making Women Modern: Middle Class Women and Health Reform in 19th Century America', *Journal of Social History*, 10 (1977), 490–507.

44. John B. Blake, 'Women and Medicine in Ante-Bellum America', *Bulletin of the History of Medicine*, XXXIX:2 (March–April 1965), 99–123.

45. Elizabeth Cady Stanton, Susan B. Anthony, and Matilda J. Gage, (eds.), *History of Women Suffrage* (New York, 1881); 'I wish,' said Mary Gove Nichols, 'to teach mothers how to cure their own diseases . . . and to increase health, purity and happiness in the family': 'To Women Who Read the Water Cure Journal', *Water Cure Journal*, 4 (1852), 68.

46. See S.W. Nissenbaum, 'Careful Love: Sylvester Graham and the Emergence of Victorian Sexual Theory in America' (PhD Dissertation, University of Wisconsin, 1968); Haller, in *American Medicine in Transition*, describes how medical sectarians acted as third party platforms by putting forward ideas, 'clamoring loudly in voices all out of proportion to their numbers, teasing and annoying the mainstream of medical thought', p. 149.

47. Thomas L. Nichols, *Forty Years of American Life* (London, 1866).

48. Benjamin Colby, *A Guide to Health* (New Hampshire, 1846).

49. Richard H. Shyrock, *Medical Licensing in America, 1650–1965* (Baltimore, 1967).

50. D.E. Konold, *A History of American Medical Ethics, 1847–1921* (Madison, WI, 1962).

51. William Alcott, 'The Right Use of Physicians', *Lib. Health*, 5 (1841), 41–5, 75–88.

52. For a full discussion, see Whorton, *Crusaders for Fitness*, 92–132; see also John R. Betts, 'American Medical Thought on Exercise as the Road to Health, 1820–1860', *Bulletin of the History of Medicine*, XLV:1 (Jan.–Feb. 1971), 138–52; and Gerald Grob, *Edward Jarvis and the Medical World of Nineteenth Century America* (Knoxville, TN 1978).

53. Rothstein, *American Physicians*.

54. Dr Worthington-Hooker, quoted in Haller, *American Medicine in Transition*, p. viii.

55. Robert Wiebe, *The Search for Order, 1877–1920* (New York, 1967).

56. Mark Twain and Charles Dudley Warner, *The Gilded Age* (1873). See also Vernon L. Parrington, *Main Currents of American Thought* (New York, 1930).

57. Ray Ginger, *Age of Excess* (New York, 1965).

58. Howard Mumford Jones, *The Age of Energy: Varieties of American Experience, 1865–1915* (New York, 1971).

59. Charles Burgess, 'The Goddess, The School Book and Compulsion', *Harvard*

Educational Review, 46:2 (May 1976), 199–216.

60. A.D. Lippe, 'Liberty of Medical Opinion and Action', *Hahnemannian Monthly*, VI (1870), 154.
61. Haller, *American Medicine in Transition*, p. 192.
62. For a discussion of these arguments see, for example, Ben Barker-Benfield, 'The Spermatic Economy: A Nineteenth Century View of Sexuality', *Feminist Studies*, 1:1 (Summer 1972), 45–75; and Smith-Rosenberg and Rosenberg, 'The Female Animal'.
63. Augustus Kinsley Gardner, *Conjugal Sins Against the Laws of Life and Health* (New York, 1870), p. 52.
64. Sigmund Freud, *Civilization and its Discontents*, trans. James Strachey (New York, 1962), p. 51.
65. See, for example, Joan Burstyn, *Victorian Education and the Ideal of Womanhood* (London, 1980); Zillah R. Eisenstein, 'Developing a Theory of Capitalist Patriarchy and Socialist Feminism', and Nancy Chodorow, 'Mothering, Male Dominance and Capitalism', in Zillah R. Eisenstein (ed.), *Capitalist Patriarchy and the Case for Socialist Feminism* (New York, 1979); Michelle Zimbalist Rosaldo and Louise Lamphere (eds.), *Woman, Culture and Society* (Stanford, CA, 1974).
66. Robert Weibe, *The Search for Order*, p. 107.
67. L.J. Deal and T.M. Logan, 'Report of the Committee to Memorialize Congress on the Cultivation of the Cinchona Tree in the United States', *Transactions of the American Medical Association*, 21 (1870).
68. Erwin H. Ackerknecht, 'The American Medical Association and the Cultivation of the Cinchona Tree in the United States', *Journal of the American Medical Association*, 123 (1943), 375.
69. J.M. Farrington, 'The Use of Alcohol in Medicine', *New York Medical Journal*, 50 (1889), 352; Haller and Haller, in *The Physician and Sexuality*, have documented the indiscriminate manner in which doctors prescribed opium and cocaine to their female patients: 'There were few cases of opium addiction which did not originate with a physician's prescription', p. 277.
70. E.F. Parsons, 'Alcohol in Therapeutics', *Proceedings of the Connecticut Medical Society, New Jersey*, 4 (1888).
71. Benoni Carpenter, 'Quackery in the Regular Profession', *Boston Medical and Surgical Journal*, 84 (1871), 312.
72. S. Weir Mitchell, *Fat and Blood* (Philadelphia, 1887); George Beard maintained that food consumed should be 'generous in quantity, quality and variety'. *Eating and Drinking* (New York, 1871), pp. 85–6.
73. Margaret Hubbard Ayer and Isabella Taves, *The Three Lives of Harriet Hubbard Ayer* (Philadelphia, 1957), p. 236.
74. George Beard, 'Physical Future of the American People', *Atlantic Monthly*, 43 (June 1879), 726; W. Wittall recommended a 'moderate rotundity . . . enough flesh to cover all the angularities'. *Health by Good Living* (New York, 1875), p. 53.
75. T.C. Grattan, *Civilized America* (London, 1859).
76. A print of John Gast's painting can be seen in *American Heritage New Illustrated History of the United States* (New York, 1963) IX, pp. 800–801; Morton Keller, *The Art and Politics of Thomas Nast* (New York, 1968); see also John Mitchell, 'Contemporary American Caricature', *Scribner's Magazine*, 6 (Dec. 1889), 728–45.
77. Gerald L. Geison, 'Divided We Stand: Physiologists and Clinicians in the American Context', in Vogel and Rosenberg, *The Therapeutic Revolution*, pp. 67–90.
78. D.W. Cathell and W.T. Cathell, *Book on the Physician Himself and Things That Concern his Reputation and Success* (Philadelphia, 11th edn., 1902).
79. Oswei Temkin, 'The Dependence of Medicine Upon Basic Medical Thought', in Chandler McBrooks and Paul Cranefield (eds.), *The Historical Development of Physiological Thought* (New York, 1959), 5–21; Roberta Park, in 'Science, Service and the Professionalization of Physical Education: 1885–1905', *Research Quarterly for Exercise and Sport*, Centennial Issue (1985) 7–20, also discusses the persistent tendency for research physiologists and medical doctors to hold substantially different views of the body.

80. Edward H. Clarke, 'Practical Medicine', in E.H. Clarke *et al.*, *A Century of American Medicine* (1876; reprint ed., Brinklow, 1962), pp. 3–72.
81. George Beard, *American Nervousness, Its Causes and Consequences* (New York, 1881); Augustus K. Gardner, *Conjugal Sins Against the Laws of Life and Health* (New York, 1870); S. Weir-Mitchell, *Lectures on the Diseases of the Nervous System, Especially in Women* (Philadelphia, 1881).
82. Edward Dixon, *Scenes in the Practice of a New York Surgeon* (New York, 1855), p. 64.
83. George Beard, *American Nervousness, Its Causes and Consequences* (New York, 1881), pp. 7–9, 185, 107, 336.
84. Dr Weir Mitchell treated nervous women by shutting them in a large bed chamber and cramming them with large amounts of rich, nourishing food. S. Weir Mitchell, *Doctor and Patient*, pp. 83–4; M.A. Hardaker, 'Science and the Woman Question', *Popular Science Monthly*, 20 (March 1882), 577–84; Henry Gray, *Anatomy Descriptive and Surgical* (London, 1877); Joseph Simms, 'Human Brain Weights', *Popular Science Monthly*, 31 (July 1887), 355–9.
85. John A. Blake, 'Women and Medicine in Ante-Bellum America', *Bulletin of the History of Medicine*, XXXIX:2 (March–April, 1965), 99–123.
86. Edward H. Clarke, *Sex in Education – or a Fair Chance for the Girls* (Boston, 1873), p. 41. See also Hamilton Osgood, 'The Need of a Radical Change in the Education and Training of the American Girl and the Physician's Duty Therein', *Boston Medical Surgical Journal*, 104 (1881), 289–92; Thomas Addis Emmett, *The Principles and Practice of Gynecology* (Philadelphia, 1879).
87. A. Hughes Bennett, 'Hygiene in the Higher Education of Women', *Popular Science Monthly*, 16 (Feb. 1880), 519–30.
88. R.V. Pierce, *The People's Common Sense Medical Adviser* (Buffalo, New York, 1889).
89. Fellman and Fellman, 32, describe Dio Lewis as a 'leftover transcendentalist whose route to the oversoul was exercise'; see also, Dio Lewis, *Our Girls* (New York: Harper and Brothers, 1871); and Patricia Vertinsky, 'Rhythmics – A Sort of Physical Jubilee: A New Look at the Contributions of Dio Lewis', *Canadian Journal of History of Sport and Physical Education*, IX:1 (May, 1978), 31–42.
90. Dio Lewis, 'The Health of American Women', *North American Review*, 135 (1882), 503–10; Beard, *American Nervousness*, p. 18.
91. For details see, for example, pertinent chapters in Betty Spears and Richard Swanson, *History of Sport and Physical Activity in the United States* (Dubuque, Iowa, 1983); Reet Howell (ed.), *Her Story in Sport* (New York, 1982).
92. Mabel Lee and Bruce Bennett, '1885–1900: A Time of Gymnastics and Measurement', *Joperd*, 56:4 (April 1985), 19–27.
93. These fears are discussed by James Reed, 'Birth Control and Social Values, 1830–1870' in Vogel and Rosenberg, *The Therapeutic Revolution*, pp. 109–33. Physicians associated birth control with threats to the social order that they served and to the profession. Had they wanted to provide reliable contraceptive means to the public, the requisite technology was available, but the perceived threats to stable family life and professional goodwill were too great. Orthodox physicians were substantially in sympathy with purity crusaders who wished to suppress birth control information and make American cities safe for middle class families. They learned that it was in the 'interest of the profession to defend the highest moral standards of the community' (see David Pivar, *Purity Crusade: Sexual Morality and Social Control, 1868–1900* (Westport, CT, 1973). Sure that all women should be willing mothers, physicians warned that sterility, insanity, and disease all resulted from birth control (Vincent J. Cirillo, 'Edward Foote's Medical Common Sense: An Early American Comment on Birth Control', *Journal of the History of Medicine*, 25 (July 1970), 341–5.
94. Horatio R. Storer, *Causation, Cause and Treatment of Reflex Insanity in Women* (Boston, 1871), p. 79.
95. The large-scale development of gynaecological surgery was a clear example of the orthodox physician's attempt to take control over the female's reproductive behaviour. Such surgery had become a thriving industry by the 1890s. Castrated women, said Dr David Gilliam, 'became tractable, orderly, industrious and cleanly':

'Oophorectomy for the Insanity and Epilepsy of the Female: A Plea for its More General Adoption', *Transactions of the American Association of Obstetricians and Gynecologists*, 9 (1896), 320–21.

96. Ralph Waldo Emerson, 'Beauty' in *The Complete Writings of Ralph Waldo Emerson* (New York, 1929), p. 611. Hogarth's line of beauty was discussed by Edmund Burke, 'Philosophical Inquiry Into the Origin of Our Ideas of the Sublime and the Beautiful', in *The Works of Edmund Burke, with a Memoir* (New York, 1836), Vol. 1, pp. 74–8.

97. General medical interest in the study of growth and physical development developed in the years after the Civil War, partly as a result of statistics collected for the Union Army which provided a massive data base for potential application by the medical profession; see John Allen Young, 'Height, Weight and Health', *Bulletin of the History of Medicine,* 53 (1979), 214–43.

98. W.S. Ruschenberger, 'Contributions to the Statistics of Human Growth', *American Journal of Medical Sciences*, 54 (1887), 67–70.

99. For a discussion of these conservative forces, see David J. Pivar, 'The New Abolitionism: The Quest for Social Purity' (PhD, University of Pennsylvania, 1965).

100. Lois Banner, *American Beauty*, pp. 154–5; Spencer Coon, 'Gibson's American Girl', *Metropolitan Magazine*, 4 (Dec. 1896). See also Anne Uhry Abrams, 'Frozen Goddess: The Image of Woman in Turn-of-the-Century American Art', in Mary Kelley (ed.), *Woman's Being, Woman's Place: Female Identity and Vocation in American History* (Boston, 1979), pp. 93–6.

101. Historical Statistics of the United States, 1789–1945, Bureau of the Census (Washington, DC, 1949), p. 45. See also Shorter, *Women's Bodies*.

102. Richard H. Shryock, *Medical Licensing in America, 1650–1965* (Baltimore, 1965), pp. 47–56.

103. Charles A.C. Reed, 'The President's Address', *Journal of the American Medical Association*, 36 (1901), 1606.

104. William Osler, *Aequimitas* (Philadelphia, 1932).

105. J.H.S. Bossard, *A Sociologist Looks at the Doctors, the Medical Profession, and the Public: Currents and Counter-currents* (Philadelphia, 1934).

106. W.F. Hartford, 'Subjective Therapeutics', *Medical Record*, LIV (1898), 158–9.

107. Nathan Allen, 'Influence of Medical Men', *New England Medical Monthly*, XI (1882–1883), 546.

108. Doctors, no less than the rest of society, consumed large chunks of evolutionary theory and interpreted it broadly. The Neo-Lamarckians, for example, interpreted evolutionary theory to suggest that the principle of acceleration and retardation was the controller of fitness among the population. This meant that historically the most recent body structures were the most susceptible to disease. The mechanics of man's and woman's upright position was relatively recent and not fully adapted to modern conditions. It contributed, therefore, to many of the diseases of the time. Especially in women, the woman's uterus was believed to have suffered most, bringing danger to mother and her unborn children. (Cora H. Flagg, 'The Pathology of Evolution', *Medical Record*, LII (1897), ·450–452. Understanding this, however, allowed physicians to treat their female patients appropriately, and to develop theories to show that certain races had better developmental potential than others. Dr J.S. Foote, 'The Ethics of Evolution', *Western Medical Review*, IV (1899), discussed how evolutionary theory implied an ascent in the development of laws to guide human conduct.

109. See Charles E. Rosenberg, 'The Bitter Fruit: Heredity, Disease and Social Thought in Nineteenth Century America', *Perspectives on American History*, 8 (1974), 189–235.

110. C.J. Devendorf, 'The Relations of the Physician to Mankind', *Physician and Surgeon*, XV (1893), 243.

111. Fellman and Fellman, *Making Sense of Self*, p. 122.

112. William James, *Psychology: Briefer Course* (New York, reprinted 1962).

113. Edwin Checkley, *A Natural Method of Physical Training; A Practical Description of the Checkley System of Physiculture* (Brooklyn, 1890), p. 125.

114. Carl Betz, *A System of Physical Culture* (Kansas City, Missouri, 1887), frontispiece; Mara L. Hatt, *The New Calisthenics: A Manual of Health and Beauty* (Boston, 1889).

115. Edwyn Sandys, 'The Place That Woman Occupies in Sport', *The Illustrated Sporting News*, 2 (21 Nov. 1903), 11.
116. Haller, *American Medicine in Transition*, p. 318.
117. Dr Dudley Sargent, regular physician turned homeopath, was one of the ablest exponents of physical exercise for women in the 1880s and 1890s as a means to effecting a higher evolution of mind and body. See D. Sargent, 'The Physical Development of Women', *Scribner's Magazine*, 5 (Feb. 1889), 181.
118. Carol Wald, quoting an advertisement of 1904, in *Myth America: Picturing Women, 1865–1945* (New York, 1975), p. 56.
119. John Haller and Robin Haller, *The Physician and Sexuality in Victorian America*, suggest that physician's opposition to bicycling was basically moralistic, and related to fears that women would neglect their duties at home. For many feminists of the time, riding a bicycle was a feminine statement of freedom from the confines of the home. See, for example, Charles E. Clay, 'Fair Riders on Modern Wheels', *Outing*, 18 (Jan. 1891), 305–7.
120. Seneca Egbert, 'The Bicycle in its Relation to the Physician', *Universal Medical Magazine*, 5 (1892–1893) 104–109; Luther Porter, *Cycling for Health and Pleasure* (New York, 1895), p. 14.
121. Whorton, *Crusaders for Fitness*, p. 322; Robert Dickinson, 'Bicycling for Women from the Standpoint of the Gynecologist', *American Journal of Obstetrics*, 31 (1895), 24–37; James Chadwick, 'Bicycle Saddles for Women', *Boston Medical Surgery Journal*, 132 (1895), 595–6.
122. Dr I. Love, 'The Bicycle from a Medical Standpoint', *Medical Record*, 48 (1895), 464.

12

The 'Amazon' and the American 'Lady': Sexual Fears of Women as Athletes

Donald J. Mrozek

Do you blame us little animals, literally aching for the freedom of kittens, puppies, and lambs, if we demand of our teachers at least five minutes gymnastic or play-exercises at the end of every hour and a few full breaths of God's pure air? Especially when you remember that soon it will not be proper for little girls any longer to romp out of doors, with the boys; indeed it will be exceedingly unladylike; for then we must turn up our hair, lengthen our frocks, put on corsets, and 'we can't be "Tomboy" any longer'.

B.F.Boller, 1900[1]

No one seemed to realize that there is a time in the life of a girl when it is better for her and for the community to be something of a boy rather than too much of a girl.

Dudley A. Sargent, 1927[2]

Some writers have said that . . . a big change took place in me. Their idea is that I used to be all tomboy, with none of the usual girls' interests, and then all of a sudden I switched over to being feminine. Well, with almost any woman athlete, you seem to get that tomboy talk.

'Babe' Didrikson Zaharias, 1956[3]

THE DIMENSIONS OF THE PROBLEM

The unequal development of athletic opportunities for women in America during the nineteenth and twentieth centuries reflected many constraining forces; but a remarkable number of them shared the underlying component of fear. According to research undertaken in the past two decades, men feared that they might be challenged or even displaced in governance of the basic social order. They feared dislocations in the work force and in electoral politics. Overall, they feared that they would lose control of public political, social, and economic affairs, which they dominated as a special masculine realm. But once the association of public life and an active manner with masculinity had been made, the entry – or re-entry – of women into these areas and the style pervading them became exceedingly problematic. Indeed, any serious challenge to this differentiation into separate male and female spheres only contributed to the underlying fear which pervaded and united all the others – the fear of losing identity and purpose. This concern was made especially vivid and concrete in the realm of sport.

Although women engaged in sport, men still dominated it, especially competitive athletics. Overall, sport thus retained the aura of a male preserve. Not uncommonly, men boasted of their involvement in sport as a proof of masculinity, especially if their gender identity seemed threatened for other reasons. The composer Charles Ives, for example, is said to have feared that his musical interests made him seem effeminate and compensated by asserting his manhood through baseball. Asked in his youth what he played, Ives mentioned no musical instrument but replied instead 'Shortstop'.[4] Ives was not unique. A prolific nineteenth-century writer of anti-masturbation literature, the Rev. John Todd, often separated himself from wife, family and home in hunting trips out in the wild; his physical removal into 'untamed' nature seems to have strengthened his sense of male identity.[5] In the years after the Civil War, health reformer James C. Jackson proposed that both girls and boys be encouraged to play outdoors so that exposure to Nature could develop their sense of 'ideality' and their inclination toward 'purity and truth'. But such activities were also clearly intended as a curative against masturbation; and the purity which boys and girls would gain through natural play was expected to strengthen their distinctive identity as men and women.[6]

The fear that woman was by nature an excessively sexual being encouraged such separate behaviour. For some men at least, as suggested by the experience of John Todd and others, there was an element of self-protection, seeing themselves as vulnerable to women rather than the reverse. The 'weakness' of the 'weaker sex' did not mean that they could not harm men; it meant rather that they were morally weak and, in that sense, out of control. Both ironically and appropriately, then, woman's role as moral guardian was elevated, at least as a goal and perhaps as an aid to social conformity. Yet it was this moral fragility which seemed to pose grave dangers for men.

Indeed, various forms of compensatory behaviour and of

self-protective hostility towards women appear deeply embedded in male experience in many cultures, as Wolfgang Lederer has suggested in *The Fear of Women*.[7] According to Lederer, the suppression of the 'precarious oscillation between love and fear' in men's feelings towards women has actually strengthened the impact of the fear and given rise to pathological consequences.[8] Among the destructive impulses that followed were an intense taboo of manners among men against 'doing things like a woman', as well as a deep resentment against the 'Amazons', whom Lederer has sharply described as 'only the church militant, the shocktroops of an ancient, world-wide system of mother-right'.[9] To the extent that women challenged the stereotype of a 'ladylike manner' in sport and physical leisure, they fell prey to such fear, partly by appearing to encroach upon the competitive, confrontational, shameless character which men supposedly brought to sporting events by virtue of their masculinity. The real differences between sensuality and sexuality fell largely out of view; and social convention – a matter of manners – thus edged into gender identification – a matter confused with sex and sexuality.

CULTURAL DIFFERENTIATION AND THE LOGIC OF FEAR

The fear experienced by men who worried over a public role for women, even if it lacked fairness, was not without a certain logic. The rationale showed itself in matters of style and manner, which were actually matters of serious substance and consequence. The focus on the manner in which men and women acted – an evident matter of style – reflected the view, as Charles Rosenberg has put it, that 'control was the basic building block of personality'.[10] By the later decades of the nineteenth century, the generalized care to govern 'the passions' – including gluttony, envy, and other excesses – narrowed into an insistent worry over sexuality.[11] On the one hand, this clearly suggested that excess had an intrinsically sexual undercurrent; and, on the other hand, it hinted that fears born in sexuality could falsely colour activities such as sport and athletics which, though intensely sensory and sensual, were not inherently sexual.

The quest for control fostered the separation of the sexes into two parallel but not identical cultures, a division which strengthened during the nineteenth century. In the twentieth century, the male solidarity which, in Lois Banner's words, 'strengthened the male tendency to see woman as a chivalric object' seemed to be challenged by the women's movement; and the male's sense of identity as well as his enjoyment of social prerogatives seemed to hinge proportionally on firm reassertion of the separate cultures.[12] To the extent that it smudged the identifying line between men and women, the emergence of women to athletic excellence could be seen as a threat to social order and as a violation of the tradition of 'true womanhood'. Moreover, some advocates of women's participation in sport may have been ambivalent presences. Dr Alice B. Stockham, for example, a Chicago physician, not only praised sport and outdoor activity as a better tonic for women than medicine but also encouraged birth control and abortion.[13] This challenge to many Americans' notion of truly feminine behaviour and womanly responsibility was especially troublesome because of the deeply rooted antipathy towards any suggestion of femininity in men. The late nineteenth-century woman was said to admire in man 'true *manliness*, and [she] is repelled by weakness and effeminacy. A womanish man awakens either the pity or the contempt of the fairer sex'.[14] It was bad enough if a man could not manage to 'behave like a man'; but his dilemma worsened if women refused to behave 'like women'.

Some contemporary observers regarded differentiation between men and women as inevitable in the socio-economic circumstances of early twentieth-century America. But its apparent causes and consequences boded ill for women's athletics. According to social scientist Anna Garlin Spencer, the 'vocational divide' did not result principally from physical motherhood but from the overriding imperative, shared by men and women, that the family be sustained. In *Woman's Share in Social Culture*, first published in 1912 and reissued in 1925, Spencer said that the man's economic and professional advancement thus assumed much greater practical importance.[15] The impact on woman was to diminish her 'personal achievement' and the 'joy of self-expression' – hallmarks of one's commitment to sport as well as purported effects of athletic success. Apart from the fatalism which tinged Spencer's thinking, her analysis pinpointed one of the most critical distinctions – while the male's individual fulfilment was taken to further the societal interest, the female's social obligations were seen as a substitute for her individual self-expression and attainment. To the extent that such 'inner-directedness' was regarded as physically inherent in women, then outer-directed activities could be regarded as deviant or suspect.

The overlays of social assumption which ultimately formed the rationale for restricting women's athletics were complex; and, although mutually supportive when seen broadly, they sometimes seemed contradictory in detail. Much of the complexity and apparent contradiction resulted from considerations of social and economic class. When commentators such as Anna Garlin Spencer spoke of women, they most commonly meant women rather like themselves –

born to some measure of comfort and to some sense of social opportunity and responsibility. In this, they resembled social commentators who spoke of sport, such as Edwyn Sandys, or political leaders who practised sport and worried over race improvement, such as Theodore Roosevelt. These were the well-bred women, marked by a sense of self-governance and reserve. Exuberance and physical display were far more the province of the poor, the immigrant, the working-class woman; and this tendency towards display itself was often taken as a mark of moral corruption. Inadequate self-control and incompetence in domestic management, for example, coupled with the unbridling of instincts for bodily display were thought to lead to such evils as prostitution.[16] To be sure, aggressive public display by women in athletics hardly constituted prostitution; but the descent into impassioned public display was suspect none the less. The absence of self-control which led to sexual depravity was too easily confused with that sensual expressiveness which had its outlet in sport. Since manners were thus a key sign of morality, the manner of one's sport and athletic practice also assumed a moral intonation.

In itself, the concern over propriety in female behaviour was hardly new. But the concern was especially strong to protect and enforce discipline among middle- and upper-class women rather than to 'redeem' the labouring poor. Discriminatory bias against poorer women had a long history, linked to suspicion of their supposed promiscuous inclinations and depreciated moral worth, whether intrinsic or induced by poverty and deprivation. As Charles Rosenberg has observed, the very fact of overt sexuality was widely regarded at the turn of the century as inimical to middle-class values. Moreover, medical practice and certainly medical prescriptions reflected class bias.[17] In addition, some historians have suggested that a disproportionate number of poorer women were subjects – or victims – of extreme surgical procedures for removal of sexual organs as a means of governing socio-sexual behaviour.[18] Any departure from the most restrained and proper behavioural code could be interpreted into a start down the road to depravity. But the middle class were inclined to view the tendency to wallow in such depravity as an attribute of their socio-economic inferiors.

Middle- and upper-class Americans had long been suspicious of physical display, especially though not exclusively among women, from the colonial period through the nineteenth century. As the lower-class appreciation of physical display created a significant commercial market for entrepreneurs such as P.T. Barnum, female behaviour again became a hotly debated issue.[19] When women had traditionally engaged in public displays, it had been crucial to preserve their image of moral uprightness. As Lois Banner has noted, Barnum had 'cloaked Jenny Lind in a mantle of respectability' during her American tour in 1850. Even so, Barnum's effort to establish perhaps the first modern beauty contest, in 1854, resulted in initial entries only from women 'of questionable reputation'.[20] It was precisely Barnum's difficulty in establishing such public display as an acceptable option for the middle- and upper-class American which suggests the strength of this modest reticence even into the twentieth century. Baring oneself literally and figuratively in public display became more feasible only when a social code for doing so descended from respectable authorities, as happened in sports which obtained middle- and upper-class approval. But even in these instances, women fared worse than men; and the tighter strictures affecting them in the nineteenth century lingered into the twentieth. After the turn of the century, the matter of gender distinction remained visible and powerful partly because distinctions according to class came under progressively sharper fire. But while class could be challenged as a creature of society, could gender and sex-based differences be challenged if they were the workings of nature?

The emergence of women to somewhat greater influence in public life during the late nineteenth and early twentieth centuries did not mean their emergence across the full range of action; nor did it eradicate the suspicion and disdain which many men and women had of the female who was physically active or 'aggressive'. Middle- and upper-class women who carved out places for themselves in the greater society did so in specialized areas, such as social and philan-thropic work or education. Their role was therapeutic rather than self-expressive; and the justification for their engagement in the outside world was social rather than individual. For all the talk of the social value of sport, the athletic hero – or heroine – was ultimately a lone figure, pursuing actions which were essentially self-aggrandizing no matter how great the protestations of team loyalty. Women's sphere surely expanded in the early twentieth century; and it included a recreational sector – even a sporting component.[21] But the quality and dimensions of that component bore only fragile similarities to that enjoyed by men. Thus, for all the enlargement of action regarded as acceptable for women, the mantle of middle- and upper-class respectability did not fall promptly on the female athlete.

In 1934, for example, Inez Haynes Irwin published *Angels and Amazons*, offering an interpretation of the rise of women to public prominence as well as suggesting what areas genuinely constituted prominence. Irwin's book, which tellingly included an acknowledg-ment of Anna Spencer Garlin, listed such callings of therapeutic intervention as doctor, minister and educator; and suitable causes included temperance and abolition. Although briefly mentioning the 'athletic craze' of the latter third of the nineteenth century, Irwin's focus swiftly turned to the traditionally important fields. Despite the rising power and scale of mass leisure culture in the decades after the First World War, serious treatment of women athletes was conspicuous by its absence.[22]

The view that the extremes of athleticism were unseemly behaviour for women was reinforced by the claims of the science of the day. Amram Scheinfeld summarized the views expounded during the 1930s in *Women and Men* (1943). Scheinfeld proposed that women were clearly inferior to men in all physical regards, such as strength and endurance. Moreover, the female body was said to 'set' sooner, while it was thought that 'her muscular system has a more limited range for development'. Scheinfeld supported his views by noting that 'hens would be no match for roosters' in some blood contests. In addition, he noted that female horses scored fewer victories at the track than males. Citing reports by Dr Calvin P. Stone of Stanford University, Scheinfeld reported that female horses won at the track at a ratio of one victory by a female to four by males. Following such evidence, Scheinfeld concluded with the 'almost universal opinion of medical authorities' that equal training of females and males for athletic competition would be detrimental to the female's ability to bear children at a later time. Thus, it appeared that the 'natural favor' accorded to males in athletics was justified again by 'natural identity' of the female attained through selected sex-related roles.[23] Female athletic excellence was possible, but only if the woman risked being considered a freak.[24]

The potential for genuine acceptance of women as athletic stars – as physically gifted beings outside of a sexual context and as persons entitled to an open range of opportunity for self-expression and the development of personality – depended on the emergence of a strong ideology which could counter the prevalent one.

By the early part of the twentieth century, sensibilities were shifting on questions of female propriety, even while concerns for the status of men lingered. The change in progress was suggested by an abrupt reversal in the *Ladies' Home Journal*'s judgement of newspaper beauty contests. As late as 1907, the magazine claimed that no woman worthy of the name would submit to sending her photograph for consideration in such a public contest undertaken by a newspaper. But by 1911, the *Journal* itself was sponsoring regional contests to find the most beautiful young women in America. Like other middle-class sponsoring agents, the *Ladies' Home Journal* found some socially elevated pretext to lend respectability to the contest. Various newspapers claimed that they were seeking appropriate models for uplifting civic sculpture or for submissions to national and international exhibitions. In its 1911 contest, the *Journal* offered as prizes portraits by Charles Dana Gibson.[25] Thus, although opportunities for public display broadened, significant constraints on the manner of display remained. This emphasis on *how* one engaged in public activities became a hallmark especially of women's sport in the first half of the twentieth century.

In essence, what took place was a change in fashion. But what made it extraordinarily important and a sensitive societal issue was that it was a change in kind – from an emphasis largely on static visual presentation to one on dynamic action in which deeds could be the measure of a woman, as they might also be of a man.

In the 1920s, a youthful appearance became fashionable for the American woman – an 'athletic' image, or at least one of fitness and health, which made action itself a sort of fashion. But the emphasis on activity was ambivalent. As Lois Banner has suggested, the energy and dynamism of the 'flapper' was sensual but, with bound breasts, not exactly sexual. Clara Bow's 'it', or sex appeal, was a vivacity coupled with 'a basic indifference to men'.[26] Though stylistically different from some of the more static images of women in the nineteenth century, this new vivacity and dynamism extended the restrictive tradition of decoration rather than that of public achievement. Put crudely, women in and after the 1920s could be much more energetic; but they might face obstacles if their actions had practical public consequences. The much vaunted liberation of women in the 1920s was, to be sure, wildly overestimated; and the actual opportunities for the sportswoman and top female athlete would depend on their hard-fought battles outside the arenas where sport was played and inside the minds and predispositions of men and women, where sport was justified.

CHAMPIONSHIP TALENT AS A SOCIAL CHALLENGE

The great female athlete in America risked being considered either eccentric, anomalous or freakish. Championship talent constituted something of a social challenge, in large measure by violating widely held notions about female 'anatomy and destiny'. Male athletes were also often treated as eccentrics, anomalies and freaks; but their process of accommodation and of emergence into acceptability proceeded at a rate which greatly outpaced that of the women. Many of the adaptive devices and coping mechanisms used by men were also used by women, but genuine respectability for the outstanding woman athlete – much more than for the refined and accomplished sportswoman – remained elusive. It was all well and good to enjoy sport if one remained a lady; but being an 'Amazon' was another matter entirely.

A measure of the deliberately outrageous had long been a part of sport in America; and the selling of sport as theatrical spectacle had exploited women as well as men, turning them into flamboyant market properties. One such woman, who was born in 1864 and named Ella Hattan, took the stage name Jaguarina and was even billed as 'Champion Amazon of the World' and 'Ideal Amazon of the Age'. Jaguarina established herself through skilled use of the sword from 1884 to 1900; and audiences were most taken with her mounted combat with the broadsword.[27] In her career, genuine athletic talent combined with exotic costume melodrama; and allusions to paganism wedged open a special niche of tolerance beyond Victorian respectability.[28] The famous wrestler Minerva, also known as 'Miss Josie' from Hoboken, New Jersey, posed in similar fashion – bold, proud, balanced and graceful. In both cases, the image of the accomplished female athlete was inseparably tied to the spectre of dominant womanhood. Minerva trounced men in some of her most popular wrestling encounters; and her status as an oddity, which helped to guard her against the general strictures of Victorianism, also gave her a tenuous exemption from gender discriminatory male dominance. So, too, Jaguarina met – and usually defeated – a string of male opponents. On 4 July 1886, she defeated Captain J.H. Marshall in mounted combat in San Francisco, although the man prevailed in a second outing. She overcame Sergeant Owen Davis, Captain E.N. Jennings, Fred Engelhardt, and Xavier Orlofsky; and, in 1887, one of her successful meetings with *turnverein* instructor Conrad Wiedemann played before the largest crowd ever then gathered in San Diego.[29]

The challenge posed by such exceptional women to their male athletic counterparts appears to have been a key to their commerical attractiveness. Newspaper accounts of Jaguarina's efforts lavished attention on her physical features, emphasizing her grace and marking her power and force as quite unexpected. Such accounts demonstrated not only the fascination with Jaguarina but the fact that there was an ambivalence in the fascination itself, rooted in the ambiguity of Jaguarina herself and of her career. Praise of her beauty conformed to stereotypes of the time. But her ability to defeat men was provocative. After one match in 1887, for example, the *San Francisco Chronicle* noted that Sergeant Owen Davis, as he was losing to Jaguarina, felt that 'it was bad enough to be beaten, but to be beaten by a woman was more than the Presidio champion's blood could brook. . .'. Sergeant Owen charged the referee, hurled insults, and threatened him before returning to defeat in the competition.[30] The commercial viability of the event, then, was not an endorsement of equality of access to sport and athletic competition; but it may even have exploited strong reservations and discriminatory instincts. It was one thing to make money from such an oddity. But it was quite a different question how well athletically gifted women would fare when competition was more straightforward – not crossing gender barriers but allowing their exuberant athletic excellence to shine through without the protective wrapping of pagan and theatrical associations. The 'Amazon' might be amusing and, perhaps, titillating as long as she remained in a realm of fantasy. But how might she be treated in the everyday world? Might not her excellence in athletics preclude her acceptance as an equal?

Recent research suggests that media accounts of prominent female athletes typically portrayed them as exceptions to the prevailing rules of femininity, regardless of the era in which they performed publicly. Eleanora Randolph Sears and Mildred 'Babe' Didrikson Zaharias, for example, seemed to deviate from commonly accepted notions about the woman's role as wife and mother, her manner of dress and suitable behaviour, her supposed physical limits, and the purported limits of her emotional stability.[31] There was a danger that female athletic excellence itself might be seen as a form of social and even personal deviation.

Sears shocked officials who picked her up for speeding, not only because she was driving the car but also because she wore masculine clothing. At sport, too, she sometimes adopted the masculine style. On 14 August 1910, reports were published that Sears rode astride while playing against men in a polo game. Also, descriptions of her play in the National Tennis Doubles Championships in the second decade of the century used adjectives stereotyped as male such as 'hard'. In the 1920s, Sears walked from Providence, Rhode Island, to Boston in 11 hours and 5 minutes. In a story in the *New York Times* on 15 December 1925, she was portrayed as superior to men. Along the way, her two male escorts began 'to feel the strain. Both Cutler and Hinckley, instead of setting the pace, lagged persistently, and Miss Sears with a grin looked over her shoulders and called: "Snap into it, boys! You offered to pace me, not chase me".'[32] For a fragile male ego, Sears could surely be something of a test.

It may have been inevitable that some would see a connection, if not an equation, between sport and masculinity and thus look askance at those women who engaged in sport with special skill and success.

Athletic clothing for women in the first decades of the century has been described by one observer as 'masculinized', at least in some sports, possibly because the women 'were entering the male domain – the sports world. . .'.[33] Meanwhile, the bloomer costume increasingly fell into disrepute. Advanced as a compromise between the demands of health and the strictures of Victorian social custom, the bloomer and its derivatives faltered before the 'mannish' simplicity of dress for riding and before functionally determined clothing such as women's one-piece bathing suits.[34] In the latter case, dedication to athletic excellence and internalized commitment hinted at male gender identification; in the former, a similar effect followed from the imitation of external style.

The social origins of those women athletes who were prominent in the first decades of the century further suggest that public excellence in women's sport lay uncomfortably on the edge of middle-class respectability. Upper-class women typically excelled in sports where the clientele was more restrictive and exclusive, such as tennis and golf. At the same time, the working class tended to provide players for games such as basketball.[35] In either case, the taste and customs of the middle class were skirted.[36]

Cases were varied. Track star Eleanor Egg, who competed in every Women's National AAU Track and Field Championship from 1923 to 1932 and set numerous track and field records, started as an acrobat in her parents' vaudeville act. She had already crossed the border into public entertainment long before setting foot on the cinders.[37]

But perhaps 'Babe' Didrikson proved to be among the most troubling – and troublesome – cases for those who believed women to be psychologically and physiologically weaker than men and so saw highly competitive sport to be properly restricted to males. Born on 26 June 1911, Didrikson was born into a culture which at once boosted commercialized sport but prized the amateur ethic, especially for women. The underlying reasons for this distinctive approach towards women's sport remain the subject of debate. But it would appear that amateurism took on a powerful romantic aura, even though public attention was drawn to professional sport. At the same time, the old consensus among various élites that amateur sport genuinely transformed personal character fell into some disrepair. Didrikson broke the mould of the idealized woman amateur – not so much by actual violation of amateur rules but by a lack of concern to seem to be a part of the system. Although Didrikson defended herself against charges that she had permitted her name and photograph to be used in automobile advertisements and forced the AAU to restore the amateur eligibility they had stripped from her, she refused reinstatement. Quoted in the *New York Times* on 6 December 1932, she said that she had preferred to make 'a few playful, and I think justified, comments on the inordinate lengths and multiplicity of their rules and regulations'.[38]

This was hardly the way to cultivate the fondness of men and women who thought female athleticism must be tightly circumscribed. Avery Brundage, for one, responded by saying 'the Greeks were right' in barring women from sport. The problem – in a societal sense – was that Didrikson did not seem to care. Such independence conflicted with the commercial promoter's desire to exert control, with the traditionalist's gender-discriminatory limitation of women's proper sphere, and with the widely held equation of female identity with marriage and motherhood. Didrikson practised sports which many educators in the 1920s and 1930s still believed interfered with successful pregnancy – shot put, javelin, and high jump – by supposedly making the chest 'inflexible'. Concerns over Didrikson's sexual identity showed themselves in frequent description of her as a 'tomboy'. Until her marriage to George Zaharias, the questions persisted, inspiring her to tell a reporter in January 1933: 'Don't ask me whether or not I'm going to get married. That is the first question women reporters ask. And that is why I hate those darn old women reporters'.[39]

Even marriage would not necessarily establish suitable sex-role identification for the woman athlete. In 'Babe' Didrikson's case, the problem may have been complicated by marriage, on 23 December 1938, to a 'fringe' sports entertainer, the wrestler George Zaharias. It was a moot point how much respectability Didrikson could win from a marital match with 'The Weeping Greek', who played a cowardly villain in the ring.

Didrikson's manner and tone as well as her actual accomplishments in sport continued to moot her gender identification. A notable instance came in an intended boxing match with Babe Ruth. 'I never met the Babe,' she was quoted as saying, 'but, gee, I'd like to put the gloves on with him for a while'. Suggesting that she might prepare in earnest and showing no apprehension at all, she added: 'Boy, how I can punch that bag'. How the two contestants might have fared and whether the event would have become an incident of the 'great male hope' will never be known. Ruth cancelled. In a charity golf match with Didrikson, comedian Bob Hope playfully added to the portrayal of her in masculine terms. 'I hit the ball like a girl,' Hope said, 'and she hits it like a man.' As Karen Epstein has observed, Didrikson was commonly referred to as an 'athlete' rather than a 'girl athlete' or 'lady athlete' and seemed to stand apart from other women intentionally.[40]

And Didrikson was no isolated case. The popular tennis star Helen Wills, much acclaimed for her 1924 match with Suzanne Lenglen of France, advocated shortened skirts, sleeveless blouses and bare legs as imperative in improving the women's game. In 1928, Gertrude Ederle received a rousing ticker tape reception in New York after swimming the English Channel, breaking the previous records of male swimmers. And Eleanor Holm was praised by sportswriter Paul Gallico as a better swimmer–athlete than any of her male counterparts. Such famous sportswomen were on the cutting edge of change, along with actresses such as Joan Crawford, Marlene Dietrich and Katharine Hepburn whom historian Lois Banner has called 'tough' and 'resilient'.[41] The adoption of 'masculine' dress and behavioural style widened the options for women, but it could not cancel out all the fears that females would themselves become 'masculinized' and demeaned.

Although Didrikson's case was highly visible given her athletic excellence and her considerable self-possession, it still suggested the dilemma which faced women athletes more generally through much of the twentieth century. They entered a sporting world riddled with stereotypical images of female athletes and restrictive assumptions about women's physical and emotional limits. Seen one way, women's ability to perform effectively in defiance of the prevailing sterotypes should have been sufficient reason to question the stereotypes. Yet, as the treatment of Didrikson suggests, it was equally possible to question the gender identity and even the sexual character of those athletes tainted by excellence. It may be argued that, great as her athletic achievements were, her final social acceptance came only when she had passed beyond athletic success and emerged as a *mater dolorosa* and moral paragon during her fight with cancer. Although not literally a mother, she had become the 'mother of us all'.

RESIDUAL FEARS AND GROWING OPPORTUNITY

In the years after the Second World War and especially from the 1960s onward, women won broader opportunities for their self-expression and for personal and professional fulfilment. That problems remained betrayed a drag-anchor of residual fears, as well as the simple fact that perfect freedom and perfect fulfilment are over-ambitious aims irrespective of gender. But in one area especially, strides were made which had special and powerful significance for the reception accorded women athletes – the realm of sexual liberation. By exploring male and female sexuality, one could not only discern prejudice and bias but could also discriminate between sex and

11. Helen Wills-Moody, champion tennis player of the 1920s and 1930s, was also admired for her beauty and femininity (Library of Congress)

12. Mildred 'Babe' Didrikson Zaharias, champion golfer, was frequently described as a 'tomboy' and broke the mould of the idealized woman amateur (Library of Congress)

13. Gertrude Ederle, long distance swimmer, seen above taking food during her unsuccessful Channel swim of 1925 – she tried again and broke the record in 1928 – had been one of the demurely dressed US Olympic team of 1924 (Library of Congress)

gender. As a result, some diminution of the traditional bias against women athletes rooted in sex roles and in sex-related physiology proved possible.

Possible – but neither automatic nor inevitable. Often changes in views came only after a long fight. And so it was no cause for wonder that athletes sometimes felt compelled to draw attention to emblems of the prevalent mainstream notion of femininity. Even in 1961, Wilma Rudolph emphasized that, although she had occasionally played basketball with her ten brothers, 'it doesn't mean that I'm a tomboy'. As recorded in a *New York Times* article, she added to her affirmation of traditional femininity by '[pointing] to her bright plaid skirt for emphasis and then fingered the delicate gold buttons on her purple bodice'. She 'glanced apologetically' at the black slippers she wore instead of high heels, which she insisted she preferred except that 'my legs get too tired if I wear them before a race'.[42]

But by the end of the 1960s and certainly in the 1970s, much had been accomplished, notably by outstanding individuals such as Billie Jean King. Such persons not only proved that women could be excellent athletes but also showed themselves to be able entrepreneurs. By developing magazines devoted to women's sport, moreover, and by similar business moves, they suggested the worthiness, if not the exact parity, of women's sport applying the full apparatus of men's sport to women's. Since sport itself had achieved recognition as serious business, moreover, it could piggyback on the general ideology of women's liberation and thus avoid being boxed off as a marginal amusement, as had happened at the turn of the century.

Billie Jean King's ability to avoid total disaster upon disclosure of her lesbian relationship while maintaining a non-traditional marriage with her husband, Larry King, suggested that sexual fears concerning women athletes had been muted somewhat by the beginning of the 1980s. Meanwhile, Dr Renee Richards overcame the initial scramble to mesh the rules of sport with the capabilities of modern medicine – for example, was a trans-sexual, now female, to be bound by prior experience and record in men's tennis? Relatively soon (and once it sank in that a sex-change operation was not likely to become a standard means for a mediocre male player to become a superior female athlete), Richards became widely recognized as an effective coach, associated with Martina Navratilova, and was often caught in close-up shots by television cameramen covering major tennis tournaments. Although it risks irony to say it of Richards, it was clearly true of King that she forced re-examination of what it meant to be female – and specifically what it meant to be a female and an athlete. Her aggressive style of play, still somewhat regrettably dubbed 'masculine' and 'a man's game', none the less became a model for other talented women, spreading a new definition of what a woman could be in the world of sport. The *New York Times* commented on King in this light on 15 May 1981, saying: 'By her brash aggressiveness, she made it more acceptable for women to push themselves'.[43] Even so, it is crucial to note that one of King's champion successors, Chris Evert Lloyd, was portrayed in the tradition of ladylike reserve and personal discipline. No single model for the woman athlete sufficed.

To be sure, the combination of women's athletic excellence and their growing activism in social, economic and political affairs did much to expand the opportunities available to the outstanding female athlete. So, too, the legitimation of sport as a component of mass entertainment and mass culture blunted the old charges of eccentricity or freakishness. But the reduction in the sex-related fears among both men and women was at least as crucial; and this required not merely a tactical victory over male social authority but, more significantly, a substantial redirection of thinking. The 'millennium' had not arrived with the likes of Billie Jean King and Martina Navratilova. But at least the residue of fear had fallen low enough so athletic excellence could hold its own against private life.

NOTES

1. B.F. Boller, 'Physical Training', *Mind and Body* 7 (April 1900), 25–6. The male adult Boller here was writing in the guise of an imaginary little girl eager for physical education and play outdoors.
2. Dudley Allen Sargent, *An Autobiography* (Philadelphia, 1927), p. 36. Physical educator Sargent specifically suggested that the girls' efforts in play and sport would make them less of a sexual threat to the coeval boys who would not as yet be able to resist curious advances from too dominating females.
3. Mildred 'Babe' Didrikson Zaharias, *This Life I've Lived* (London, 1956), p. 103. She also noted that Mary Lena Falk was known as 'the tomboy from Thomasville, Georgia' and Patsy Berg as 'the Minnesota Tomboy'.
4. Frank R. Rossiter, *Charles Ives and His America* (New York, 1975), pp. 31–2.
5. A useful study of John Todd appears in G.J. Barker-Benfield, *The Horrors of the Half-Known Life, Male Attitudes Toward Women and Sexuality in Nineteenth Century America* (New York, 1976). An extended speculation on the relationship of such thinking to the gender-typing of public action and to male dominance in sport appears in Donald J. Mrozek, *Sport and American Mentality* (Knoxville TN, 1983), pp. 232–3.
6. James C. Jackson, *The Sexual Organism and Its Healthful Management* (Boston, 1861; reprint, New York, 1974), especially pp. 54–5 concerning play. It must be emphasized, however, that Jackson's primary remedy for masturbation was not exercise but diet, including the avoidance of horseradish and spices which he thought confirmed the practice of 'secret vice'. Concerning such remedies to masturbation, see Jackson's chapter, innocently entitled, 'Masturbation, How It Arises, How It is Kept Up', pp. 60–86.

7. Wolfgang Lederer, *The Fear of Women* (New York, 1968).
8. Ibid., pp. vii–viii.
9. Lederer, *The Fear of Women*, pp. 36, 105.
10. Charles Rosenberg, 'Sexuality, Class and Role' in *No Other Gods, On Science and American Social Thought* (Baltimore, 1961, 1962, 1976), p. 75.
11. Ibid.
12. Banner, *American Beauty*, p. 244.
13. Alice B. Stockham, *Tokology: A Book for Every Woman* (Chicago, 1886). Also see Stockham, *Karezza, Ethics of Marriage* (Chicago, 1896).
14. Rosenberg, *No Other Gods*, p. 79.
15. Anna Garlin Spencer, *Woman's Share in Social Culture* (Philadelphia, 1912), pp. 149–51. It should be noted that Spencer was adopted a strongly accommodationist or 'conservative' viewpoint; and, although she recognized the 'spinster' as demonstrating female equality with men in some 'specialized' tasks, she clearly agreed with the view that the mother and housewife 'did something far more vital for race development' (p. 150).
16. Ibid., p. 115.
17. Rosenberg, *No Other Gods*, p. 80, pp. 54–70.
18. See, for example, Barker-Benfield, *The Horrors of the Half-Known Life*.
19. See, for example, Lois W. Banner, *American Beauty* (New York, 1983), pp. 254–255. It is worth noting, also, that Barnum was a key promoter of wrestling events. In making no distinction between saleable sport and other commercially viable forms of entertainment, Barnum was both out of step with the sport 'reformers' of the last third of the nineteenth century and a harbinger of a crucial – perhaps even predominant – thrust in sport and entertainment during the twentieth century.
20. Banner, *American Beauty*, p. 255.
21. Concerning the reluctance of prominent women to support strong athletic competition for women and girls, see Banner, *American Beauty*, pp. 286–7.
22. Inez Haynes Irwin, *Angels and Amazons, A Hundred Years of American Women* (Garden City, NY, 1934). Also see Margaret W. Rossiter, *Women Scientists in America, Struggles and Strategies to 1940* (Baltimore, 1982). The difficulty of pursuing 'the possibilities of independence' is a theme in Peter Gabriel Filene, *Him/Her/Self, Sex Roles in Modern America* (New York, 1974), p. 52 and *passim*.
23. Amram Scheinfeld, *Women and Men* (New York, 1943), pp. 274–80.
24. Scheinfeld also said that menstruation severely inhibited athletic participation, noted that the promoters of the 'Aquacade' at the New York World's Fair had kept extra swimmers ready so that women could be kept out of the pool for four days during their menstrual cycles, but that some women still seemed oblivious to the 'fact' that they were supposed to perform badly at such times and managed somehow to overcome their purported debility. Scheinfeld, *Women and Men*, p. 281.
25. Banner, *American Beauty*, pp. 257–8.
26. Ibid., p. 278.
27. Lynn Emery, 'World Renowned Champion Amazon: Jaguarina' (paper presented at the 11th annual conference of the North American Society for Sport History, Mont Alto, PA, May 1983).
28. The use of pagan imagery as a means of exempting oneself from the strictures of Victorian culture is discussed in Mrozek, *Sport and American Mentality*, pp. 212–13.
29. Emery, 'World Renowned Champion Amazon'.
30. Ibid., 8.
31. See, for example, Karen V. Epstein, 'Social Perceptions of Four Prominent Female Athletes During the Twentieth Century in the United States' (paper presented at the 11th annual conference of the North American Society for Sport History, Mont Alto PA, May 1983).
32. Ibid.
33. See Emelia-Louise Kilby, 'Changing Clothes in Women's Sports: 1895–1940' (paper presented at the 11th annual convention of the North American Society for Sport History, Mont Alto PA, May 1983).

34. Ibid.
35. See, for example, Epstein, 'Social Perceptions of Four Prominent Female Athletes'.
36. As Lois Banner has suggested, it was possible to stage a female beauty pageant in Rehoboth Beach, Maryland as early as 1880 without scandal or interference, largely because it was a working-class resort. In Atlantic City, however, it took much effort and a considerable length of time before a format could be developed which fused the lower-class 'carnival' and the upper-class 'festival' and added the overlay of health consciousness. See Banner, *American Beauty*, especially pp. 266–7.
37. See J. Thomas Jable, 'The Acrobat on the Athletic Field: Eleanor Egg, New Jersey's Early Track and Field Champion and Record Holder' (paper presented at the 11th annual convention of the North American Society for Sport History, Mont Alto PA, May 1983).
38. See Epstein, 'Social Perceptions of Four Prominent Female Athletes'. Also, concerning her career, see Zaharias, *This Life I've Led*; William Oscar Johnson and Nancy P. Williamson, *'Whatta-Girl', The Babe Didrikson Story* (Boston, 1975).
39. Quoted in Epstein, 'Social Perceptions of Four Prominent Female Athletes'.
40. Ibid.
41. Banner, *American Beauty*, pp. 275–6.
42. Quoted in Epstein, 'Social Perceptions of Four Prominent Female Athletes'.
43. Quoted in ibid.

Select Bibliography

The bibliography that follows has been supplied by the contributors. In some instances the same work appears more than once.

CHAPTER 1

Jill K. Conway *et al*, *The Female Experience in 18th and 19th Century America* (Princeton, 1985), especially section VI.

Carl N. Degley, 'What Ought to Be and What Was: Women's Sexuality in the 19th Century', *American Historical Review*, 79 (1974), 1467–90.

Anita C. Fellamn and Michael Fellman, *Making Sense of Self: Medical Advice Literature in Late 19th Century America* (Philadelphia, 1981).

Harvey Green, *Fit for America: Health, Fitness, Sport and American Society: 1830–1940* (New York, 1986).

John S. Haller and Robin M. Haller, *The Physician and Sexuality in Victorian America* (Urbana, 1974).

Mary Hartman and Lois Banner (eds.) *Clio Consciousness Raised: New Perspectives on the History of Women* (New York, 1974).

Donald J. Mrozek, *Sport and American Mentality: 1880–1910* (Knoxville, 1983).

Charles E. Rosenberg, *No Other Gods: On Science and American Social Thought* (Baltimore, 1976).

Barbara Welter, *Dimity Convictions: The American Woman in the 19th Century* (Athens, Ohio, 1976).

James C. Whorton, *Crusaders for Fitness: The History of American Health Reformers* (Princeton, 1982).

CHAPTER 2

Sara Delamont and Lorna Duffin (eds.), *The Nineteenth Century Woman: Her Cultural and Physical World* (London, 1978).

Sheila Fletcher, *Women First: The Female Tradition in English Physical Education 1880–1980* (London, 1984).

Joan N. Burstyn, *Victorian Education and the Ideal of Womanhood* (London, 1980).

Louise Michelle Newman (ed.), *Men's Ideas/Women's Realities: Popular Science, 1870–1915* (Oxford, 1985).

Carol Dyhouse, *Girls Growing Up in Late Victorian and Edwardian England* (London, 1981).

Rosalind Rosenberg, *Beyond Separate Spheres: Intellectual Roots of Modern Feminism* (New Haven, 1982).

CHAPTER 3

Roberta Frankfort, *Collegiate Women: Domesticity and Career in Turn-of-the-Century America* (New York, 1977).

Jean E. Friedman and William G. Shade, *Our American Sisters: Women in American Life and Thought*, 3rd ed. (Lexington, MA, 1982).

Ellen W. Gerber, Jan Felshin, Pearl Berlin, and Waneen Wyrick, *The American Woman in Sport* (Reading, MA, 1974), especially Chaps. 1–4.

Daniel Walker Howe (ed.), *Victorian America* (Philadelphia, 1976).

John A. Lucas and Ronald A. Smith, *Saga of American Sport* (Philadelphia, 1978), especially Chapters 15 and 20.

Donald J. Mrozek, *Sport and American Mentality, 1880–1910* (Knoxville, TN, 1983).

Roberta J. Park, 'Embodied Selves': The Rise and Development of Concern for Physical Education, Active Games and Recreation for American Women, 1776–1865', *Journal of Sport History*, V (Summer 1978), 5–41.

Benjamin G. Rader, *American Sports: From the Age of Folk Games to the Age of Spectators* (Englewood Cliffs, NJ, 1983).

Research Quarterly for Exercise and Sport, Special Centennial Issue (April 1985). (Published by the American Alliance for Health, Physical Education, Recreation, and Dance).

Rosalind Rosenberg, *Beyond Separate Spheres: Intellectual Roots of Modern Feminism* (New Haven, 1982).

Betty Spears and Rickard A. Swanson, *History of Sport and Physical Activity in the United States* (Dubuque, IA, 1978).

CHAPTER 4

Paul Atkinson, 'Fitness, Feminism and Schooling', in Sara Delamont and Lorna Duffin (eds.), *The Nineteenth Century Woman: Her Cultural and Physical World* (London, 1978), pp. 92–133.

Dorothea Beale, Lucy H.M. Soulsby, and Jane Frances Dove (eds.), *Work and Play in Girls' Schools* (London, 1901).

Jan Felshin, 'The Triple Option . . . For Women in Sport', in M. Marie Hart (ed.), *Sport in the Socio-Cultural Process* (Dubuque, IA, 1972), pp. 431–7.

Sheila Fletcher, *Women First: the Female Tradition in English Physical Education 1880–1980* (London, 1984).

Ellen W. Gerber *et al.*, *The American Woman in Sport* (Reading, MA, 1974).

Deborah Gorham, *The Victorian Girl and the Feminine Ideal* (Bloomington, IN, 1982).

M. Pointon, 'Factors influencing the participation of Women and Girls in Physical Education, Physical Recreation and Sport in Great Britain during the period 1850–1920', *History of Education Society Bulletin*, 24 (Autumn 1979), 45–56.

CHAPTER 5

C. Crunden, *A History of Anstey College of Physical Education 1897–1972* (Anstey College of Physical Education, 1974).

S. Delamont and L. Duffin (eds.), *The Nineteenth Century Woman: Her Cultural and Physical World*, (London, 1978).

C.Dyhouse, *Girls Growing Up in Late Victorian and Edwardian England*, (London, 1981).

H. Eisenstein, *Contemporary Feminist Thought* (London, 1984).

S. Fletcher, *Women First: Female Tradition in English Physical Education 1880–1980* (London, 1984).

V. Klein, *The Feminine Character: History of an Ideology* (London, 2nd edn., 1971).

J. May, *Madame Bergman-Österberg: Pioneer of Physical Education for Girls and Women* (London, 1969).

S. Rowbotham, *Hidden from History* (London, 1973).

E. Whitelegg, *et al.* (eds.), *The Changing Experience of Women* (Oxford, 1982).

CHAPTER 6

Sheila Fletcher, *Women First: The Female Tradition in English Physical Education 1880–1980* (London, 1984).

Sheila Fletcher, 'The Educational Service of the Race: The High Calling of the Gym Mistress in the First Half of the Twentieth

Century' (proceedings of the Annual Conference of the History of Education Society of Great Britain, December 1984).

Rudolf Laban, *Modern Educational Dance* (London, 1948).

Peter McIntosh, *Physical Education in England since 1800* (London, 1968).

Jonathan May, *Madame Bergman-Österberg: Pioneer of Physical Education for Girls and Women* (London, 1969).

George Newman, *The Building of a Nation's Health* (London, 1939).

Josephine Tey, *Miss Pym Disposes* (London, 1957).

Ida Webb, 'Women's Physical Education in Great Britain 1800–1965' (unpublished Leicester M.Ed. thesis, 1967).

CHAPTER 8

R. Twopeny, *Town Life in Australia* (Middlesex, 1973).

T.D. Jaques and G.R. Pavia, *Sport in Australia* (Sydney, 1976).

R. Cashman and M. McKernan (eds.), *Sport in History* (St Lucia, 1979).

R. Cashman and M. McKernan (eds.), *Sport: Money, Morality and the Media* (Sydney, n.d.)

J. Daly, *Elysian Fields – Sport, Class and Community in Colonial South Australia* (Adelaide, 1982).

Ailsa Zainu'ddin, *They Dreamt of a School* (Melbourne, 1982).

N. MacKenzie, *Women in Australia* (Melbourne, 1962).

B. Haley, *The Healthy Body and Victorian Culture* (Cambridge, MA, 1978).

CHAPTER 9

Jean Cochrane, Abby Hoffman and Pat Kincaid, *Women in Canadian Life: Sports* (Toronto, 1977).

Helen Gurney, *Girls' Sports: A Century of Progress in Ontario High Schools* (Don Mills; 1979).

Helen Lenskyj, ' "Feminity first": sport and physical education for Ontario girls, 1890–1930, *Canadian Journal of the History of Sport* 13:2 (1982), 4–17.

Helen Lenskyj, 'The Role of Physical Education in the Socialization of Girls in Ontario, 1890–1930' (unpublished Ph.D. dissertation, University of Toronto, 1983).

Helen Lenskyj, 'A kind of precipitate waddle': early opposition to women running', in Nancy Theberge and Peter Donnelly (eds.), *Sport and the Sociological Imagination* (Fort Worth, 1983), pp. 153–61.

Helen Lenskyj, 'We Want to Play . . . We'll Play: Women and Sport in the 20s and 30s', *Canadian Woman Studies* 4:3 (1983), 15–18.
A.E. Marie Parkes, *The Development of Women's Athletics at the University of Toronto* (Toronto, 1961).

CHAPTER 10

Mary Beth Norton, 'The Evolution of White Women's Experience in Early America', *American Historical Review*, LXXXIX (1984): 593–619.
Jennie Holliman, *American Sports (1785–1835)* (Durham, NC, 1931), Chapter 11.
Julia C. Spruill, *Women's Life and Work in the Southern Colonies* (Chapel Hill, NC, 1938), Chapter 5.
Jane Carson, *Colonial Virginians at Play* (Williamsburg, VA, 1965).

INDEX